ALEXANDER WAUGH

THE HOUSE OF

WITTGENSTEIN

Alexander Waugh is the grandson of Evelyn Waugh and the son of columnist Auberon Waugh. He has been chief opera critic at the *Mail on Sunday* and the *Evening Standard*, and is also a publisher, cartoonist, and award-winning composer. He has written several books, including *Fathers and Sons* (a history of his literary antecedents), *Classical Music: A New Way of Listening*, *Time*, and *God*. He lives in Somerset, England, with his wife and three children.

THE HOUSE OF

WITTGENSTEIN

THE HOUSE OF
WITTGENSTEIN

A FAMILY AT WAR

ALEXANDER WAUGH

Anchor Books
A Division of Penguin Random House LLC
New York

FIRST ANCHOR BOOKS EDITION, APRIL 2010

The Library of Congress has cataloged the Doubleday edition as follows:
Waugh, Alexander.
The house of Wittgenstein : a family at war / by Alexander Waugh.
p. cm
Includes bibliographical references and index.
1. Wittgenstein family. I. Title.
CT1097.W58W38 2009
929'.20943613—dc22 2008033312

Anchor Books Trade Paperback ISBN: 978-0-307-27872-2
eBook ISBN: 978-0-385-52672-2

www.anchorbooks.com

147028622

FOR SALLY

Es gibt eine Unzahl allgemeiner Erfahrungssätze, die uns als

gewiß gelten. Daß Einem, dem man den Arm abgehackt,

er nicht wieder wächst, ist ein solcher.

There are an enormous number of general empirical

propositions that count as certain for us. One such is that

if someone's arm is cut off it will not grow again.

—LUDWIG WITTGENSTEIN,

ON CERTAINTY 273, 274

❖ ❖ ❖

CONTENTS

FAMILY TREE *x*

PART ONE ◆ A DIRTY THING TO DO *1*

PART TWO ◆ A NASTY MESS *59*

PART THREE ◆ THE NEW DISORDER *125*

PART FOUR ◆ CONNECTION AND MELTDOWN *199*

POSTSCRIPT *282*

ACKNOWLEDGMENTS *285*

NOTES *287*

BIBLIOGRAPHY *315*

INDEX *323*

THE HOUSE OF

WITTGENSTEIN

❖ ❖ ❖

Anna Wittgenstein b. 1840, d. 1896	Marie Wittgenstein b. 1841, d. 1931	Paul Wittgenstein (industrialist) b. 1842, d. 1928	Josephine Wittgenstein b. 1844, d. 1933	Ludwig "Louis" Wittgenstein b. 1845, d. 1925
= Heinrich Emile Franz (judge) b. 1839, d. 1884	= Moritz Pott (iron merchant) b. 1839, d. 1902	= Justine Hochstetter b. 1858, d. 1918	= Johann Nepomuk Oser (professor of chemistry) b. 1833, d. 1912	= Maria Franz b. 1850, d. 1912

Hermine "Mining" Wittgenstein b. 1 Dec. 1874, Teplitz d. 11 Feb. 1950, Vienna	Dora Wittgenstein b. 1876 d. 1876	Johannes "Hans" Wittgenstein b. 1877, Vienna 1902, went missing	Konrad "Kurt" Wittgenstein b. 1 May 1878, Vienna d. Oct. 1918, Italian Front, suicide	Helene "Lenka" Wittgenstein b. 23 Aug. 1879, Vienna d. Apr. 1956, Vienna
				= Max Salzer (government official) b. 3 Mar. 1868, Vienna d. 28 Apr. 1941, Vienna

Maria Salzer b. 6 Mar. 1900 d. 14 Aug. 1948	Friedrich "Fritz" Salzer b. 11 Feb. 1902 d. 22 July 1922	Felix Salzer (musicologist) b. 13 June 1904 d. 12 Aug. 1986	Clara Salzer b. 7 Sept. 1913 d. 29 Oct. 1978
			= Arvid Sjögren

Hermann Christian Wittgenstein
(land agent)
b. 1802, d. 1878

= Franziska "Fanny" Figdor
b. 1814, d. 1890

| Karl Wittgenstein (industrialist) b. 8 Apr. 1847, Gohlis d. 20 Jan. 1913, Vienna = Leopoldine "Poldy" Kalmus b. 14 Mar. 1850, Vienna d. 3 June 1926, Vienna | Bertha Wittgenstein b. 1848, d. 1908 = Karl Kupelwieser (lawyer and company director) b. 1841, d. 1925 | Clara Wittgenstein b. 1850, d. 1935 | Lydia Wittgenstein b. 1851, d. 1920 suicide = Gen. Josef von Siebert b. 1843, d. 1917 | Emile "Millie" Wittgenstein b. 1853, d. 1939 = Theodore von Brücke (judge) b. 1853, d. 1918 | Clothilde Wittgenstein b. 1854, d. 1937 |

| Rudolf "Rudi" Wittgenstein b. 27 June 1881, Vienna d. 2 May 1904, Berlin suicide | Margaret "Gretl" Wittgenstein b. 19 Sept. 1882, Vienna d. 27 Sept. 1958, Vienna = Jerome Steinberger/ Stonborough b. 1873, New York d. 15 June 1938, Vienna | Paul Wittgenstein (pianist) b. 5 Nov. 1887, Vienna d. 3 Mar. 1961, New York = Hilde Schania b. 26 Dec. 1915, Rannersdorf d. 31 Mar. 2001, Pennsylvania | Ludwig "Lucki" Wittgenstein (philosopher) b. 26 Apr. 1889, Vienna d. 29 Apr. 1951, Cambridge |

| Thomas Stonborough b. 9 Jan. 1906, Berlin d. 14 Feb. 1986, Vienna | John Jerome "Ji" Stonborough b. 11 June 1912, Vienna d. 29 Apr. 2002, Dorset | Elizabeth Wittgenstein b. 24 May 1935, Vienna d. Feb. 1974, New York | Johanna Wittgenstein b. 10 Mar. 1937, Vienna | Paul "Louis" Wittgenstein b. 30 Nov. 1941, New York |

THE HOUSE OF
WITTGENSTEIN

PART ONE

A
DIRTY THING
TO DO

1 VIENNESE DEBUT

Vienna is described—over-described—as a city of paradox; but for those who do not know this or have never been there, it may be pictured as a capriccio drawn from the flat sound bites of the Austrian Tourist Board, a place defined by its rich cream cakes, Mozart mugs and T-shirts, New Year's waltzes, grand, bestatued buildings, wide streets, old fur-coated women, electric trams, and Lipizzaner stallions. The Vienna of the early twentieth century was not marketed in this way. In those days it was not marketed at all. Maria Hornor Lansdale's once-indispensable guide of 1902 draws a portrait of the Hapsburg capital that is at once grubbier and more dynamic than anything suggested in our modern guidebooks. Her book describes parts of the Innere Stadt or city center as "dark, dirty and gloomy" and of the Jewish quarter she wrote: "The interiors of the houses are unspeakably squalid. As one ascends the stair the rickety banister sticks to one's fingers, and the walls on either side ooze. Entering a small dark room the ceiling is covered with soot and the furniture crowded close together."

A German might step onto a Viennese streetcar and find himself unable to exchange a word with any of his fellow passengers, for the city then was home to a rapidly expanding population of Magyars, Rumanians, Italians, Poles, Serbs, Czechs, Slovenes, Slovaks, Croats, Ruthenians, Dalmatians, Istrians and Bosnians, all of whom lived together apparently in happiness. An American diplomat describing the city in 1898 wrote:

> A man who had been but a short time in Vienna, may himself be of pure German stock, but his wife will be Galician or Polish, his cook Bohemian, his children's nurse Dalmatian, his man a Servian, his coachman a Slav, his barber a Magyar, and his son's tutor a Frenchman. A majority of the administration's employees are Zechs, and the Hungarians have most influence in the affairs of the government. No, Vienna is *not* a German city!

The Viennese were regarded abroad as a good-natured, easygoing, and highly cultured people. By day the middle class congregated in cafés, spending hours in conversation over a single cup of coffee and a glass of water. Here newspapers and magazines were provided in all languages. In the evenings they dressed for dancing, for the opera, the theater or the concert hall. They were fanatical about these entertainments, unforgiving of the poor player who forgot his lines or the singer who sang sharp, while idolizing or deifying their favorites. The Viennese writer Stefan Zweig remembered that passion from his youth: "Whereas in politics, in administration, or in morals, everything went on rather comfortably and one was affably tolerant of all that was slovenly and overlooked many an infringement, in artistic matters there was no pardon; here the honour of the city was at stake."

❖ ❖ ❖

ON DECEMBER 1, 1913, there was cold sunshine over most of Austria. By the evening a mist had spread from the northern slopes of the Carpathian Mountains down to the rolling hills and verdant lowlands of the Alpine Foreland. In Vienna, the air was still, the streets and pavements quiet and the temperature uncommonly cold. For the twenty-six-year-old Paul Wittgenstein this was a day of high excitement and excruciating tension.

Clammy fingers and cold hands figure in every pianist's worst dream—the slightest sheen from the glands of the pads can cause the fingers to slip or "glitch," accidentally hitting two adjacent keys at once. The sweaty-fingered pianist is slave to his caution. If his hands are too cold, the finger muscles will stiffen. Coldness in the bones does not drive sweat from the skin and in the worst instances the fingers may be immobilized by cold while remaining slippery with sweat. Many concert artists spend a nervous hour or two before a winter recital with their hands plunged into a basin of hot water.

Paul's concert debut was scheduled to start at 7:30 p.m. in the Grosser Musikvereinsaal, a hallowed place, of near perfect acoustic, where Brahms, Bruckner and Mahler heard many of their works performed for the first time. It is from here—the "Golden Hall"—that the famous New Year orgy of waltzes and polkas is annually broadcast to the world. Paul did not expect his debut to sell out. The auditorium had a seating capacity of 1,654, with 300 standing places. It was a Monday night, he was unknown, and the program he had chosen to perform was unfamiliar to the Viennese public. He was, however, well acquainted with techniques for papering a house. As a boy he had been sent by his mother to buy 200 tickets for a concert in which a family friend was playing the violin. The man at the ticket office dismissed him as a tout, shouting in his face: "If it's tickets for resale you're wanting you can go elsewhere!" Paul returned to his mother, begging her to appoint someone else to the task. For the first time in his life he felt ashamed of being rich.

If the hall was going to be half empty, at least those seats that were occupied should be filled with as many allies as possible. He wanted to create an atmosphere that would give the impression of strong public support. The Wittgenstein family was large and well connected. All siblings, cousins, uncles and aunts were expected to attend and to applaud uproariously at the end of each piece regardless of how they felt he had played. Tenants, servants and the servants' distant relations, many of whom had never before attended a concert of serious music, were plied with tickets and summoned to appear. Paul could have hired a smaller hall but was advised that the critics might not show up if he did so. He needed Max Kalbeck of the *Neues Wiener Tagblatt* and Julius Korngold of the *Neue Freie Presse* to be there. These were the two most influential music critics in Vienna.

Every detail was carefully considered. A concert with the Vienna Philharmonic Orchestra would have cost him nearly twice as much as the less prestigious Tonkünstler Orchestra, but money was no object. "Quite apart from the price," he later wrote, "I would not hire the Vienna Philharmonic. Probably they won't play as you want them to do, it will look like a horse which you can't ride; and then if the concert is a success, people might say it was only due to the orchestra's merit." He chose the Tonkünstler.

The conductor, Oskar Nedbal, was twelve years older than Paul, an ex-pupil of Dvořák, a composer and a first-class violist who had joined the Tonkünstler Orchestra in 1906 after ten years as conductor of the Czech Philharmonic. On Christmas Eve 1930, he threw himself head first from a fourth-story window of a hotel in Zagreb and was heard of no more.

Paul's program was unusual, obstinate and provocative. He wanted to present four consecutive works for piano and orchestra—four virtuosic concertos in a single evening. Irrespective of success or failure, this young man's debut would long be remembered as an audacious gymnastic spectacle.

Works by the inebriate Irish composer John Field, who had died in Moscow of cancer of the rectum in 1837, had long fallen from fashion in Vienna. Nowadays "Drunken John" is best remembered as the man who invented the nocturne—a form of short piano reverie later popularized by Chopin. Paul's valet and cook were probably not the only ones in the audience that night never to have heard of him. Even among the musical cognoscenti of 1913, few would have rated Field as worthy of the Golden Hall, for Vienna had a musical heritage of its own, the most illustrious of any city in the world, and to those raised on a diet of Mozart, Haydn, Beethoven, Schubert, Brahms, Bruckner and Mahler (all of whom had lived at one time or another within the city walls), Field's music would have seemed at best an insipid curiosity, at worst a bad-taste joke.

History does not record how Paul felt in the hours leading up to the concert or his state of mind as he dressed in his tails, warmed his hands in the green room, climbed the steep steps onto the concert platform and took his bows before an audience of friends, strangers, critics, mentors, teachers and servants, but he never succeeded in controlling his nerves. Later he was observed to bash the walls with his fists, tear up his music or hurl furniture across the room in the fraught final minutes before walking onto the stage.

The Field Concerto is in three movements lasting a total of thirty-five minutes. If Paul failed to notice at the time, he must have been informed afterward that Julius Korngold, chief critic of the *Neue Freie Presse,* had left the auditorium during the applause and had not returned to hear his renditions of Mendelssohn's Serenade and Allegro giocoso, the Variations and Fugue on a Theme of Czerny by Josef Labor, or Liszt's crashing bravura Concerto in E flat. As he and his family scoured the papers and music journals in the days following the concert, this critic's curious behavior must have weighed heavily on their minds.

Ludwig, Paul's younger brother, was not in Vienna to hear him play. Three months earlier he had moved from England (where he had been studying philosophy at Cambridge) into two rooms of a postmaster's house in a tiny village at the bottom of a fjord, north of Bergen in Norway. According to the diaries of his closest friend, his decision to exile himself was "wild and sudden." In September he had stated that he wished to withdraw from a world in which "he perpetually finds himself feeling contempt for others and irritating others by his nervous temperament." He was also at this time suffering (as he often did) from delusions of his own death. "The feeling that I shall have to die before being able to publish my ideas is growing stronger and stronger in me every day," he wrote to his tutor and mentor at Cambridge. A fortnight later a shock spurred him on his course of action—it took the form of a letter announcing that his sister Gretl and her husband Jerome were coming to live in London. "He can't stand either of them and he won't live in England liable always to visits from them," his friend recorded. "I am leaving at once," Ludwig exclaimed, "because my brother-in-law has come to live in London and I can't bear to be so near him."

The whole family wanted Ludwig to come to Vienna for Paul's concert and for Christmas, but he was resistant and the obligation to conform weighed heavily upon him. His family depressed him, the previous Christmas had been horrific, he was in low spirits and his philosophical work was advancing at a snail's pace. "UNFORTUNATELY I have to go to Vienna for Christmas," he wrote to a friend. "The fact is my mother very much wants me to, so much so that she would be grievously offended if I refused. She has such dreadful memories of just this time last year that I do not have the heart to stay away."

2   THAT TIME LAST YEAR

Christmas at the Wittgensteins' Winter Palais on the Alleegasse in Vienna's Wieden district was, by tradition, an extravagant and ceremonious affair to which the family attached the greatest significance; but the Christmas of 1912 (the year before Paul's concert debut) was different from all the rest, for on that occasion the family's energies and enthusiasms were subdued by the grim realization that its head (Paul and Ludwig's father Karl Wittgenstein)—stout-chested and leathery of complexion—was dying in his bedroom upstairs. He was suffering from cancer of the tongue and a month earlier had submitted himself to the scalpels of the distinguished Viennese surgeon Baron Anton von Eiselsberg. To gain access to the lesion Dr. von Eiselsberg had needed first to remove a large section of Karl's lower jaw. Only then was he able to proceed with the extirpation of the neck glands, the floor of the mouth and whatever was left of Karl's tongue after previous surgical raids. His bleeding was staunched by a team of assistants using the modern technique of electrical cautery.

Karl had smoked large Cuban cigars all his adult life and continued to use them even after the first symptoms of his disease had been diagnosed seven years earlier. Then he was advised by doctors not to move in order to effect a cure. By the end, he had endured seven operations, but the cancer continued to outmaneuver every stratagem that Dr. von Eiselsberg could devise against it, shifting in a sequence of malignant sideways steps from thyroid to ear to throat and eventually to his tongue. His final operation took place on November 8, 1912. Eiselsberg had warned him that there was a risk of his dying under the knife and on the evening before, as the doctors were sharpening their tools, Karl and his wife Leopoldine retired to the opulent gloom of the *Musiksaal.* He took out his violin, she sat at the piano, and together they played through some of their favorite works by Bach, Beethoven and Brahms in a long, unspoken farewell to one another.

The next morning, in the center of his plain, well-lit, clean-tiled theater, Dr. von Eiselsberg cut the tumor from Karl's mouth. Perhaps this time he had finally succeeded in eradicating the last traces of the cancer, but for Karl—flat, speechless and entrapped by the curse of a secondary infection—it was already too late. He left the clinic to die at home. And thus it was that on Christmas Day 1912, as he lay outstretched, weakened and feverish upon his bed, his family was gathered round in a mood of grim expectation.

3 KARL'S GREAT REBELLION

Hermine (pronounced *Hermeena*), nicknamed Mining, was the firstborn of Karl's nine children and his favorite child. Named after her grandfather, Hermann Wittgenstein, her birth marked a turning point in Karl's business fortunes and as a consequence he always treated her as a lucky mascot. She was thirty-nine years old at the time of his dying, unmarried, still living at home and still at his beck and call. In character she was inward looking, a repressed person, whose movements were stiff, whose stance was erect and whose manner (to those who did not know her well) appeared to be arrogant or aloof. In fact she suffered from low self-esteem and was ill at ease in the company of strangers. When Brahms came to dinner and she was allowed to sit with him at the top table, she became so agitated with nervous tension that she had to leave the room and spend most of the evening vomiting into one of the Palais lavatories. Photographs of the youthful Hermine portray her as alert, feminine, perhaps even pretty, but an instinctive need for privacy put her always on her guard against the approaches of men. They say she had one or two suitors in her prime but none so ardent as to relieve her of her maidenhood.

As the years piled on she withdrew from all but her closest circle of friends and family, her smile shortened and she grew self-conscious, gracious, vigilant and schoolmarmish. On the hottest days, she dressed in the heaviest and most somber clothes, brushing her hair flat back against her head and pressing her ponytail into a tight coil at the nape of her neck. Her ears were broad and heavy and her nose uncommonly prominent—both features inherited from her father. In her last years she resembled a handsome army officer in the first gloat of early retirement, a bit like Captain von Trapp in the film version of *The Sound of Music*.

Despite her inhibitions, Hermine was a talented pianist and a good singer, but her main passions were for painting and drawing. Since the early 1890s, when her father bought the Palais (for 250,000 florins off a bankrupt property developer who had built it for himself twenty years earlier), Hermine had helped and encouraged him in amassing his art collection. At first she was allowed to choose which works to buy and decide where and how they should be displayed—her father jokingly referred to her in those days as "my Art Director"—but as his instinctive bossiness took over, her role diminished and eventually faded into the shadows of his domineering enthusiasm. She remained, however, her father's close companion, accompanying him on arduous trips of inspection to his factories and rolling mills around the Hapsburg Empire, superintending his business receptions, suggesting countless improvements to his hunting estate in the mountains and, in the weeks before his final operation, sitting patiently by his bed jotting autobiographical notes that he dictated to her in wheezing, staccato gasps:

1864 Advised to leave school. Should have continued private studies until graduation.

Ran away from home in January 1865.

Lived two months in a rented room on the Krugerstrasse.

Took with me a violin and 200 florins that belonged to my sister Anna.

Noticed in a newspaper ad a young student's request for support and gave him some money in exchange for his passport.

At the frontier, in Bodenbach, officials asked to see all passports.

Forced to wait in a large room.

Called individually to be scrutinized by two frontier guards.

The false passport just happened to be all right.

The so-called "advice to leave school" took the form of what Germans and Austrians call a *Consilium abeundi*—Karl was effectively expelled. Hermann Christian Wittgenstein, though frequently furious at his son's dilatoriness, attempted on this occasion to limit his reproach. Karl had always given cause for concern; he had always been a stubborn, single-minded and difficult child and there had been many occasions on which the need to reprimand him had arisen—the time, for instance, when he had pawned his violin to buy a glass-cutting apparatus; the time he fiddled with the tower clock to make it strike every fifteen minutes and rouse the household at regular intervals throughout the night; the time when he "borrowed" one of his father's coaches, took his sister and her friend out for a spin, drove too fast and crashed on a bridge, breaking his sister's friend's nose. And what about the time when he ran away from school to the neighboring town of Klosterneuburg? He was only eleven, had jettisoned his expensive overcoat in order to pass for a street urchin and was recognized begging in a coffeehouse doorway by the town mayor. Held overnight, he was returned the following morning to his furious parents.

Hermann adored, petted and indulged his eldest son Paul, slipping him secret gifts and grooming him as heir to his fortunes, but with Karl, his third son, he could never get along. From the start the relationship was frosty, distrustful and antagonistic, and so it would remain until the day of Hermann's death in May 1878. Hermine cited differences in personality between her father and grandfather. They were too dissimilar— chalk and cheese as the English say; *Tag und Nacht* (night and day) as she would have put it. Karl was humorous, unpredictable and free spirited, his father Hermann ponderous, parsimonious and rigid. In other respects they were of similar mold; both were domineering and unyielding and it was by reason of these common failings (more perhaps than by reason of their differences) that their great enmity arose.

When Karl ran away for the second time, he did so suddenly, without warning and without note of explanation. It was January 1865. He was seventeen years old. At first it was supposed that he had had an accident. The weather was bad—blizzards and subzero temperatures. Ice covered the streets of Vienna and all roads leading out of the city were blocked by drifts of heavy snow. Karl's photograph was distributed among policemen who confidently predicted his imminent return, but as the days stretched into weeks and the weeks turned to months, Karl was nowhere to be found, and tension in the Wittgenstein household had risen to such a pitch that soon it became impossible to mention the boy's name in front of his parents.

From the frontier checkpoint at Bodenbach, Karl had made his way to the port of Hamburg, where he boarded a ship bound for New York. He arrived there in the early spring, penniless and with nothing but the clothes on his back and an expensive violin under his arm. First he took a job as a waiter in a restaurant on Broadway, but left after a fortnight to join a minstrel band. Following President Lincoln's assassination at Ford's Theatre on April 14, all theater and music performances were banned throughout the Union and Karl's group was forced to break up. Soon he found himself piloting a canal boat of pressed straw from New York to

Washington, where he remained for six months serving whiskeys in a crowded "Nigger-bar."

> Main activity was to distinguish between one black man and the next, to know who had paid and who hadn't. The owner of the bar himself could not tell the blacks apart.
>
> Made my first decent pay there.
>
> Newly dressed and equipped, returned to New York in November and wrote home for the first time.

The dying man's memory was not quite precise. His first letter—a few laconic lines—was actually sent, three months earlier, in September 1865 and was addressed to a Wittgenstein servant with whom he was on friendly terms. The effect was instant: a flurry of letters issued from his siblings and from his mother in Vienna, but nothing from his father, with whom he remained in deep disgrace. At first he felt too ashamed to respond to any of them and his silence prompted his sister to write a begging letter urging him to make contact with his parents. Karl responded, not to them, but to her: "I cannot write to my parents. Just as I would not have the courage to stand before them now and ask their forgiveness, I could do so even less on paper, paper that is patient and does not blush. I shall only be able to do it when the occasion will permit me to show them my improvement."

For months the stalemate persisted while his mother, eager for word from her wayward boy, continued to ply him with letters and remittances of money. Still he refused to respond to her directly. On October 30 he wrote to his brother Ludwig (nicknamed Louis):

> Mother's letter made me terribly happy; as I read it my heart was beating so strongly that I could not go on . . . At the moment I carry food and serve drinks. The work is not difficult, but I have to keep going until 4 a.m. . . . . I have only one desire—you can probably guess it—to be on better terms with Father. As soon as I have entered a business I shall write to him but business is very bad here so you should not be surprised that I have not yet found myself another job.

Karl's lassitude was both mental and physical. He felt depressed, and for six months had been suffering from a grotesque form of diarrhea (possibly dysentery) that had left him weak spirited and emaciated. Only by strenuous effort could he muster the strength to write to his mother:

> You may think that I am a rotten son for thanking you only now after I have received several letters from you and not yet written myself but I cannot find the inner peace I need in order to write to my parents. Every time I think of you and of my sisters and brothers I feel shame and regret . . . dearest mother, please talk to Father in my favour and be assured of the sincerest gratitude of your son.

Direct correspondence with his father remained out of the question, at least before he had found himself employment on a level higher than barman. Returning from Washington to New York, he took a job teaching mathematics and violin at a Christian school in Manhattan. Unable to control his pupils, he transferred to an asylum for destitute children at Westchester for a short spell as nightwatchman. After that he went to teach at a smart college in Rochester where the food was good and the salary, for the first time since he had been in America, reasonable. Only now could he turn his thoughts to Vienna and to his father.

4 ENTREPRENEUR

There were no red carpets or silver bands to welcome Karl home on his return from New York in the spring of 1866, and the very sight of him served only to deepen the distress that his flight had caused within his family. He was in a shocking state: skinny, delirious and bedraggled, speaking a garbled mixture of incorrect German and Yankee slang.

His mother had written to warn him that he was expected to take a job in agriculture on his return. "If it is Father's urgent wish that I should work on a farm, I shall of course do it," Karl had told his brother Louis. On arrival, still in disgrace, he was dispatched to one of his father's rented farms near the small market town of Deutschkreutz, in what was at that time a part of German West Hungary. Here it was hoped he might recover his energies and develop some enthusiasm for his father's line of business.

Hermann Wittgenstein was no ordinary farmer. He had never plowed a field or milked a cow, for his business successes were rooted in a partnership with his in-laws, rich Viennese merchants called Figdor. At the time of Karl's birth in 1847, he was a wool trader living at Gohlis, near Leipzig in Saxony. Four years later he moved with his wife and children to Austria, where he acted as factor, or estate manager, transforming the dilapidated inheritances of flaky aristocrats into thriving concerns in exchange for a percentage of the profit. The money he made from this, and from his collaboration with the Figdors (who traded the coal, corn, timber and wool that these estates produced), was prudently invested in Viennese property.

Though frugal to a fault, Hermann lived with his family in considerable style. In Austria he took a lease on the famous palace at Bad Vöslau, moving three years later to the huge, cubed, towered castle of Vösendorf (now a town hall and bicycle museum) nine miles south of Vienna. Later, he occupied the main portion of a rented castle at Laxenburg, originally built to house the Empress Maria Theresa's Prime Minister, Anton von Kaunitz. His youngest child, Clothilde (who ended her days as a reclusive morphine addict in Paris), was the only one of Hermann's eleven children to be born in Austria. Karl was the sixth in age, and his parents' third and youngest son.

Hermann Wittgenstein never lavished money upon his children for he was determined that they should make their own way in the world. Of his three sons, he considered Karl to be the most feckless, but strict parsimony, combined with incessant reprobation and disparagement of Karl's abilities, succeeded only in kindling within the boy's hardening heart a steely ambition to prove his father wrong.

At the end of his career Karl liked to hear himself described as a "self-made man," but the term was only partially accurate. His vast fortune was certainly earned by his energy and business aptitude, but like many soi-disant "self-made" men Karl tended to overlook the fact that he had married a lady of considerable fortune, without whose bountiful trust fund he might never have succeeded in making the first leap from business employee to capitalist owner.

The story of Karl Wittgenstein's rise from rebellious American barman to multimillionaire Austrian steel magnate may be succinctly summarized. After the year spent farming at Deutschkreutz he enlisted at the Technical University in Vienna, acquiring there only as much knowledge as he felt might later be of use to him, skipping afternoon lectures and taking a low-paid work-experience job at the factory of the Staatsbahn (National Railroad Company). In 1869 he left the university without qualifications and spent the next three years employed in various jobs—as assistant design engineer at a naval shipyard in Trieste; at a turbine construction firm in Vienna; with the Hungarian North-East Railroad at Szatmár and Budapest; at the Neufeldt-Schoeller Steel Works at Ternitz; and finally at the spa town of Teplitz (or Teplice), where he was hired, initially on a part-time basis, to help draw up plans for a new rolling mill. The manager took him on as a favor to the family, expecting little of him, but soon Karl's energy, originality of mind, and ability to find quick solutions to a wide assortment of business and engineering problems earned him a full-time salaried position at the mill.

Feeling at last secure, with an annual income of 1,200 gulden, Karl resolved to ask for his sweetheart's hand in marriage. She, Leopoldine Kalmus, was the sister of a woman who rented a wing of the castle at Laxenburg. Karl's mother cautiously welcomed the news of her son's engagement, but was unsure if he would make a good husband. To her future daughter-in-law she wrote: "Karl has a good heart but he left his parents' home too early in life. As to the final improvements in his upbringing, reliability, order, self-control, all this, I hope, he will learn in your loving company."

Hermann, who had yet to meet Miss Kalmus, was less positive. Her father (deceased) had been a wine merchant. By blood she was half Jewish and by faith a Roman Catholic, offending at a stroke his Protestant ethic and his anti-Semitic sensibility. In point of fact Leopoldine was a distant cousin of Hermann's wife, Mrs. Wittgenstein—both could claim descent from a Rabbi Isaac Brillin in the seventeenth century—but Hermann may not have known this at the time. In any case he had long made it clear to his children that he did not wish them to marry Jews. Of the eleven, only Karl disobeyed. Hermann had a legal right to forbid the marriage and it fell to Karl to request his father's formal permission. He duly went through the motions but did so in such a sloppy and inconsiderate manner as to throw his father into a rage.

Hermann was lying in bed complaining of backache when his son arrived in high spirits from Teplitz. Karl offered a massage to soothe the pain and no sooner was his father flat down, groaning into his pillow, than Karl casually let slip the information that he was en route to Aussee, where he intended to propose to Miss Kalmus. Whether the matter of her faith was raised at that moment, history does not relate, but as Karl was extolling the beauties and virtues of his bride-to-be, Hermann cut him short. "Well, they are all like that at first," he said, "until they shed their skins!" Only once the engagement had been publicly declared would the old man write to his future daughter-in-law:

> Dear Miss,
>
> My son Karl, unlike his brothers and sisters, has always, from his earliest youth, chosen to follow his own direction. In the end this has not perhaps turned out to be such a grave disadvantage. He even asked for my consent to the engagement, though only when he was already on his way to ask for your hand. Since he is so full of praise for you, and since his sisters warmly concur in their appraisal of you, I do not feel that I have the right to make difficulties, and so I can only wish that your desires and hopes for a happy future be met. Let this expression of my sincere frame of mind suffice at least until I have had the opportunity to make your personal acquaintance.
>
> Yours truly,
> H. Wittgenstein

Karl and Leopoldine were married on St. Valentine's Day, February 14, 1874, in a side chapel of St. Stephen's, the great Catholic cathedral of Vienna. It was a windy day. On the cathedral roof polished, colored tiles gleamed like the scales of an exotic fish while high on the front portal, among carved figures representing ugliness and evil, the face of a Jew in his *pileum cornutum* leered down on Hermann and his guests as they filed through the door. When the service was over, everyone assembled to cheer the bride and groom—but Karl, in a fury at his coachman's sloth, smashed his fist against the carriage window shouting: "To hell with you! Are you going to drive off?" The force of this blow shattered the glass and gashed his hand, spilling blood across the clean interior of the coach.

❖ ❖ ❖

THE COUPLE WENT TO LIVE AT EICHWALD, near Teplitz, but Karl's remunerative job there did not last as long as he had expected. Soon, he found himself embroiled in an internal dispute at the climax of which he resigned in protest at the chairman of the board's rough treatment of his friend, the managing director. For a year he remained unemployed (it was at this time that Hermine was born) and in the summer of 1875 he took a desultory job as an engineer with a company in Vienna. After a year in the capital, the hostile chairman at Teplitz himself resigned and Karl was reinstated at the old firm, this time with a seat on the board. The mill's fortunes were in a parlous state but he managed to turn them round by securing a hefty order for railway tracks against stiff competition from Krupp. This he achieved by chasing the Russian financier, railroad builder and trusted counselor to Tsar Alexander II, Samuil Poliakov, halfway around Europe and getting him to agree to the purchase of much lighter and cheaper rails than his rivals were offering. The Russians, at war with the Turks, needed the rails for a military campaign in the Balkan Peninsula. Karl's deal stipulated that he would continue manufacturing rails until such a time as Poliakov telegraphed him to stop. When the order finally came through Karl reported to the Russians that his company had several thousand of their rails in his yard ready for shipping—a lie of course—but it ensured that the final payment was much bigger than it otherwise would have been.

In his business dealings Karl was an opportunist whose great fortune was accumulated as much by the successful outcomes to the risks he took as by his hard work and lively intuition. He made promises, unsure as to how he could ever fulfill them, he agreed to buy companies and shares with money he did not possess, and he offered for sale stocks that had already been promised to other clients. In the end he trusted always to his wits to extricate himself from the problems he created. "An industrialist must take chances," he wrote. "He must be prepared to gamble everything on a single card when the moment demands, even at the risk of failing to reap the fruits that he had hoped to gain, losing his initial stake and having to start again from scratch."

In 1898, aged fifty-one, he returned to Vienna after a long holiday abroad to announce his retirement from business. With immediate effect he withdrew from all of his directorships and executive positions, choosing, in the years that followed, to keep a beady eye on the industry from his office in the Krugerstrasse that was always kept open "just in case the Minister of Commerce should drop in for my advice." At the time of these resignations he was at the peak of his career. In the course of it he had been owner or principal shareholder of the Bohemian Mining Company, the Prague Iron Industry Company, the Teplitz Steel Works, the Alpine Mining Company and a host of lesser factories, rolling mills, and coal and metal mines throughout the empire. He had occupied seats on the boards of at least three major banks as well as a munitions company and possessed, scattered within his three main Austrian residences, magnificent and valuable collections of furniture, art, porcelain and autograph musical manuscripts.

For as long as his health permitted, Karl dedicated part of his retirement to his private pleasures—hunting, shooting, fencing, riding, commissioning and collecting art, writing articles on business and economic affairs, playing the violin and, in the summer, taking long walks through the Alpine countryside. It would be idle to speculate on how much money he was worth. Karl Menger, a cousin, wrote that his fortune before the First World War "had been estimated at 200 million kronen—the equivalent of at least that many dollars after World War II." But these figures are meaningless. He was stupendously rich.

5 MARRIAGE TO AN HEIRESS

Jerome Steinberger was the son of a bankrupt kid-glove importer from New York. His father, Herman, had committed suicide on Christmas Day 1900. One of his Steinberger aunts had thrown herself into the Hudson River. It is thought that an uncle, Jacob Steinberger, may also have killed himself in May 1900. Jerome made audacious attempts to rescue the family firm but failed, changed his name to Stonborough and took a course in humanities at a college in Chicago. His father, an immigrant from Nassau in Saxony, was rumored to have insured his life for $100,000. His sister, Aimée, married William, the black-sheep brother of the powerful Guggenheim clan.

In 1901, styling himself Dr. Stonborough, Jerome traveled for the first time to Vienna and, a year later, returned to the city to study medicine. It is not known where, how or even if he converted from Judaism to Christianity, but on January 7, 1905, twelve weeks after his sister's Jewish marriage in New York, he was back to Vienna, on one of the coldest days in Austrian history, shivering before the altar of a Protestant church on the cobbled Dorotheergasse, with a tall, nervous, twenty-two-year-old Viennese bride at his side.

Her friends called her Gretl, though she had been christened Margherita and would, in due course, anglicise the spelling of her name to Margaret. She was Karl and Leopoldine Wittgenstein's youngest daughter. Among her aunts and uncles ranked judges, soldiers, doctors, scientists, patrons of the arts and government administrators—all of them prominent. Affixed to the walls of the church above the spot where she and Jerome exchanged their vows were three polished plaques, each of them sponsored by a member of the family: "Thy Kingdom Come," "Blessed are they that hear the word of God, and keep it," "Let all that breathes praise the Lord. Alleluia!"

What induced Jerome and Gretl to take a romantic interest in one another is not obvious. They came from different backgrounds. Hers was musical, his was not; while she embraced the company of others, he was inclined to shun it. Both, however, took a keen interest in matters medical and scientific—she, as a teenager, had embroidered a cushion for her bedroom that depicted a human heart complete with coronary vessels and arteries. After his father's bankruptcy Jerome must have been excited at the prospect of sharing in her vast fortune; she was, after all, the daughter of one of the Hapsburg Empire's richest men. And it may equally be possible that she, in her turn, was attracted to those qualities in him—his impatient, domineering personality, commanding presence, unpredictable mood swings—that most reminded her of her father. These speculations may, in the case of Gretl and Jerome, be wide of the mark, but similarities of personality did exist between Jerome Stonborough and Karl Wittgenstein, and, even if Jerome had not been primarily motivated to marry Gretl for her fortune, he could not have failed to be impressed by her father's luxurious, treasure-filled palace in Vienna.

Gretl was nine years younger and several inches taller than her new American husband, dark-eyed, dark-haired and of pale complexion. It would be misleading, on the strength of surviving snapshots, to describe her as beautiful, at least in the conventional sense of the term, but the photographic art may have been unjust to her as many who knew her personally attested to her striking and attractive looks. "She possessed a 'rare' beauty," said one, "and was elegant in an exotic manner. Two arches on her forehead formed by her hair growing to a point made her appearance unique." Gustav Klimt struggled to capture these elusive nuances in a full-length portrait commissioned by Mrs. Wittgenstein shortly before her daughter's marriage.

Gretl loathed the finished picture, blaming Klimt's "inaccurate" depiction of her mouth, which she later had repainted by a lesser artist. Even then, the picture failed to please, so she left it to molder, unhung and unfeted, in her attic. Visitors to the Neue Pinakothek gallery in Munich, where the picture presently hangs, might enjoy trying to work out for themselves why the sitter was so displeased with it. They may point to the rings of gray under Gretl's eyes, identify her expression as tired, doubtful, possibly frightened; they may observe how she stands self-conscious and discomfited, in a flamboyant, ill-fitting, shoulderless white silk dress, or remark on the pallor of her hands clasped in a neurotic twist of fingers at her stomach. But by examining the portrait, however intently, the visitor will never learn the reasons for all this—reasons that were unconnected to any apprehensions that she may have been feeling about her marriage to Jerome, or even to her awkwardness at having to sit for the sexually predatory Klimt. In May 1904, at the time Klimt started work on the painting, Gretl's brother, her closest sibling in age and the boon companion of her teenage years, had suddenly, theatrically and very publicly poisoned himself.

6 THE DEATH OF RUDOLF WITTGENSTEIN

At the time of his demise Rudolf Wittgenstein, known in the family as "Rudi," was twenty-two years old and a student of chemistry at the Berlin Academy. By all accounts he was an intelligent, literate, good-looking man with grand passions for music, photography and the theater. In the summer of 1903, anxious about an aspect of his personality that he termed "my perverted disposition," he sought help from the Scientific Humanitarian Committee, a charitable organization that campaigned for the repeal of Section 175 of the German Criminal Code—a draconian law against *die widernatürliche Unzucht* (unnatural sexual acts). The same organization published an annual report of its activities under the florid title *Jahrbuch für sexuelle Zwischenstufen unter besonderer Berücksichtigung der Homosexualität* (Yearbook for Transsexuality with Specific Consideration of Homosexuality) and it was in one of these volumes that a case study, written up by the distinguished sexologist Dr. Magnus Hirschfeld, described in detail the problems of an unnamed homosexual student in Berlin. Rudi, fearing that the article had identified him as the subject, immediately set himself upon his fatal course of action. That, at least, is one version of the story. The facts that follow are less contentious.

At 9:45 on the evening of May 2, 1904, Rudi walked into a restaurant-bar on Berlin's Brandenburgstrasse, ordered two glasses of milk and some food, which he ate in a state of noticeable agitation. When he had finished he asked the waiter to send a bottle of mineral water to the pianist with instructions for him to play the popular Thomas Koschat number "Verlassen, verlassen, verlassen bin ich":

Forsaken, forsaken, forsaken am I!
Like a stone in the roadway, for no lass loves me!
I shall go to the chapel, to the chapel way off,
And there on my knees, I'll cry my heart out!

In the forest stands a hillock where many flowers bloom,
There sleeps my poor lass, whom no love can revive.
Thither my pilgrimage, thither my desires,
There I'll feel keenly, how forsaken I am.

As the music wafted across the room, Rudolf took from his pocket a sachet of clear crystal compound and dissolved the contents into one of his glasses of milk. The effects of potassium cyanide when ingested are instant and agonizing: a tightening of the chest, a terrible burning sensation in the throat, immediate discoloration of the skin, nausea, coughing and convulsions. Within two minutes Rudolf was slumped back in his chair unconscious. The landlord sent customers out in search of doctors. Three of them arrived, but too late for their ministrations to take effect.

A report in the next day's paper indicated that several suicide notes had been found at the scene. One of them, addressed to his parents, said that Rudi had killed himself in grief at the death of a friend. Two days later his mortal remains were taken from a Berlin morgue back to Vienna to be buried without honor; for his father Karl, the pain and humiliation were unspeakable. No sooner were the burial rites concluded than he hurried his family from the cemetery, forbidding his wife from turning to look back at the grave. In future neither she nor any member of the family would be permitted to utter Rudolf's name in his presence again.

Eight months after the funeral, as Gretl and her new husband were leaving the church in which they had just been married, the bride placed her frozen wedding bouquet into the hands of a trusted friend with instructions to take it to the place where her brother was buried, and to strew her flowers, in memory, upon his grave.

7 THE TRAGEDY OF HANS

Karl's decision to forbid any mention of Rudolf was actuated, not by a lack of feeling on his part, but by a surfeit of it, which, unleashed, might prove destructive. There were practical considerations too, a desire to pull his family together and stop them from mourning, something that only a stiff-lipped resistance could achieve. But if his intention was to bind the surviving members of his family closer together he could not have failed more signally, for the effect of his censorship created an atmosphere of unbearable tension in the home, causing a split between the Wittgenstein children and their parents that time would never heal. Karl was blamed (but not to his face) for loading his sons with excessive career pressure, for insisting that none of them should pursue any profession that did not involve the two disciplines that had made him his fortune—engineering and business. Mrs. Wittgenstein, Leopoldine (or Poldy as she was called within the family circle), was also accused by her children of failing to stand up to her autocratic husband, of being mouse-like, indecisive, and insecure. More than forty years after her brother's death Hermine recorded with bitterness:

> When my seven-year-old brother, Rudi, had to take his public school entrance examination, he was so unhappy and afraid that the examining teacher told my mother: "He is a very nervous child; you should be careful with him." I have often heard this sentence repeated with irony, as if it were nonsensical. My mother could not seriously consider that one of her children could be overly nervous; that, for her, was out of the question.

Family discussion of Rudi's suicide was forced by Karl's ban into furtive conclaves, with the inevitable consequence that the facts mutated over time in the manner of a Chinese whisper. It was rumored, for instance, that he had killed himself because his pampered Viennese upbringing had inadequately prepared him for the rigors of student life in Berlin; that he had killed himself because his father had refused to allow him to train as an actor, or because he had contracted a venereal disease that had sent him off his head. All these things and many more were said, some of them, no doubt, inaccurate and disheartening, and yet they were as nothing compared with the distorted tattle that emanated from the disappearance of another brother, Johannes (known as Hans).

As Oscar Wilde might have remarked, "To lose one son, may be regarded as a misfortune, to lose two looks like carelessness." As strange as this may appear, Rudi's suicide was not the first such tragedy to befall the House of Wittgenstein, for two years earlier Hans, Karl's eldest son, had vanished without trace. He too was a forbidden topic of conversation.

Surviving photographs of Hans in his youth, with angled head and intense squinting eyes, suggest that he may have been a little imbecilic, perhaps what is nowadays termed an idiot savant—defined as a backward child who displays an uncommon talent in some restricted area such as memorizing or rapid calculation. He was certainly shy—painfully so—and his inner world was intense. Physically large and ungainly, stubborn and resistant to discipline, he was regarded by his eldest sister as "a very peculiar child." The first word he ever spoke was "Oedipus."

From his earliest youth he followed a strange impulse to translate the world around him into mathematical formulas. As a small boy strolling with his sister through a Viennese park one afternoon he came across an ornate pavilion and asked her if she could imagine it made of diamonds. "Yes," Hermine said, "wouldn't that be nice!"

"Now let me have a go," he said, and setting himself upon the grass proceeded to calculate the annual yield of the South African diamond mines against the accumulated wealth of the Rothschilds and the American billionaires, to measure every portion of the pavilion in his head, including all of its ornament and cast-iron filigree, and to build an image slowly and methodically until—quite suddenly—he stopped. "I cannot continue," he said, "for I cannot imagine my diamond pavilion any bigger than this," indicating a height of some three or four feet above the ground. "Can you?"

"Of course," Hermine said. "What is the problem?"

"Well, there is no money left to pay for any more diamonds."

For all his mathematical savvy Hans's abiding interest was in music, for which he displayed prodigious and phenomenal talent. At four years old he could identify the Doppler effect as a quarter-tone drop in pitch of a passing siren; at five, he flung himself to the ground in tears crying "Wrong! Wrong!" as two brass bands at opposite ends of a long carnival procession played, simultaneously, two marches in different keys. When the family went out to hear the famous Joachim Quartet in concert at the Kleiner Musikvereinsaal, Hans refused to come. He was not interested in musical interpretation, instead he lay on the floor at home with the parts of the score that were being performed at the concert spread out in front of him. Without ever having heard the piece he was able, simply from his study of the single, separately printed sheets, to construct in his head a clear impression of how all four musical lines would sound together and, from that, to play the whole from memory on the piano to his parents on their return.

Although left-handed, Hans could play the violin, organ and piano to a deft standard. Julius Epstein, Mahler's teacher and a distinguished professor of piano at the Vienna Conservatoire, once hailed him a "genius," but Hans's musical interpretations, for all their dexterity and flashes of warmth, were marred by extreme violence and spontaneous eruptions of tension, typical of his nature from its earliest years. Hermine blamed this on the strained, simmering atmosphere of the Wittgenstein home, concluding:

> It was tragic that our parents, in spite of their great ethical seriousness and sense of duty, did not succeed in creating some sort of harmony between themselves and their children; it was tragic that my father had sons who were as different from him as if he had found them in an orphanage! It must have been a bitter disappointment to him that none of them would follow his path and continue the work of his life. One of the greatest differences—and one of the most tragic—concerned his sons' lack of vitality and will for life in their youth.

So what exactly happened to Hans? A short piece in the *Neues Wiener Tagblatt* of May 6, 1902, explained: "Industrialist Karl Wittgenstein has suffered a terrible misfortune. His eldest son, Hans (24), who has been in America for about three weeks on a study trip, has had a canoeing accident." The date of this short notice suggests the possibility that Rudi may have chosen the second anniversary of his brother's "terrible misfortune" as a significant date on which to end his own life in Berlin. But if Hans had indeed killed himself on May 2, 1902, the Wittgensteins were still a long way from admitting it publicly, and this all too brief report, which gives no indication of Hans's eventual fate, was by no means the last word on the matter. Family gossip has since produced many alternative explanations. Some say he fled to America, others to South America, one report has him last seen in Havana, Cuba. His name does not appear on any of the extant passenger lists. Maybe he traveled on a false passport. It is known that he was sent by his father in his early twenties to work at production plants in Bohemia, Germany and in England, where he was expected to take on duties and responsibilities that he greatly resented and from which he failed to reap any noticeable benefit. Instead of working he preferred to play music.

On his returns home Hans's relationship with his father was, by turns, sulphurous and tempestuous. Karl was a frightening man, even in a cheery mood. As Gretl wrote in a private notebook: "My father's frequent joking didn't seem funny to me, only dangerous." Karl, a poor judge of character, nursed an intense desire for his eldest son to excel in business, to shine as an entrepreneur and industrialist, to mirror his own soaring achievements—but the higher you soar, the smaller you look to someone who cannot fly and Karl, though musical himself, abhorred Hans's morbid obsession with music and eventually forbade him from playing any instrument except during strictly designated hours. Karl's own youthful rebellion against his father had led directly to his great success in business, but it was unwise of him to assume that Hans was made of the same mettle, and shortsighted to suppose that relentless paternal pressure upon such a young, volatile and unstable man would lead to any but the most catastrophic consequences.

The consensus of opinion points to his having dodged his father by fleeing abroad sometime in 1901. Hans had put on weight in his early twenties, had grown obsessed with the gloomy nihilistic philosophies of Arthur Schopenhauer and was, according to one report, "known to be homosexual." Some claim that he lived to the age of twenty-six. One source records that he died at the Everglades in Florida, another that "in

1903 the family was informed that a year earlier he had disappeared from a boat in Chesapeake Bay and had not been seen since. The obvious conclusion to draw was that he had committed suicide."

But do parents "obviously conclude" that their child has killed himself when they are informed that he was last seen in a row boat a year earlier? Would it not be more typical for any parent caught by such strained and unusual circumstances to wait patiently, hoping, expecting, hour by hour, year by year, for a knock at the door? At what point does a parent concede, without corpse or witness, that his son has not simply run away and hidden himself but has actually committed suicide?

Sailing off in a boat is just about the only theme consistent with most variants of the tale. Some say that Hans shot or poisoned himself in the boat, others that he scuttled it in order to drown himself. One of his nephews believed that the boat must have capsized during a tropical storm on Lake Okeechobee: "Of course a man can take a pistol out on the lake and kill himself, but unless very drunk, no one would seek that damn lake as a place to leave life." A letter from one of Hans's aunts suggests that the family sent an employee out to the Orinoco in Venezuela in search of him. A boat, an unspecified date, at least five different locations—the truth is unlikely ever to emerge.

Hans may, of course, have lived a full life abroad and in secret from his family in Vienna, but the most likely scenario is that he did indeed commit suicide somewhere outside Austria, that the family had prior intimations, or direct warnings, of his suicidal intent, and that the spur that induced them to declare openly that he had taken his life was the very public death in Vienna, on October 4, 1903, of a twenty-three-year-old philosopher called Otto Weininger.

The Weininger story is quickly told. He was an intense, clever, misguided young man, small and simian of aspect, from a family of rigid moral outlook. His father was a goldsmith. His short life was lived at the poles of self-hatred and self-worship with no saner resting place in between. "I believe that my gifts are such," he wrote, "that in some way I can solve all problems. I do not think that I could ever be wrong for any considerable length of time. I believe that I have deserved the name Messiah (Redeemer) because I have this nature."

In the spring of 1903 Weininger published his magnum opus, a long treatise called *Geschlecht und Charakter* (Sex and Character) which took a tough line on women (he was a misogynist) and on Jews (of which he was one). As the book was passing through the presses he remarked to a friend: "There are three possibilities for me—the gallows, suicide, or a future so brilliant that I don't dare to think of it." In the end a hostile press reception determined him on the second option. On the evening of October 3 he took a room in a house on the Schwarzspanierstrasse where the Austrian poet Lehnau had for several years repined and where, on March 26, 1827, Beethoven had died. No sooner were the letting terms agreed with his landlady than Weininger asked for two letters to be delivered to his family and, shortly after 10 p.m., retired to his room, locked the door, took out a loaded pistol, pointed the barrel at the left side of his chest and fired. When his brother arrived the next morning in urgent reaction to the letter he had just received, the bedroom door had to be kicked in; inside he found Otto sprawled in a pool of his own blood, fully clothed and still breathing. The young philosopher was rushed unconscious by voluntary ambulance to the Vienna General Hospital, where, at 10:30 that morning, he died.

Weininger's suicide caused a significant stir in Viennese society. The newspapers ran pages of commentary about him, and his reputation rose from that of obscure controversialist to national celebrity in a matter of days. Copies of *Geschlecht und Charakter* started to sell in great numbers. It is rumored that some of the Wittgensteins attended his funeral at the Matzleinsdorf Cemetery, which took place, like Christ's crucifixion, during a partial eclipse of the sun. All the Wittgensteins read his book.

Recent studies have documented the way in which high-profile "media" suicides can be held responsible for triggering so-called copycat deaths. In the month of August 1962, for instance, the U.S. suicide rate increased by 303 (a jump of 12 percent) after Marilyn Monroe took her fatal overdose. But this is not a new phenomenon. The suicide rate soared also in Vienna following the sensational double suicide of Crown Prince Rudolf and his mistress Marie Vetsera at Mayerling in 1889, and over a hundred years before that Goethe's novel *Die Leiden des jungen Werthers* (The Sorrows of Young Werther) had to be banned in cities across Europe when it was decided that the fictional hero's suicide was responsible for a spate of copycat deaths among the lovelorn young men of Italy, Leipzig and Copenhagen.

And thus it was in Vienna after Otto Weininger's death in October 1903. If Hans Wittgenstein really killed himself, the deed was most probably enacted while Weininger was still alive, but the acceptance of his fate, the declaration of it by his family in Vienna, came afterward, in the immediate wake of Weininger's public death—a wake whose silent ripples reached far beyond the Schwarzspanierstrasse, perhaps even to the very edges of that little restaurant table in the Berlin *Gaststube* where, seven months later, Rudolf sat edgily eyeing his last glass of milk.

8 AT HOME WITH THE WITTGENSTEINS

The Wittgenstein Winter Palais on the Alleegasse, which Jerome Stonborough first visited sometime between the dramas of Hans's disappearance and Rudi's suicide, must have seemed of a different order of opulence to anything that he had experienced as a glove importer on Broadway. That first visit was likely to have been as a guest at one of the Wittgensteins' private concerts to which he would have been invited as a new friend of Rudolf Maresch, a doctor married to one of Gretl's cousins.

The front elevation, which stretched more than fifty yards along the Alleegasse, was from the outside both imposing and austere: nine bays on the first floor, seven below, with high arches at either end. Jerome entered by the gate on the right-hand side, through heavy oak doors, attended by a uniformed porter whose simple task was to rise from his stool and bow to arriving guests. In the forecourt, he could not have failed to notice a colossal fountain statue (the work of the Croatian expressionist Ivan Meštrović) nor, on entering the gloomy high-ceilinged hall, an elaborate mosaic floor, carved paneling, frescoes depicting scenes from Shakespeare's *A Midsummer Night's Dream* and an imposing piece by Auguste Rodin. Straight ahead of him, between two stone arches, six steps, supported by marble balustrades, ran up to impressive glass double doors. These were attended (on the near side) by a full-sized statue of a Teuton doffing his cap in a gesture of welcome, and opened (on the far side) by a liveried valet, garbed, as one Palais guest remembered, in "a uniform reminiscent of an Austrian hunting outfit from the Steiermark." From here visitors were led up a long flight of wide, red-carpeted, marble steps (illumined in the daytime by sunlight streaming through the domed glass roof high above) to a cloakroom where servants waited to take the coats.

Private concerts took place sometimes in the Hall but more often in the *Musiksaal* on the first floor. This was the most splendid of all the Wittgenstein salons. Here, plush hunting tapestries were draped from ceiling to floor, except at one end where the whole wall was taken up with the pipe case of a two-manual pedal-organ, richly decorated with paintings of knights and minstrels in the Pre-Raphaelite style. In the center of the room two Bösendorfer Imperial grand pianos faced one another, keyboard to keyboard, while from a high black plinth frowned the squatting, naked figure of Ludwig van Beethoven, carved from a single block of white marble by Max Klinger in preparation for his celebrated Beethoven Monument. A set of ten gilt standard lamps was distributed around and about, but they were seldom switched on as the room was usually kept in darkness. Even by day its shutters were closed, the sole source of light being that of two small lamps clipped to the lecterns of each piano. If Jerome had needed the "rest room" he could not have found himself in a more convenient spot, for it was one of Karl Wittgenstein's obsessions that each of the main rooms of his house should have a lavatory leading off it, wherein the taps and sinks were ornately gilded.

The Wittgensteins' musical soirées were, in the words of Hermine, "always festive occasions, almost solemn, and the beautiful music was the essential thing." The quality of music making was first class, as the musicians who played there ranked among the most distinguished of their day. The violinist Joseph Joachim, a pupil of Mendelssohn and the first to play Brahms's Violin Concerto, was a first cousin of Karl's and he (remembering to pick from among his many violins the famous Guarneri del Gesù violin of 1742 that Karl had generously loaned him) played always two or three times a year at the Palais and used the *Musiksaal* for rehearsals whenever his quartet was in Vienna. The guests—scientists, diplomats, artists, writers and composers—were as distinguished as the musicians assembled to entertain them. Brahms came to listen to a performance of his Clarinet Quintet here; Richard Strauss attended several concerts in the *Musiksaal* and so did the composers Schoenberg, Zemlinsky and Gustav Mahler, although the last of these was not invited back after insulting his hosts by storming off in pique muttering, "Nothing more should be played now that we have heard the Beethoven 'Archduke' Trio." Another regular visitor was Eduard Hanslick, Wagner's nemesis, regarded until his death in 1904 as the most powerful and most feared music critic in Vienna. To a letter from Mrs. Wittgenstein inquiring about his health, Hanslick replied shortly before he died:

> *Dear and esteemed and gracious lady,*
>
> *Your letter, so beautiful, touched my heart with such warmth, a sentiment that it happily and gratefully retained for the whole day. Those splendid evenings for which I have you to thank passed in lively reminiscence before my eyes. The magnificent music, the toasts, anticipated with pleasurable excitement, given by your sage and eloquent husband, the deep pleasure you took in rapt attention to the music and the rest!*
>
> *My health, which seems to maintain a certain equilibrium, allows me to hope that I shall be able to thank you in person in May for so kindly inquiring about me.*
>
> *With the greatest respect, yours Ed. Hanslick*

If Jerome was made to feel insecure in such rarefied Viennese milieus, he would not have admitted to it at the time (this would happen later); instead his awkwardness erupted in fits of brooding jealousy at the apparent ease with which Gretl chatted to other men during the period of their courtship. She interpreted these moods as a manifestation of his earnest love and not (as hindsight would later assure her) as a serious warning of the psychosis that would darken, destabilize, subsume and eventually destroy her marriage. Gretl's obstinacy had inspired her to marry someone from far outside the Wittgenstein circle, but Jerome Stonborough was not only a stranger to the Wittgensteins, he was a stranger to all of Vienna, a stranger even in his native America, a man of no particular domain, unaccountable, hard to please and hard to measure. Karl may have been dimly satisfied to learn that his son-in-law was a man of means whose sister was married to a Guggenheim, but a few inquiries among his smart friends in America (these included the steel billionaires

Andrew Carnegie and Charles Schwab) would surely have alerted him to Jerome's change of name, to the Steinberger bankruptcy and to the ineffable feebleness of William Guggenheim.

When Gretl bought a bijou castle on the shores of Lake Traun, Marguerite Cunliffe-Owen, a gossip columnist writing under the nom de plume Marquise de Fontenoy for the *Washington Post,* tried, without success, to find something out about her mysterious husband:

> Who is Dr. Stonborough? He is the purchaser of the villa and also the Chateau Toscana, which belonged to the long-missing Archduke John of Austria, and to his mother, the late Grand Duchess Maria Antonia of Tuscany. Dr. Stonborough is described in the announcement of the purchase as "the well-known American multimillionaire." But I cannot find his name in any of the standard works of reference, nor even in that Locator which gives the names of the members of the leading clubs, and of the so-called smart sets of all the principal cities of the United States.

As for Gretl's siblings they detested their new brother-in-law with an intensity that grew with the passing years; her two youngest brothers, Paul and Ludwig, known collectively as *die Buben* (the Boys), especially so. When Jerome first met them they were teenagers, but still being treated by the rest of the family as something of a collective afterthought.

9 THE BOYS

In adult life Paul Wittgenstein was far more famous than his younger brother, but nowadays it is the other way around: Ludwig, or Lucki to the family, has become an icon of the twentieth century—the handsome, stammering, tortured, incomprehensible philosopher, around whose formidable personality an extraordinary cult developed in the years that followed his death in 1951—a cult, incidentally, whose membership includes many who have never opened his books or tried to understand a single line of his thought. *"Schmarren!"* (Trash!), is how Paul described it all. But such criticism did not dent the brothers' friendship. When Ludwig's treatise, *Tractatus Logico-Philosophicus,* was first published (a book in which the author claimed in his preface to have found the final solution to most of the world's most puzzling philosophical problems), he presented a copy to Paul, inscribing it: "To my dear brother Paul for Christmas 1922. If this book be worthless, may it soon vanish without trace."

At the time of Gretl and Jerome's courtship, Paul—attractive, neurotic, learned, nature-loving and intense—was seventeen years old and on the point of taking his final school examinations at the classical Gymnasium in Wiener Neustadt. Ludwig, a year and a half younger, was lodging during term time with a family called Strigl in the provincial town of Linz where, by day, he attended lessons at the *Staatsoberrealschule,* a semiclassical state secondary school of 300 pupils. According to the recollection of one of his fellow pupils, the majority of the school's teachers were

> mentally deranged, and quite a few ended their days as honest-to-God lunatics; their collars were unkempt . . . Their external appearance exuded uncleanness, they were the product of a proletariat denuded of all personal independence of thought, distinguished by unparalleled ignorance and most admirably fitted to become the pillars of an effete system of government which, thank God, is now a thing of the past.

That pupil—just six days older than Lucki—was Adolf Hitler.

It is unlikely that either Ludwig or Hitler had, at that time, the slightest inkling of the potential rise of the other. At school both were misfits; both insisted on addressing their fellow pupils with the formal German *Sie* as opposed to the informal *du* used by everyone else. Hitler, who suffered a hereditary weakness of the lungs, was regarded by his teachers, not as a future *Führer* of Germany, but as a problematic dunce who failed even to achieve his final-year certificate, while Ludwig, whose corresponding ailment was a painful extrusion of the intestines (commonly called a hernia), was at best considered an average scholar whose grades, in most subjects, gave frequent cause for concern.

At home in Urfahr, a suburb of Linz, Hitler's mother indulged her son with unquestioning confidence in all his abilities, while in Vienna the

Wittgenstein family was slow to acknowledge any of the talents of its two youngest members. Paul's piano playing—which inspired most of the young man's waking thoughts—was dismissed as unsubtle and obsessive. "Not as accomplished as Hans," they said; but Paul had at least succeeded, where his younger brother had failed, in gaining entry to the academic Gymnasium at Wiener Neustadt. Ludwig, who had constructed a working model of a sewing machine from wooden sticks and wire at the age of ten and whose interests during his youth were more practical and technical than academic, managed to pass his entrance examination to the far less academic *Realschule* only after a period of intense extra tuition.

At first Karl had tried to stop Paul and Ludwig from going to school at all, insisting that they be educated, like the rest of his children, privately at home in the subjects of Latin and mathematics. The rest (geography, history, science, whatever) they would have to pick up for themselves by reading books, for school time, in Karl's view, was wasted time; much better, he believed, for his children to take a healthy walk or engage in sport. It was only after Hans's disappearance, when the atmosphere of the Wittgenstein home had become insufferable, that Karl finally relented, allowing his two youngest boys to enter the public school system. But by then it was already too late—too late for Ludwig to pass his exams, and too late for either to be properly trained in the art of human relations. Their private tutoring had always kept them apart from other children of their age, and although their mother had tried to encourage them to play with the servants' children, her ploy failed to impress either and was greatly resented. Playmates were few and as a consequence all the Wittgenstein children developed into hardened individualists, who struggled throughout their lives to make and maintain meaningful relationships.

In boyhood Paul and Ludwig fought with each other as most brothers fight. At one time they vied jealously for the attentions of a boy called Wolfrum. Paul, a natural anarchist and mischief-maker, enjoyed leading his younger brother into trouble, but they were close in age and, in those days, close also in friendship. How severely their brothers' suicides affected them cannot be gauged. As the family's two youngest members, they must have been sheltered to some degree from the worst of the fallout. They were also considerably younger than Hans and Rudolf. Ludwig maintained a few good memories of Rudolf, but of Hans (who was twelve years his senior and who disappeared from home when he was just thirteen) one suspects that he remembered little. But the *Buben* cannot have remained entirely oblivious to the chronic atmosphere of their home during those years and both of them would, at various stages in their lives, come dangerously close to killing themselves. Ludwig, in a scribbled reminiscence of his childhood, claimed to have first indulged thoughts of suicide in his tenth or eleventh year—in other words in 1900 or 1901, *before* the Hans and Rudolf tragedies.

The Wittgenstein story is one of many suicides—an aunt and a cousin also ended their lives in this way—but it should not be inferred (as is sometimes stated) that this way of death was considered acceptable, honorable or even normal to an early-twentieth-century Viennese. Karl, as has been shown, was ashamed of both Hans's and Rudolf's behavior; Otto Weininger's father felt the same about his son; even Weininger himself wrote shortly before his death: "Suicide is not a sign of courage but of cowardice, even if it is the least of the cowardly acts." Ludwig was ashamed at times of not having killed himself, but the reason why he and indeed Paul never did so was precisely because they lacked this form of cowardice. "I know," wrote Ludwig, "that to kill oneself is always a dirty thing to do. Surely one *cannot* will one's own destruction and anybody who has visualized what is in practice involved knows that suicide is always a rushing of one's own defenses. But nothing is worse than to be forced to take oneself by surprise." This ambiguous attitude, shared by Paul, was a far cry from the sense of shame that their father felt about the suicides of Hans and Rudolf.

Many years after the events with which this chapter chiefly deals, when Paul was retired and living in New York he used, every day, to take long walks from his nineteenth-floor apartment at Riverside Drive up to George Washington Bridge, across to the other side and back again. On one such occasion his attention was drawn by a crowd that had assembled upon the bridge in order to dissuade a desperate man from throwing himself off. When he realized what they were up to, Paul burst through the mob waving his walking stick. "If this man wishes to die, let him do so. What business is it of yours to tell him how he should or shouldn't end his life?" In the fracas that followed, the man, finding himself no longer at the center of attention, silently withdrew from his precarious position on the bridge and was neither seen nor heard of again.

Like all the Wittgensteins, Paul and Ludwig were exceptionally musical. Ludwig learned to play both violin and piano and later trained himself as a clarinettist; but he always felt overshadowed by his elder siblings. He once dreamed that he was standing on a station platform overhearing Paul telling Hermine how thrilled Jerome had been by his (Ludwig's) musical gifts. The next morning Ludwig wrote it down:

> It seemed that I had sung so wonderfully during the Bacchante by Mendelssohn the day before . . . I had sung extraordinarily expressively and with particularly expressive gestures. Paul and Hermine appeared to agree entirely with Jerome's praise. Jerome apparently said again and again: "What a talent!" . . . The whole was underpinned by smugness. I woke up and was irritated or rather ashamed at my vanity.

From earliest youth, Paul contemplated a career as a concert pianist, in stubborn defiance of his father's wishes. Not just his father but his whole family tried to dissuade him from it. They told him that he was no good. "Does he have to pound the piano like that?" his mother used to ask. Even if he were a better player, he was told, it would be unseemly for a boy of his class and background to take up a career as a performing artist. Despite the vehemence of their entreaty Paul would not be deflected. In the holidays he took lessons from Marie Baumayer—a family friend and one-time pupil of Clara Schumann, rated in her day as one of Vienna's foremost interpreters of Schumann and Brahms—but his most cherished ambition was to be accepted into the classes of the colossus of piano pedagogy Theodore Leschetizky.

Odd perhaps that Karl Wittgenstein—accomplished bugler, violinist, cousin of Joachim, a man who counted Brahms and Strauss among his friends, whose collection of original handwritten musical manuscripts was among the finest in the world, a man who, during classical concerts, would wipe the tears from his eyes with his index finger and proudly submit the glistening digit for his wife's inspection—odd that he, of all people, should have been so violently opposed to his sons' entering the music profession. Like many great men of commerce he had a shallow understanding of the psychologies at work in his family and was able to appreciate his sons only by measuring their achievements against his own. If they turned out to be less energetic, less able, less courageous or willing to take a risk than he, then they were deemed to have failed. The pressure on the Wittgenstein brothers—Hans, Kurt, Rudi, Paul and Ludwig—to make their own mark in the great iron, steel, arms and banking business that he had founded contributed to a nervous and self-destructive strain in all five of them.

10 THEIR MOTHER

Mrs. Wittgenstein's besetting sin was that she failed, on the one hand, to protect her children from the wrath and impatience of their father and, on the other, to compensate them with much warmth or motherly indulgence of her own. She was a small woman of long nose and round face—an intensely introverted and nervous character, detached and dutiful. In adult life she suffered regular attacks of migraine and phlebitis, a complication of the arteries, nerves and veins of her legs. "We simply could not understand her," wrote Hermine in a memoir intended for private circulation, "and she, furthermore, had no real understanding of the eight strange children that she had brought into this world; with all her love of humanity she seemed to have no real understanding of people." As Gretl remembered her: "My mother's devotion to duty made me too uncomfortable and I found her agitated character beyond enduring. She suffered from a constant overstress of nerves."

Mrs. Wittgenstein's adult life was spent in sacrifice to the demands of her husband and her own geriatric mother, leaving her eight surviving children to scramble from the emotional void as best they could.

> From a very early stage [wrote Hermine] we children had the impression of a strange state of tension in our home, a lack of relaxation that did not emanate solely from my father's agitation. My mother

was also very excitable, though she never lost her quiet friendliness in confrontation with her husband or her mother.

According to Hermine their mother's neurotic obsession with wifely duty led to the eventual eradication of all traces of what must once have been her original personality: "I believe that our mother, as we knew her, was no longer completely herself . . . among other things we could not understand why she had so little will and opinion of her own, and we did not reflect on the impossibility of maintaining a will and opinion of one's own next to my father."

An example given by Hermine: Mrs. Wittgenstein one evening retired to bed with her feet swaddled in a cloth that had been accidentally soused in pure carbolic acid, a very weak solution of which was believed at that time to offer relief from the discomfort of new shoes. During the night the acid burned itself into her flesh so that by morning it had caused a deep and repellent wound that would not heal for weeks. All night long she lay awake and in agony but dared not move or make a sound for fear of disturbing her husband's sleep.

One by one, all eight of the Wittgenstein siblings came to realize that the best (perhaps the only) way to communicate with their mother was through music—for that was the solder that welded each disparate member of the family to her and to one another. In youth Mrs. Wittgenstein had taken piano lessons from the struggling Hungarian composer Karl Goldmark (long before he had made a big name for himself with his opera *Die Königin von Saba*). Although her hands were tiny and her physical movements awkward, Goldmark managed to show her how to play gracefully, to sight-read almost anything, to improvise long pieces, to pick out tunes by ear and to transpose effortlessly out of one key into another. Too shy to perform in public, she enjoyed playing duets, chamber music or musical games with her family, and it was in this shared wordless activity that her maternal detachment was least disconcerting to her children. "It would have been impossible for her quickly to comprehend any complicated spoken sentence, and yet it was easy for her to read a complicated musical piece from the score or to transpose it into any key." Musical expression came naturally to Mrs. Wittgenstein and, when she played, "her face developed a new kind of beauty."

Since the Wittgenstein siblings were brought up both to recognize and to idolize classical composers and musical performers, and since their best means of communication with their mother was through the wordless medium of music, it is hardly surprising that each of them should have pursued music with an enthusiasm that, at times, bordered on the pathological. When music was around them they were at their freest and at their most amicable. To witness the exuberance and passion of Paul, Ludwig, Hermine, Leopoldine, Karl or any of them singing or playing together, any visitor might have been forgiven for assuming that these querulous, volatile and complicated people formed one of the happiest and most united families of the Hapsburg Empire. Their performances were intense, glowing and passionate and as one enthusiastic guest at the Palais recalled long after the great building had been reduced to rubble and all of the Wittgensteins were gone: "They rocked with the rhythm of the dance, showing everyone just how much they enjoyed it."

11 THE OTHER BROTHER

Since Hans's disappearance in 1903, Konrad, or Kurt as he was known within the family, became by default the eldest of the Wittgenstein sons. He, like all of his siblings, was also a gifted musician who could play both piano and cello with flair and who took pleasure in duetting with his mother. But, unlike the others, he did not rate seriousness high among the virtues. At five foot six he was several inches shorter than either Ludwig or Paul, with fair hair, blue eyes and a prominent scar on his left cheek. By nature he was flip and jocular and, in the opinion of his family, lightweight and slightly babyish. After a period of study at the Technical University in Hanover from which he qualified as an engineer in 1899, Kurt volunteered for a smart dragoon regiment as a one-year conscript. At soldiering he did not excel (his final Military Academy report concluded that he was "not suitable" for active service) but by 1903 Kurt had succeeded nevertheless in registering himself as an officer in the Reserves. From the army he went straight into the steel business and in 1906, backed by his father with an income of 20,000 kronen, he set up a rolling mill with a partner, Sebastian Danner, at Judenburg on the banks of the River Mur. This was the first mill of its type to use electric arc furnaces that generated a more consistent and controllable heat than the old coal-fire variety and produced a molten metal that was no longer affected by impurities emanating from the heat source. More than a hundred years after its foundation Kurt's steel plant remains in business, boasting from its Internet Web site that the name Stahl Judenburg (Judenburg Steel) "stands for quality, flexibility, reliability and the systematic development of competence"—not perhaps epithets that can be easily applied to its founder.

Kurt was never married. It is said that he failed in two courtships. He did not enjoy adult conversation and with strangers and guests sometimes appeared awkward or rude. He found happiness in piano-playing, hunting, fast motorcars, toys and the company of children. His family dismissed him as a *Kindskopf*—an overgrown child. In a letter to Ludwig, Hermine wrote of him: "there is no depth to his character, but since you don't expect to find any, you don't miss it either." As a deathbed companion to his ailing father, Kurt was far from ideal.

12 THE MIDDLE SISTER

In August 1879, fifteen months after Kurt was born, the Wittgensteins had a third daughter, christened Helene, and subsequently nicknamed Lenka. She was the "third" daughter because between her and the eldest, Hermine, came little Dora, who died of complications in her first month. At the time of Karl's dying Helene inhabited a large apartment on the Brahmsplatz, a few streets from the Wittgenstein Palais in the Alleegasse. Plain, Rubenesque and often smiling, she was married in 1899 to a pillar of the Austrian Protestant establishment called Max Salzer, a minister in the government's finance department. After his retirement from the ministry he was chosen to run the Wittgenstein family fortune. Later he became senile and the family allowed him to continue his ministrations while ignoring all his advice. Max's brother Hans Salzer (married to a

Wittgenstein cousin) was a pulmonary surgeon of international renown. Helene had four children. She sang beautifully, played the piano to a high standard and laughed more than was usual for a Wittgenstein. From the outside she may have seemed the most settled and relaxed of her siblings, but she too suffered from tensions of a pathological and neurotic kind. She was terrified of thunderstorms and was also anemic. With her children she was exceedingly strict. Of her two sons, the elder died from paralysis caused by polio at the age of twenty, while the younger, Felix Salzer, became a famous musicologist, who estranged himself from his parents at an early age. Life in the Salzer household was not always joyful.

13 PAUL'S EARLY TRAINING

A strange quirk of Austrian mentality in the last decades of the Hapsburg Empire manifested itself in society's reluctance to trust to the abilities of young men. The writer Stefan Zweig, a Viennese contemporary of the Wittgenstein siblings, complained of the "inner dishonesty" that refused to acknowledge a young man's manhood until he "had secured a 'social position' for himself—that is, hardly before his twenty-fifth or twenty-sixth year." While a father would refuse consent for his daughter to marry a man still in his mid-twenties, employers equally deemed young men unfit for serious office. "All those qualities of youth," wrote Zweig, "freshness, self-assertion, daring, curiosity, youth's lust for life—were regarded as suspect in an age that only had use for 'substance.' "

The visible effects of this attitude were bizarre. Whereas, in most societies, the old make efforts to appear younger than they are, in Vienna young men went to inordinate lengths to make themselves look old. A thick beard, a long dark coat, a sedate walk, a slight paunch and a walking stick—these were props that the young men of Vienna needed to gain the respect of their elders. Shops sold them gold-rimmed spectacles (which they didn't need for their sight) and bottles of quack unguent that boasted "Rapid Facial Hair Growth." Even schoolboys refused to carry satchels lest they be recognized as schoolboys.

For this reason the Viennese concert-going public was reluctant to buy tickets to hear musicians under the age of forty—never mind that two of the city's greatest composers, Mozart and Schubert, never reached that age. Great music must be interpreted by mature artists, they assured themselves—an attitude that goes some way to explaining why Paul's concert debut took place at the late age of twenty-six. But the obstacle that was even tougher than contemporary prejudice was his own family. Paul's debut would never have taken place in December 1913 if his father had still been alive.

In the long argument that raged in the Wittgenstein household over whether Paul should or shouldn't, could, couldn't, must or mustn't become a concert pianist, one person, perhaps above all others, helped to shift the tide in Paul's favor. His name was Theodore Leschetizky, a Polish octogenarian erotomaniac, hailed as the smartest piano teacher of his age. His pupils included Artur Schnabel, Ignaz Paderewski (who later became prime minister of Poland) and the brilliant, if volatile, Ignacy Friedman. In his youth Leschetizky had taken lessons from Karl Czerny, a pupil of Ludwig van Beethoven. His teaching method, insofar as he had one, was to insist on beautiful tone production, a virtue that he encouraged from his pupils by exposing them to the vagaries of his chameleon temperament. During lessons he could be despotic, irascible, sarcastic and volatile, or, without warning, effusive, sweet natured or embarrassingly tender and generous.

He liked to enter his students' minds, to explore their private and spiritual lives and to share in their innermost secrets. His prettiest female pupils were subjected to excruciating conversations about sex, during which he found it difficult to keep his hands off them. In the spirit of this grand passion Leschetizky married four of his pupils in succession, the last (who enjoyed a brief concert career as "Madame Leschetizky") when he was seventy-eight years old.

To be accepted at Leschetizky's classes, prospective pupils were required to audition in front of him. "Were you a child prodigy? Are you of Slavic descent? Are you a Jew?" he would ask as they entered the hall. If the answers were "yes," "yes" and "yes" he grinned broadly and the audition got off to a good start. One hopeful came to him with a Beethoven piano sonata and when he had finished playing it the master proffered his hand and with a cold, gnomic smile said, "Good-bye!" The prospective student was astonished. "Good-bye!" Leschetizky repeated. "We shall never meet again at the piano. A man who could play that with such bad feeling would murder his own mother."

If the master had detected promise, he would send the applicant for one or two years' preparatory study with one of his assistants. The most prestigious of these was Malwine Bree. Paul seems to have fixed things in a different order, having enrolled with Miss Bree at the age of eleven without auditioning for Leschetizky first. In her youth, she too had studied with Leschetizky (with whom she had fallen in love) and also with Liszt. At various times in her life she counted Wagner, Anton Rubinstein and Mark Twain among her friends and she married a Viennese physician, Dr. Moritz Bree, who was fleetingly a famous poet. By the time Paul first met her she was widowed and her professional life was entirely dedicated to the service of Leschetizky. She groomed his pupils assiduously in piano technique and reverence for the master, and in 1902 wrote, with his approval, a book on his pedagogic methods that would ensure his international reputation for decades after his death.

In September of 1910, after Paul had completed his military service, Mrs. Bree pronounced him ready to transfer to the master. At home he was already considered good enough to accompany his cousin, the famous violinist Joseph Joachim, and to play duets with Richard Strauss on his visits to the Palais. Leschetizky had high hopes of Paul's career and if he occasionally wearied of his student's hard-edged pianism (he dubbed Paul "the Mighty Key-Smasher") or if Paul sometimes resented his master's narrow musical tastes (Leschetizky considered Bach and Mozart not worth learning), their relationship progressed to firm friendship. Paul, to his dying day, professed an unwavering admiration for his old master: "he was both an artist and a teacher at the same time," he remembered. "To find these two qualities of intelligence and artistic inspiration (each of them rare) in *one* person is as rare as an eclipse of the sun and moon together."

Leschetizky was not the only father figure in Paul's life for both he and his younger brother Ludwig befriended, adulated and revered a blind organist and composer called Josef Labor. Labor was a small man, not quite a dwarf but nearly so, who wore a bushy moustache and let his thick hair grow wild around his shoulders. A disconcerting glimmer of blind white eyeball showed through the slits of his half-shut eyelids, and the skin of his face was sallow and gray. A long chin and pointed bird-bill nose completed the image, confirming an impression of a menacing gowk from a nightmare or fantasy horror film. He was however a wise, intelligent and kind-hearted man. Ludwig regarded Labor as the greatest living composer, indeed as one of the six great composers of all time—Haydn, Mozart, Beethoven, Schubert and Brahms being the other five. Paul also held him as both man and musician in the highest regard. "What binds you and me together," Ludwig wrote to his brother, "is our shared interest in Labor's music."

No one listens to Labor nowadays. If he is remembered at all, it is as a brief mentor to Arnold Schoenberg, or as a composition tutor to Mahler's future wife, the semi-deaf seductress Alma Schindler. When Alma applied for lessons with Alexander Zemlinsky, Labor was heartbroken. In her diary she recorded the emotion of her last session with him:

> Labor. He's lost for ever. Has abandoned me. "I can't do it," he said, "either Zemlinsky or me. But both—no." I was sobbing quietly. He must have noticed . . . Otherwise he was uncommonly sweet—soothing my wounds. At the time it hurt me deeply. I've been studying with him for six years—haven't learned all that much, but always found him a warm-hearted sympathetic friend. And a true artist as well. A dear kind fellow.

Labor, blinded at the age of three by an attack of smallpox, was educated at the Institute for the Blind in Vienna and later studied piano and organ at the Vienna Conservatoire. He lived for a while in Lower Saxony, where he was court organist to the libidinous King Georg V of Hanover. The king, who was also blind, became a close friend and when he was forced to move to Austria in 1866, Labor came with him.

Paul went to him for "music theory" lessons, which consisted of long conversations about music, art, theater, philosophy, politics and life in general. While bravely resigned to his blindness, Labor had the ability to reduce those around him to tears of sympathy that sometimes spurred them to charitable action on his behalf.

"You know, ever since I can remember, I've always wished for an organ, but never had the money," Labor told Alma Schindler. "I've given up all hope now—in the next world perhaps." Alma wrote in her diary that evening: "God willing, if ever I were really well off—the first thing I'd do would be to buy Labor an organ!" In the end it was Paul's mother, Leopoldine Wittgenstein, who paid for Labor's new Rieger-Jaegerdorf organ, and Karl, who, on Labor's seventieth birthday in June 1912, paid to have many of his finest compositions published by Universal Edition in Vienna. Ludwig tried (without success) to get Labor's music performed by musicians in Cambridge. In Vienna the Wittgenstein family promoted regular "Labor Evenings"—concerts dedicated to the performance of his works. At such events the family servants—cooks, gardeners, huntsmen and chambermaids—were all urged to attend and, in the words of Gretl's younger son, Ji, "commanded to applaud super-vigorously (They did!!!) and blind Labor was delighted that the public was so enthusiastic."

"I could never hear enough of Labor's music," Hermine admitted, "for it touched me often to tears—tears which I let freely course down my cheeks, since I knew he could not see them." The Wittgenstein family was besotted by him. He became their property—their in-house composer, musical adviser, recipient of their charity, friend and all-round philosophical and psychological guru. When a public charity calling itself the Labor-Bund was set up to publish more of his music, promote concerts and erect a statue of the composer in front of the Konzerthaus, the Wittgensteins were very jealous.

14 LUDWIG'S PREDICAMENT

Between his three surviving sons Karl could choose no heir. Kurt was lightweight, Paul and Ludwig both worryingly neurotic and fundamentally uninterested in business. By the time of his dying, none of them was married. He had hoped that at least one might succeed as an engineer and for a while it seemed that Ludwig alone might have made it. In 1906, shortly after leaving school, Ludwig had read a book called *Populäre Schriften* (Popular Writings) by the renowned Viennese physicist Ludwig

Boltzmann, which contained an essay on aeronautics in which it was suggested that any advancement of this burgeoning science would require the attentions of "heroes and geniuses"—the former to test-fly the planes and the latter to understand how and why they worked. Reading this at the height of the Weininger cult and knowing also that Weininger had himself attended several of Boltzmanm's lectures, Ludwig (the young aspiring hero-genius) promptly applied for a place in Boltzmann's class at the University of Vienna. Had he succeeded, he would have sat on a classroom bench next to Erwin Schrödinger (winner in 1933 of a Nobel Prize for his work on quantum mechanics), but both students' aspirations were dashed when on October 5, 1906, the great physicist, while holidaying at the seaside resort of Duino near Trieste, hanged himself in his hotel bedroom as his wife and daughter were splashing about in the warm waters of the bay. So Ludwig went instead to the Technical High School of Berlin–Charlottenburg to study hot-air balloons. This he later claimed to have been a complete waste of his time. A year later, with encouragement from his father, he moved to Manchester in England, first to experiment with kites on the Derbyshire moors and afterward to engage as a research student at Manchester University investigating propellers. The female students at Manchester appalled him, as he was irritated by their flirtatious manner with the professors. "All the women I know are such idiots," he said.

By June 1911 Ludwig had patented a small refinement to the propeller of his day, but his engineering enthusiasms (for which he later claimed to have possessed "neither taste nor talent") were waning and by the end of the year he resolved to seek out Bertrand Russell in Cambridge, to see if he might not prefer to study philosophy.

Boltzmann, Weininger and Beethoven ranked among the icons whom Ludwig most admired and whom he most wished to emulate. Each exemplified to him genius in its purest form, not limited by literary, artistic or scientific achievement, but extending beyond that, to embody in his mind the very essence of genius as expressed by force of personality. In the case of Weininger Ludwig repudiated much of his philosophy but continued nevertheless to insist on his genius. "His greatness lies in that with which we disagree," he once said. "It is his enormous mistake that is great." Ambitious, unstable and driven by a neurotic urge for self-improvement, Ludwig needed geniuses to worship as much as he desired to be regarded as one of them himself. "Improve yourself, that is the only thing you can do to better the world," he said.

Having thrown himself at Bertrand Russell's feet, Ludwig soon discovered that, without having completed a single significant piece of written philosophical work and while still only in his mid-twenties, he was being hailed by many of the brightest minds of Cambridge University as a genius. "Perhaps the most perfect example I have ever known of genius as traditionally conceived, passionate, profound, intense and dominating," is how Russell later described him.

Ludwig's seduction of Russell may be followed through an entertaining series of letters that Russell sent to a "very tall [woman] with a long thin face something like a horse, indomitable courage and a will of iron." She was the daughter of a duke and the wife of a brewer, his mistress at the time, Lady Ottoline Morrell. He first wrote to her about Ludwig in a letter of October 18, 1911, in which he described the aspiring young philosopher as "an unknown German, speaking very little English but refusing to speak German" who had interrupted a private tutorial in his rooms. Ludwig, uncertain whether to commit himself to philosophy at Cambridge or to return to his aeronautical experiments in Manchester, insisted on being allowed to sit in on Russell's famous philosophy classes. The don graciously obliged, but soon became apprehensive when Ludwig started stalking him around the rooms and colleges of the university. Suddenly and unexpectedly he would appear in Russell's rooms, just as he was changing for dinner, or at midnight as he was climbing into bed, insisting on talking philosophy late into the night and threatening to kill himself if Russell turned him out. Russell consequently endured hour upon hour of Ludwig, pacing around his rooms "like a caged tiger," testing his patience to the uttermost, stuttering and blathering long and incomprehensible monologues on the subject of logic and mathematics.

"My German friend threatens to be an infliction," a wearied Russell wrote to Lady Ottoline; "he came back with me after my lecture and argued till dinner time—obstinate and perverse, but I think not stupid." In subsequent letters Ludwig is described as "very argumentative and tiresome. . . . a bore . . . excitable and rather sad . . . In his flat moments he talks slowly, stammering, and saying dull things . . . My German engineer

I think is a fool. He thinks nothing empirical is knowable—I asked him to admit that there was not a rhinoceros in the room but he wouldn't," and a fortnight later: "My ferocious German came and argued at me after my lecture. He is armour-plated against all assaults of reasoning. It is really rather a waste of time talking to him." Meanwhile Russell's philosophical colleague, George Moore, became so perplexed, intrigued, excited and irritated by Ludwig that he contemplated keeping a diary entitled "what I feel about Wittgenstein."

The same happened to Russell, who within a few months was enthralled by his young student. "I am getting to like him, he is literary, very musical, pleasant mannered and I *think* really intelligent." Should he then return to his aeronautical studies or plug on with philosophy? As Russell later recalled, Ludwig put the question in typically obtuse form: At the end of his first term he came to me and said: "Will you please tell me whether I am a complete idiot or not?" I replied "My dear fellow, I don't know, why are you asking me?" He said "Because if I am a complete idiot I shall become an aeronaut; but if not I shall become a philosopher." I told him to write me something during the vacation on some philosophical subject and I would then tell him whether he was a complete idiot or not. At the beginning of the following term he brought the fulfilment of this suggestion. After reading only one sentence, I said to him: "No you must not become an aeronaut." And he did not.

❖ ❖ ❖

BACK IN VIENNA, Karl was bitterly disappointed to receive news that his last and youngest son had, like all the others, spurned his chances of becoming a great engineer. Cambridge, however, rejoiced. Russell was particularly delighted. Still no clearer in his understanding of Ludwig's philosophical message, he felt abundant admiration for his young student, and wrote to his horse-faced mistress to tell her so:

> He has pure intellectual passion in the highest degree; it makes me
> love him . . . He is the young man one hopes for. But as is usual with
> such men, he is unstable, and may go to pieces . . . in discussion
> with him I put out all my force and only just equal him. With all my
> other pupils I should squash them flat if I did so. When he left I

was strangely excited by him. I love him and feel that he will solve the problems that I am too old to solve.

Russell's joy in Ludwig soon came to the attention of others at Cambridge, among them the economist John Maynard Keynes, the historian Lytton Strachey and various members of the so-called Cambridge Conversazione Society, a secretive conclave of intellectual, left-wing and mainly homosexual men, which wanted to have Ludwig elected to the membership as a fellow "Apostle." Russell (known as Bertie by his friends) guarded Ludwig's company jealously and, although himself a signed-up Conversazione Society Apostle, was disturbed by the prospect of having to share his *trouvé* with the others. In November 1912 Strachey wrote to another society member, Saxon Sydney Turner:

> The poor man [Russell] is in a sad state. He looks about 96 with long snow-white hair and an infinitely haggard countenance. The election of Wittgenstein has been a great blow to him. He dearly hoped to keep him all to himself, and indeed succeeded wonderfully, until Keynes at last insisted on meeting him and saw at once that he was a genius and that it was essential to elect him . . . Their decision was suddenly announced to Bertie, who nearly swooned. Of course he could produce no reason against the election except the remarkable one that the Society was so degraded that his Austrian would certainly refuse to belong to it . . . Bertie is really a tragic figure, and I am very sorry for him, but he is most deluded too.

All his life Ludwig had been unsettled by feelings of self-hatred, psychological loneliness and urges to kill himself. In 1912 he was once again contemplating suicide, even while conceding that his work was worthwhile. He was pleased to have given up aeronautics, pleased to have a voice in the world of Cambridge philosophy and to be adulated by a small but influential clique of philosophers. In the figure of David Pinsent, a clever, easy-going student of maths at Trinity College, Ludwig had also found his first real friend. By his own bleak standards the year 1912 was probably one of the happiest in Ludwig's life.

15 THE NEWLYWEDS

In the octave of years that passed between her 1905 marriage to Jerome Stonborough and her father's final illness in 1913, Gretl had not been altogether happy either. Since the death of Rudolf, she had connected herself, umbilically, to her sister Hermine, upon whom she depended for guidance and friendship as well as moral support and motherly love. "I do not think that my marriage [to Jerome] will change anything between you and me," she wrote on the evening after her wedding, "because I am completely unchanged . . . I live at all times of day with you at the Alleegasse." She had left Vienna in a state of high anxiety. The first stop on the long honeymoon trip was a visit to the Wittgenstein summer retreat, a panoramic estate called Hochreit situated on a high ridge where the Traisen and Schwarza valleys meet among the Mittelgebirge mountains of Lower Austria. "The parting was terribly hard," she wrote to Hermine, "far worse even than I had feared; truly I have been heavy-hearted ever since. On the journey I had a private cry . . . So it was an abysmal first evening." From the Hochreit she and Jerome traveled to Venice and from thence to Cairo and up the Nile on a boat to Aswan and Luxor. Jerome was thrilled by the Sphinxes and the great temple at Karnak, but Gretl was not. "The Egyptian ruins do not impress me at all and the Nile is rather boring." At least she seemed to be pleased with her new husband. "He is quite changed. Imagine, he is not jealous any more and is smiling from morning to evening."

Shortly after their return to Europe in the late spring of 1905, Gretl and Jerome moved to Berlin, where he had decided to embark upon a study of chemistry. As a wedding present Karl had paid for the couple's rented flat near the Tiergarten to be kitted out by the controversial interior decorators Joseph Hoffmann and Koloman Moser. The result, a mixture of stark modernity and nursery kitsch, greatly pleased her and as soon as work on the flat was completed she too decided to enroll in a course of study at the Scientific Institute. In Vienna she had found few members of her own sex able to share in her excitement about science, but to her surprise and disappointment there were ten female students in her embryology and histology class in Berlin and she loathed them all. "Six of these women are Russian Jews," she complained. "They are dirty, careless and mainly dressed in transparent things. Then there are the others, blonde Germans who smile all the time. None of them has a natural relationship with men. They are all poor, ugly and miserable little souls."

In 1906 Gretl gave birth to a son who was christened Thomas (nicknamed Tommy), and a year later the Stonboroughs, abandoning Berlin, went for a long and luxurious visit to their Guggenheim in-laws in New York. On their return to Europe they set up a new home in Switzerland. It was a feature of Jerome's neurosis that he could never stay in the same place for long. He and his family were constantly on the move, with the excuse always that he had to study another science with another professor at another university. For all his university meanderings he never seemed to gain any qualifications. In Switzerland he enlisted at the Federal Technical College in Zurich to study with Professor Richard Willstätter, who in 1915 was awarded the Nobel Prize for chemistry for his investigations into chlorophyll. Gretl tried to enlist on a course in physics and mathematics at the University of Zurich but was told she had first to pass her *Abitur* (final-year school exams). She did so, but no sooner had she enrolled than Jerome let it be known that he desired to move again, this time to Paris.

In the French capital, where they rented a luxurious flat on the Rue de la Faisanderie, Gretl signed up for another scientific course. "I cannot tell you how much I enjoy learning," she wrote to Hermine. "If only one could prescribe study to every human being. I am sure that it is a universal cure for all dissatisfaction and a good replacement for a husband and a child!" Six long years after the birth of Thomas, she and Jerome had a second son called John Jerome, whom they nicknamed Ji or Ji-Ji.

16 KARL'S LOSS OF CONSCIOUSNESS

Let us now return to the deathbed scene that was abandoned, some while back, with Hermine sitting by her father's side taking autobiographical dictation, as Karl's life dangled by a thread in an upstairs room at the Palais over Christmas 1912. When a person is unquestionably dying and everyone around him knows it, even those who love him most begin to hope that the final curtain will hurry up and fall. The Wittgensteins were growing impatient. Ludwig was eager to return to Cambridge, to his new friends and, above all, to his philosophy. "On arriving here I found my father very ill," he wrote to Russell. "There is no hope that he may recover. These circumstances have—I am afraid—rather lamed my thoughts & I am muddled although I struggle against it." But Karl, fragile as he was, somehow survived Christmas and Boxing Day and into the New Year. By January 6, 1913, Ludwig had to concede that he would not be able to get back to Cambridge for the start of the new term "as the illness of my poor father is growing very rapidly." To his moral science tutor he wrote four days later: "Although it is certain that he will not recover, one can not yet tell whether the illness will take a very rapid course or not. I will therefore have to stay here another ten days & hope I shall then be able to decide whether I may go back to Cambridge or must stay in Vienna, until the end." On the same day he informed Russell:

He is not yet in any great pain but feels on the whole very bad having constant high fever. This makes him so apathetic that one cannot do him any good by sitting at his bed etc. And as this was the only thing that I could ever do for him, I am now perfectly useless here. So the time of my staying now depends entirely upon whether the illness will take so rapid a course that I cannot risk leaving Vienna.

This comedy of vanities, shuffling visitations and bedside vigils went on for another week until, on 20 January, Karl finally lost consciousness, and submitting to the inevitable, graciously breathed his last.

Dear Russell,
    My dear father died yesterday in the afternoon. He had the most beautiful death that I can imagine; without the slightest pain and falling

asleep like a child! I did not feel sad for a single moment during all the last hours, but most joyful & I think that this death was worth a whole life. I will leave Vienna on Saturday the 25th & will be in Cambridge either on Sunday night or Monday morning. I long very much to see you again.

Yours ever,

Ludwig Wittgenstein

17   IN MEMORIAM K.W.

Karl Wittgenstein's obituaries, as all obituaries tended to be in those days, were dignified and complimentary. None of them mentioned his price-fixing, his cartels or his squeeze on the workers that had so vexed the left-wing press at the time of his grand resignation. Instead they dwelt upon his charitable giving, focusing especially on his legacy as a patron of the arts, without whose spontaneous generosity the famous Secession building on the Friedrichstrasse would never have been built. "Karl Wittgenstein was a man of unusually creative energy and strong organisational talent," reported the *Neue Freie Presse.* "The Austrian Iron industry, which thirty years ago was in a less than advanced state, had him to thank for its dramatic progress." The last paragraph was a warm tribute:

> Karl Wittgenstein had a wild temperament and an extraordinarily rapid grasp of a subject, brilliantly quick-witted in discussions and a charming sense of humor. He was often irascible but never bore a grudge; always willing to help his friends and even those who held opposing views valued his traits of character. His charitable largesse was frequently carried out in secret; he promoted young talent and was always ready to support artistic endeavors.

The autobiographical notes that Karl had dictated to Hermine were in no fit state for publication. Instead the family decided to honor his memory with a privately printed edition of his politico-economic writings and pieces he had written about his travels. On January 25, 1913, he was buried in a plot long reserved for himself and his family, occupying a prime position in the grand, hierarchical cemetery and tourist center known as the Zentralfriedhof. The Wittgenstein family crypt, a crumbling octagonal edifice of once-modern design, can be located at a distance of forty paces from the graves of Beethoven, Schubert, Brahms and Johann Strauss. Soon after Karl's death, his son Rudi's mortal remains were moved from their original place of burial to be next to his. Rudi is the only one of the five Wittgenstein sons to be interred here. Next to Karl now lies the body of Leopoldine, his wife, and on the other side that of an eagle-nosed servant who went by the name of Rosalie.

18 PAUL REVIEWED

Paul's concert debut on December 1, 1913, with which this story opened, was considered a huge success by his family, by his friends and perhaps also by the Palais servants, even before the first reviews started to appear in the papers. Albert Figdor, an eccentric billionaire cousin, wrote to him on the day after the concert to say that he was overjoyed by the success of it and that all of Vienna was praising him. "Please accept the enclosed joke as a small token of my affection." His present was an original autograph manuscript of a humorous canon by Felix Mendelssohn.

Paul was acutely sensitive to the opinions of others—furious about praise when he believed it to be unmerited, and indignant about negative criticism of any kind. He preferred his performances not to be discussed at all. Most of all he was allergic to the views of his younger brother, for though Ludwig conceded an admiration of Paul's technique, he was seldom enthusiastic about the manner of his interpretation. Ludwig was hypercritical of all musicians, even the best (he once interrupted the famous Rosé String Quartet during one of their rehearsals to tell them they were playing a Schubert quartet all wrong), but his low opinion of Paul's musicianship, though typical of his fastidiousness, agitated his elder brother beyond endurance. While Paul was practicing at home one evening he suddenly stopped playing and rushed through to the next-door room where Ludwig was sitting minding his own business, and shouted at him, "I cannot play when you are in the house as I feel your scepticism seeping towards me from under the door."

"My opinion of your playing is, in and of itself, UTTERLY IMMATE-RIAL," Ludwig insisted, but Paul, who would never let the matter drop, came to the conclusion that his younger brother could not stand his musical performances.

In the Volksgarten Café on the Burgring, Ludwig once tried to explain his position. He began, as tactfully as he was able, by comparing Paul's piano playing to the performance of a fine actor who regards the text of a play as a springboard from which he can express to the audience aspects of his own personality, and went on to admit that Paul's musical interpretations were spoiled (for him at least) by the intrusion of too much ego into the music. "You do not, I believe, seek to hide behind a musical composition but want to portray yourself in it. If I wish to hear a composer speak (which I often do) I shall not turn to you."

Like most performing artists, Paul affected to despise professional critics, even though he later became one himself. "From an artistic point of view they are not important," he wrote to his agent. "What does it matter what so-and-so thinks or makes believe to think? Unfortunately though, from a practical point of view, they are of the utmost importance," and it was precisely for want of good press reviews that he had planned his Musikverein debut in the first place. Max Kalbeck, the distinguished sixty-three-year-old critic and Brahms scholar, was the first to appear with a highfalutin piece in the *Neues Wiener Tagblatt* on December 6:

> Any young man, a member of Viennese high society, who launches himself on the public in the year 1913 as a piano virtuoso with a concerto by John Field must either be a fanatical enthusiast or a very self-confident dilettante. But Herr Paul Wittgenstein—for it is he of whom we speak—is neither one nor the other but (better than either as far as we are concerned) a serious artist. He undertook this hazardous adventure without knowing quite how risky it was, driven by a pure love for the task and guided by the honourable intention of placing before the public a test, both reliable and rare, of his eminent skills.

Kalbeck's review winds on in verbose, affected prose that would be considered unprintable in modern times. It is perhaps for this reason that his Boswellian eight-volume biography of Brahms, written over fifteen years between 1898 and 1913, though still the seminal source of Brahms scholarship, has never been translated into English. Of Paul's concert the great critic continued:

> Under the fading light of our feelings, well-loved figures of antiquity hovered before us and initiated us into the secrets of poetic twilight. A dryly written composition had unexpectedly blossomed into a poem. Inside that immaculately clean technique, which seems to us today as cool as inorganic matter, lives a tender and sensitive soul and we felt its warm breath.

Kalbeck was a friend of the Wittgensteins—a regular guest at their Alleegasse music evenings—and his rave review of Paul's performance may have been biased. His description of Paul's "immaculately clean technique" and "the pure and faultless luster of the pianist's delicate, soft and sparkling touch" may be compared with comments from another unsigned review published in *Das Fremdenblatt* on December 10 which stated that "further practice would add greater perfection to his abilities and refine his performance," and that his playing was "particularly careful and exceedingly cautious." But the *Fremdenblatt* critic went on to add that "the force with which the notes were struck and the unassuming precision of a healthy rhythmical sense legitimise his performing in public" (hardly consistent with his point about "cautiousness"), and that the programme's considerable hurdles were "cleared by a performer who was obviously firm in the saddle."

Julius Korngold, the all-important critic of the *Neue Freie Presse* who had mysteriously walked out of the concert after listening only to the first piece, eventually produced a short paragraph for his newspaper that attempted to justify his behavior: "The debut of the young pianist Paul Wittgenstein aroused lively interest . . . [his] freshly acquired technique, his sheer joy in music making and his classically trained feeling for style could all be sympathetically indulged without the need for taking further risks." Korngold's review, appearing a full three weeks after the concert, refreshed the young pianist's confidence and bolstered him with renewed authority to continue in pursuit of his chosen career. Paul had fought hard against his family's objections, sometimes rebelling against and sometimes making concessions to his father's tyranny. On Karl's insistence he had enrolled at Vienna's Technical University in 1910 and soon afterward taken a job (much resented) as a banking apprentice in Berlin. Now at last he had secured a victory for his pianism. The Korngold review may have been late in coming and slapdash in its execution, but that did not matter, for it was a final and very public vindication of Paul Wittgenstein's talent that succeeded not only in filling him with hope and confidence but also in alleviating the gloom of a family Christmas which, that year, everyone had been dreading.

On December 3, 1913, two days after Paul's triumphant debut, a short piece appeared in the pages of *Srbobran,* the Chicago journal for émigré Serbs in America:

> The Austrian Heir Apparent has announced his intention of visiting Sarajevo early next year. Every Serb must take note of this . . . Serbs, seize everything you can lay your hands upon—knives, rifles, bombs and dynamite. Take holy vengeance! Death to the Hapsburg dynasty and eternal remembrance to the heroes who raise their hands against it.

PART TWO

A NASTY MESS

19 MONEY MATTERS

Karl Wittgenstein's estate was divided equally between his wife and six surviving children. Gretl had opted for a hugh cash settlement and promptly bought herself a villa and a castle and some land at Gmunden for 335,000 Austrian kronen, but no sooner had she invited the architects and decorators to doll the place up than Jerome, restless as usual, was insisting on a move to England. So in April 1914 the Stonboroughs packed their bags and went to live in a Jacobean manor house at Besselsleigh near Abingdon in Oxfordshire. Jerome, having slightly more experience of business than his wife, took command of her considerable investments, transferring the bulk of her liquid fortune to the American stock market. Paul and his other siblings divided among themselves their late father's Austrian properties as well as his large portfolio of foreign stocks held at the Central Hanover Bank in New York, the Kreditanstalt and Blankart depots in Zurich and at the Dutch bank Hope & Co. in Amsterdam.

Each of the siblings was made exceedingly rich by their father's demise, but the money, to a family obsessed with social morality, brought with it many problems. Each was generous, donating large sums, often secretly, to the arts, to medicine, to friends and to other worthy causes. Ludwig distributed 100,000 kronen among various Austrian "artists." These included the architect Adolf Loos, the painter Oskar Kokoschka and the poets Rainer Maria Rilke and Georg Trakl. The last of these killed himself with an overdose of cocaine in the following year. Seventeen other recipients wrote thank-you letters to Ludwig, most of which he repudiated as "extremely distasteful" on account of their "ignoble almost fraudulent tone." Hermine, in a muddled quasi-philosophical way, tried to draw some distinction between the sort of money that she called "ethical" and the sort she labeled "bourgeois." Gretl dreamed longingly of a life without any money at all. "It would be healthy," she wrote in her diary, "if destiny would kick me off the high life from which I could never voluntarily depart. Maybe, but only maybe, I would then become a human being. But

I am not brave enough. As things stand now I can see the right path clearly in front of me but I cannot decide to take it."

Paul believed that strong government was more important than any amount of personal wealth and gave large sums to anticommunist and anti-anarchist political organizations. For a rich young man wanting to make his way as a concert pianist, things were not as easy as they may have seemed. When people in the classical music business smell money (which isn't very often), they are drawn to it like wasps to a jam pot. If a performer is rich enough to stage his own concerts, however good he is at playing his instrument, he will find himself in the dispiriting position of being invited to play only on a no-fee basis, or in consideration of sponsorship. This was to prove a problem for Paul that lasted the whole of his performing life. In the months following his debut promoters and agents buzzed around eager to partake of his fortune, but on the advice of his blind and wise mentor, Dr. Labor, he held them at bay:

> Nothing [said Labor to Alma Schindler] is more dangerous for a
> young talent than not allowing it to mature. For all young artists
> the example of Rubinstein and Goldmark should be held up as the
> direst warning—two such talents—ruined because they did not wait
> until they were ready. Rubinstein bestowed his spring buds upon us
> all, but never brought forth fruit.

In the six months following his debut Paul played no more than a handful of concerts. There was an evening of chamber music by Mendelssohn and Labor with the well-known violinist and friend of the family Marie Soldat-Roeger. Hermine, in attendance with her mother and sisters, wrote to inform Ludwig that Paul had played "very beautifully and had received praise from all sides." At Graz, in February 1914, he gave a solo recital, which was complimented by the fastidious critic of the *Grazer Tagespost*. Another chamber concert in March was followed, three weeks later, by a second high-profile outing at the Musikverein. This time the Vienna Symphony Orchestra, conducted by the Slovakian pianist and composer Rudolph Réti, played Josef Labor's Variations on a Theme of Czerny, an anodyne nocturne by Field and a handful of studies by Chopin. These scattered events may appear insignificant, but to Paul they were the necessary rungs in a ladder of experience that he hoped might lead him towards his long-cherished goal of a busy international career. But neither Paul nor anyone else in the complacent, easy-going, coffeehouse atmosphere of Habsburg Vienna had reckoned on that summer's catastrophic interruptions.

20 PRELUDE TO WAR

When news reached Vienna, on June 28, 1914, that the heir to the Hapsburg throne, Archduke Franz Ferdinand, had been shot in the neck by a juvenile anarchist at the Bosnian town of Sarajevo, there was no wailing or rending of veils. The Austrians, by and large, took it on the chin, for the Emperor's nephew had never been popular. The reasons for this were neither political nor considered, but instinctive and emotional—the people had long ago made up their minds that he was fat and ugly and ungracious. The Archduke had married morganatically, that is to say he had espoused a woman deemed by Hapsburg house law to be too lower class to attend state occasions and too lower class to bear future heirs to the Imperial throne. In order to marry her, Franz Ferdinand had been forced to renounce the right of any future issue to the Austrian throne. The public knew that the Emperor disliked his nephew intensely, and since the old man's life had been full of woe—his brother was put to death by firing squad in Mexico, his sister-in-law lost her marbles, his wife was murdered by a rough brute in Geneva, and his only son was the Prince Rudolf who had apparently shot himself in a suicide pact with his mistress—public sympathy was all with the Emperor against his ponderous and overbearing heir. Stefan Zweig, who on several occasions observed the Archduke in his box at the theater, remembered his sitting "broad and mighty, with cold fixed gaze."

> He was never seen to smile and no photographs showed him relaxed. He had no sense of music and no sense of humour, and his wife was equally unfriendly. They were both surrounded by an icy air; one knew that they had no friends and also that the old Em-

peror hated him with all his heart because he did not have suffi-
cient tact to hide his impatience to succeed to the throne.

In a photograph taken on that fatal day at Sarajevo the Archduke and
his wife are both, contrary to Zweig, depicted with broad grins on their
faces, but their last, perhaps their only, smiles came too late to warm the
hardened hearts of the Viennese, as did the news of Franz Ferdinand's
last utterance, gasped at his Archduchess as she sat grim-faced and upright behind him in their carriage: "Sopherl! Sopherl! Don't die! Keep
alive for the children . . . It is nothing! It is nothing! It is nothing!" She
could not hear him, for she was already dead.

Historians have suggested that within the psyche of the men and
women of all German-speaking lands was a will to war, that the artists
and composers and writers were demonstrating a restless predilection for
the destruction of their states. This instinct drove them to an atavistic,
primeval savagery. Shortly after the outbreak of war the German writer
Thomas Mann explained:

> This world of peace, which has now collapsed with such shattering
> thunder—had we not all of us had enough of it? Was it not foul with
> all its comfort? Did it not fester and stink with the decomposition
> of civilisation? Morally and psychologically I felt the necessity of
> this catastrophe and that feeling of cleansing, of elevation and liber-
> ation, which filled me, when that which one had thought impossi-
> ble really happened.

And yet in the immediate aftermath of the Sarajevo assassination the
public showed itself to be more concerned with the funeral arrangements—particularly the vexed question of whether the Archduchess's
corpse was grand enough to be buried with that of her husband in the Ka-
puzinergruft, or Imperial Crypt—than with the possibility or probability
of any war proceeding from it. On a higher, governmental level, however,
things were a little different. Franz Conrad von Hötzendorf, Chief of the
Austro-Hungarian General Staff, and Foreign Minister Leopold Berchtold seized upon the Archduke's murder as an opportunity to humiliate
Serbia and strengthen Austro-Hungarian influence in the Balkans. The

Serbian government, they claimed, had had a hand in the assassination and must therefore be punished. The inevitable rejection, by the Serbs, of an unacceptable Austrian ultimatum on July 25 led to Vienna's declaration of war against Serbia on the 28th.

The rest—an extraordinary scrimmage of nations roused to action in the name of honor—is, as they say, history. On July 31, Germany declared war on the Russians, who were mobilizing troops in Serbia's defense; France, in honor of its agreement with Russia, moved against Germany; Germany, to protect itself against the French, invaded Belgium, whereupon the British (who had not the slightest interest in the Serbian quarrel) declared war on Germany in defense of Belgium's neutrality. On August 5, Austro-Hungary declared war on Russia; on August 6, Serbia on Germany; and the day after that Montenegro declared itself against the Austro-Hungarians and the Germans. On August 10, France declared war on Austro-Hungary and on August 12 Great Britain did the same. By August 23 Japan, thousands of miles away, had pitched in against Germany with the immediate effect that Austro-Hungary, in honorable defense of its ally, declared war on Japan. On August 28, two short months after the Sarajevo shootings, Austro-Hungary declared war on Belgium. More countries would follow, for events were proceeding at a horrifying pace, but even before the last of these belligerent nations had time to throw itself into the ruckus, disaster had struck the House of Wittgenstein.

21 SIGNING UP

With regard to their conscription, the circumstances of the three surviving Wittgenstein brothers—Kurt, Paul and Ludwig—were each very different. Kurt was thirty-six years old when war broke out and was living in New York. He had arrived aboard the newly built German liner *Imperator* on April 9, 1914, with the purpose of exploring opportunities for investment in the American and Canadian steel business. For a while he stayed at the Waldorf Hotel, before moving to the Knickerbocker Club on East 62nd Street. He made friends in high society, bought himself a luxurious automobile, took several holidays at the Virginia spa resort of Hot Springs and settled into his New World lifestyle with apparent ease. When the news of war in Europe reached him, he was on his way back to New York from Cranbrook, a steel-manufacturing town in British Columbia, intending to sail back to Austria at the beginning of July, but the American authorities would not let him leave. When he presented himself at the Austrian Consulate in Manhattan he was put to work by the Consul General, Alexander von Nuber, in the organization's propaganda department, whose task it was to persuade the American people, the American press and more importantly the American administration to support the Austro-Hungarian cause in the war.

Paul and Ludwig were with their sisters and their mother at Hochreit, the family's mountain retreat, when news of war reached them. In a rapture of patriotism, they rushed back to Vienna to find the popular mood on the streets frenzied and excitable. Every butcher and cobbler, every doctor and teacher was experiencing what Stefan Zweig described as "an exaltation of his ego," imagining himself a hero. Women were urging their husbands into uniform, class barriers were falling, people spoke warmly to strangers in the shops and joked heartily over the imminent demise of the Serbs.

Ludwig wanted to sail for Norway but, when he found his exit from Austria barred, volunteered for civilian duties instead. Unlike his brothers Paul and Kurt, Ludwig had managed to avoid military service. In 1868 the Austrian government had introduced a compulsory conscription of three years for every young male, but the costs had proved exorbitant. Instead of revoking the law, all kinds of formulations were devised (including the drawing of lots) whereby a man might wriggle out of this irksome duty. In the event only one in five eligible men ever made it into uniform and, of those, only a small proportion served the full three-year term demanded by the law. With no previous service record, Ludwig had no regiment to which he could report, and since he had suffered two hernias in his groin the previous year he was, in any case, deemed unsuitable for active service. Determined to play his part, he decided to enlist as a volunteer soldier, and on August 7 was called up as a private in a garrison artillery troop that was to form part of the Austro-Hungarian First Army, destined for the borders of Hapsburg Poland and Russia known as the Galician front.

Like many of the young German men of 1914, Ludwig was spiritually exhausted and in need of theater. Early that year he had fallen out with Bertrand Russell and had written to him insisting that their friendship be terminated. "My life has been one nasty mess so far—but need that go on indefinitely?" He had also, by his frantic manner, lost the friendship of the Cambridge philosopher George Moore, and was uncertain even about the future of his relationship with his closest companion, David Pinsent. "I keep on hoping that things will come to an eruption once and for all so that I can turn into a different person," he wrote, and so the war, which on June 28 seemed little more than an inconvenience to Ludwig, was transformed, within a matter of days, into a welcome opportunity for challenge and personal liberation. "I knew very well," Hermine wrote, "that Ludwig was not only concerned with defending his fatherland, but that he felt an intense desire to burden himself with some difficult task, and to accomplish something other than purely intellectual work."

If he was refreshed by the outbreak of hostilities, Ludwig nevertheless entertained little hope of the great Austro-Hungarian victory that the masses, on both sides of the conflict, were predicting with the oft-repeated phrase: "It'll all be over by Christmas." In a scribbled note written shortly after the war had begun, Ludwig admitted that the situation was "terribly sad." "It seems to me as good as certain that we cannot get the upper hand against England. The English—the best race in the world— *cannot* lose. We, however, can lose and shall lose, if not this year, then next year. The thought that our race is going to be beaten depresses me terribly."

David Pinsent wrote in his diary of Ludwig's volunteering for the army: "I think it is magnificent of him to have enlisted—but extremely sad and tragic . . . He writes praying we may meet again some day. Poor fellow—I hope to God we shall." They never did. Pinsent was killed in an airplane crash in France in May 1918.

22 DISASTERS

Paul went along with the majority of his Austrian compatriots in supporting the Austro-Hungarian monarchy, believing that his moral and civic duty was to defend the honor of the Hapsburgs for which he would, if necessary, lay down his life. But, like his younger brother, he was not so easily swept by the tide of national optimism. He too nursed a fatalistic view of Austria's prospects, and openly asserted what the Emperor had said in private to his Chief of Staff just days before signing his declaration of war, that "if the Monarchy must perish it should at least perish with decency." War for Paul offered no opportunity for self-improvement but was a question of personal and national honor. His sister Gretl, however, welcomed the international crisis on Paul's behalf. "Aid has come to us from an unexpected quarter," she wrote to Hermine on August 22. "If they come back in one piece, this war will have done many of those I know a lot of good—and that includes Paul and [my friend] Willi Zitkovsky."

Paul had completed his military service five years before the declaration of hostilities, passing as a junior officer in the Reserves, attached to the same smart cavalry regiment as his brother Kurt. On the whole, his military reports had been creditable. In the winter of 1907 he was issued with four demerits and fined for "lack of attention in the riding school and laziness in theoretical instruction," but his final report of 1909 had concluded that, as a cadet officer—"single, finances in order, with a monthly allowance of 600 kronen"—he was of "most honourable, firm character, quiet, serious and good-natured."

Four hectic days after Austria's declaration against Serbia, Paul found himself once again dressed in the colorful regimental garb of the 6th Dragoons. As a second lieutenant he was entitled to a black crested helmet, trimmed in brass, embossed on the front with the badge of the Imperial Eagle and, on either side, with images of a lion in violent disagreement with a serpent. His breeches were of madder red and his tunic pale blue but beaded in red, denoting his officer status. He wore a red cartridge belt (another sign that he was an officer), black leather thigh-length "butcher's boots" and a large, dark brown, double-breasted greatcoat. His weaponry, which like his uniform was indicative of rank, consisted of a Roth-Steyr pistol, a Mannlicher carbine rifle, a saber in a steel scabbard and a bayonet. Paul and his fellow officers may have looked splendid perched on their saddles, in all this colorful regalia, but the kit of both man and animal were relics of a previous century, unsuitable for the exigencies of modern combat. Their shiny metal badges and bright colors were easily visible to the enemy; their rifles and sabers too heavy; their jackets and coats (in comparison to those of other armies) badly stitched; even their saddles were thoughtlessly constructed. Designed to give the cavalry a good seat on parade, they rubbed hard against the skin of the horses' backs, so that within the first week of engagement a large section of the Austrian cavalry was put out of action as hundreds of officers were forced to return from their sorties on foot, leading their horses by the reins.

The Austro-Hungarian army of 1914 was ill equipped, incompetent, ill trained, undersized, unready and yet overenthusiastic for battle. The soldiers' contagious eagerness to start fighting right away led to many grave errors. In the first few days of engagement they managed to shoot down three of their own airplanes, so that the order had to be repeatedly given that no planes should be fired upon. At Jaroslawice on August 20, two Austrian cavalry divisions advancing in parallel lines wheeled around and started fighting each other. Too proud or too exhilarated to stop, the Austrians carried on with their battle till interrupted by the arrival of a Russian infantry unit that put them all to flight. Nothing, however, compares to the dithering of Conrad von Hötzendorf over where he should send his army in the first days of mobilization. His problem—hard to solve—is at least easy to explain. The Austrians had to fight a two-front war. In the northeast the Russians had fifty infantry divisions ranged against them. In the south, Serbia had eleven. The total strength on the Austro-Hungarian side was only forty-eight divisions. Thus Hötzendorf's army was too small for the war that he had elected it to fight—smaller even than it had been in 1866 at the time of its crushing defeat at the hands of the Prussians, and this, despite a total population increase of twenty million since that date. Hötzendorf needed therefore to decide whether first to smash up the Serbs with say twenty divisions, posting the rest of his army to Galicia to hold the Russians, or to send a greater force against the Russians, leaving a smaller defense force in the south to contain the Serbs. In the end he chose the latter course but not before changing his mind more than once and, in so doing, throwing the whole railway system of the Austro-Hungarian Empire into disarray.

Paul and Ludwig were both dispatched to the Galician front in the north, Paul with the Fourth Army, Ludwig with the First. But Hötzendorf's indecision meant that both of them reached their unloading stations (in Paul's case the wrong one) nearly a week after they were supposed to be there. Several trains shunted along at less than walking speed. Others broke down. One took forty hours to get from Vienna to the San, three times longer than normal; several stopped for six-hour lunch breaks despite having mobile kitchens on board. In the confusion at least one signalman shot himself, and one train, packed with soldiers, was returned to the very station from which, days earlier, it had departed amid the clamor of trumpets, bunting, waving hands and fond farewells.

Ludwig reached his posting on August 19 and was immediately assigned to minor tasks aboard a captured Russian riverboat, the *Goplana*, patrolling the Vistula. Paul was supposed to have arrived at Zólkiew, near Lwów (or Lemberg), on August 12, but owing to the confusion was not unloaded until August 20 some sixty miles west at Jaroslaw on the San. From there he proceeded on horseback in a northeasterly direction with the soldiers of the 5th Cavalry Brigade under the command of Major General Otto Schwer von Schwertenegg, reaching Lubaczów on the morning of August 20 and Zamość two days later on the evening of the 22nd. Hötzendorf, aware that Wenzel von Plehve (a Russian commander of German descent) was mobilizing 350,000 soldiers of the Russian Fifth Army westward to stop them, continued blithely predicting a swift advance of Austro-Hungarian troops into Russian territory.

On August 23, Paul's fourth day in Galicia, he and six men under his command were ordered north across undulating wooded terrain toward the village of Izbica. Their mission was to reconnoiter enemy positions and report back to the squadron commander, Captain Erwin Schaafgotsche, at a field camp located between Izbica and Krasnystaw. After a few miles Paul and his men turned east to Topola and then proceeded to move cautiously in the direction of the Russian border and the fast-assembling ranks of enemy troops.

From the woods outside Topola the view extends for several miles eastward across the plain of Grabowiec. From here a vast number of Russian troops could be observed mobilizing rapidly in a southwesterly direction toward Zamość. Paul and his men took careful note of their numbers, their armaments and the direction in which they were headed. The citation for the medals that Paul received for his role in this action indicates that they were awarded not only in consideration of the usefulness of the information he had gleaned, but for outstanding personal valor. He bravely rescued two of his men when they came under fire from a forward-placed Russian scout troop or sniper team and ordered a counterattack to delay the Russians while the positions of their army were being surveyed. "As regards my allegedly heroic deeds," he later wrote to his mother, "there was nothing of that about them. You won't believe it but I know it."

During the encounter Paul was wounded—hit by a bullet that shattered the elbow of his right arm. Later he could recall nothing between the sensation of a sharp and excruciating pain and his waking up on a field-hospital camp bed, but his men had pulled him back to safety, retreating quickly through the woods until they were out of range of enemy fire. There they applied a makeshift tourniquet to Paul's upper arm to staunch the bleeding. The journey back to Izbica was several miles and they needed urgently to find an ambulance corps or a field hospital on the way. At some point either Paul or some of his men succeeded in passing to Captain Schaafgotsche the crucial military intelligence that they had gleaned at Topola—information that later proved vital to the Austrian defense of Zamość.

By the time he was brought into the field hospital, situated within the walls of the fortress town of Krasnystaw, six miles north of Izbica, Paul had already lost consciousness. Either that or the shock subsequently obliterated his memory of events and helped him to forget any medical consultation or warning that most of his right arm would have to come off. All that he remembered was that when he regained consciousness the shock of discovering the mutilation to his arm was compounded by another, perhaps equally disturbing, shock: that during the course of his operation, as the doctors were filling his lungs with anesthetic doses of morphine, scopolamine, nitrous oxide or ethyl chloride, as they were slicing a circular incision round the skin of his upper arm, as they rolled back the flesh to create a flap, as they sawed through the exposed bone, discarded the amputated limb, folded and stitched the loose flaps back over the end of the stump—as all these things were carrying on, the Russian Fifth Army in its first major incursion into Hapsburg-Polish territory was storming the walls of Krasnystaw, so that by the time Paul regained consciousness the enemy had taken the town and was swarming with loaded guns and harsh hysterical voices through the corridors and wards of his hospital. Paul, his fellow patients, the surgeons, doctors, orderlies and nurses were being held at gunpoint as prisoners of war, now in the power of a hostile government, and soon to be bustled across enemy lines, thousands of miles from their homes, to prison camps in Russia and Siberia.

23 PRISONER OF THE RUSSIANS

There were no train lines and few roads on the vast exposed lands stretching eastward out of Krasnystaw. Those captives deemed fit enough to march were forced to do so, sometimes up to fifteen miles a day, sometimes at the point of a Cossack saber, nourished only by one slice of bread and a bowl of cabbage soup, served in the morning of each day. For two or three weeks they marched until they reached a depot from which transport by rail could begin. In their first Galician offensive the Russians took 100,000 Austro-Hungarian prisoners of war. These, added to the large numbers of their own wounded and the straggling hoards of displaced Poles wandering hither and thither in search of food and shelter, created a vast, untidy migration of despairing people for whom the Russians were unprepared and ill equipped to cater.

Surviving accounts of the long march to the interior attest to the kindness and consideration of the Russian doctors, to the help, also, of the Russian peasantry who often took pity, giving bread and clothing to bedraggled Austrian and German POWs as they passed through their villages, but many report as well on the cruelty, crookedness and avarice of the rank-and-file Russian soldier. Article 4 of the Hague Convention, to which all belligerent nations were bound, stipulated that prisoners of war were to be treated humanely. They were to be held in the power of the hostile government, not in that of the individuals or corps who had captured them. With the exception of arms, horses and military papers, all personal belongings were to remain the property of the captured soldier. In reality, soldiers of the Russian army, themselves underpaid, underfed and terrified, ransacked the pockets of their prisoners, removing money, letters, watches, notebooks, cutlery and anything else that took their fancy. At POW hospitals, Russian guards made away with any clothing that they could lay their hands on—coats, shirts, boots and even blankets disappeared from the patients' wards and, since hospitals received payments based on the number of patients coming in and going out, dishonest clerks saw to it that even the most severely sick prisoners were moved needlessly about from one hospital to another, crawling sometimes barefoot and at night (so that the Russian people might be spared the sight of them) to freezing railway and tram stations, shuttling for weeks between Russian cities, often only to be returned to the very hospital from which they had started out.

In this way Paul found himself, in the long months after he was taken prisoner, shunted from Chelm to Minsk to Kiev, to Orel, to Moscow, to Petrograd and to Omsk in the cramped, overcrowded, foul-smelling and vermin-ridden conditions of the *tjeploshki*. These were the boxcars, wagons and cattle trucks, forty to fifty of which, linked together, formed a typical POW transport train. In the middle of each stood an iron stove and a bucket for a lavatory. Two rows of plank bunks were fixed to either side, and a separate space, with its own bunk, was provided for the armed guard. Typically each car held thirty-five to forty-five prisoners, sleeping often six to a bunk. As one Austrian POW remembered it: "Everybody had to face either to the left or to the right side, squeezed tight to one another. Turning over had to be done all at once, for only by keeping our bodies in strictly parallel formation could we all fit the available space."

There was little to cheer Paul as he lay on the bare board of a *tjeploshka* trundling across 7,000 miles of alien terrain. For days on end he lay, pressed against other prisoners, the wound festering on his arm, his eyes wide open, in a carriage filled with vermin. He remembered with particular repulsion the rats running over his body and confided years later to a close friend "how they still recurred as my sporadic nightmare and how grateful I am that my blood was immune from insect bites. Other prisoners had found bugs and lice intolerable but I could brush them away unstung."

Harder to dispel were the physical and psychological traumas Paul suffered in the weeks and months after his operation—traumas that were amplified by the practical difficulties that he had to face in adapting his disability to everyday life. Suddenly he was unable to tie his shoelaces, to cut his food or dress himself in the morning. Géza Zichy, an acquaintance of Paul's who lost his right arm in a hunting accident at the age of fifteen, recalled his first attempts to dress himself: "It took three hours, but I did it. I used the door knob, the furniture, my feet and my teeth to achieve it. At meals I ate no food that I could not cut myself, and today I peel apples, clip my fingernails, ride, I am a good shot and have even learned to play the piano a little."

The causes of a disorder known as phantom limb pain, which affects all amputees, are still not clearly understood by the medical profession. Some believe that the brain continues to operate from a blueprint of the whole body even when parts of it have been removed. Others that the brain, frustrated at receiving no response from the missing limb, bombards it with too many signals, thus aggravating the nerves that originally served it. Whatever the cause, the symptoms are acute—a searing pain in the missing limb, a sensation that the absent fist or elbow is clamping tighter and tighter until it is about to explode, or that the whole limb is somehow inextricably twisted or bent. Looking to see that the arm is no longer there does not relieve the victim, for the pain will persist even when his eyes have confirmed that it cannot possibly be.

It was not until three weeks after his capture that Paul was permitted to write home for the first time. All prisoners' letters were subject to Russian censorship, but it was not for this reason that they tended to a cheerful tone. Quite apart from the obvious motive of not wishing to upset their families with details of their desperate state, many prisoners felt shame, even guilt, for having betrayed or dishonoured their families and comrades in arms by leaving the front line. The Swedish Red Cross nurse Elsa Brändström, known as the Angel of Siberia, did more than anyone to alleviate the suffering of Austro-Hungarian POWs, and told in her memoirs the pitiful story of one Austrian cadet: "A young man lay in the corner. No dumb animal in his father's farm had ever perished in such filth. 'Give my love to my mother; but never tell her in what misery I died' were his last words."

The reluctance of prisoners to tell the truth about the grueling circumstances of their captivity led to further problems with the mail, for all outgoing letters were checked not only by the Russians but also by the Kriegsüberwachungsamt, or KÜA, the censorship department of the War Supervisory Office in Vienna. With so many cheerful missives arriving from Russia (75,000 in the month of December), an order was given out on Christmas Eve 1914:

> Letters have been received lately from our prisoners of war in enemy countries. In some of these letters the writers describe life in captivity in a very favourable light. The spreading of such news among the troops and recruits is undesirable. The military censors are therefore to be instructed that such letters of our prisoners of war as may, by their contents, exercise an injurious influence are to be confiscated and not to be delivered to their addressees.

From the middle of August until the first week of October Mrs. Wittgenstein had remained in an anxious state. She had recently suffered an acute attack of phlebitis and her doctor had ordered her to hold her legs in a horizontal posture at all times. This prevented her playing the piano—the best method she knew for calming her nerves. Of Paul she had heard nothing for six weeks, his last letter being a complaint that none of hers were getting through to him. It was not until October 4 that she finally received, in barely legible scrawl, the news that he was still alive. Paul's letter to his mother has been lost, but Mrs. Wittgenstein's letter, in which she relays the news to Ludwig, survives:

> *My dear beloved Ludwig,*
>
> *I have written you many letters and cards with my thanks for all yours and for the telegram. I do hope that they have reached you at last. They bring you the most tender greetings and kisses from me, and all your sisters' love; and assure you that we are all well here and in Gmunden. A terrible misfortune has befallen our poor Paul who lost his*

right arm in one of the battles at the end of August [sic]. He wrote to me himself with his left hand on 14 September from the officers' hospital in Minsk and his news arrived three days ago. He also wrote that he was being looked after extremely well. You can imagine how I feel not being able to go to him. God protect you, my beloved child. I wish you could sense it whenever I think of you. For all your dear letters, be tenderly embraced by your Mama.

Leopoldine's card failed to reach Ludwig on his riverboat until October 28, by which time she had already posted him another: "I've not heard any more from Paul since the 4th," she wrote, "the day on which, after six weeks of waiting in vain, I received his letter from Minsk with the news of his serious injury. I imagine you must have received the card I wrote telling you that the poor boy has lost his right hand." Ludwig's immediate response can be found in his diary of October 28:

Received a lot of mail today, incl. the sad news that Paul has been seriously wounded and is in captivity in Russia—but, thank God, being taken good care of. Poor, poor Mama!!! . . . At last a letter from Norway in which I am asked for 1,000 kronen. Is it possible for me to send it to him? Now that Norway has joined with our enemies!!! This is, in any case, a frightfully sad business. I keep having to think of poor Paul who has so suddenly lost his career! How terrible. What philosophy is needed to get over it! If only this can be achieved in any other way than suicide!! . . . Your will be done.

On the following day Ludwig recorded: "Headache and tiredness in the morning. Thought a lot about Paul," while in Vienna his mother and sisters augmented their panic by imagining that Paul might now try to kill himself.

24 KURT WITTGENSTEIN IN AMERICA

For all her anxiety about the welfare of her sons, Mrs. Wittgenstein was equally concerned that the honor of the Wittgenstein family should at all times be upheld. She felt proud of Ludwig for having volunteered himself for the army and of Hermine and the Stonboroughs for volunteering themselves for hospital jobs. Her pride was also stirred by initial reports of Paul's heroism for which, she hoped, he might one day be decorated. In this she was encouraged by his former commanding officer, Colonel von Rettich:

November 11, 1914

My Dear Mrs. Wittgenstein,

I have obtained your address from Erwin Schaafgotsche. As former Colonel of the 6th Dragoons, I would like to offer my sincerest sympathy to you over the severe wounding of your son. You may be proud of him because the information he obtained as leader of a military patrol frustrated the efforts of the Russians to attack us at Zamość. He has rendered outstanding service, for which I sincerely hope he will receive official recognition in due course. This is however not possible at the present time, for though your son was captured owing to his being wounded, it must yet be proven that this was due to no fault of his own. As this fact appears to have been established already he should find no further obstacles on his return. I have learned that the healing of his wound is progressing satis-factorily.

With my deepest respects, I remain, most sincerely yours,
Alfred von Rettich

Kurt, however, was a thorn. "Poor sidelined Kurt," as his mother referred to him, was not able to pull his weight on the front line. That he was safe in America was of no consolation to her or to her daughters in Vienna. In his letters home Kurt gave them the impression that he was doing everything in his power to return to Austria and reenlist in the army. Neither his age nor his less than satisfactory military service record counted against him. America's policy toward the conflict in Europe was officially neutral, so that U.S. residents (of whatever duration) were forbidden from actively taking sides in the European war. Kurt, as a reserve officer in the Austro-Hungarian 6th Dragoons, was consequently prohibited from leaving America as his stated intention was to rejoin the Austrian army.

He and his colleagues at the Austrian Consulate General involved themselves instead in a clandestine and illegal racket in false foreign passports, using them to repatriate U.S.-resident Austrians who, like Kurt, had found themselves stuck on the wrong side of the Atlantic. Kurt's letters home revealed none of this, only that his American work was dull and that he wished to God he were in Europe fighting like his brothers for his country. His mother and sisters—particularly Hermine—felt the dishonor of his absence keenly: "I am most anxious at the moment for Kurt," she wrote to Ludwig. "He will have a bad time if everyone else has played their part and suffered, except for him! He'll feel as though he has been permanently marked down." And later: "I'm always having to think of poor Kurt and how terrible it is that he is not experiencing these times as we are; you can hardly call what he is doing in America really living."

But Kurt's American existence may have been livelier than his sister had realized. His job—in what the *Providence Journal* described as "Consul General von Nuber's New York office of spies and tricksters"—presented him with varied opportunities. He played the piano, for instance, in a concert of Austrian and German folk music at the Aeolian Hall, hosted dinners at the Knickerbocker Club to raise money for a campaign to rouse Austrian expatriates, and gave interviews to American newspapers. But, despite his keenest efforts, American public opinion continued to swing to the side of the Entente Allies and away from Germany and the Central Powers. "It is not difficult to find a reason for the pro-British sentiment in America," Kurt indignantly told a reporter from the *Washington Post* in January 1915. "The British have been manufacturing sentiment over here in diverse ways . . . I believe the American people are coming to realise their error, however."

Not so one of them, an elderly lady of German extraction living on Manhattan's Upper East Side called Delia Steinberger (Jerome's widowed mother), who felt so strongly pro-British and anti-German that she had her surname changed (fifteen years after her son had done the same) to the more English-sounding Stonborough, falsely claiming, on her U.S. census return, that both her parents had been born in England.

Kurt paddled bravely against the powerful current of American anti-German feeling: "The reports I have from home are entirely satisfactory," he told the *Post,* "and I am confident that we must win." The Russians had been "hammering away" at the "practically impregnable" fort of Przemyśl for months to no effect and so long as Przemyśl continued to hold out, the enemy stood "no chance." But his patriotic optimism was ill founded. At the time of his speaking the casualty rate among the original infantry units of the Austro-Hungarian army was 82 percent. Two months later on March 22 the Austro-Hungarian commander Hermann Kusmanek surrendered the fort at Przemyśl, leading 119,000 of his men on the long march into Russian captivity.

Kurt kept his job in New York for another two years, despite surges of public pressure to have him and his colleagues at the Consulate expelled from America. First there was the scandal concerning fake passports; this was followed by public outrage at the revelation of millions of dollars secretly channeled by the Germans to Austrian diplomats for war propaganda in America; and then a story that the Austrian Consulate was paying for advertisements that threatened the livelihood of Austrian workers in American munitions factories. These advertisements, which were printed in dozens of American newspapers, read as follows:

> The Imperial and Royal Austro-Hungarian Embassy, acting under orders from the home Government, gives notice by this announcement to all Austrian and Hungarian citizens that all workmen who are employed in factories in this country which are making either arms or ammunition for the enemies of their country are committing a crime against the military safety of their fatherland. This crime is punishable by ten to twenty years' imprisonment and, in especially aggravating circumstances, with the penalty of death. Against those who violate this order, the whole weight of the law will be brought in the event of their return to their own country.

Each successive scandal renewed the calls to have all Austro-Hungarian diplomats expelled from the U.S. In 1915 the Austrian Ambassador in Washington, Konstantin Dumba, was expelled, but nothing was done about the rest of them, until America joined the war in the spring of 1917, when all diplomatic relations between the two countries were finally severed.

On the afternoon of May 4 that year at Hoboken Pier, Kurt, along with Dumba's replacement as ambassador, Count Adam Tarnowski, the Consul General from New York, Alexander von Nuber, and 206 so-called "enemy officials" under the surveillance of a cohort of American secret service agents, boarded the Holland-America liner *Ryndam,* bound for Holland. At Halifax the ship was held over for five days as British intelligence officers interrogated everyone on board. After that she was permitted to sail on to Rotterdam under a safe-conduct pass, proceeding north of the Faroe Islands to avoid the submarines and mined zones.

Mrs. Wittgenstein, who seems to have known nothing of her son's American expulsion and had not heard a word from him in several months, was as surprised as she was delighted to read his telegram of May 17: "ARRIVED ROTTERDAM TODAY IN GOOD HEALTH. WEDNESDAY VIENNA. KURT."

Hermine, bored stiff in her voluntary job as a supervisor at an outpatient clinic, greeted the news of her brother's return with enthusiasm. "I've just learned that Kurt has arrived in Rotterdam," she wrote to Ludwig. "I'm very happy for him, I can tell you! His situation after the war would have been extremely uncomfortable!"

25 ARRIVAL IN SIBERIA

For his twenty-seventh birthday on November 5, 1914, Paul was cooped up in a freezing, slowly moving cattle wagon. One-armed and distressed, he had been shunted from hospital to hospital for nearly three months, so that by the time he had passed the Urals into the vast and empty steppe of Western Siberia it was winter and the weather was biting cold. With temperatures dropping as low as 76 degrees below zero, the sliding doors of the *teploshki,* which had been rolled open in the morning hours of the early autumn—affording him welcome ventilation and spectacular views of the great sunflower plains of the Volga—were now kept firmly closed. Sickness, despair and filthy odors suffused the darkness within. When a man died his corpse remained on board until the next change of guard—sometimes several weeks later. In February 1915 two boarded-up wagons arriving at the southeastern city of Samara were found to contain sixty-five prisoners, only eight of whom were still alive. The carriages were shunted a mile out of town, where Russian guards with axes and spades removed the fifty-seven frozen bodies and threw them into a hole dug by the side of the track. This was not uncommon. Boarded-up wagons arriving at Moscow and Omsk thought to contain valuable goods turned out, upon inspection, also to be filled with frozen corpses.

In accordance with Article 17 of the Hague Convention, Paul was entitled, as a junior officer, to payment of fifty rubles a month with which to buy food, soap and other necessities. In reality the money was seldom received. To avoid payment Russian officials ensured that prisoners were transferred out of camp on the day before their pay was due. In transit, the duty for distributing the prisoners' cash fell to the transport commandant of each train. Some were honest, but many sought to embezzle the money, claiming inability to find the correct change. On such occasions prisoners were left with no nourishment, having to subsist, sometimes for days on end, on nothing but *kipiatok*—boiling water provided free of charge at each station along the line.

As a junior officer Paul received marginally more humane treatment from his captors than that which they meted out to the rank and file. POW officers were not obliged to work for the Russians, but soldiers in the ranks were put to manual labor—25,000 of them perished constructing the Murman Railway in the winter of 1914–15.

Omsk, a city situated at the confluence of the rivers Om and Irtysh in the *gubernia* or province of Akmolinsk some 1,600 miles east of Moscow, is the capital of Western Siberia. In 1914 it had a resident population of 130,000 which, within four years, was increased by 96,000 prisoners of war. In the ten months to August 1915, some 16,000 of them died there. On his arrival at Omsk station, Paul was hauled off the train in a blizzard and escorted under armed guard to a modern vodka distillery recently converted into a POW hospital. Others from the same train were escorted to prison camps outside the town, some as many as thirty miles away. Frozen, homesick, underdressed, many of them died before reaching their destinations.

At the entrance to the hospital Paul was handed a blank postcard on which to write to his family informing them of his new location before being pushed into a communal bathroom on the ground floor where his face and hair were shaved, his clothes were taken for disinfection and he was ordered to bathe. Though bitterly cold, the hospital at Omsk was preferable to many of the places of internment that Paul had visited en route. All the Russian hospitals were suffering from a shortage of bandages and medicine, but at least Omsk was cleaner than the one at Orel (where Paul had been placed in the same ward as typhoid and diphtheria victims); it was less crowded than the hospital at Moscow (which held 4,000 patients); and safer than the Nikolai in Petrograd, where the guards were insanely brutal. It was here, in the officers' ward, that an Austrian captain was bayoneted in the back for attempting to go to the lavatory. The sentry's blade punctured his lung and in a hasty court judgment he (the guard) was acquitted of wrongdoing, while the severely wounded officer and three invalid prisoners who had testified on his behalf were each sentenced to six years' hard labor.

26 THREE SOURCES OF INSPIRATION

Paul's decision to continue his career as a concert pianist, despite the loss of his right arm, was taken in the early days of his captivity, long before he had reached the hospital at Omsk. The alternative to success was not failure but death, and although his mother and sisters anxiously scoured letters from Russia for hints that he might be contemplating suicide, the trauma of his condition had, if anything, made him more determined than ever to return to his homeland and resume his concert career. He had been groomed by his father to confront fear and despise self-pity, and these lessons were taken to heart. In a solitary effort of will, he trained himself to understate the gravity of his condition and to dismiss, often quite rudely, the sympathy of friends and their well-meaning offers of help. If, at any stage, he had feared for his future as a five-fingered pianist, at least he would have relished the opportunity to face that fear down. The means by which he put his courage to the test often disconcerted his friends. He would astound them by swimming, one-armed, far out to sea in lightning storms, by striding within inches of the upper edges of the great cliffs of Dover or by balancing along the high iron-framed railway track that crosses the marshes at Southwold. His secretary once screamed when she came into his New York apartment to find him tightrope-walking along a thin balcony parapet with a drop, on one side, of 200 feet to the concrete pavement below.

There were, of course, other role models, beside his father, whose example inspired Paul's resolve to continue playing the piano. His blind mentor Josef Labor was one of them, Count Géza Zichy another. Though Paul had not yet met this eccentric and ebullient Hungarian aristocrat, he knew of him by reputation. Liszt had been dazzled by Zichy's one-armed piano playing; so too had the critic Eduard Hanslick, who described him in the Viennese press as "the greatest marvel of modern times on the piano." In 1914 Zichy, moved by the plight and sheer number of amputees returning from the front, wrote a self-help book, complete with photographic examples, showing the amputee how to eat a crayfish using his teeth, how to crush meat rather than cut it, how to wash a single hand by rubbing it with soap against the chin and how to get in and out of his underpants: "You must learn how to put your pants on by yourself," he insisted. "It would be too humiliating to have to ask someone else's help." Zichy's manual contained a preface by Dr. von Eiselsberg, the surgeon who had operated unsuccessfully on Karl's tumor in November 1912. "This book will comfort the amputee," Eiselsberg had written, "and it will also show him that, with an iron will, even the terrible loss of an arm may be borne more easily." In May 1915 the Count gave a piano recital in Berlin before an audience consisting entirely of one-armed soldiers. Paul knew nothing of this, but a copy of Zichy's book had been sent to him in Russia and when he and Zichy eventually met, Paul, though scathing of his artistry, was much inspired by his energy and enthusiasm.

A key source of inspiration to Paul in his darkest hours of captivity was Leopold Godowsky, a virtuoso Lithuanian, believed by many to possess the finest technique of any living pianist. Godowsky had created a sensation at his Viennese debut in 1904, playing his own firework version of Strauss's "Blue Danube" Waltz, as well as a short sequence of Chopin Studies spectacularly rearranged for the left hand alone. It is likely that Paul attended this concert. If not he would certainly have heard about it. "I can assure you I am the topic of Vienna," Godowsky wrote to a friend. "The criticism I got is in the *Freie Presse,* the most important daily in Austria. The critic, I am told, is the terror of Vienna. All my friends are jubilant over the article he wrote and they say this will settle my name here."

After that Godowsky was invited back to Vienna many times, and early in 1909 he accepted the prestigious post of Director of the Piano School at the Imperial Academy of Music with the highest salary of any piano teacher in Europe. Godowsky's controversial left-handed arrangements of Chopin Studies were published between 1894 and 1914. Paul did not own copies of these pieces before the war but he knew all about them, and it was while recuperating in the hospital at Omsk that one day he carefully marked out the image of a piano keyboard in charcoal on an empty crate and, for the first time, attempted to figure out how Godowsky had succeeded in arranging Chopin's tempestuous "Revolutionary" Study for the left hand alone.

Paul had worked on this piece in its original two-handed form with Leschetizky and performed it at least twice in public—once at Graz in February 1914 and once at the Vienna Musikverein in March—so he knew the notes by heart. The puzzle was how to join the passionate, restless theme of the right hand to the rapid figurations of the left in such a way that both tune and accompaniment could be played simultaneously with only five fingers of one hand. Many pianists would have dismissed the idea as an impossibility, but Paul, aware that Godowsky had achieved it ten years earlier, was determined to figure out how.

Day after day and for hour upon hour, he addressed himself to this arduous and improbable task, tapping his freezing fingers on the wooden box, listening intently to the imagined music sounding in his head and creating, in the corner of a crowded festering invalids' ward, a tragicomic spectacle that aroused the sympathy and curiosity of his fellow prisoners and all the hospital staff.

27 A GLIMMER OF HOPE

Paul's relentless finger-tapping came to the attention of a thirty-two-year-old Danish diplomat called Otto Wadsted on one of his routine visits to the hospital. The Danes, neutral in the war, maintained a consulate at Omsk from which they were able to monitor the condition of prisoners and report to the Danish Red Cross. Consul Wadsted ran a dedicated office, taking pains to visit all the camps as regularly as the Siberian authorities would allow, aiding and befriending many of the Austro-Hungarians and Germans imprisoned there. A highly cultivated man, he was fluent in both French and German, widely read, a keen amateur painter and an enthusiastic violinist. Moved by Paul's plight and concerned for his physical and mental condition, he interceded with the Military Governor of Omsk, General Moritz, to ensure that as soon as he was discharged from hospital Paul could be transferred to a place of internment where there was a piano. In the first years of the war, Omsk was not equipped to accommodate the huge and sudden influx of prisoners from the west and so long as the concentration camps outside the town were still in the process of construction, captives were held in whichever buildings came to hand. These, in January 1915, included a circus, a cellar, a brothel and a disused slaughterhouse, as well as several hotels and private dwellings.

In Vienna Mrs. Wittgenstein had succeeded in opening a line of communication to Paul via her nephew Otto Franz, a diplomat working at the Austrian Embassy in Copenhagen. Franz was in direct contact with the Danish Foreign Office, which in turn received regular bulletins from Wadsted's Consulate at Omsk. In this way Franz was able to telegraph his aunt in Vienna on February 20, 1915: "Paul transferred to small hotel Omsk as of second half of January. Freedom of movement within the town. Has to report three times a week." Paul had already written to his mother to impart the same news, but his letter of February 2 failed to reach Vienna until March 28:

> My dear, well-beloved and darling mother,
>   I have already been discharged from hospital as being in good health

and, thanks to the intercession of the Danish Consul, have been given per-
mission to remain here and live in town, which I am very happy about.
So, the best thing is to write via registered mail via Copenhagen to the
following address: Lieutenant P.W., prisonnier de guerre, Nomera
Stepanovskaya, Omsk . . . I'm well: I'm even playing the piano. Am
enormously pleased at every bit of news from home and sincerely thank
all those who have written to me. My greetings to all! And to you, my
dear mother, the most tender embraces from your son,
    Paul.

Twenty officers were billeted in the same hotel, sharing four to a room. All but two of them were Austro-Hungarians. Prisoners here were permitted to visit the town. At first, if they gave their word that they would return, they could come and go as they pleased, but their strict code of honor required them to attempt escape at all times. Too many tried to escape, and in the end exasperated Siberian officials restricted them to two town visits a week in groups of six under the strict supervision of an armed guard.

Every day for three months Paul practiced on a shabby, untuned upright piano that some say was brought to the hotel by a sympathetic Russian guard and according to others had been sitting disused in a closet in the hotel. His aim was to rearrange as many pieces as he could remember by heart into workable performing versions for the left hand. By late February he was able to write to his mother that he was feeling "splendid" and that if he were allowed to stay in the hotel he would have every reason to be happy. Mrs. Wittgenstein wrote to her youngest son: "Paul seems to be practising industriously. What a blessing for him!" Hermine was not so sure, for she feared that failure to succeed as a pianist could only prove devastating to Paul. "You were quite correct to suppose that he has already formed an opinion about his misfortune," she informed Ludwig, "and even though I fear that his sole aim is still to become a virtuoso I am nevertheless happy for him that he doesn't have to look for a completely new field of activity."

By the beginning of April 1915 Paul's confidence in his piano playing was such that he was able to send a message to his mother, via Consul Wadsted, via the Danish Foreign Office, via Otto Franz, to ask her to inquire of Josef Labor if he would compose a piano concerto for the left hand. Ludwig, on military duty in Vienna, had spent two days with Labor at his flat on the Kirchengasse on January 4 and 5, and the idea of composing a piano concerto for the left hand (something that had never been done before) may have been cooked up between the composer and the philosopher at this time, for when Mrs. Wittgenstein passed Paul's message to Labor he was able to tell her that he had been working on the piece for some time already.

Labor's blindness prevented him from writing down his own music; instead he composed by touch at the piano, feeling his way round the keyboard and memorizing each part, then playing it back to an amanuensis who took it down by ear. In the early days the composer's mother did this for him, later his sister Josephine, but by 1900 the task was always undertaken by one of his doting pupils called Rosine Menzel. By mid-May, Mrs. Wittgenstein found "dear Labor fully immersed in his composition for Paul—It is touching to see with what love and joy he sets about his work." The piece he planned was a *Konzertstück* or short concerto-like piece in the key of D major, consisting of an introduction, five variations on an original theme, an intermezzo and a cadenza in improvised style. His aim was to send the music out to Paul in Siberia as soon as it was ready, but circumstances changed and the score, which was completed in June 1915, remained in Vienna until Paul's return.

Toward the end of March a letter from Consul Wadsted to the Royal Danish Embassy in Petrograd was intercepted by the Russians. It contained complaints about the manner in which Austro-Hungarian prisoners were being treated at Omsk—complaints that Wadsted had already voiced to the face of Alexei Plavsky, the commandant of the prison camps at Omsk. Plavsky, a choleric old general, anxious lest news of his rough and illegal treatment of prisoners should come to the attention of a higher authority, instituted a conspiracy against Wadsted, accusing him of acting as a spy for the Germans. Bogus witnesses were brought forth. A young Austrian officer, imprisoned at the same hotel as Paul, was sentenced to death for colluding. Pressure was applied to the Danish Embassy in St. Petersburg to have its Consulate at Omsk closed down and Consul Wadsted recalled. By chance the case came to the attention of Princess Cunigunde von Croy-Dülmen, a tenacious German aristocrat working as a volunteer POW camp inspector for the Red Cross. Acting above and beyond the call of duty, the Princess hired, at her own expense, a famous Russian defense lawyer who succeeded in exposing Plavsky's conspiracy and getting the Austrian officer's death sentence commuted to two months' imprisonment.

Unfortunately none of this happened in time to prevent Paul and his fellow officers of the small hotel from being transferred to a more secure and far nastier camp in the center of Omsk. Russian policy dictated that prisoners of Slav origin were to be treated with greater leniency than those of Germanic blood. This, it was hoped, would encourage the Slavs to switch sides and fight for the Russian army against the Hapsburg forces. The original plan was to hold all of them in European Russia so that the traitors among them could quickly and easily be deployed against the Austrians on the Galician front. German and Austrian POWs, or *germanskis* as the Russians called them all, were to be sent to Siberia and provinces farther east, but, owing to the large numbers of captives and the incompetence and crookedness of the Russian system, thousands of Slav prisoners ended up with the *germanskis* in Siberia. General Moritz, the district Military Governor, had been accused, during the Wadsted conspiracy, of colluding with the Danish Consulate in placing Austrian and German officers at all the best places of internment while cramming the Slavs (contrary to official policy) into the crueler and more punitive prisons. Worried that his German surname and friendly associations with Wadsted's Consulate might make him suspicious in the eyes of Russian authority, Moritz hastily ordered that all *germanskis* interned at hotels and private houses be transferred to harsher camps to allow POWs of Slav origin to take their places. For Paul and the other officers at Nomera Stepanovskaya, this was a bitter blow.

28   BURIED ALIVE IN THE KREPOST

What Paul could not have known was that his transfer out of the hotel at Omsk would probably have taken place with or without General Moritz's intervention on behalf of the Slavs, for at the same time General Plavsky was under siege from the townsfolk of Omsk demanding that crippled POWs be removed from their streets. The daily spectacle of legless, armless, earless and noseless *germanskis* was proving detrimental to local morale. For this reason, Paul (along with 800 amputees) was moved into the town prison to be out of the sight of the sensitive townsfolk of Omsk.

The Krepost ("fortress" in Russian) is famous even today as the criminal dungeon into which the exiled Fyodor Dostoevsky was thrown in the middle of the nineteenth century, and which he later used as the setting for his novel, variously translated into English as *Buried Alive in Siberia* and *The House of the Dead.* In spirit little had changed there since Dostoevsky's day. The POWs of 1914 called it "the big mousetrap"—a place of utmost horror. Built in the eighteenth century as an army barracks, few traces of the original structure remained standing, for when Paul arrived there it consisted of several low, wooden and brick shacks and an exercise yard, surrounded by a twenty-one-foot-high wooden palisade fence with six watchtowers for armed guards. Each shack was a single narrow, leaking, unheated room that held seventy prisoners with nowhere else to go. Nurse Brändström, who inspected the Krepost when Paul was there, reported to the Red Cross in Geneva, "as the weeks and months go by men of the highest culture, tortured by homesickness, are treated as were Russia's worst criminals seventy years ago." It was, she wrote, "universal opinion that even in Siberia the Krepost of Omsk is unique." In his memoirs (published in Berlin in the spring of 1918) the German officer Julius Meier-Graefe described it as a "dung-shack, an ice hole, a place to catch typhoid and other maladies, an establishment for lice. The Krepost is the endmost, a meanness, a dishonour to Russia."

For a Russian POW camp to be even barely tolerable the prison commandant (or *nachalnik*) and his assistant (*praporshchik*) needed to demonstrate qualities of kindness and competence. This sometimes happened, but not at the Krepost. Here the commandant, conscious of his social inferiority to the educated prisoners under his charge, issued pointless and sadistic commands purely to assert his power over them. He addressed them all as "German swine," had them stripped and horsewhipped in front of him, constantly searched, forced to run the gauntlet of Cossack knouts for minor offenses, and deprived of all manner of basic needs. One officer told a Red Cross inspector that he had been held in an unlit, unheated cell for thirty days simply for quipping that a place as unpleasant as the Krepost should be built in Germany for Russian prisoners. Another was beaten up and punished with three months' solitary confinement for making a sketch of the prison in oils. At the time of Paul's arrival all musical instruments were confiscated and the prisoners forbidden from singing or whistling. "Sheer malice" Paul called it at the time. He cursed the governor privately, and took to teaching his fellow prisoners French instead.

With over 1,000 interns the Krepost, originally built for 300 criminal prisoners, was grossly overcrowded. Those who could find no place on one of the hard bunks were forced to sleep on the bare asphalt floors. Bunks were placed edge to edge so close that the narrow gangway between them was scarcely wide enough for one person to pass. There was nowhere to sit and no furniture on which to put things. Prisoners were expected to eat their meals lying down or perched on the rungs of the bunk-bed ladders. The food was disgusting, for although it was prepared by the prisoners themselves, the daily meat ration, to which each officer was entitled, was sold by the prison guards for profit and substituted with scrag ends, boiled head, ear or hooves. Even the tea was made from water that some insane Krepost commandant had insisted be dragged up by the prisoners in buckets from the exact spot in the river where all the town's sewage was disgorged. For lavatories the prisoners had to make do with holes in the ground. Amputees with one or no legs needed to be supported by their comrades to use them and when a delegation of prisoners came forward to ask permission to construct a lavatory seat from a wooden box their request was sadistically turned down.

In the midst of all this homesickness, degradation and despair, some of the crippled officers of the Krepost were clinging to a distant hope. Paul was one of them. He had heard of Pope Benedict XV's initiative to bring the leaders of opposing belligerent nations to some agreement over the exchange of severely wounded and disabled prisoners. At first it was envisaged that some prisoners might even be home by Christmas, but negotiations dragged on and for months there was no news of a breakthrough.

That Paul was being considered as a possible exchange prisoner was known to him at least two months before he was transferred to the Krepost. Having heard nothing from him since January 3, his mother in

Vienna continued to pester her nephew for news. Consul Wadsted telegraphed Franz by return: "GOOD NEWS. NAME APPEARS ON A PRELIMINARY LIST OF PRISONERS TO BE EXCHANGED. FINAL DECISION SOON. GOOD LUCK." Mrs. Wittgenstein wrote immediately to Ludwig: "You can imagine how happy I am! Even though it will require much more patience, as long as the matter has been put into motion, there is reason to hope that we may see Paul again in the foreseeable future."

As the months passed with no announcement from the Vatican, Mrs. Wittgenstein's patience continued to fray. At the end of May she reported: "I have had good news from Paul, as far as his health is concerned, but not a syllable about the exchange. It makes one despair!" And when she discovered that he had been hauled before the prison commandant and ordered into confinement for a month, she was beside herself with agitation. The reasons for the disciplinary action are unknown, though it is possible that he was one of eleven officers punished at that time for failing to report an attempted breakout. Whatever the reason, Paul, without a piano, new to the Krepost and low in spirits, took it badly. Hermine confided to Ludwig:

> Mama is, of course, really upset about it and it's very fortunate that Paul mentions the kindness of the Danish Consul to which he attributes significant preferential treatment and he makes a number of light-hearted remarks, which at least soften the overall sad impression a little.

Another cause for concern was the tone of Paul's letters home in which he had started making dangerously subversive remarks, which Mrs. Wittgenstein feared might lead him into further trouble with the prison authorities. In one of them, which by a stroke of fortune seems to have eluded the notice of the Russian censors, he wrote that his only real concern was for an Austrian victory in the war and that he would willingly donate one million gold kronen to support the Austrian troops.

What Paul did not mention in his letters home, as he knew it would distress his mother gravely, was that a typhus epidemic had broken out among the prisoners. This disease, which killed indiscriminately, hung over the Krepost like a nameless horror. It was carried by body lice, from which Paul believed himself immune. Its early symptoms—a high fever with severe pain in the muscles and joints—are followed by dark-red rashes that spread rapidly from the victim's bottom and shoulders to the rest of his body. In the second week the infected person loses control of his bowels and becomes delirious. Within days he is most likely to be dead. By Easter 1915, when the epidemic was at its height, some twenty to thirty men were removed from the Krepost every day and brought into hospital. None of them returned. Neither of the two hospitals in Omsk could cope with the daily intake from the camps in the region as doctors, nurses and attendants themselves started to fall victim to the disease. One especially galling incident is preserved in the diary of Hans Weiland, an Austrian officer held at Krasnoyarsk:

> The men lie side by side pressed closely against each other in tiered rows of bunks. The air, a repellent, almost sweet stink, is thick enough to cut. Water drips continuously from the ceiling . . . Then, late in the evening, a guard comes to me with an order from the camp commandant: the company is to provide five attendants immediately for the typhus hospital; the other attendants are either sick or dead . . . There is a sudden silence; everyone is thinking it over; everyone holds back. This message is the way to death, a deliberate parting from family, wife, children, life. Nobody volunteers. I repeat the request and explain the need for this duty to be carried out. The hazy atmosphere makes it impossible to see across the room; you can hardly see the next man's face. You can almost hear the breathing and the pulse beats in the silence. Then a young fellow from the Sudetenland calls out from his bunk: "I'll go; it has to be." He stands in front of me, says quietly that his mother is old but if he has to die then his brother will probably come home from the war and look after her. Four other men follow his lead with hardly a word. They go to the hospital, take over the nursing duties, become ill and all five die. Heroes!

29 A CHANCE OF ESCAPE

In the summer of 1915, after months of querulous, drawn-out negotiation, the first batch of sick and wounded prisoners was finally exchanged out of Russia, but Paul Wittgenstein, whose name had been on the list since January, was not among them. His mother had been sending him too much money in the post and the Russians, intercepting and stealing it, were anxious not to forfeit their income. In the meantime, two captives, who had been with Paul in the Krepost and had succeeded in getting themselves exchanged out of Omsk, came to see Mrs. Wittgenstein in Vienna. One of them, Captain Karl von Liel, had been wounded in September 1914 and as he lay on the ground unable to move was mutilated by the enemy. Two fingers of his right hand and four of his left were cut off. "This amazing individual," Leopoldine told Ludwig, "is in good spirits despite having to undergo every possible type of operation here to fit prosthetic attachments." Captain von Liel told Mrs. Wittgenstein that, when last seen, Paul was looking well, healthy and cheerful, that he was now good enough at Russian to translate the newspapers for those men who had not made such progress, that he was teaching French to a former fellow pupil of his old school, and that both teacher and pupil were taking their lessons very seriously.

> I was extremely pleased [Mrs. Wittgenstein wrote] that both the
> exchanged officers spoke of Paul with great respect and love and
> praised his kindness, decency and idealism. Captain von Liel asked
> Paul whether he would rather the war had not broken out and that
> he still had his arm but Paul said he would rather things were as
> they were. That's really splendid!

When a second officer from Omsk, Lieutenant Gürtler, told Mrs. Wittgenstein about the money and why Paul was not being exchanged, she thought to herself, "If this is really an obstacle to Paul's release, it would surely be possible to come to some arrangement." If she succeeded in doing this the process certainly took its time, for at the beginning of October she was informed that Paul was scheduled not for exchange but for transfer from Omsk to some other prison camp in the south. "Perhaps we may have to be grateful for that," she wrote to Ludwig, "but while we still had hope that he might be imminently considered for exchange, this represents a dreadful disappointment!"

It was not until the very end of the month that she received a telegram from Otto Franz bearing the good news that Paul and six other invalided officers had been sent for examination before a committee in Moscow. "That represents at least a glimmer of hope!" she wrote. There was, of course, still plenty of room for pessimism and Hermine felt it strongly: "As to whether Paul will be exchanged? I've really very little hope, and I find the prospect of Mama's disappointment really terrible."

The medical commissions to which prospective exchange prisoners were sent were degrading affairs. Invalids arrived in a state of optimism, having traveled thousands of miles from camps in the east, only to be informed that they were not ill enough to be exchanged and must return to the prisons from whence they came. In Kazan, prison doctors were held liable for the expense of an invalid's return journey, which made them understandably reluctant to recommend anyone for exchange in the first place. Prisoners who made it to Moscow or Petrograd found themselves at the mercy of unscrupulous medical NCOs operating a reign of terror. At Lazaret 108 in Petrograd, the Angel of Siberia had reported:

> They sold their patients' food. Prisoners who still had their wedding rings, watches and so forth had to give them up. Those who refused and thereby made themselves disliked were kept as a punishment from the medical commission which, from time to time, held the decisive examination. In this way men might remain up to ten months in the hospital while trains of exchange prisoners departed with a half or a third of their full complement.

As soon as Paul arrived in Moscow he was examined by doctors to confirm that he qualified as a "severely wounded or disabled prisoner of war whose disablement permanently prevented his military service," questioned by military interrogators and warned that, if he were ever to rejoin the Austro-Hungarian ranks and be recaptured in action by the Russians, he would face summary execution.

From the moment Mrs. Wittgenstein knew that Paul was up before the exchange tribunal she became very anxious and she remained in this state for a fortnight, during which time her legs were more painful than ever, and her boon companion and former servant Rosalie Hermann had started to cough in a noisy and alarming way. But she waited and waited until news of her captive son came at last to Vienna. The details of her reaction are preserved in a letter she sent Ludwig:

> My dear, good Ludwig,
>
> Just imagine: early on the 9th—after we had heard nothing of Paul for a long time other than that he was in Moscow to be examined, we read that he was among the group that was being exchanged and which had arrived at the Finnish-Swedish border post in Haparanda on the 8th. On the afternoon of the 9th we had a telegram from Paul from Ljusdal in Sweden. Yesterday, we learned that the group had passed through Sassnitz and today Paul is already in Leitmeritz. Today I had a report from Stradels and Wolframs; both were at the station at midnight to greet him and they assure me that he looks in splendid form, very well and in the best of moods. Paul now has to spend a period in quarantine in Leitmeritz. If this lasts any great length of time, I think Hermine will go to see him there. If only you, my dear good Ludwig, could come again, that would be a real blessing for me. I shall have to do without poor sidelined Kurt but as far as you are concerned, I hope I will be lucky enough to have you here in the foreseeable future. Apart from a few bouts of catarrh and my ankle, we are in good health.
>
> With the tenderest embraces from your mother.

30 FAMILY REUNION

Neither of Paul's two surviving brothers was in Vienna on November 21, 1915, to welcome him back from captivity. Kurt was still languishing in New York and Ludwig on active duty as an engineer in an artillery workshop at the train station at Sokal, a Ukrainian town fifty miles east of Zamość. The veins in Mrs. Wittgenstein's legs were bulging and far too painful for her to consider the 400-mile round trip from Vienna to Leitmeritz, where Paul was detained for ten days in quarantine, so Hermine went alone. On the journey out she feared that she might not recognize her brother when she saw him, expecting to be greeted by a depressed, emaciated and somehow damaged figure, but she was relieved and surprised by his good spirits, writing immediately to her mother and siblings: "Paul's appearance and nature are so unchanged (apart from his arm of course). Seeing him again was not much different than if he had been on a long journey and we were telling each other all the latest news and couldn't stop talking."

Meier-Graefe wrote that the Krepost scarred a man for life, and although Paul was altered by his Siberian ordeal he managed, for a while at least, to conceal the worst of it from his family. Mrs. Wittgenstein wrote of their reunion: "I took much delight in Paul's calm and composed disposition . . . He really looks very well and is astonishingly cheerful and hasn't lost any of his ability to tease." Hermine reported that "he speaks of his misfortune in such a matter-of-fact way. You never get the feeling that you have to be careful in what you say for fear that one thing or another might hurt him, and this makes it enormously easy."

But despite Paul's ease of manner he was suffering acute physical discomfort. The doctors at Krasnystaw had accomplished their task imperfectly and in their anxiety over Russian troop movements had failed to cut skin flaps large enough to cover the exposed bone of his right arm adequately. As a result the scar at the end of the stump was stretched too tight and had started to adhere to the bone. The nerve ends, trapped between bone and skin, were extremely sensitive. On his return to Vienna Paul took the problem immediately to Dr. von Eiselsberg's surgery on the first floor of a rickety eighteenth-century building close to the Ringstrasse. Among the staff there were eight unpaid volunteers, one of whom, recently joined, was Paul's bald and moody American brother-in-law, Jerome Stonborough.

Paul's operation was not as straightforward as Jerome had explained it to his mother-in-law, nor, as he had asserted, did it involve the simple removal of a growth. The doctor had to reopen the wound, cut some of the dense membrane, known as the periosteum, away from the end of the bone and scrape about half an inch of marrow out of the inside with a curette. Only then could he restitch the wound in such a way that the soft tissue at the end of the stump would remain freely movable over the end of the bone. For two weeks after the operation Paul was in great pain, suffering from loss of appetite and unable to sleep. The doctors ascribed this to the effects of the anesthetic, though it might equally have been caused by depression. His intention was to have a prosthetic arm fitted as soon as the stump was healed, but this was never done and, for the rest of his life, Paul instead wore the empty sleeve of his jacket neatly tucked into his right-side hip pocket.

As soon as he was feeling strong enough to reenter the swing of life, he did so with vibrant energy, walking each morning through the Baumgartner Wald and the steep parkland of the Wittgenstein estate at Neuwaldegg. He practiced with his left hand, tying ties and shoelaces, doing up and undoing buttons, cutting meat, peeling apples, swimming, riding, writing and reading. He studied the self-help books that were published to cater to the thousands of amputees returning each month from the front and set up a modus operandi with his batman, Franz. In the afternoons, he practiced long hours at the piano, started to organize (as he vowed he would in his letter from the Krepost) his million-kronen donation to the Austrian troops, and took steps—despite the threats of execution that he had received at the tribunal in Moscow—to rejoin the army and return once again in uniform to the chaos of the eastern front.

31 A TRANSFORMATION

Ludwig was not given leave to join his family for Christmas in 1915. Having recently been promoted to *Militärbeamter* (military official), he remained at Sokal singing "Stille Nacht" in the officers' mess instead. In July he had taken three weeks' leave (suffering from shock but not gravely injured) after accidentally blowing himself up in the workshop. As yet, he had not been posted to the front but craved the experience and had surprised his senior commanders with requests for dangerous action. He had been involved in what might loosely be described as a "skirmish" while serving as a searchlight operator on board the river ship *Goplana*. Six weeks after the outbreak of war he and the crew had been forced to abandon ship and flee a sudden Russian advance. "I am not afraid of being shot," he wrote, "but of not fulfilling my duty properly. God give me strength! Amen. Amen. Amen." The enemy kept coming. Ludwig and his comrades (men whom he had earlier described as "a bunch of pigs . . . unbelievably crude, stupid and malicious") were forced to retreat for thirty sleepless hours. "Have been through terrible scenes," he wrote. "I feel very weak and see no hope anywhere. If my end is coming now, may I die a good death, attending myself. May I never lose myself." Two days later he added: "There is nothing between us and the enemy . . . Now I should have the chance to be a decent human being, for I am standing eye to eye with death. May the spirit bring me light."

In his memoirs Meier-Graefe recalled telling a Russian guard that he was being transferred to Siberia. The guard looked at him sympathetically and shuddered: "In Siberia, all men search for God." As far as Paul was concerned there was no need to postulate the existence of any deity, and he neither found nor sought to find one in Siberia. Though he had been brought up as a Catholic, his line on religion broadly followed that of his idol, Arthur Schopenhauer, reams of whose philosophical writings he could quote by heart. "Religion is the masterpiece of the art of animal training, for it trains people as to how they shall think." From this position Paul never wavered.

Ludwig on the other hand, a philosopher of logic and language, now reunited in friendship with the atheists Bertrand Russell and George Moore, was a lost soul who, during the early months of the war, may not have been consciously searching for God but found him nevertheless in a little bookshop in the Baroque city of Tarnów, twenty-five miles east of Kraków. It was here that he bought a book simply because it was the only one in the shop—and this in itself he believed to be a sign. It was a German translation of *The Gospel in Brief* by Leo Tolstoy—a redaction of the four New Testament gospels, which excluded all those parts of the original of which Tolstoy did not approve—sections on Jesus's birth and genealogy, his miracles (walking on water, turning water into wine, raising the dead and so on), his beating up of a fig tree, his fulfillment of Old Testament prophecies and his resurrection. The work had a profound effect on Ludwig, who devoured it with fervor, carrying his copy wherever he went. "This book virtually kept me alive," he told a friend afterward. His comrades at the time, seizing upon this eccentricity, nicknamed him *"der mit dem Evangelium"*—"the man with the gospel."

Tolstoy's vision (if that is the term) was broadly anti-church. He believed that Christ preached a message that had been corrupted by exegesis, that Christianity (that is to say his own Tolstoyan version of it) was "neither pure revelation nor a phase of history but the only pure doctrine which gives meaning to life." The message was simple—that man has a divine origin, "the will of the Father," which is the source of all human life. This he must serve. Doing this obviates any need for him to satisfy the desires of his own will and is a "life-giving" process. A true Christian must therefore imitate the ways of Jesus, renounce physical gratification, humble himself and draw himself close to the spirit. This is precisely what Ludwig attempted to do, but he was not always very successful at it:

> From time to time I become an *animal* [he wrote in his notebook]. Then I can think of nothing but eating, drinking, sleeping. Terrible! And then I suffer just like an animal, without the possibility of internal salvation and am then at the mercy of my appetites and aversions. The authentic life is then unthinkable.

In the preface to his slim philosophical treatise, *Tractatus Logico-Philosophicus,* Ludwig acknowledged that some of his ideas may have been drawn from other writers, adding: "It is a matter of indifference to me whether the thoughts that I have had have been anticipated by someone else." There are many similarities between this work and Tolstoy's *Gospel in Brief.* Both books are laid out in six sections (though Ludwig added a seventh to the *Tractatus* consisting of a single, now famous, proclamation, "That which we cannot speak about we must pass over in silence") and both works are presented as a sequence of connected, numbered, gnomic utterances. Consider these from Tolstoy:

1.1.   The foundation and beginning of all things is the understanding of life.

1.2.   The understanding of life is God.

1.3.   All is built upon the understanding of life, without which there can be no living.

1.4.   In this is true life.

1.5.   This understanding is the light of truth.

And these from the opening page of Ludwig's *Tractatus*:

1.   The world is all that is the case.

1.1.   The world is the totality of facts not of things.

1.11.   The world is determined by the facts and by their being *all* the facts.

1.12.   For the totality of facts determines what is the case.

1.13.   The facts in logical space are the world.

Common to both texts is the notion of eternal life belonging only to the present. As Tolstoy put it:

7.   This present life in time is the food of the true life.

8.   And therefore the true life is outside time; it is in the present.

9.   Time is an illusion in life; the life of the past and the future clouds men from the true life of the present.

Ludwig's *Tractatus* expresses the same idea, but perhaps a little more succinctly:

6.4311 . . . If we take eternity to mean not infinite temporal duration but timelessness, then eternal life belongs to those in the present. Our life has no end in just the way our visual field has no limits.

Ludwig's family was alarmed, disconcerted, alienated and embarrassed by his sudden conversion. Hermine, Gretl and Paul read Tolstoy's *Gospel* in an attempt to understand him better. Hermine, often overwhelmed by Ludwig's intellect and struggling to keep up with him, read several other books by Tolstoy as well. Gretl studied Ernest Renan's hugely popular *Life of Jesus* to see if it was compatible with Tolstoy. Paul took a teasing, controversial and not altogether sympathetic line. "Even if Paul should by chance ever like the same book as Ludwig, he would always look for and find something essentially different in it," Gretl told Hermine. Of all Ludwig's siblings she was the one who came closest to sharing in Ludwig's new spirituality, but Tolstoyan Christianity was not a religion in the sense of a shared communion. What *The Gospel in Brief* offered to Ludwig, as a young man crippled by conflicting urges to narcissism and self-loathing, was the long-sought opportunity for radical self-improvement—a thorough rinsing of all those parts of his personality that he found most distasteful, and an opportunity for conscious self-elevation and transfiguration from mere mortal to immortal Jesus-like, prophet-like, perfect human being. "There are two godheads: the world and my independent I," Ludwig wrote in his notebook in July 1916. "For life in the present there is no death." According to Dr. Max Bieler, an officer serving with Ludwig at Sokal in the autumn of 1915, "Ludwig had all the characteristics of a prophet."

When Ludwig's *Tractatus* appeared in print after the war, it confounded the expectations of the small circle that had grown to admire his ideas on logic and many, including Bertrand Russell, found the work's "urge toward the mystical" incomprehensible and rather depressing as though it were not a philosophical tract but some impenetrable Gospel according to Ludwig:

> 6.521 The solution of the problem of life is seen in the vanishing of the problem.
> (Is not this the reason why those who have found, after a long period of doubt, that the sense of life became clear to them have been unable to say what constituted that sense?)

32 GRETL'S ISSUES

When war broke out the Stonboroughs had hoped to return to England. Gretl, by virtue of her marriage to Jerome, had become an American citizen, but as a Wittgenstein she was driven by strong patriotic urges to do her duty by Austria. Whatever assistance she could give to her country she preferred it on a grand scale and wished, by her largeness of heart, her ingenuity of mind and her vast fortune, not just to lend a hand, but to influence things in a major way, to win the war for Austria. She needed to feel engaged "with all my strength. To do my utmost both physically and mentally," which is why she was not at all happy in the voluntary work she had undertaken, organizing meals for between eighty and a hundred men a day at a small hospital in Ischl.

> This war affects me just as it does you [she wrote to Hermine]—I can achieve nothing, absolutely nothing. But I would give a lot to be able to contribute something to this campaign. It seems so dreadful that one could have lived through such a thing and yet not actually lived through it.

Gretl left the hospital after catching an infection from one of her patients and was advised by her doctor never to return. Now she could apply her mind to higher things, but first she had to struggle with the dead weight of a marriage that was not working well. Her problem was that she was an irritating person. Her opinions, her modes of expression and her manner of dress all tended to grate on people's nerves—her mother's, Ludwig's, Paul's and especially her husband Jerome's. Hermine, who admitted on occasion to wanting to slap Gretl in the face, was nonetheless her sister's staunchest ally, constantly reminding others of her "inner greatness."

> I can hardly say how much I love and admire Gretl [she wrote to Ludwig]. Why then does she possess such characteristics as give rise to sharper censure than is received by many people who do not act

as well and generously in greater matters as she does? That always hurts me immeasurably.

But neither Gretl's manner nor her reserved attitude to sexual matters can be held entirely responsible for the failures of her marriage, for Jerome—morose, tetchy, paranoid, prone to grandiose delusions—was an impossible husband. At the beginning of 1916 he was in a particularly bad way, terrified by and obsessed with the notion that America was planning to join the war against the Austrians. He talked and thought of little else. For days on end he would disappear only to return, sometimes in the middle of the night, shaking, staring ghoulishly into space, silent and motionless, or exploding suddenly into aggressive rages. His behavior tested Gretl's nerves to their limits. Unsure how to cope, she tried to intellectualize the problem, seeing her husband as a split personality with an "inner life" that was "once clear and is now confused" and an "outer life" that "no longer takes place (as it used to) between things, but is now oriented among people." Such cryptic assertions did little to improve the situation—nor did a move in October 1915 from Gmunden to a gracious rented apartment in the Palais Erdödy on the Krugerstrasse. She could, of course, sue for divorce, but whenever the idea was mooted Jerome threatened to take the boys, Thomas and Ji, to America with him. What was the matter with Jerome? At first Gretl tried to work it out for herself by reading books on psychology and psychiatry. Nothing came of it and many years later she was persuaded to send him to the famous neurologist Julius Wagner-Jauregg, who had recently won a Nobel Prize for his controversial treatment (injecting psychotic patients with tuberculin and malaria parasites) that was proving effective in cases of syphilitic *dementia paralytica*. It is not known whether Jerome was suffering from syphilis, but his erratic behavior and psychotic paranoia rank among the classic symptoms of that disease. Pierre Stonborough (his grandson) stoutly denies the possibility, but no alternative explanation has been offered for Jerome's psychosis. Whatever the truth of it, Wagner-Jauregg had no success and Jerome's condition continued, off and on, until the day of his death.

33 PAUL'S ONE-HANDED DEBUT

In the early months of 1916 each member of the Wittgenstein family was suffering from one health problem or another. Mrs. Wittgenstein's legs were still "terribly painful." She had had them operated upon and was confined to a wheelchair for the weeks of her recuperation. She was also worried about her eyesight and the rapid advancement of what seems to have been some form of macular degeneration—a loss of central vision— that would eventually leave her completely blind. Helene was in bed with stomach cramps "and associated complaints," Gretl was worried about her palpitating heart, Ludwig was losing his mind on the eastern front, and Hermine, Jerome and Paul all had problems concerning their fingers. By coincidence, Hermine and Jerome each had an infected swollen finger on his/her right hand so that both had to be discharged from their voluntary hospital duties. Paul had slipped and fallen over in the bathroom, landed on his hand and broken a finger bone. It was a bitter blow. For almost a month he was unable to play the piano and, more than anything, he was looking forward to trying out the new piece that Labor had composed especially for him. Labor too was disappointed, for it was not until March 11 (two and a half months after the accident) that "my apostle, Paul" was able to give a first rendering of the work at a private concert in the *Musiksaal* of the Wittgenstein Palais. A young student of Leschetizky played the orchestral part on a second piano, but the great Polish pedagogue was himself unable to attend as he had died four months earlier while Paul was awaiting his release from the quarantine hospital at Leitmeritz. The concert was a grand success. Paul played beautifully and the whole piece, to Labor's unconcealed delight, had to be encored.

On October 28, Paul gave a performance of another work by Labor, a quartet in which the piano part had been arranged for one hand by the composer's acolyte Rosine Menzel. Again the concert was a private affair at the Wittgenstein Palais and again Paul played "very beautifully, with great warmth and fire." The composer was deliriously happy. Even Hermine, whose reaction to Paul's playing was typically negative, rejoiced in his interpretation of two short Mendelssohn pieces that she felt he had executed "very well and with feeling."

Paul's case has naturally made me very upset [she told Ludwig] and as much as I would like to deny him the right to pursue music on account of many rough patches, I am equally happy to grant him that right for the sake of a piece played with feeling.

Among those present in the audience was the lean, elegant figure of Hugo Knepler, a popular Viennese impresario who had helped to stage and promote one of Paul's chamber concerts before the war. Knepler (who was murdered in 1944 at Auschwitz) was given the task of organizing the first public performance of Labor's *Konzertstück* and on December 12, 1916, in the same hall (the Grosser Musikvereinsaal), with the same conductor (Oskar Nedbal) and the same orchestra (the Wiener Tonkünstler) that Paul had used for his two-handed debut exactly three years earlier, the public heard, for the first time, some music composed for orchestra and a left-handed pianist.

Paul had worked with obsessive diligence and determination, practicing sometimes as many as seven hours at a sitting, to be ready for this concert. "It was like trying to climb a mountain," he later admitted; "if I could not reach the summit by one route I would climb down and start again from the other side." He had received a few useful tips from Count Zichy and from his former teacher Malwine Bree, but the artful pedaling and fingering techniques that he employed to create an illusion of not just two but sometimes three or four hands playing, were entirely of his own invention. He placed himself at the instrument, not opposite the middle of the keyboard, where a two-handed pianist normally sits, but far to the right so that he could strike the highest notes without twisting his body to reach them. By constant exercise he developed a formidable strength in his fingers, wrist and upper arm; he played sometimes with his fist or with two fingers on one note for extra force; he learned to use his thumb and index finger to carry a melodic line while his middle, ring and little fingers accompanied at a different volume. His most far-reaching innovation was a combined pedaling and hand-movement technique that allowed him to sound chords that were strictly impossible for a five-fingered pianist to play. By striking a chord loudly in the middle register, using a subtle "half-pedal" technique with his right foot, and by following immediately with a barely audible pianissimo note or two in the bass, he was able to deceive even the sharpest-eared critic into thinking that he had played a chord with his left hand alone that required a span of two and a half feet across the keyboard.

The main difficulty he faced was to make his music sound complete in itself. It simply would not do to be "half as good as a two-handed pianist" and yet his phenomenal achievement in disguising the loss of his right hand served only to create a new set of vulgar problems. There was a danger, for instance, that the public, seeing the name "Paul Wittgenstein" on a billboard, would buy tickets not in order to appreciate the music but to see the spectacle, as though he were some kind of cheapjack conjuror or amusement park exhibit. It was precisely for this reason that Ludwig could not bear to attend his brother's public concerts.

On the plus side Paul was not displeased to discover that his predicament—that of a young wounded war hero with a prodigious artistic talent—was deeply attractive to women. Successful classical musicians were lionized in Vienna as in no other place in the world, and Paul's pitiful condition, his stubborn masculine determination and, one supposes, his colossal bank balance made him the idol of every soft-hearted female in the city. Women of all ages, types and sizes gathered around the piano to talk to him and to admire his playing, always sincere in their appreciation of his talent. "Although it was only elderly and weak women yesterday," Hermine informed Ludwig, "he could also have young and pretty ones, so pleasant and charming is he to the ladies (almost as conciliatory towards them as he can be abrupt and arrogant towards men)." One wonders if Hermine were not, in her heart, a little jealous. "A lady recently told me with tears in her eyes how touching she found Paul's playing; whoever would have thought it! But we are delighted to realise how wrong we were!"

The poster advertising Paul's left-handed concert debut made no mention of the fact that the starring artist had lost an arm, but simply listed the repertoire he intended to play (Labor's concerto, three of Godowsky's arrangements of Chopin Studies, pieces by Bach and Mendelssohn and the Liszt *Rigoletto* Paraphrase) with a small line underneath explaining that some of the pieces were to be performed in arrangements for the left hand. Ludwig, who had recently been promoted in rank to officer cadet in the Reserves, was for once able to attend. Paul, clearly nervous, complained afterward that he had performed badly and made too many mistakes, but Labor—who was "all fired up and dead keen as regards Paul"—complimented him extravagantly. A week later Julius Korngold's equivocal review was published in the *Neue Freie Presse* in Vienna:

> Paul Wittgenstein does not play the piano with one hand in a way one plays in a world where two hands are needed for such a task, but in a way one would play in a world where people only had one hand. His playing should then only be evaluated on its own terms . . . Wittgenstein's interpretations are those of a spirited and sensitive musician. Let us, after his debut, crowned with success, clasp the courageous hand, which he has learned to use so skilfully. The sounds produced by his left hand do not betray the artist's melancholy at no longer possessing a right hand, rather they express his triumph at being able to bear his loss so well.

34 WAR IN EUROPE RAGES

Despite the long hours that Paul spent preparing his one-handed concert debut he managed to find time for "welfare" work. He had vowed to donate one million kronen for the troops and saw to it that this pledge was properly fulfilled by organizing the making and distribution of thousands of army greatcoats. In Russia he had been horrified by the flimsiness of the Austrian jackets compared with those worn by the enemy and was convinced that the plight of POWs during the eight-month Siberian winters was made intolerable by them. From factories in Bohemia he ordered thousands of bales of strong, warm, gray material, but was dismayed to find the operation hindered by a shortage of tailors—most of them were dead, wounded or still fighting on the front. With characteristic determination he advertised in cities around the monarchy for old tailors to come out of retirement and work for him. In this way the job was done and tens of thousands of greatcoats finally delivered to a storehouse in Teplitz ready for distribution via Sweden to POW camps in Russia and Siberia. In 1916 Paul's million-kronen contribution represented one-twentieth of the total national expenditure on POW clothing aid for that year.

Ludwig also elected to donate a million kronen toward the Austrian war effort but being on active duty was unable to supervise it. His idea—less practical than Paul's—was to build a giant new mortar cannon. The biggest in the Austrian army was the massive 305mm Skoda that weighed 22.9 tons and could throw an 842-pound shell 13,000 yards at the rate of ten rounds per hour. These were the finest heavy howitzers produced in the war, but Ludwig, with characteristic obstinacy, didn't think them good enough, and had the money transferred to a fund in Vienna to be spent on the development of a better weapon. It was never used. Ludwig was not concerned to follow up the matter and when Hermine, many years later, attempted to trace what had become of his donation she was told that the whole lot had disappeared in the hyperinflation of the 1920s.

At the end of March 1916, Ludwig was given the opportunity to prove himself at the front, being assigned to the duties of an artillery observer at Sanok, east of Kraków. His new position did not however alleviate relations with his comrades-in-arms as he remained consumed with disgust for himself and by intense loathing of those around him. "Within myself I am full of hatred and cannot let the spirit come to me. God is love." The men of his unit, he claimed, detested him simply because he was a volunteer, but more likely they were put off by his self-obsession and lofty manner. In his notebook Ludwig conceded: "So I am nearly always surrounded by people that hate me. And this is the one thing which I still do not know how to take. There are malicious and heartless people here. It is almost impossible to find any trace of humanity in them."

Despite these inner tensions Ludwig proved himself as valiant in battle as his elder brother. Of course he was desperately afraid, but fear in the face of death was, he had decided, "the sign of a false, i.e., a bad life." From June to August he was caught on the wrong side of the Brusilov Offensive, the huge and well-planned forward strike by the Imperial Russian army under its regional commander Alexei Brusilov, which resulted in the loss of 1.5 million Austro-Hungarian troops (including 400,000 taken prisoner) and thus put the Austro-Hungarians on the defensive for the rest of the war.

In a moment of piety Ludwig decided he would not accept promotion to the rank of officer and was only persuaded to recant his position by the earnest entreaties of his family. "Perhaps you are not such an odd person as I think," Hermine wrote to him, "but I am worried that you might regard promotion as some kind of shirking from hard work and fail to see that it might be a question of life and death . . . I don't think it's a laughing matter!" Paul reminded him of the dangers of being captured: "It would have meant certain death for me if I had had to suffer the treatment meted out to the rank and file who were taken prisoner in Siberia." In the end Ludwig accepted his destiny, rising to the rank of lieutenant in the Reserve. He continued, however, to pester higher command with requests for postings to places where the fighting was most dangerous, for his new spirituality demanded of him that he test himself to the uttermost, and that he accede always to his own highest standards. In May 1916 he duly volunteered to man an observation tower upon which he knew that he would frequently come under enemy fire. "Perhaps nearness to death will bring light into my life," he pondered. A year later he enlisted Paul's help in demanding of various senior officers that he be allowed to transfer from the artillery to the more dangerous infantry. As a member of an officers' club in Vienna, Paul was able to use his connections to advance his brother's cause, but in the end nothing came of it. Meanwhile, in action against British troops, Ludwig was commended for his "courageous behaviour, calmness, sang-froid and heroism" under fire and awarded the Militär-Verdienstmedaille—the Military Merit Medal with Swords on the Ribbon. By the end of the war he had been decorated many times.

In March 1916, Paul was finally decorated for his bravery in the opening month of the war with the Military Cross (class III), and was promoted to first lieutenant (retroactive from September 1915). In October he received a further medal, the Military Cross (class II), pinned to his chest by the thirty-five-year-old Grand Duke of Mecklenburg, a lovelorn German aristocrat who, fifteen months after the ceremony, took his dog for a walk in a wood near Neustrelitz and shot himself in the head.

For more than two years President Woodrow Wilson had done his best to steer a neutral course between lobby groups demanding that the United States join the war on one side or the other, or stay out of it altogether, but when, on March 18, 1917, three American merchant ships were sunk by German submarines, the President's burgeoning resolve to support the Allied Powers was stiffened. On April 2, Congress met in special session and two days later the Senate passed a resolution in favor of war by ninety votes to six. In the House of Representatives, after a seventeen-hour debate, it was agreed by 373 votes to 50. The public galleries of both Houses echoed to wild cheering as the motions were carried, but Wilson returning to the White House buried his head in his hands and wept. "My message was one of death for young men. How odd it seems to applaud that."

Jerome Stonborough reacted to the news from America by insisting that he and his family leave Austria right away. Gretl demurred, arguing that she had things to do in Vienna and didn't wish to emigrate, but her husband was adamant and on April 14, eight days after President Wilson's declaration, they arrived at a hotel in Zurich in neutral Switzerland. Exile from Austria did not suit Gretl's bossiness as she liked to believe that she was always at the center of things and always useful. Her social life in Austria was a whirl of politicians, high-flying diplomats, well-known artists, composers and performers from whom she was loath to be separated.

Arriving in Switzerland, Gretl sank into a depression, lying in bed all day, for weeks on end, rising only for short walks or to inspect a Picasso that she was tempted to purchase. At times she was overwhelmed by acute feelings of loneliness, homesickness and aggressive patriotism. Stress caused her heart to fibrillate and each time this happened she said to herself, " 'Oh my God! It's starting' and I die the thousand unnecessary deaths that every coward dies." Her depressions were aggravated by acute hypochondria and a paranoid fear of dying. "I am always thinking of death and picturing my own end," she wrote in her journal. "I do not dare to think of returning home as I am sure I will die before I get there." Like

Ludwig she too sequestered herself behind the altar rails of Tolstoyan Christianity. "I am well, apart from my health, because I have a clear conscience. As Tolstoy writes: 'bound by the flesh but free through the spirit.' "

For Jerome, the move to Switzerland served only to refuel his neurotic restlessness, and within a few months he moved the family from Zurich to the fortified lakeside town of Luzern, where they stayed at the Hotel National. But as soon as they arrived in any new place Jerome was once again making plans to remove to somewhere else. Under these conditions there could be no permanence in their lives and as they dashed from St. Moritz, to Bad Tarasp-Vulpera, to Bern, to Ouchy near Lausanne and back again to Luzern, the strain in Gretl and Jerome's relationship came once again close to breaking point.

Jerome insisted that he needed to take their elder son, Tommy, off to America for an indefinite period. Gretl tried her best not to react to this provocation, for the boy, then aged eleven, was beginning to show signs of emotional instability and the last thing she wished was for him to be uprooted from a German- to an English-speaking school; but seeing no point in engaging herself in battle with someone to whom she felt bound for the rest of her life, she failed to take any action. "What can I do then?" she asked her sister. "If I rebel divorce would be the only consequence. Jerome talks about divorce all the time but I am against it for the sake of the children. For theirs and for his own sake, because he does not know what he is talking about."

By moving to Switzerland in April 1917, Gretl just missed her brother Kurt's eagerly awaited return from New York. "Kurt is back home just the same big child as when he left three years ago. But that doesn't matter at the moment," Hermine reported. "He comes home on Sundays and dashes around with the children . . . Let's hope things always go smoothly for him!" Kurt's initial training as an infantry officer at the Danube town of Stockerau ten miles north of Vienna lasted for two months. On July 15, 1917, he was sent on a six-week training period behind the lines. His mother never mentioned her sorrow at his parting except on the occasions when her legs were hurting too much for her to be able to restrain herself. In the Wittgenstein family difficult feelings were subsumed by playing beautiful music, and just before Kurt left for battle he and his mother practiced a Schubert quartet for many hours together on the piano. "Thank God that such things exist," wrote Hermine. "They are a blessing whatever life brings!"

36   PAUL'S ALTERED CHARACTER

The mask of cheerfulness with which Paul had greeted his family on his return from Siberia could not be worn for long for, despite his determination to bear his sorrows with fortitude, one piled upon the other until the cracks began to show. Memories of his father, of his suicidal brothers Hans and Rudi, guilt at having deserted his comrades in the Krepost, the grim realization of his present armless condition, thoughts of his wrecked career, of Ludwig's unstable mind, of the starvation and disease that were overtaking Vienna, frustrations of every kind—artistic, familial, sexual— not to mention the endless, slow, slow losing of the war, these were the things that preyed upon him and sought eventually to destroy his moral equilibrium.

Since his return to Vienna in November he had been attending also to the gradual disintegration of Rosalie Hermann, a tall, bony and much admired former servant of his grandmother's with whom he had been especially close since his childhood. Paul was her favorite among the Wittgenstein children, and he in turn looked on her with the same degree of fondness with which many sons are able to look upon their mothers. Rosalie had been employed as Mrs. Wittgenstein's mother's maid for fifty-two years and Frau Kalmus had bequeathed her enough money and furniture to live independently in a plush flat on the Brahmsplatz, but when Rosalie's coughing fits began and her health was failing Mrs. Wittgenstein had her moved into a grand bedroom at the Alleegasse Palais. Here, every day, Paul brought her fresh flowers, sat by her bedside, recounted stories, told her jokes, read her books and played her music. Rosalie's dying was attenuated over many months of high fever and unsightly swellings, during which time she impressed the whole family with her stoicism in the face of death. In May 1916 she went into hospital. When she died she was buried with honor next to Karl in the Wittgenstein family tomb. Under her mattress she had left a thank-you letter addressed to Mrs. Wittgenstein. Rosalie was a peacemaker among querulous people and Paul felt her loss deeply.

After her death Paul's agitation and irritability increased. In the company of his family, of strangers or of guests his frustrations vented themselves in violent clashes. Hermine and Mrs. Wittgenstein worried at the frequency of his "crazy moods," and, shortly before her departure for Zurich, Gretl gave him a thorough ticking-off. To her surprise Paul's response was both apologetic and contrite. He explained to her, in touching tones, how much he was suffering from his own irritability and how he believed her reprimand to be wholly appropriate. Hermine wrote to Ludwig: "If necessary Gretl's rocket will be repeated and possibly, as Paul has already requested, with even greater severity." Ludwig was astounded. "I cannot begin to imagine it. But there are still things in this world that are unimaginable." For a while Gretl's forthright ministrations seemed to do the trick and Hermine reported that her brother was "completely changed," but no sooner were the Stonboroughs departed for Zurich than Paul was back to his old ways.

Ludwig's solution was for Paul to move out of the Palais and find himself an apartment elsewhere in Vienna, but Hermine, shuddering at the prospect of life on her own with her mother, insisted that he stay. "Between Mama and me there is no contact without friction," she wrote. "If it were just me at home it would be really dead." When Paul was behaving well he was capable of cheering up the Palais in a way that Mrs. Wittgenstein and Hermine were not. They were too reserved, too anxious. Hermine's taciturnity was, in her own view, contagious, while Mrs. Wittgenstein "can't get much pleasure from strangers if they have no connection with her children." Paul, on the other hand, was energetic and his busy life ensured a coming and going of interesting people that would enliven their days. He could cheer his mother by playing piano duets with her. So it was agreed that he would stay, for, despite his bouts of madness, his presence at the Palais was deemed a bonus. After all, "The hours passed in stimulating company at home would not be greatly diminished by the odd (or even by several) unpleasant scenes," Hermine conceded.

On the second floor of the Palais, Paul arranged a bachelor suite for himself. Approached by a separate staircase with windows looking on to the courtyard and gardens below, it consisted of a sitting room (with dining table), a bathroom and a bedroom, into which he could withdraw and have meals brought up to him by the servants. One of the Palais's seven grand pianos was installed and on "crazy days" Paul practiced undisturbed, furiously pounding the keys with his left hand for hour upon hour—behavior that reminded Hermine of her father. "Unfortunately, to my really great distress, [Papa's] restlessness shows itself in Paul's piano playing. When I hear him practicing upstairs not a single bar accords with my way of thinking and feeling and that is a torture for me and a lasting source of sorrow."

Like his father, Paul had scant control of his temper and his brothers were just the same. When all three were together, the rowing was always at its worst. They yelled at one another, sometimes for whole afternoons, moving from room to room as they did so, and as much as Mrs. Wittgenstein liked the idea of seeing them all together the reality of it strained her nerves. Paul generally was held to blame.

Like Ludwig, Paul was at his happiest when he was busy and he loved especially to be away from home. In the year-long wait to rejoin the army he performed several concerts outside Vienna. Labor's concerto had opened doors for him, and his playing was now regarded by the authorities as a source of inspiration to flagging morale. Not all crippled soldiers were so lucky. Those who returned from the front with their faces shot to pieces were held behind locked hospital gates where the public was not able to see them. Paul, though, was encouraged to vaunt his fighting spirit, and in the early months of 1917 he performed with striking success to audiences of troops, invalids and steel workers at Wrocław, Kladno, Teplitz, Brno and Prague. On at least three of these occasions he played Labor's new piece, and the delighted composer started on a second left-handed piano concerto ready to perform in the summer.

In March 1917 Paul made his Berlin debut at the Beethoven-Saal. The German capital was at that time one of the major musical centers of the world and Berliners' appetite for music was insatiable. By 1939 the city boasted no fewer than 81 orchestras, 200 chamber groups and over 600 choirs. To be well received as a concert pianist in Berlin and Vienna was to have succeeded upon the world stage. Paul had not been back to Berlin since his years of banking apprenticeship and had mixed feelings about the place. He had enjoyed the music, but derided the boardinghouses on the Kurfürstendamm and the Tauentzienstrasse as "abominable places full of cheap knickknacks, cheap paintings, unliveable and overused at the same time; middle class in the worst sense of the word."

The hall, which he expected to be half empty due to sloppy publicity, was in fact full and the audience discerning and appreciative. On his return to Vienna, he was grilled by Hermine and his mother for news of how it had gone, but his pathological need for privacy denied them the intelligence they sought and it took five days to glean from his chirpy manner that it had all been a huge success. Hermine was overjoyed on her brother's behalf. The Berliners, she felt, had judged Paul entirely on the quality of his playing, unlike the dreadful Viennese who were always more interested in the stump of his right arm than his music. "And that is really something!" she said.

37 ENDGAME

The death on November 21, 1916, of Emperor Franz Joseph served only to dampen Austrian morale. He had ruled for sixty-eight years and, despite his aversions to innovation and his much derided obsession with petty court protocol, the longevity of his reign had lent him an air of authority that had grown with familiarity and custom. He symbolized perhaps more than he achieved but at least he guided Austria and sixteen other subject states through a long period of peace and stability. Stefan Zweig called the time in which he grew up before the First World War "The Golden Age of Security" and few in 1916 could remember an Austria that was any different; but by November of that year the people had grown war-weary and dispirited. No amount of trumpet noise or funeral pomp could rouse them from their negative stupors or restore to them their previous sense of national pride. Everything the army had fought to protect and uphold now seemed irretrievably lost. The comfortable, immutable, Epicurean, easygoing life of the Austrian people, ruffled already by the storm of two years' war, was now, upon the death of their octogenarian emperor, transformed into the "world of yesterday."

The Wittgensteins, though broadly monarchist in temperament, were not aristocrats nor did they move in court circles. Some of Karl's descendants believe that he was offered the nobility "von" but declined it on ethical grounds. In truth he felt underrated by the Austrian establishment and was greatly excited by the smallest attention he could get from the Hapsburgs. He was delighted that the Emperor once noticed his good seat when riding and put great store on a royal visit to one of his factories. When his boys were young Karl would pick them up by their ears. If they kept quiet he shouted "Hochgeboren!" (well bred!), but if they cried or squealed in pain he yelled "Nichtgeboren!" (lower class—literally "not-born").

If Hermine and Paul felt the passing of an era at the death of their emperor they did not express it. They did, however, make a conscious effort to disconnect from their past by redecorating and restructuring their two palaces at the Alleegasse and at Neuwaldegg. Hermine hoped that the new designs would help her mother "loosen her ties to Papa," but in the end all the siblings were pleased to rid these places of certain decorative vestiges of Karl's overbearing personality.

At court the Emperor was succeeded by his grand-nephew, Archduke Karl von Hapsburg-Lothringen, known during his brief reign as Emperor Charles I, who immediately tried to sue for peace, but who by the end of 1917 had succeeded only in ceding most of Austria's military command to the Germans. In the meantime, on the eastern front, his dilapidated and dispirited army managed by a miracle to win the war against Russia. This had more to do with the state of internal Russian politics than the superiority of Austrian arms. In February a revolution had deposed the Tsarist regime, and the new provisional government, in order to bolster its popularity at home, had ordered a great offensive against the whole Galician sector. After ten days of spectacular territorial gain, the exhausted Russian soldiers suddenly lost their enthusiasm and refused to fight on. The Austro-German armies routed them in a fierce counterattack that forced them to retreat to positions 150 miles east. This catastrophic humiliation led many in Moscow to call for the war to be immediately ended and when the head of the provisional government, Alexander Kerensky, refused to capitulate, chaos ensued. Latvians, Estonians and Lithuanians started calling for their independence from Russia, while the powerful Bolsheviks, who favored an end to the war, quickly seized control in the so-called October Revolution. Two months later, on December 15, Lenin's envoy Leon Trotsky effectively ended his country's participation in the war by signing an armistice with the Central Powers at Brest-Litovsk.

These great events inevitably made an impact on the lives of each of the Wittgenstein brothers. Ludwig, during the July offensive, had retreated with his Austrian comrades from a forward position at Bukovina to the western side of the Lomnica River, and when the Russian spirit suddenly withered and the Austrian rout began, he joined in the counterattack assisting in the recapture first of Czernowitz and then of Bojan at the end of August—actions for which he was once again decorated. When the Russians were finally withdrawn from the war, the Austrian forces were able to turn their attentions from the eastern front to the south, and in the spring of 1918 Ludwig was posted to the Alpine front near Asiago in Vicenza.

Oblivious to the threat of execution, Paul was determined to rejoin the war from the moment he returned to Vienna in November 1915 and, like his brother, demanded a posting to a place where things would be most dangerous. Unlike Ludwig, however, his motives in wishing to return to action were entirely patriotic and had nothing to do with spiritual self-improvement. When he was awarded his medals in March 1916, Paul was ordered into retirement with an annual pension of 1,696 kronen, but he was having none of it. He was determined to fight on, and after a long period of lobbying generals at his club in Vienna and twisting the arm of his red-nosed retired uncle, Cavalry General Josef von Siebert, he finally received his call-up papers in August 1917. His mother and sisters were in general agreement that he had made the right decision, though Hermine hoped he would not be sent too close to the front. "One hardly knows what is the best thing to wish for Paul," she wrote. "What another wound would mean for him now that he is only half a man hardly bears speaking about, when you consider how passionately he loves playing the piano. He lives only for it and through it." When orders were sent for him to report to army headquarters at Villach in Carinthia he was "somewhat put out that it was nothing more dangerous."

For several weeks Paul was deputed to minor office tasks at Hermagor, a small town to the west of Villach, which made him restless and irritable, but from late September 1917 he was assigned to Fourth Army Command Headquarters at Wladimir Wolynski in the western Ukraine, where he was given employment in the communications office. Here he discovered that he could operate with one hand the Hughes type-printing telegraph machine, which had a small keyboard very similar to that of a piano, consisting of fourteen white and fourteen black keys. Paul's fellow officers were astounded to find that he could type messages on it with one hand faster than they could manage with two.

At the end of February 1918 he was granted several weeks' leave as the Austro-Hungarian Fourth Army, under its competent but incapacitated commander Karl Graf von Kirchbach auf Lauterbach, was being dissolved. At home Hermine found him "very pleasant and approachable." For once there was no friction between Paul and Kurt—at least she did not notice it—but, as she told Ludwig, "It was a good thing that your more finely tuned apparatus was not present—it would most certainly have detected a slight tension and have inflamed it as a result—the two brothers are so different."

Returning to duty, Paul was posted to the fortress town of Riva on the northern shores of Lake Garda as adjutant to the fifty-five-year-old General Anton von Schiesser. Though it was captured by the Italians in November 1918, Schiesser's courageous and determined defense of the town (for which he was subsequently ennobled) made him a national hero.

In retirement at Innsbruck he was saluted as he walked the streets and when he died in 1926 a plaque celebrating his deeds at Riva was appended to the house of his birth at Schenkenfelden. An official army report on Schiesser from 1918 describes him as "a very efficient, lively and energetic general. Faithful in his duties . . . an athletic and strong-willed commander."

Paul's posting to Riva brought all three Wittgenstein brothers to within a hundred miles of one another on the Italian front, but this did not last for long. For some unknown reason Paul was discharged from the military in August 1918. He was determined to serve, and after the war took pride in his military record, so it is inconceivable that he was dismissed, or left for any dishonorable reason. Ill health may have had something to do with it for, in the middle of July while on leave with his family at Neuwaldegg, he collapsed with a high fever that lasted several weeks.

It is possible that by the time he was recovered the situation at Riva was too chaotic for him to return and that no new position presented itself in the few months of the war that remained.

It is equally possible that Paul's illness (a violent influenza) was the same virulent strain, known as Spanish flu, that would go on to claim more than twenty million lives in a Europe-wide pandemic. The disease was officially acknowledged to have reached Vienna in October, when among those killed were the twenty-eight-year-old artist Egon Schiele and his pregnant wife Edith. Not everyone who contracted the disease died from it, and it was soon discovered that a transfusion of blood from someone who had survived the disease was the best cure. In the worst cases a victim's face would turn blue, he would cough blood and soon his lungs would be swamped by his own body fluids. Edith Schiele's first symptoms appeared on October 26 and she died on the 28th, while her husband, nursing her over those three days, got a blue face on the 28th and died on the 31st. That same month five servants in the Wittgenstein household contracted the virus. Mrs. Wittgenstein and Hermine were spared.

At the same time as Schiele and his wife were dying in Vienna, Corporal Adolf Hitler, fighting the British at Ypres, was rendered blind and speechless by a chlorine-gas attack on his line. "When this happened," he told an interviewer in 1923, "I saw my future. These questions flashed through my mind: 'You never feared death—Why? You are still alive when others around you fell—Why?' And I told myself, because fate has singled you out to accomplish something. I resolved to consecrate my life to my country—to the task of driving out the enemies within her borders."

On the Italian front, meanwhile, Austro-Hungarian troops were fast becoming dejected and defeatist. They had lost 100,000 soldiers trying to force their way into northern Italy at Lombardy, Trentino and across the lower Piave. On the western front the Germans too were struggling and could ill afford to send troops to their aid. South of the river, the Italian commander General Armando Diaz planned a forward offensive of five armies that would divide the Austrian forces in two, by advancing in a line from Monte Grappa to the mouth of the Piave. By October 27, with the help of a British corps under Lord Cavan, Diaz had secured a strategic foothold on the left bank of the river. This success caused mutiny to break out among the Austrian ranks and on the 28th the Austrian High Command ordered a general retreat. This gave the Italians the confidence to surge forward and succeed in their aim of splitting the Austrian army. On November 3 an armistice was signed at Villa Giusti near Padua. With twenty-four hours between signature and the agreement officially taking effect, the Italians continued rampaging forward in order to seize as much land as possible in advance of territorial negotiations. Many Austrians, unaware that an armistice had been signed, pointlessly lost their lives defending against the Italian attack. Thirty-eight thousand casualties were reported on the Italian side, but 300,000 Austro-Hungarians were taken prisoner, of whom General Anton von Schiesser was one and Ludwig Wittgenstein another. It was somewhere in the middle of all this chaos that Kurt Wittgenstein met his end.

Nobody from the Wittgenstein family in Vienna seems to have known of Kurt's death until sometime in December. The first that Ludwig knew of it was from a letter that his mother wrote to him at his POW camp near Como on December 27.

> *My dearest son,*
>
> *After the dreadful anxiety we were suffering for your sake, your card dated 6th November which we received on 6th December did us infinite good; and today's news by telegraph is doubly cheering because it is up to date. You can't imagine how overjoyed we were. There was general delight involving the whole family. Whatever shall we do when we expect to see you back here? We are well and all is well with the Salzers. But we have suffered a severe loss. Our dear Kurt fell in the very last days of the war at the end of October. I embrace you, my dearest beloved son, with the tenderest love and my only wish is that you should remain in good health and that you may return home in the not too distant future. With her every thought, your mother is with you today.*

Clearly there had been worry in Vienna that Ludwig, who had been out of contact since December 6, might also have been killed or even have killed himself, for Hermine wrote to him at the same time as her mother: "I'm indescribably happy to know that you're alive! Kurt fell on 27th November. Mama very distressed but brave and cheered by your news. All in good health here; also good news from the Stonboroughs, nothing but good news to report. . . ."

It may be noticed that Hermine and her mother each give different dates for Kurt's "fall." Mrs. Wittgenstein says "end of October" and Hermine "27th November." In a further letter dated January 10, 1919, Hermine writes, "Kurt fell on 27th September, it's very sad." The most probable date for the death is the end of October as Mrs. Wittgenstein originally asserted, most likely on the 27th, the day that Lord Cavan and General Diaz secured their bridgehead on the Piave and the Austrians started to mutiny. On the Italian front the fighting was over by November 27, so Hermine's date must be wrong.

Perhaps more interesting than the day Kurt died are questions as to why and how it happened. In her memoirs Hermine wrote, "My brother Kurt shot himself without visible reason on a retreat from Italy in the last days of the First World War." This ignores the fact that explanations for his suicide were sought at the time and that various conflicting stories have since filtered down through different branches of the family. One version that Paul gave to his friend Marga Deneke in the 1920s was written up in 1961 shortly after his death. This then may loosely serve as Paul's version:

> A special poignancy marks Kurt Wittgenstein's death for he was safely installed in an office in the USA but, supported by his family, he deployed every available means to get himself recalled for military service in Austria. An army order commanded him to expose his battalion to complete annihilation before a battery of enemy guns. Knowing that no conceivable military advantage was involved, he disobeyed the order. Then fear of a court martial preyed upon his mind. It became too much for him and he killed himself. This was on the eve of surrender in 1918. In the confusion of these days there would have been no inquiries. The waste of it all was bitter.

This version, however, conflicts with that of Gretl's son, Ji Stonborough, who was told (possibly by his mother) that Kurt had shot himself, like many other Austrian officers, in the twenty-four-hour period after the signing of the armistice of November 3 because he refused to be taken prisoner by the Italians. If this were indeed the case then the story may have been changed to save Ludwig's blushes, since he had accepted surrender to the Italians and had himself been taken prisoner at the same time.

Another version recorded by Paul's daughter Johanna, following her interviews with family members in Austria in the 1980s, broadly supports the Deneke account, adding a little more detail. Kurt, she says, was ordered to lead his men across the River Piave. There followed a heated exchange with his commanding officer in which he shouted: "I am not offering my men in vain. The war is already lost." At that point he drew his pistol from its holster and threatened the officer that if he did not remove himself immediately from his sight he would be shot. The astonished commander withdrew, loudly hissing threats about a court martial. Kurt then summoned his men, instructed them all to go home, and minutes later shot himself.

A fourth version suggests that it was the men, not Kurt, who rebelled; that it was he who ordered them to action and they who refused to obey by deserting him on the field. Standing alone with an 11mm Gasser revolver in his hand, with no men to support him and in the face of a heavy Italian bombardment, he was forced to take a rushed decision between three galling alternatives: to desert with his men; to fight on alone and be shot or captured by the enemy; or to put a bullet through his head. He chose the last, dispatching himself in a sudden burst of fury.

Perhaps it is of little matter now which of the above scenarios comes closest to the historical truth for in November 1918, as far as the surviving members of his family were concerned, Kurt—childish, light-hearted, frivolous Kurt—was (for the time being at least) the family hero. Like so many of the eight and a half million soldier victims of the Great War he was given no funeral and his remains lie today at some undiscovered, unmarked spot somewhere along the banks of the Piave. To Paul, a fourth son suddenly finding himself head of the family, to Ludwig incarcerated at a camp in Italy, to Gretl, exiled in Switzerland, and to Mrs. Wittgenstein and her daughters Hermine and Helene at home in Vienna, the news of Kurt's death recalled from within suppressed memories of unspeakable tragedy; but this time at least there was a difference, for with the bitter news came also a faint reassurance: that, unlike the wretched fates of Hans and Rudolf, Kurt's suicide could be counted as an "honourable death."

Paul and Ludwig's belief in his heroism never wavered, but Hermine's, for some unknown reason, did. In her fairytale memoirs many pages are devoted to effusive praise of her worthy aunts and uncles, to family connections and to her beloved Rosalie. There is a whole chapter also on Ludwig, whom she describes as "the most interesting and worthwhile of my brothers"; she leaves a fond and puzzled description of Hans in youth but says next to nothing about Paul or Rudolf. Her portrait of Kurt is squeezed to a single paragraph in which she portrays him as a "relaxed" person, a "typical rich bachelor without serious duties" with a "harmless, cheerful disposition" and a "natural and delightful musicality" who, despite all this, appeared to carry "the germ of disgust for life within himself." No mention of any heroism in 1918, not a whisper; if anything she deplored his suicide as an act of weakness. To her brothers' intense irritation she frequently compared them unfavourably to their father. "Papa would not have done it this way; if Papa were only here he would have . . ." Did Kurt, she mused, "finally die from a lack of the 'hard must,' a conception my father so much wanted to impart to his sons; or was it simply a lack of endurance which seized the upper hand at one moment, and certainly not the most difficult one in the war?" This she never knew.

Many die too late, and some die too early. Yet strange soundeth the precept: "Die at the right time!" Die at the right time: so teacheth Zarathustra.

PART THREE

THE
NEW
DISORDER

38 AFTERMATH

By mid-November 1918 the fighting was at last over. In defense of empire two million Austro-Hungarian soldiers had lost their lives in violent clashes with Russians, Italians, Serbs and Rumanians across a front that ran from the Alpine barrier of northern Italy to the undulating landscape of central western Poland. More than two million had been imprisoned in Russia and Siberia, and three million severely wounded. The mighty monarchy in whose honor these actions had been fought had collapsed and disintegrated, and with it Austria's long epoch of grandeur had come to a sorry end. On November 11, Charles I, Emperor of Austria, King of Hungary and Bohemia, relinquished "every participation in the administration of the state" and, four months later, without formal abdication, departed by train with his black-clad wife, Empress Zita, for the Swiss border station at Feldkirch and a life in exile. His short reign had been spent in pursuit of peace. He was the only leader of a belligerent state to ban the use of poison gas. In 1921 he was deported to the Atlantic island of Madeira where, a year later, he died of pneumonia.

With the demise of the last emperor a new era was born in Austria as the once-proud state transformed itself into a small, weak and unstable republic. None of the new political parties was in favor of national independence, as everyone feared that the country would be too weak to survive on its own. Some, like Adolf Hitler, agitated for *Anschluss* (connection with Germany) even though this had been specifically prohibited under the terms of the armistice. Others, like Paul Wittgenstein, hoped for a restoration of the old order, but the Czechs, the Poles, the Southern Slavs and the Hungarians recoiled at the suggestion of a return to Hapsburg rule and rejected economic union with Austria on the basis that the country was now too poor.

Vienna, once the hub of the monarchy's free-trade area and the heart of a spreading European empire, was caught unprepared for the turn of events. The old railway system upon which the Hapsburg economy had depended ground to a halt as each newly formed state claimed ownership of the rolling stock. Food and raw materials, once supplied to the Viennese from Hungary, were stopped by the new administration in Budapest to extract better trade terms in the future and to avenge past wrongs. The coal that had once been brought to Vienna by rail from the Bohemian lands was similarly embargoed by the new Czechoslovak regime in Prague. Many Viennese lost their lives in the harsh winter of 1918–19 and starvation in the city affected most of its two million inhabitants. Within one year of the war's end, 96 percent of Austrian children were officially classed as "undernourished." In the streets the gaunt faces of a ravenous population cast a darkening pall over the city's spirit as the black-net widow's veil came to be recognized as the sign of a touting prostitute.

In the countryside the peasant farmer, circumventing a government law of maximum tariffs, sold his highly prized bread, milk and eggs secretly to the man from the town for an extortionate sum, but when that same peasant arrived at the shops, gleeful, with his fist full of cash, hoping to buy tools, pots, hammers, scythes and kettles, he was dismayed to discover that the shopkeeper had been forced to quadruple prices in order to pay for his bread, milk and eggs. In the feverish atmosphere of hyperinflation the burgher and the peasant soon came to an understanding that money didn't work and that goods must be traded by exchange for other goods. Antiques, leatherbound books, jewelry and works of art were thus passed from the bourgeois to the peasant in exchange for a weekly food ration. During the war the value of the Austrian krone had fallen sixteen-fold due to the government's extravagant printing of banknotes to pay its bills, and by August 1922 paper money was virtually worthless as consumer prices rose to a level 14,000 times higher than they had been before the war.

With Kurt's death shares in his steel plant at Judenburg went to his business partner Sebastian Danner, while his properties in Austria and his portion of the family trust was divided by his siblings. One million kronen was left to charity. Paul, as executor of the will, had the idea to spend it all on garden allotments for the poor. Driven by his conviction that cultivation of the soil was a healing occupation, that it would improve the moral and physical well-being of the Viennese, help them fight starvation and offer a sensible alternative to Bolshevism, Paul encountered many difficulties. Buying the land and resolving how it should be distributed proved to be insurmountable problems, and he eventually handed the million to the worthy burghers of the city council, who failed to accomplish anything with it.

In Switzerland Gretl had complained of feeling lonely, cut off from her family and vexed at having no useful occupation or outlet for her patriotism. In point of fact she had made many friends, one of whom was Napoleon's great-grand-niece Princess Marie of Greece, who lived for a while in the same hotel in Luzern. Like many of Jerome and Gretl's friends, Princess Marie had connections in high diplomatic and political circles. She was a one-time mistress of the French Prime Minister Aristide Briand, and later introduced Gretl to her hero Sigmund Freud, from whom she had originally sought advice about her frigidity. Wherever Jerome and Gretl found themselves, in Vienna, Berlin, London or Bern, they tended to make friends with the American ambassador or American consul there. These ties—which have the faint whiff of espionage about them—were later to prove extremely useful.

One of the Stonboroughs' friends in Switzerland was the American Envoy and Minister Plenipotentiary Pleasant Stovall, with whom Gretl pleaded for help in sending a special train from Switzerland to Vienna containing 161,472 cans ($10,000 worth) of condensed milk for the starving children of the old empire. At first American officials were opposed to any activity within the neutral states that might benefit Germany or Austria, and Jerome berated Gretl for drawing attention to herself by trying. U.S. diplomats were suspicious of the Stonboroughs' close friendship with Princess Marie of Greece, but when Gretl and Jerome assured them that they would move out of the Hotel National, they came at length to be trusted. The U.S. administration had reasons of its own for wanting to feed the starving Austrians, and the U.S. Legation in Switzerland eventually agreed to offer Gretl a helping hand. The condensed milk that her money bought was theoretically enough to keep 4,000 children nourished for a month, but the Austrian authorities never acknowledged receipt and one wonders, in an age of pillage and acute starvation, whether it ever reached its intended destination.

By August 1919, much to the disapproval of her brother Paul, Gretl was appointed special representative of the American Relief Administration, or ARA, a U.S. government organization originally set up to supply the Allies with surplus American food under the banner "Food Will Win the War." As soon as she had returned to Vienna, Gretl met the ARA's chairman, Herbert Hoover (later thirty-first U.S. President), who was seeking to distribute 500,000 tons of food among the starving population of Austria. To many, the operation may have seemed nothing more than a pleasant, altruistic, humanitarian gesture by a conquering nation toward its recently defeated enemy, but the scheme was in reality motivated in Washington by the unspoken political aim of halting the advance of communist revolution from the east. According to White House theory a starving population was more likely to embrace a socialist ideology than a well-nourished one. So when, in December 1919, Gretl was sent by the ARA to the United States to help raise money for Austrian famine relief, she was (wittingly or unwittingly) operating as an American government agent in a covert U.S. operation to stem the spread of European Bolshevism.

39 FAMILY TENSIONS

Early in 1938 Ludwig, chatting with one of his Cambridge disciples, Theodore Redpath, asked him: "Have you had any tragedies in your life?"

"It depends what you mean by tragedy," Redpath replied.

"Well I don't mean the death of your grandmother at the age of eighty-five," said Ludwig. "I mean suicides, madness or quarrels."

By this definition Ludwig's own life was a tragic one and so too were the lives of all the Wittgensteins. As the suicides and madness increased in the family, so too did the quarreling. Ludwig and Gretl were rivals. He resented her because she was controlling and patronizing, she resented him for being disrespectful and ungovernable. When the Palais at Neuwaldegg was being cleared of Karl's influence, Gretl had stipulated that Ludwig should have no hand in the redecoration as his intransigent tastes were "not even the best of a rotten bargain." In Switzerland Gretl had been touched by the long letters Paul had written her with his left hand, but even before her return to Vienna in June 1919 she found a cause to quarrel bitterly with him.

Paul's mistake was to have authorized the investment of a large part of the family's domestic fortune in government war bonds without consulting her. Although most of Gretl's wealth was invested in the American stock market, she had inherited a share of Kurt's estate, which remained in Vienna, superintended by Paul as nominal head of the family. The value of the bonds plummeted to such an extent that, by the time Gretl got to hear about it, they were worth less than the coupons would have been worth as paper. Most of the Wittgensteins' great domestic fortune was irretrievably lost. Gretl was infuriated by the waste, but this, she claimed, was the least of her concerns. Paul had been "utterly thoughtless," for allowing the story to get into the newspapers, which she feared would get her and her husband, as American citizens, into serious trouble with the U.S. authorities. At a time when she was desperately trying to prove her loyal American credentials to the diplomats in Bern, the last thing she wanted was for them to discover that she and her family had been financially supporting the enemy from neutral Switzerland during the war. In a rage she wrote to Hermine: "Good old Paul has managed one piece of hare-brained nonsense after another, putting on Papa's airs and graces, and without a thought in his head has put me in the most terrible position." Jerome meanwhile was pacing around their Swiss hotel bedroom bellowing like a buffalo: "It is no way to do business!"

"And he is right!" Gretl insisted. "And I of course will always take Jerome's side."

Relations between Gretl and Paul were not soothed by her return to Vienna in June. Jerome had not wanted to go but was hoping to travel directly from Switzerland to America instead. They did as she insisted, but moods were fraught when they got there. After an absence of two years she wrote in her diary: "Everything in the Alleegasse was just as before . . . Big quarrel with Paul about politics in the evening." Paul had criticized her condensed-milk charity operation and deplored her working for the Americans. Politically she was anti-Bolshevik but in favor nevertheless of the new left-wing socialist republic. "The Austrians are desperate," she complained, "they preferred the old sloppiness to the new disorder but the new disorder contains new seeds unlike the old one . . ." Earlier she had written to her sister Hermine: "I have always had red tendencies and now I have become even redder. I am afraid that I think in a different way than you all do and do not know if I shall be sensible enough to hold my tongue." Tongue-holding was never Gretl's virtue, and her outspoken "red tendencies" grated against Paul's staunch right-wing monarchism. But politics alone could not be blamed for the Wittgensteins' failure to get along with one another for whatever the subject of conversation—art, music, books, money, personal plans—they always found cause to quarrel, and when all five siblings were together, things were at their most fractious.

> It is not in the nature of us 5 siblings to be social together [Ludwig wrote to Hermine]. You are able to have a conversation with me or Gretl, but it is difficult for the three of us together. Paul and Gretl even less. Helene fits well with any one of us but it would never occur to you, Helene and me to come together as a group. We are all rather hard, sharp-edged blocks who find it difficult to fit together snugly . . . we are only sociable with each other when we are diluted by friends.

The siblings' social incompatibility forced them to use the Palais as a hotel, avoiding where possible communal activity, bagging rooms for private conclaves with their own invited guests. One such, a woman invited to stay by Paul, remembered the tension in the Alleegasse when, after lunch, Ludwig asked *his* guest, Marie Baumayer, to play the piano for him after lunch. The two of them withdrew to an adjacent room.

> Hearing the music in the next-door room made me long to listen more closely, but I gathered "Lucki" did not tolerate intruders. Perhaps least of all someone who was Paul's friend. Patriotism and family pride held the Wittgensteins together, but each brother and sister kept firmly to his own ideas.

Ludwig, along with hundreds of thousands of Austrian soldiers, was held captive in Italy long after the armistice. The Italians used their prisoners as bargaining chips in negotiation to gain disputed territory north of the Piave. Nor did the cease-fire do much to end Ludwig's personal quest for absolution. Even in a prisoner-of-war camp he maintained a

Christlike determination to push himself through every conceivable test, rejecting officer privileges and demanding of his guards that he be transferred from the officers' prison to a nearby rank-and-file camp where a typhoid epidemic had broken out. When well-connected friends in Switzerland wrote to officials at the Vatican begging their intercession to release Ludwig (on the compassionate grounds that his mother had already lost three sons and had only one cripple left at home) he was brought before a medical tribunal, where he made it plain that he would not be released before any one of his fellow prisoners. His moral drive, intense seriousness, arresting looks and personal magnetism attracted disciples in prison camp as on the battlefield. One of them, Franz Parak, who was held with Ludwig at Monte Cassino, worshipped the young philosopher, greeting his every statement with sighs of adulation. This irritated Ludwig, who claimed that the soldier reminded him of his mother and, to Parak's bitter regret, never wished to see him again after their release.

Arriving in Vienna at the end of August 1919, Ludwig went straight to his bank to tell them that he did not want his money anymore and that his intention was to rid himself of all of it. The manager was alarmed—"financial suicide!" he called it—and Herr Trenkler, manager of the family assets, threw his arms in the air when Ludwig demanded that he draw up the necessary papers so that not a single brass heller remained in his possession. On the same day Ludwig had written to a friend: "as far as my state of mind is concerned I am not very well." He was clearly in a wretched state but his resolve was adamantine and no one could deflect it. When he told his family what he planned to do they too were extremely worried on his behalf, though Hermine was more appalled by his new choice of profession than by his scheme of self-impoverishment. "A man with your philosophically trained mind working as an elementary school master is like a precision instrument being used to open a wooden crate," she said. He is said to have answered: "And you remind me of someone looking through a closed window unable to explain the strange movements of a passer-by, unaware that a storm is raging outside and that the person is only with great effort keeping himself on his feet."

Tolstoy's influence lay behind Ludwig's decisions to discard his fortune and take up teaching, for the great Russian novelist had fifty years earlier cast aside his own aristocratic fortunes for a life of ascetic self-denial and humble toil. Jesus's injunction to renounce wealth is given in *The Gospel in Brief* as a commandment in the fourth chapter—"Do not lay up store on earth. On earth the worm consumes and rust eats, and thieves steal." Curiously Tolstoy's redaction did not include any of the original Biblical passages in which Jesus requires that a person's wealth be handed specifically to the poor. The most famous of these appears in the Gospel of St. Matthew as the story of a rich young man to whom Jesus says: "If you wish to be perfect, go and sell your possessions and give the money to the poor, and you shall have treasure in heaven; then come follow me."

Ludwig decided to give his fortune to his three rich siblings, Paul, Hermine and Helene. Gretl was excluded from the handout on the basis that she was much richer than the others because most of her fortune, safely invested on the American stock market, had not been affected by the deleterious forces of Austrian hyperinflation. This, however, was not made clear at the time. Hermine, for one, believed that Gretl had been cut out simply because she and Ludwig were on bad terms. It has been suggested that he gave his fortune to his siblings (instead of the poor) for reasons of convenience, since much of it was bound in shared real estate. This may be partly the case, but it was also true that he believed money to be corrupting and that since his siblings had so much of it already, they, he reasoned, could hardly be corrupted any further.

The row that ensued about Ludwig's money affected the whole family. Karl's eldest brother, Uncle Paul, was furious with those of Ludwig's siblings who had accepted his money and accused them of taking advantage of their younger brother who was clearly sick. They ought, he insisted, to have laid some secret fund aside in case he changed his mind and wanted his money back. Hermine, who admitted doing "everything to fulfil Ludwig's wishes down to the smallest detail," argued that her greater knowledge of her brother's state of mind left no alternative but to do as he asked. Uncle Paul, who loved his own possessions so greatly that he left instructions for several of them to be buried with him in his coffin, neither could nor would try to understand his nephews and nieces and in high moral dudgeon cut himself off from those he accused of having profited by Ludwig's madness.

40 ANTI-SEMITICS

The threat of a Bolshevik takeover in Vienna felt very real. The Russian Revolution according to Paul "began with the Jews . . . Under the Tsarist regime they were suppressed, and at least the poor among them have reaped benefits from the overthrow and, as in Vienna, they compose a large part of the leadership." There were many Jews in Vienna before the war—10 percent of the population according to some estimates—and their numbers were greatly increased during the conflict and in the months that followed it. Multitudes of Galician Jews had sought refuge in the city from the Russian invasion of Poland and in 1919 a further influx poured in from Hungary after the fall of the Jewish Bolshevist leader, Béla Kun. Kun's short hold on power was repressive and on his expulsion all Hungarian Jews—not just those involved in his government—were subject to brutal reprisals. Many of them, including Kun himself, fled to Austria. There and in Berlin he attempted, without success, to foment a Marxist revolution. Kun's days ended in the USSR, where he was murdered by Stalin's assassins.

The arrival in Vienna of Kun and his communist plotters did nothing to allay suspicions among the Viennese that the Bolshevik movement was Jewish led and that it might, at any moment, seize the reins of power in Austria. This fear led to a sharp increase in anti-Semitism in Vienna.

> Is there any shady undertaking, any form of foulness in which at
> least one Jew does not participate [Hitler asked in *Mein Kampf*]?
> On putting the probing knife carefully to that kind of abscess one
> immediately discovers, like a maggot in a putrescent body, a little
> Jew often blinded by the sudden light.

Hitler claimed in his autobiography of 1924 that, although he had been aware as a young man of the "moral pestilence" of the Jewish hold over the press, art, literature, the theater and white-slave trafficking ("It was worse than the Black Plague of long ago"), it was not until he discovered the extent of Jewish participation in the political life of Vienna that a Damascene conversion took place within him. "In the face of that revelation the scales fell from my eyes," he wrote. "My long inner struggle was at an end . . . The knowledge [that the Jews were responsible for communism] was the occasion of the greatest inner revolution that I had yet experienced. From being a soft-hearted cosmopolitan I became an out-and-out anti-Semite."

And so it was that this soi-disant "soft-hearted cosmopolitan" from Upper Austria resolved, in the years following the Great War, that his life's great mission should be to rid the world of a "noxious bacillus":

> Should the Jew, with the aid of the Marxist creed, triumph over the people of this world, his crown will be the funeral wreath of mankind . . . And so I believe today that my conduct is in accordance with the will of the Almighty Creator. In standing guard against the Jew I am defending the handiwork of the Lord.

People nowadays draw little distinction between the anti-Semitism of a generalized joke or complaint against Jews and the anti-Semitism of the medieval autos-da-fé and Nazi extermination camps; the one, it is argued, proceeds from the other as sure as night follows day. Let us not consider these arguments but only observe that in Vienna, long before Hitler had any power or influence, the former type of anti-Semitism (that is to say the generalized grumbling against Jews) was extremely common and that the Austrian administration, to this day, makes a distinction between Hitler's yobbish anti-Semitism and the so-called "gentlemanly anti-Semitism" of Vienna's turn-of-the-century mayor Karl Lueger, whose name is commemorated in modern Vienna by the Dr.-Karl-Lueger-Ring, by the Dr.-Karl-Lueger-Kirche at the Zentralfriedhof, by Dr.-Karl-Lueger-Platz, and by a prominent Karl Lueger monument standing at the start of the Stubenring.

The Wittgensteins were not anti-Semitic in the Hitlerian sense of the term for, like their hero the anti-Semitic philosopher Jew Otto Weininger, they deplored any form of persecution, and yet, out of the context of their time, judged by today's standards, the family's attitude to the Jews would be considered questionable. Their grandfather, Hermann Christian Wittgenstein, refused to allow his children to marry Jews. Karl, his son, remarked that "in matters of honour one does not consult a Jew." In a letter from Hermine to Ludwig we find the casual aside, "the woman is particularly likeable, although of course Jewish," for she believed that the "Aryan and Jewish races are diametrically opposed as regards merits and deficiencies, and that they must combat each other either openly or furtively." Paul believed, like his father, that "dishonesty lies at the heart of every Jew," and his friend Marga Deneke explained that "If he ever named Jews it was with the hatred of the dog for the wolf." Ludwig, much influenced by Weininger's curiously elaborate anti-Semitism, would have "nothing to do with the communist Jews," and believed that the Jews in general were "unnatural creatures" by virtue of their having lived in "foreign states under foreign laws and living conditions and restraints," and (again like Weininger and also like Richard Wagner in the previous century) Ludwig judged the Jews to be incapable of creating "original" (as opposed to "reproductive") art. In December 1929 he recorded a dream about a Jewish car-driver who opened fire with a machine gun killing a passing cyclist and a young, poor-looking girl. Ludwig, in the dream, thought to himself: "Must there be a Jew behind every indecency?"

In a passage uncomfortably reminiscent of some of Hitler's rhetoric in *Mein Kampf,* Ludwig compared the Jewish people to a *Beule* in Austrian society. Wittgenstein scholars have been squabbling among themselves ever since about whether he intended by this German word to mean a "boil," a "pustule," a "tumor," a "bump" or a "swelling." In any case it was clearly not intended as a compliment.

41 SEX LIVES

Of the sex lives of the three Wittgenstein sisters, things may be succinctly recapitulated thus: Gretl was sexually aloof and may, like her friend Princess Marie of Greece, have sought Sigmund Freud's advice on the matter. Hermine (it is supposed) never experimented and possibly recoiled at the thought. Helene's sex life is reckoned to have been the most normal of all eight siblings. She had four children (the first born in 1900) and was greatly upset, some twenty years after her marriage to Max Salzer, to discover that she was pregnant once again in 1919.

About Paul's erotic life very little is known until the early 1930s. He was aware that one day a biography might come to be written about him and, as a neurotically private man, did his best to conceal his tracks from future investigation by keeping as much of his life as possible secret even from his brothers and sisters. "In truth," his nephew Ji Stonborough later recalled, "he led two or three lives of which we in the family only knew one." In the 1950s he was approached by Hollywood moguls wanting to make a film about his life. He told them to go away, and when later contacted by a writer seeking help with a proposed biography of his brother, Paul replied curtly offering the minimum assistance:

> Concerning the biography of my brother: I really believe that Ludwig would have resisted ANY biography. For biography is indiscretion. A biography without indiscretion is worthless. But since all men of note have to have biographies written about them, then I suppose my brother will also have to suffer the same indignity. In any case it is better that the facts be right than they be wrong or, even worse, just silly rumours.

Paul made it clear that he never wished to have a biography written about him unless it concerned itself solely with his artistic life. None of his incoming correspondence (except letters from composers and musicians, and an incomplete batch from his brother Ludwig) can be found. Other, personal letters may still exist and may yet turn up, though it is suspected that they were destroyed in accordance with his wish that his life remain private. What then can be said about Paul's sex life before 1930? He was certainly heterosexual and, as can be gathered from clues in Hermine's letters to Ludwig, he was attractive to and attracted by a great many women.

Viennese women, it would seem, were particularly alluring in the first years of the twentieth century, as Paul was reaching puberty. The following description of them appears in Maria Hornor Lansdale's 1902 guide to Vienna and the Viennese:

> Observe attentively the passers-by on a Vienna Street . . . The women have the vivacity of the Slavonic races; their hair is superb and their

teeth even and as white as milk; they are well formed, slender, nervous; their feet are pretty, with well-arched insteps, altogether unlike the Bavarian goose-foot, or the elephant pad of the Prussian.

According to Ji Stonborough, Paul "had endless mistresses and all from the scum of this or that country. The servants knew all about it but we in the family had few suspicions. He bought houses for the mistresses." Stonborough perhaps gives away the lie by acknowledging that the family had few suspicions. How then did he know? Later in life Ji conceded: "I disliked Paul intensely and, I admit, I did not like Ludwig much either."

That Paul kept mistresses for whom he bought houses is certainly possible, as this was common practice among the rich Viennese bachelors of his day. It is also possible (though there is no evidence for this) that he visited prostitutes before the war. At that time in Vienna "female wares were offered for sale at every hour and at every price, and it cost a man as little time and trouble to purchase a woman for a quarter of an hour, an hour or a night, as it did to buy a packet of cigarettes or a newspaper." These lines were written by Stefan Zweig, who was from the same generation as Paul, was brought up in the same city, of similar education and social background. In his autobiography, *The World of Yesterday,* Zweig describes a veil of pseudo-morality that repressed normal sexual relations between young Viennese men and women and led to a boom in prostitution and syphilis in the city:

> Try as I might I cannot recall a single comrade of my youth who did not come to me with pale and troubled mien, one because he was ill, or feared illness, another because he was being blackmailed because of an abortion, a third because he lacked the money to be cured without the knowledge of his family, a fourth because he had to pay hush-money to a waitress who claimed to have had a child by him, a fifth because his wallet had been stolen in a brothel and he did not dare to go to the police.

Zweig also records that Viennese fathers of a certain class, in order to discourage their sons from visiting brothels, would engage pretty servant girls in the house with the task of educating them by sexual experience. There is no means of discovering whether Karl adopted such a system for Hans, Kurt, Rudi, Paul or Ludwig—we must rely upon our hunches.

As to Ludwig's erotic life, this has been the subject of much heated and acrimonious debate in the years since his death. Like his sister Gretl, he seems to have found sexual arousal disturbing and, having discovered Tolstoy's *Gospel in Brief,* was pleased to try as hard as he could to stick to the letter of the commandment written in Chapter 4: "Do not seek delight in sexual gratification . . . All sensuality destroys the soul, and therefore it is better for you to renounce the pleasure of the flesh than to destroy your life." In 1931 he proposed marriage to a Swiss woman, Marguerite Respinger, on condition that they be excused sex together.

In the aftermath of Ludwig's death the keepers of his flame and the holders of his copyrights concealed evidence in their archives which could have proved that he had been homosexual. As one of them wrote at the time: "If by pressing a button it could have been secured that people would not concern themselves with [Ludwig's] personal life, I should have pressed that button." In 1973 an academic from California State University, William Warren Bartley III, bypassing the Wittgenstein estate, published a book about Ludwig in which it was claimed that during his period of teacher-training in Vienna he would regularly walk to the famous Prater park where "rough young men were ready to cater for him sexually. Once he had found this place Wittgenstein found to his horror that he could scarcely keep away from it." With this a torrent of rebuke cascaded upon Professor Bartley's head. Among those to join the ruckus was Ji Stonborough, who tried to injunct publication of his book through the courts, while sending a bombastic piece to the periodical the *Human World,* in which he threatened to vomit on the hat of the publisher, described the work as "a book of obscene denigration . . . a farrago of lies and poppycock" and dismissed the author as a "slovenly and prurient rogue." Stonborough's indignation failed however to close the case. Author Ray Monk, researching his comprehensive biography *Ludwig Wittgenstein: The Duty of Genius* (1990), was given unrestricted access to all the so-called "coded remarks" of Ludwig's notebooks. Among them he found a confession of a physical relationship with a friend, Francis Skinner, in 1937: "Lay with him two or three times. Always at first with the feeling that there was nothing wrong in it, *then* the shame." Whether this indicts Ludwig of homosexual activity with rough men in the Prater seventeen years earlier is, of course, quite another matter. Frustratingly Professor Bartley refused to reveal his sources for the story and is now dead, so while some continue to disbelieve it, others (Ray Monk being chief among them) hold to the view that if Ludwig's compulsive visitations to the park ever happened, his behavior there was probably not participatory but voyeuristic.

42 A LITTLE TEACHING

The Stonboroughs' campaign to raise money in America for the Austrian famine was not entirely successful. When they arrived in December 1919 Jerome made a long statement to the *New York Times* and Gretl was described, in the *Chicago Tribune,* as an Austrian countess, which was amusing enough, but then they found that most of the Christian and Jewish German-Americans among whom they were campaigning were reluctant to give money to erstwhile enemies of America, and Jerome, who had been longing to return to the land of his birth, collapsed, within days of his arrival in New York, into a mood of deep depression and nervous paranoia. At every turn he threatened suicide. Gretl, exasperated, had him put under the permanent surveillance of a psychiatric orderly. For two months his neurotic behavior persisted. Only by February was he beginning to show slight signs of improvement, but Gretl remained "very unhappy about his condition," writing to Hermine that "during the day he was almost normal, only the nights are still terrible."

In America, the Stonboroughs must have decided that their marriage was finally over for when they returned in July 1920 Gretl took an apartment in the Palais Schönbrunn, while Jerome rented a separate flat in the Palais Erdödy where his neighbor in the same building was Albert Henry Washburn, American Ambassador to Vienna. But Jerome soon grew tired of Vienna and found himself an expensive flat in Paris. Over time the Stonboroughs accrued many secrets. In her memoir Hermine does not reveal why a "slightly psychotic" blackmailer came to Gretl's house one day, threatening to throw a stick of dynamite at her unless she paid him more money, but the story was offered as an illustration of her sister's pluck, for Gretl told the extortionist to go ahead and throw his bomb as she was not afraid.

With Jerome spending most of his time buying art in Paris and their eldest son Thomas at Cambridge University, Gretl decided to adopt a boy as a companion for her eleven-year-old son Ji, and in January 1924 she went to Berlin and returned not with one but with two aristocratic youths. They were brothers whose father had been killed in the war and whose mother was impoverished and sick. Jochen and Wedigo von Zastrow were twelve and thirteen years old at the time and Ji did not immediately take to either of them. Jerome was furious with Gretl when he heard what she had done and refused to speak to the Zastrow boys, or even to acknowledge their presence, for almost six years.

Gretl saw little of her eldest sister in Vienna for Hermine, with her low self-esteem, was refusing to heed anyone's advice. If she had ever seriously entertained the idea of marrying and having a family she realized now that she had probably missed the boat. In December 1919 she was forty-five years old and more aware than ever that her destiny was to be a maidish one: to look after her aging mother (by whom she was permanently irritated), to offer emotional succor to her younger siblings (of whom she was a little jealous), to keep the Palais open for their guests, and the Hochreit available for her Salzer, Stonborough and Zastrow nephews and nieces to enjoy in their long summer holidays. In life Hermine was lonely, and this she resented. When she felt that her siblings showed insufficient enthusiasm for her drawings, she tore them up in despair and after a while stopped painting altogether on the basis that it was a "pointless and egocentric" pastime. To force herself out of the house and to imbue her life with purpose she found herself a job as an apprentice mistress at a day-care school for children whose parents had been killed in the war. This shortly led to her setting up her own Occupational Institute for Boys in a former military hospital barrack at Grinzig. Over sixteen years the venture cost her several hundred thousand kronen and she frequently lost control of her boys. But it was a job that took her away from her mother and, although she did not love the work, it offered consolation and distraction in an otherwise empty life.

Ludwig, true to his word, spent his postwar years as a humble teacher. Having completed a training course on the Kundmanngasse, he took a job for the summer holidays of 1920 as an assistant gardener at a monastery in Klosterneuberg, sleeping nights in the potting shed. At the beginning of September, he applied, under a false name, for a teaching post at Reichenau, was awarded the job but declined it when his identity was discovered. Gossip soon spread that mad Ludwig had disowned his family. When Paul came to hear of it he sent an avuncular letter of reproach to his younger brother:

> It is out of the question, really completely out of the question that anybody bearing our name and whose elegant and gentle upbringing can be seen a thousand paces off, would not be identified as a member of our family. Even changing your name as an *ultima ratio* would gain you nothing. It is a fact, however hard it may seem, with which you must come to terms and which, as harsh as this may sound, you will have to get used to.

Ludwig failed to reply, and Paul sent a "supplement" three days later:

> That it was unavoidable that your origins and the family to which you belong should become public knowledge . . . I've already mentioned in my letter. If it hadn't been Mautner [the wife of Karl Wittgenstein's former employee] then it would have been the woodman who worked for us on the Hochreit; or the teacher who was formerly employed at the Alleegasse or a waiter in the public house who had once been a waiter in the company hotel at Kladno or in the community inn at Miesenbach, or a factory worker who had once been employed by Uncle Louis in Koritschan or Friesach or a farm girl who had previously been a milkmaid in the Trauch and who recognised you and all sorts of other possibilities. That you can neither simulate nor dissimulate anything including a refined education I need hardly tell you. Precisely for this reason it would have been more sensible if you had said straight away who and what you were. You then would have taken the sting out of the exaggerated rumours right from the start.

By the time that Ludwig was getting his brother's letters, in November 1920, he was reemployed (under his real name) as a schoolteacher in the tiny mountain village of Trattenbach. He stayed there for two years, then taught briefly at Hassbach near Neunkirchen, followed by two further years at Puchberg-am-Schneeberg and finally from November 1924 to April 1926 at a small elementary school in the village of Otterthal in Lower Austria.

All this time he ate and drank little and continued to wear his old army uniform on an almost daily basis. "Why should you care about clothing?" asks Tolstoy's *Gospel*. "Do not trouble and worry yourselves; do not say that you must think of what you will eat and how you will be clothed." Aware of his propensity to squabble with his siblings in Vienna, Ludwig kept, for the most part, out of their way.

> But I tell you [says the *Gospel in Brief*] that everyone is worthy
> of judgement who gets angry with his brother. And still more to
> blame is he who abuses his brother . . . And so it is the first com-
> mandment: do not be angry, do not abuse; but having quarrelled,
> make peace in such a way that no one may have cause for offence
> against you.

These were bad years for Ludwig. More than ever he was plagued by demons, unsettled by violent memories of war and grieving over the death of his closest friend. "Every day I think of Pinsent. He took half my life with him. The devil will take the other half." This bleak mental state can be observed through a series of confiding letters that he sent to an intellectual army friend, Paul Engelmann. "I have continually thought of taking my own life, and the idea still haunts me sometimes. I have sunk to the lowest point" and "I am in a state of mind that is terrible to me." He hoped and believed that teaching might save him from all of this, for he needed to be working every day "or else all the devils in hell will break loose inside me." As usual, he was consumed with self-loathing and described himself to Engelmann as "morally dead," "base," "stupid and rotten," and, despite Tolstoy's injunction, he could not prevent himself from detesting most of the people around him. The Trattenbachers were "obnoxious, good-for-nothing and irresponsible," the Otterthalers "inhuman beings" and the people of Hassbach "repulsive grubs."

In November 1922 *Tractatus Logico-Philosophicus,* his mystical-philosophical treatise upon which he had been working on and off throughout the war, was finally published in a German edition with an English parallel text and an introduction by Bertrand Russell. Ludwig's philosophical friends, who were at once nonplussed and deeply impressed by it, pleaded with him to abandon teaching and return to Cambridge. Ludwig was painfully aware that his work, though short and simple in layout, would be misunderstood by everyone, and this irked him. The main difficulty in the *Tractatus* was caused by his blunt refusal to define his terms or to elucidate his points with examples. He tried to explain the meaning to Paul Engelmann, who later conceded that it "went far beyond my own mental grasp." His former Cambridge colleague George Moore thought he could understand it when Ludwig went through the work with him line by line, but as soon as he had parted company from the author found himself totally muddled and quite unable to explain it to anyone else. In the end Moore had to concede that it was the indomitable force of Ludwig's will which convinced him that his friend *must* be right, whether he could understand him or not.

Even Gottlob Frege, the great German logician to whom Ludwig had sent a copy in the summer of 1919, failed to progress beyond the first page and wrote to Ludwig in frustration: "You see, from the very beginning I find myself tangled in doubt as to what it is you want to say and can make no headway with it." Ludwig complained to Russell: "he doesn't understand a word of it . . . it is very hard not to be understood by a single soul!" But Russell also was forced to admit that, after several readings, there were many "important" points that he was still unable to grasp. Ludwig tried to explain them to him, but was not entirely successful. Later he attempted to ban Russell's explanatory introduction from the first edition on the grounds that, in German translation at least, it revealed nothing but "superficiality and misunderstanding." In his notebooks Ludwig recorded a nightmare in which people failed to get his meaning, and yet he remained incapable of explaining his thoughts clearly to others. To his perpetual irritation, the central thesis of *Tractatus Logico-Philosophicus,* which concerned the limitations of language, seemed to be all too vividly demonstrated by its own impenetrability.

> My propositions serve as elucidations in the following way [Ludwig wrote at the end of the *Tractatus*]: anyone who understands me eventually recognises them as nonsensical, when he has used them, as steps, to clamber up beyond them. (He must, so to speak, throw away the ladder after he has climbed up it.)

Things were not made any clearer with an explanation that he gave to his literary friend Ludwig von Ficker: "My work consists of two parts: the one presented here plus all that I have *not* written. And it is precisely the second part that is the important one." The young Cambridge philosopher and mathematician Frank Ramsey traveled to Puchberg to talk through the work with him, spending four to five laborious hours each day going over it point by point. After two days the two men had managed only seven pages. Ramsey wrote to his mother from Austria:

> It's terrible when he says "Is that clear?" and I say "no" and he says "Damn it's horrid to go through that again." Sometimes he says: "I can't see that now, we must leave it." He often forgets the meaning of what he wrote within 5 minutes . . . Some of his sentences are intentionally ambiguous having an ordinary meaning and a more difficult meaning which he also believes.

Undeterred, Ramsey returned to Cambridge bemused, exhausted, but by now a confirmed Wittgenstein disciple. In the July 1924 edition of the philosophical journal *Mind,* he wrote a glowing review. "We really live in a great time for thinking," he added in a letter that same summer, "with Einstein, Freud and Wittgenstein all alive, and all in Germany or Austria, those foes of civilisation!"

Ramsey, like Russell, Moore, Engelmann and others, had fallen under the spell of Ludwig's striking looks, manner and extraordinarily persuasive personality. From these small beginnings was the great industry of Wittgenstein exegesis born. Thousands of books have since been written to explain the meaning of the *Tractatus,* each different from the last. Ludwig himself later disavowed parts of it in his posthumously published *Philosophical Investigations,* but still this brief, gnomic work of the First World War continues to give the philosophical world a great deal of gristle to chew upon and in this sense, at least, the influence of Wittgenstein the philosopher has been considerable.

There were of course at that time (and still are, now) many doubters—those who roll their eyes and mutter about "the Emperor's new clothes!" Ludwig's uncles, aunts and extended family of Austrian cousins were among those who were the least impressed. Many of them were simply embarrassed by what they perceived to be his eccentric behavior and thought it perverse that he, the dupe of the family—an elementary school teacher—should be honored as a great philosopher abroad. "Shaking their heads, they found it amusing that the world was taken in by the clown of their family, that *that* useless person had suddenly become famous and an intellectual giant in England."

Ludwig's nuclear family also continued to worry about him, but he had shut himself off from them, refused to answer their letters and often returned unopened the food parcels that Paul and Hermine sent him. Their best way of reaching him was through covert association with his friends. One of these was Dr. Hänsel, whom Ludwig had met during his Italian imprisonment, and whom he now treated as some kind of mentor batman, seeking his moral advice on the one hand, while ordering him on the other to send books and supplies and run errands for him on a daily basis. Another of Professor William Bartley III's sins was to have revealed in his book on Wittgenstein that the highly moral Dr. Hänsel was the author of a polemical treatise, *Die Jugend und die leibliche Liebe* (Youth and Carnal Love), which railed against homosexuality and masturbation. Hermine, who would never have read such a book, corresponded regularly with him about her youngest brother and was always grateful for his reassuring responses. "It is not easy having a saint for a brother," she told him. "There is an English proverb: 'A live dog is better than a dead lion' to which I would add, that I should rather have a happy *person* for a brother than an unhappy *saint.*"

In November 1923, Paul, who deemed the heart to be more important than the intellect, was distressed to learn that Ludwig was suffering from a painful colonic ulcer and, aware that he could do nothing directly for him, gingerly approached another of Ludwig's friends, Rudolf Koder:

Dear Mr. Koder,

I have a request and would be most pleased if you could help me. My brother Ludwig suffers from colitis, which is very dangerous when left untreated for too long as it weakens the body and attacks the nerves, even worse when the patient is tired or stressed. Because of this my brother looks terrible, run down and exhausted. This could be remedied by a special diet. The doctor says that he should, for example, eat plenty of gruel and barley soup, that he mustn't move about too much but rest and stay calm, but Ludwig complains that the whole thing is too expensive and causes too much bother.

May I ask you, dear Mr. Koder, to exert some influence on him to persuade him to take this diet. You must of course not tell him that I told you to do so. You must ask him as a friend how he is and then tell him what he should be eating and to be wary of the serious consequences of his condition. If his servant is not able to produce the right gruel soup I would be prepared to send all necessary ingredients to you, dear Mr. Koder, and then maybe he would believe that you had made it yourself. I cannot imagine that the ingredients are very difficult to obtain for such a simple dish. I trust to your diplomatic skills. You would receive our deepest thanks for this. Sorry to bother you but I could think of no other way. Maybe you will manage with your good influence that which my sister and I have been unable to achieve.

I thank you in advance. PW

Years later, Ludwig was remembered by an old man from Kirchberg as "that totally insane fellow who wanted to introduce advanced mathematics to our elementary school children." To others, particularly his brighter pupils, he was recalled with affection as an outstanding teacher. He taught them architectural styles, botany and geology, he brought a microscope from Vienna, made model steam engines; showed them how to dissect a squirrel, and boil the flesh off a fox in order to reassemble its skeleton. But for all his enthusiasm and ability, Ludwig was a tyrannical, impatient and often violent teacher. One girl whose hair he had pulled in a rage found it falling out in clumps that very evening when she combed it, another was hit so hard that she bled behind the ears. When, in April 1926, he boxed a weak and unintelligent eleven-year-old several times round the head, the boy collapsed unconscious on the floor. In a panic, Ludwig dismissed the class and carried the boy to the headmaster, bumping, en route, into the father of the girl whose ears he had previously caused to bleed. The man lost his temper, accusing Ludwig of being some kind of animal trainer rather than a teacher, and insisted on calling the police. As he rushed off to raise the alarm, Ludwig put down the unconscious boy and fled from the village. The law soon caught up with him and he was summoned to appear at the district court of Gloggnitz on May 17. At the hearing he lied to the court—something that he deeply regretted for the rest of his life—and the judge, suspecting that he might be too deranged to be held accountable for his actions, ordered an adjournment until such a time as the accused had been psychologically examined. Ludwig waited in Vienna for the doctor's summons. "I'm curious to know what the psychiatrist will say to me," he wrote to his friend Koder, "but I find the idea of the examination nauseating and am heartily sick of the whole filthy business."

43   PAUL'S RISE TO FAME

Despite the family's huge loss of fortune following Paul's ill-advised investment in government bonds, the Wittgensteins remained—by the impoverished standards of most of Vienna's middle class—extremely rich. The reasons for this were foreign investments. From the bequests of his father and three brothers, augmented by Ludwig's benefaction of 1919, Paul found himself in possession of an impressive asset portfolio. In Vienna's 1st District he owned an immense block of shops, offices and apartments in the fashionable Kohlmarkt as well as a big building at No. 1 Plankeng (since demolished and rebuilt as a modern hotel). In the 2nd District he owned an apartment block on the Stuwerstrasse and another with shops at street level at Mariahilferstrasse 58 in the 7th. Of the family dwellings he owned half of the Palais on the Alleegasse (Hermine owned the other half) and one-third of the Palais and estate at Neuwaldegg (Hermine and Helene holding the other two-thirds); but Paul's rented properties were not the cause of his wealth in the troubled years after the war, for the government had put a strict bar on rent increases so that, as the price of everything rose 14,000 times, rents remained stuck at pre-inflationary levels. By 1922 a whole year's rent on a family apartment would earn the landlord just enough to buy himself dinner at an averagely priced restaurant.

In 1912, maybe sensing some national collapse, Karl had invested a considerable part of his personal fortune in foreign stocks and shares. After his death this portfolio was managed on behalf of his heirs by his religiously minded brother Louis, as a *stille Gesellschaft*—a silent or sleeping partnership—at the Dutch bank Hope & Co. The scheme was set up to save tax. The bank knew the name only of Louis, as trustee, but was not privy to those of the Trust's individual owners. In 1919, fearing a Bolshevik uprising in Austria, and by virtue of his owning an estate whose lands spread across the border into the newly created Kingdom of Yugoslavia, Louis adopted foreign citizenship. In this way he was able, as trustee of the family fortune, to transfer the whole lot abroad. This clever move endowed the Wittgensteins with power to pay for things in Swiss francs or U.S. dollars at a time when the domestic currency of Austria was practically worthless.

After his return from soldiering in 1918, Paul became withdrawn and cautious concerning his future career as a pianist. It was rumored that he had shaved off all his hair and locked himself into a distant room of the Palais, where he practiced for nine hours a day, refusing to see anyone, even the servants, who were under strict orders to push his food through a crack in the door and leave without entering. This was an exaggeration. His hair was indeed cropped extremely short, as it had been in Siberia. It is also true that the strain of playing the piano with one hand had forced him into a radical revision of his technique, and that between August 1918 and April 1922 he did not give any large-scale public performances. Hermine was probably referring to this period in Paul's life when she wrote that he had come so close to suicide that "it is perhaps only due to an accident that [he] remained in this world and finally came to terms with life."

Doubts flooded his mind as to whether his one-handed piano enterprise was ever going to work. He gave a few private performances in the Alleegasse Palais during this period and was egged on by his ever-enthusiastic mentor Josef Labor, who continued to ply him with new works, some especially written for his disability, others being rearrangements for one hand of music he had previously composed for two. These included two trios, a quartet, a quintet divertimento, a third piano concerto and a fantasie for piano solo.

Paul knew, however, that he could not survive off Labor alone, and yet was able to find little else to play. In an effort to build a concert repertoire he had scoured the antiquarian music stores of Paris, Vienna, Berlin and London for works written for the left hand alone. Predictably he found only a small handful of pieces: two short works by Scriabin composed after he had sprained the wrist of his right hand, an arrangement by Brahms written for Clara Schumann, six studies by Saint-Saëns; the Godowsky arrangements of Chopin, one and a half pieces by Charles Alkan and some mediocre things by unknown and untalented composers such as Alexander Dreyschock, Adolfo Fumagalli and Count Zichy. As to Paul's own arrangements of works by Mozart, Mendelssohn, Liszt, Wagner and others, these had taken him a great deal of time and effort to compose and, while they helped him to improve his technique, he was among the first to recognize that they were not especially good. Moreover they were arrangements, and as such they were compromised versions of original works. "Interesting, but not as good as the original," people would say. If there were to be any hope for Paul's one-handed career he would need to commission new works from great composers.

On June 29, 1922, Josef Labor celebrated his eightieth birthday. In Vienna, the occasion was marked with a week-long binge of his music culminating in a premiere performance at the church of Sankt Josef ob der Laimgrube, of a Mass that he had composed in 1918. All the Wittgensteins attended. Four days earlier Paul had contributed to a concert in Labor's honor at the ceremonial hall of the Hofburg Palace and on the twenty-third gave a "very nice" performance of the concerto that Labor had composed for him in 1915 with the Vienna Ladies' Symphony Orchestra under Julius Lehnert. The composer, however, was too ill to attend. His friends thought he might be dying.

Labor's health had been in steady decline for years and it was now obvious (if it had not been so earlier) that the Wittgensteins' championing of his work was not going to make him an international celebrity during his lifetime, that he did not have many new pieces left in him and that Paul's career could not be sustained by playing his music and his alone. The name Josef Labor on a concert program was box-office death even then, and although Paul played his music with tremendous passion, audiences often found it bewildering. Even Ludwig admitted that his music was "subtler than anything else" and therefore "particularly hard to understand."

But just as everyone was expecting his death, the blind old master was advised by a homeopath to change his diet and suddenly rallied. The Wittgensteins were overjoyed. "Labor's feeling well again!" exclaimed Hermine, while her mother enthused: "One cannot praise enough the miracle which the homeopath has achieved in his case. The complete change of diet has immediately improved his physical and emotional state and Labor has become his old self, the youthful musician."

Indeed, Labor felt so well on this new diet that he started immediately working on another piano concerto for Paul.

> *My dear Labor,*
>   *The joy it gives me to know that you are again engaged in writing something for me needs to find some expression and I should like to give you a little something to make you happy. Please be so kind as to accept the enclosed package from your ever faithful former pupil, Paul Wittgenstein.*

The package is said to have contained a lock of Beethoven's hair, but despite this characteristic act of generosity the blind composer remained a jealous man. If there were any truth in the notion that the Wittgensteins felt a sense of "owning" Labor, the same certainly pertained in reverse. Paul was *his* prodigy, and the old man did not approve of his "ever faithful" former pupil's plan to commission new works from a raft of other composers more distinguished than himself. His resistance took time to overcome, but when engaged on his final concerto for Paul the eighty-year-old composer acknowledged that it would be his last large-scale work for the left hand and gave his solemn sanction for Paul to commission other works from whomsoever he chose.

Between December 1922 and Easter 1923, Paul approached three prominent composers and one less well known, with invitations to write concertos for piano and orchestra (left hand) in exchange for highly prized U.S. dollars, and by the late spring of 1923 all four of them (Paul Hindemith, Erich Wolfgang Korngold, Franz Schmidt and Sergei Bortkiewicz) were working industriously on his behalf. Since the purpose of each commission was to advance Paul's career, the choice of composers needed to be carefully made. His favorite music—upon which subject he was a recognized expert—was that of the early Romantic, late Classical period. He detested so-called modern music and although he was personally acquainted with Arnold Schoenberg (another protégé of Labor's), as well as other members of the Second Viennese School, he would never have considered commissioning music from any of them.

Erich Korngold, the son of Julius, chief music critic of the *Neue Freie Presse,* was still in his twenties when Paul commissioned him, but the Viennese public had already embraced him as their greatest musical prodigy since Mozart. Mahler proclaimed him a genius at ten, and Richard Strauss, hearing two works composed at the age of fourteen, confessed to mixed feelings of awe and fear. With his opera *Die tote Stadt* (first performed in 1920) Korngold achieved world renown. His music may have been a little more modern than Paul would have liked, but for $3,000 he could at least be sure that the work would reach a wide audience, for as the precocious composer had himself confirmed: "Every conductor in Germany will automatically perform a new piece by me."

The works of Franz Schmidt were, and still are, very highly rated in Austria and it is a shame that his beautiful, natural, personal and instinctive music is so infrequently performed elsewhere in the world. By commissioning a new work from Schmidt (price $6,000) Paul could guarantee himself dates in the major venues of German-speaking countries.

Hindemith, a rising young German of the avant-garde, was a riskier choice. Whereas Paul was convinced that music should appeal to the heart, Hindemith's works of that period were aggressively cerebral. He first met Paul at a concert in Vienna in December 1922, at which he was playing the viola part of his own Second Quartet. That this dense, tortured work should have appealed to Paul's conservative tastes is surprising. With the money that Paul offered him, Hindemith planned to buy and restore a fifteenth-century watchtower, known as the Kuhhirtenturm, in the Sachsenhausen district of Frankfurt. This he succeeded in doing, but the tower was blown up by Allied bombers in 1943.

The fourth composer on Paul's list, Sergei Bortkiewicz, wrote attractive music in the tuneful Romantic idiom of Tchaikovsky, Liszt and Rachmaninoff. He came from the landed gentry of Kharkov in the Ukraine and, after troubled times in Berlin, Russia and Turkey, settled in Vienna in the summer of 1922. Since his death in 1952, Bortkiewicz's music is all forgotten, except by a small claque of ardent campaigners.

As the four men set about composing their concertos, Paul, with equal energy, devoted himself to arranging their premieres. The Hindemith (*Piano Music with Orchestra*) was scheduled for the beginning of the new season in Weimar and Vienna, the Bortkiewicz would be premiered in Vienna in November 1923, Schmidt's piece (a set of variations on a theme taken from Beethoven's "Spring" Sonata) was booked for its first airing three months later in February 1924, and Korngold's concerto for September. The stage was set and Paul had much to look forward to, but first he had to concentrate on the world premiere of his blind mentor's Third Piano Concerto on November 10, 1923, with the Vienna Symphony Orchestra under Rudolf Nilius at Vienna's recently built Grosser Konzerthaussaal. It was Labor's last completed work, composed in his eighty-first year, and Paul thought very highly of it.

As each of the composers submitted his score, arguments broke out. Hindemith had anticipated problems even before sending his first draft. Writing on May 4, 1923, he warned Paul: "I think I should have everything ready by the end of next week. I would be sorry if you weren't pleased with the piece. It may perhaps sound a little strange to you at first, but I have composed it very lovingly and like it myself very much." In the same letter he asked if Paul could advance him at least half the money right away so that his builders could start work on the watchtower. Paul replied that he was frightened that he might not understand the new work. Soon Hindemith was able to dispatch a first draft with a note attached:

I hope that your terror will have abated once you have looked through the score. It is a simple and thoroughly uncomplicated piece and I firmly believe that after a while it will give you pleasure—perhaps you might be a little horrified to start with but that does not matter—you will most definitely understand the piece.

As far as the money was concerned Paul behaved honorably, paying in full, on time, and receiving in exchange the manuscript, the orchestral parts and exclusive performance rights in the work for his lifetime, but he was horrified by Hindemith's music. After many hours of diligent practice he decided that the piece was simply incomprehensible and canceled the scheduled premiere. Hindemith's piece, *Piano Music with Orchestra,* remained undiscovered and unperformed until December 2004.

With the composers Korngold and Schmidt, Paul also had arguments. In both cases he felt that the composers had overscored their works and that the piano could not be heard above the sound of the orchestra. Although Josef Labor had been upset by cuts that Paul had made in his music, the question of balance never arose as he always wrote for a small chamber orchestra. Schmidt, eager to please, acquiesced in Paul's demands and accepted many changes. Korngold, however, was affronted. His concerto was scored for a massive band including four horns, three trumpets, contrabassoon, harp, celesta, glockenspiel and xylophone. Paul complained that "the contrast between the sound of the piano and the sound of the orchestra is so great that the piano sounds like a chirping cricket," and drew heavy red lines through the parts that he did not like. Korngold was indignant at these mutilations, but Paul wrote to assuage him.

> *Dear Herr Korngold,*
>
> *Please find enclosed the second score of your concerto. As far as the brackets which I have written in are concerned, I would ask you, even if it goes very much against the grain, to have them copied out as well. If I play the piece with you conducting, you can nonetheless, as you see fit, still have the bracketed sections played. But if I were to play the piece behind your back, then I would leave out the bracketed instruments. Don't take fright at the ravages and don't be angry with yours sincerely, Paul Wittgenstein*

The premiere of Franz Schmidt's Beethoven Variations on February 2, 1924, was an elevating success. The critic of the *Neues Wiener Tagblatt* praised the composer for his "supremely musical talent," adding that "Paul Wittgenstein, who achieved with one hand the polyphony of two, was encored together with the conductor in a storm of triumph which he had inspired."

The Korngold piece, a tense fusion of rich noise and deliberately ugly eroticism, was even more successful. The premiere in the Golden Hall was conducted by the composer, and the program included other firsts of works by Karl Prohaska, Hugo Kauder and Alma Mahler, but it was the Korngold Concerto that stole the headlines. The critic of the *Neue Freie Presse* hailed it as an "astonishing, concisely crafted and truly inspired work," pointing out (as if he knew about Paul's quarrel with the composer over balance) that "Paul Wittgenstein ensured, with verve, that his solo instrument retained the predominance it deserved." The critic of the *Neues Wiener Tagblatt* filed an eccentric rave review that appeared in the newspaper eight days later:

> Paul Wittgenstein, having been robbed of his right arm—one might even say robbed of more than his life—by an idiotic shot during the war, but overcoming fate by sheer artistic heroism, has become a virtuoso of the remaining left hand and has raised his one-sidedness to a state of completion, indeed of unattainability. And now the great brotherhood of the artistic heart has come to his aid: Korngold dedicated this concerto to him . . . Paul Wittgenstein played "his" work with a technique to which joy had lent wings: with your eyes shut you would have guessed that two hands were needed. We were all replete with the joy of a great talent.

Paul had ensured that the scores and parts belonged to him and had negotiated exclusive performing rights to all these works. Concert promoters were eager to stage them and he soon found himself in demand at concert halls throughout Europe. This gave him the confidence to invite Richard Strauss, the world's most successful living composer, to attend the Korngold premiere, and to ask him whether he too might consider composing a left-hand piano concerto.

Paul knew Strauss slightly because he had stayed with his parents at the Alleegasse Palais on his occasional visits to Vienna before the war. This did not, however, entitle him to a cheap deal. "Strauss is very avaricious," Paul reported; "he certainly thinks of money-making, but he does that *before* and *after* composing, not *while* he composes. And that's the important point." In the end Strauss accepted the commission for a sensational advance of $25,000, and set to work composing an intense, brooding concerto, which he entitled *Parergon zur Sinfonia Domestica,* by which he meant an adjunct, or companion piece, to a symphony that he had composed twenty years earlier. Both the *Sinfonia Domestica* of 1903 and the new *Parergon* shared thematic material and in musical circles rumors quickly spread that Strauss had taken a fortune off Paul only to rework an old piece. Paul defended the composer, arguing that the criticism was "unjust" and that the concerto "has great beauties." This did not, however, prevent him from berating Strauss for perceived inadequacies in his score. Once again Paul insisted that the orchestra was too heavy and that the piano part was drowned out. After many painful discussions Strauss reluctantly agreed to transfer an important theme from the orchestral score to the piano part and to allow Paul to thin the texture himself by deleting lines from the score. The *Parergon* contains a breathless solo part of the utmost variety and technical difficulty, but Paul complained that it was not brilliant enough. He wanted something that would create a sensation, something far more dazzling, and pushed Strauss to rework it. In a typical trilingual explanation Paul later revealed that the *Parergon* "had to be changed *de fond en comble* as they say in French to make *ein brauchbareres Kon-zert* out of it" (changed from top to bottom to make a decent concerto of it).

Strauss seems to have taken Paul's criticisms in good heart, although some of the alterations that the pianist demanded were far too complicated to resolve in the short time before the Dresden premiere, scheduled for October 6, 1925. Instead he offered to compose a second left-hand concerto entitled *Panathenäenzug* (pan-Athenian procession), which might better suit Paul's needs. Whether the composer demanded a further $25,000 for it is not known, but it seems likely that he did, for shortly after the Berlin premiere Strauss started building himself a mansion on Vienna's Jacquingasse known as Richard Strauss Castle.

Panathenäenzug, an enchanting, humorous, quasi-jazzy piece, suffered once again, in Paul's view, from clumsy orchestration. "How can I with my one poor hand hope to compete with a quadruple orchestra?" he asked. The premiere with Bruno Walter and the Berlin Philharmonic on January 15, 1928, was a critical flop. Paul was sneeringly referred to as "Dr. Strauss's left hand" and the Berlin critics asserted that the music at last proved what they had long suspected: that the sixty-four-year-old composer was suffering from premature dementia; and that the pianist was nothing but a rich dilettante. Adolf Weissmann, critic of the *Berliner Zeitung am Mittag,* was especially hostile: "It is easy to understand that this pianist who had the misfortune to lose his right arm in the war does everything to stay in the limelight. It is hard to understand however how Strauss could have produced such an absolute failure . . . this *Panathenäenzug* goes beyond the limits of our endurance."

Paul shrugged off the Berlin reviews as "uninteresting opinions of uninteresting persons, written with the presumption and arrogance of an infallible pope," and Strauss wrote to console him: "I am so sorry that the Berlin press tore you and my piece so to shreds. I know that the *Panathenäenzug* is not bad, but I didn't think it was so good that it would be accorded the honour of unanimous rejection." Two months later in Vienna *Panathenäenzug* was a critical and public success. Paul was lauded in the pages of the *Neues Wiener Tagblatt* for his "astonishing bravura" and by an ecstatic Julius Korngold in the *Neue Freie Presse*:

> Paul Wittgenstein finds here a wealth of activity for his fabulous left hand. It dominates the keys, dominates the orchestra. Astonishing the energy and skill of the artist who, if we close our eyes, deceives us into imagining a two-handed pianist: indeed sometimes in the power of his attack, into imagining two two-handed pianists. He was a roaring success with the audience.

The price of these commissions may have been exorbitant but the effect was exactly as Paul had planned. Within five years he was being acclaimed as a serious, major artist on the international concert scene. News of the Strauss commissions was reported in newspapers all around the world and by the end of the decade he had appeared on concert platforms with conductors Erich Kleiber, Bruno Walter and Wilhelm Furtwängler in

Berlin, with Fritz Busch in Dresden, with Pierre Monteux in Amsterdam, with Sir Henry Wood in London, with Adrian Boult in Birmingham, with Felix Weingartner in Basel, with Rhené-Baton in Paris and with Richard Strauss as a conductor in Trieste, Turin and Prague. A United States concert tour was set for October 1928. The *New York Times* reported that "Paul Wittgenstein has been much sought here for his American debut." Audiences adored him. His presence on stage was commanding. When he played softly he melted the hearts of everyone who heard him, while his wiry, leaping, percussive *fortissimi*—which so irritated his family when they heard him practicing at home—provided a thrilling, anarchic spectacle in the formal setting of a large concert hall. The sheer speed at which he was able to move his fingers across the keyboard was breathtaking. Paul may have bought his way to fame but, with dedication, skill and artistry that were a match for any living pianist, he had earned his right to it. By 1928 he had climbed with his single hand to the top of the tree; he was living his dream, and for the time being at least appeared to be happy. "Having to work," he wrote in September 1927, "and moreover to earn money—so much the more if it be for a good purpose—is the best thing on earth."

44 THE DEATH OF MRS. WITTGENSTEIN

In the years following the First World War the Wittgensteins suffered a number of blows. Karl's brother-in-law, the cognac-nosed General von Siebert, died in 1920. Soon afterward his wife, Aunt Lydia, put her head in a gas oven because she could no longer cope with caring on her own for their deaf-and-dumb daughter. The following year, in July 1921, Helene's twenty-year-old son, Fritz Salzer, died of polio, which had developed in the days before his death into acute flaccid paralysis of all four extremities, lungs and heart. On April 26, 1924—Ludwig's birthday of all days—the old and beloved Josef Labor died after a week's fever at his home on the Kirchengasse. Hermine sketched him on his deathbed with tears filling her eyes. A septet that he was halfway through composing for Paul lay unfinished on his desk. Less than a year later Karl's brother, Uncle Louis, drew his last breath and one of Mrs. Wittgenstein's nephews died in a mountaineering accident. All these incidents, especially the death of Labor, affected her adversely; but, in truth, she had never recovered from the shock of Kurt's suicide in 1918.

To have three sons commit suicide must strain the nerves of even the steeliest mother. The deaths of Hans and Rudi had tainted her soul with ineradicable sorrow, shame and guilt, but in the case of Kurt her burden was far worsened by the fact of her having actively encouraged him to return to Austria to fight, like his brothers, for the honor of a now-vanished empire. News of Kurt's death seems to have broken her heart; from that moment her health and spirits slumped along a trajectory of slow and irreversible decline. Within four years her legs were crippled, her eyes almost blind and her mind decrepit and senile. All interest in life had deserted her. Her family tried to rekindle the old spark by fostering a closer friendship with a grumpy, slightly insane but once distinguished soprano called Marie Fillunger. To this end they rented her a flat on the Landstrasse-Hauptstrasse from which she could visit their mother every morning and enliven her with talk of Brahms and Joachim and the good old days. Mrs. Wittgenstein had met Miss Fillunger apparently for the first time only after Karl's death, though it is possible that Ludwig knew her from his student days in Manchester, where she was a singing teacher at the Royal Manchester College of Music and where she lived with her lesbian lover, Eugenie Schumann (the composer's daughter), a few streets from Ludwig's lodgings on the Wilmslow Road. Grumpy Miss Fillunger's companionship briefly enlivened Mrs. Wittgenstein, whose deadened eyes apparently lit up as she accompanied her in songs by Schumann and Brahms. Mrs. Wittgenstein's piano playing was no longer accurate and Miss Fillunger's robust voice had lost the luster that had once inspired Brahms to entrust her with the premieres of many of his greatest works, but the relationship between the two old ladies was, according to Hermine, delightful. "My mother tried to smooth the surface of this very rough diamond with friendliness and humour and she was rewarded for this with Miss Fillunger's most unsentimental love."

By the spring of 1926, as Ludwig was disgracing himself with knock-out blows to the students of Trattenbach, Mrs. Wittgenstein was too far gone to feel the dishonor. Her eyes stared disconcertingly through and beyond the faces of the doctors, family and the friends who came to visit her.

To calm her frequent fits of agitation they played her records. Short bursts of soft music had a calming effect, but in her final crankiness she could no longer distinguish between a phonograph and a live performance. Suspecting that musicians were present in the room, she would interrupt in order to thank them and, when she had had enough, would turn to the phonograph and ask it in her most gracious tones: "Gentlemen, I am old and sick and easily tired, so for heaven's sake, please do not hold it against me if I ask you to stop."

In mid-May she was staying at the white, bright and airy Wittgenstein palace at Neuwaldegg when her health took a further turn for the worse. On the 22nd she was needy and frightened and Hermine had to hold her hand for the whole afternoon; on the 26th things were bad again all day—she kept screaming that someone was trying to kill her, alternately grumbling, whimpering and begging for mercy. Her family gathered around. Two days later in the afternoon she fell asleep only to awake next morning with a fever. For three days thereafter she lay in a coma. Those days "were very good to me," Gretl explained in a letter to her elder son. "It was weird. Mama slept very deeply. Her soul seemed very far away. We sat on her bed and her quasi-death seemed beautiful to me because it brought good thoughts to mind." After a surge in her pulse on June 2, Mrs. Wittgenstein's children decided to stay all night by her bed and at seven the following morning she stopped breathing and they all crawled exhausted to their rooms. Paul, at the moment of his mother's death, resolved that he would never visit Hochreit again for as long as he lived—and he honored his vow. Ludwig wrote to a friend, "It was a gentle death," and Gretl told her son, "It was a very beautiful night!"

> Yes [Hermine wrote in her memoir], it can be said that my mother had been, in many respects, almost something of a saint, and she was loved as such, honoured and mourned by an infinite number of people. This picture, however, would not be complete if I failed to mention some eccentricities that made life difficult for my mother and often made it difficult for us children just being with her.

45 FROM BOOM TO BUST

Mrs. Wittgenstein was seventy-six years old when she died and two days later, on the warm afternoon of June 5, 1926, her boxed-up corpse was placed next to the remains of her husband and her old servant Rosalie Hermann in the family grave at Group 32b, no. 24, in Vienna's Zentralfriedhof. Close and opposite (Group 15e, no. 7) lay the mortal remains of Josef Labor, the inspiration of her days.

In September, Paul played Franz Schmidt's Beethoven Variations with the Vienna Philharmonic, with the composer conducting. The pianist Marie Baumayer wrote to Hermine: "Paul played so splendidly today; more beautifully than ever. It was magnificent and the Philharmonic players were terrific as well. How Mama would have been delighted." But in truth Mama's mind in its last years was too far gone to enjoy any of Paul's successes in the concert hall or to feel any tinge of regret at Ludwig's ignominy. A letter from Dr. Hänsel to Ludwig two months after her death suggests that court proceedings were still continuing against him for concussing his pupil at Otterthal in April. After that the trial on his case goes dead. Either it was abandoned or records were artfully removed from the slate. In either case it is probable that Paul, Gretl, Hermine, Helene and the Wittgenstein fortune had a hand in covering it up. The chief witness, Josef Haidbauer, the boy who was knocked unconscious, died shortly afterward of hemophilia. Even if Ludwig had wished to return to teaching, it is unlikely that he would have been offered another job.

Mrs. Wittgenstein left her youngest son some money in her will but Ludwig, true to form, refused to accept any of it. On leaving the school at Otterthal, he accepted, once again, a job as assistant gardener, this time at the monastery of the Brothers of Mercy at Hütteldorf on the outskirts of Vienna, where he pondered two options: to become a monk or to commit suicide. Aware of his distress, Gretl offered him a chance to work with the architects Paul Engelmann and Jacques Groag on a luxurious modern-style palace that she was building for herself on the Kundmanngasse. Fearful that he might quarrel with her and with his coworkers Ludwig initially refused, but subsequently changed his mind. Proudly describing himself as "Ludwig Wittgenstein, Architect," he proceeded to make exacting demands, haggling over every millimeter of every lock and radiator fitting, insisting that a recently plastered ceiling be undone and raised by a few centimeters, so that by the time the task was completed it had run overtime and over budget and everyone involved was thoroughly depressed and exhausted. A locksmith "jumped with fright" when Ludwig bawled at him and Jacques Groag wrote a letter complaining, "I come home very depressed with a headache after a day of the worst quarrels, disputes, vexations, and this happens often. Mostly between me and Wittgenstein." When Gretl eventually refused to pay for any more of Ludwig's expensive adjustments, he went off and bought himself a lottery ticket ("a tax on unfortunate, self-conceited fools" as Sir William Petty once described it) in the vain hope of winning enough to pay for the work himself.

The house, from the outside, consisted of three stark, unadorned rectangular blocks. Hermine, who disliked it intensely, recorded in her memoir that "two great people [Ludwig and Gretl] had come together as architect and client, making it possible to create something perfect of its kind." She claimed that it fitted her sister like a glove, but when her nephew Tommy Stonborough came to sell it after his mother's death he did so on the grounds (since contested) that Gretl had always loathed it.

The plain right-angled contours of Gretl's new house were certainly not to everyone's taste. Paul thought it was abysmal, and so did Jerome. The work was completed in 1928 and on Christmas Eve of that year the family gathered there to celebrate. Gretl felt the Christmas had been "shit" and "a dismal failure." Jerome ostentatiously handed presents to everyone except the Zastrow boys, whom he still refused to acknowledge. The next day he accepted Paul's invitation to dine at the Palais in the Alleegasse (now renamed Argentinierstrasse), which alarmed Gretl, as she knew that the atmosphere there irritated him and usually sent him crazy. She was right to have worried. All through dinner Jerome railed against her pretentious new house and with "Ludwig Wittgenstein, Architect" sitting directly opposite, she found herself twisting in agonies of embarrassment. On the way home in the car she confronted him: "How could you have said all that!" The effect was like throwing a lighted match into a can of petrol, she explained to Tommy: "all the anger that he felt against himself exploded on to me and the world. I felt my mistake but was too exasperated to hold myself back. Poor Ji struggled to control his tears."

Ludwig was sensitive. His dislike of family contention (even though he was often the cause of it), and the siren call of the philosophical brotherhood, finally persuaded him to return to Cambridge to work on "visual space and other things," and so he left Vienna in early January 1929. At the same time Paul, with whom he was now on excellent terms, went to Munich to give a performance of the Bortkiewicz Concerto. Gretl stayed in Vienna living the high life, befriending important people, planning private concerts and receptions at her new house. For ten months things went smoothly for her until, in late October, a telegram arrived from New York informing her that her American stock portfolio had imploded and she had lost most of her fortune in the Wall Street Crash.

Of course it was all Jerome's fault—or so Gretl's brothers and sisters told her. He was inept and incompetent with money and should never have been allowed near her fortune. They expected her to take a tough line with him—to give him one of her famous "tickings-offs." Instead she insisted: "He is my husband and I cannot destroy a human relationship over money." She calculated that she would be left with an income of around $30,000 a year, that she would have to rent out the new house in Vienna, dismiss all but three of her servants, sell some pictures of Paul and Hermine to pay off the rest, and move into a smaller flat. At first she announced that she would refuse offers of help from her siblings but in the end accepted from Paul, Hermine and Helene a share of the fortune that Ludwig had given them in 1919, from which she was originally excluded.

At the time Gretl claimed "not to be unhappy at all." She said she had too much money anyway, "more than I should have." She enjoyed a challenge and this was certainly one. "Don't ask for life to be easier if you are capable of being strong," she would say. Jerome, however, was not made of the same mettle, nor was he capable of such strength as hers, and the loss of his wife's fortune—which forced him to consider giving up his flat and luxurious lifestyle in Paris—sent him, once again, into a spiral of mental decline. Gretl put him into the Cottage Sanatorium on the

Sternwartestrasse, where he was subjected to several weeks of Dr. Wagner-Jauregg's shock treatments. After that she took him to Egypt to recuperate.

Everyone was nervous about the following Christmas (1929). It had all gone so badly wrong the year before. As early as November, Ludwig wrote to Hermine and Paul suggesting they each bring a friend to dilute the tension. Nobody wanted Jerome to come as he was in double disgrace, for losing his wife's fortune and for behaving like a pig last time round. Gretl was traumatized by her family's naked hostility toward him, but eventually she succeeded in persuading Ludwig to get him invited. Under instruction from his wife to be on his best behavior Jerome acquitted himself well. Christmas, for once, was peaceful and intimate, and Jerome had the grace to say hello to the Zastrow boys for the first time in his life.

46 MORE ON PAUL'S CHARACTER

Once or twice a year, every year, Paul visited a friend in England, Marga Deneke. They were close, though unlikely to have been lovers. She kept a framed silhouette of Paul on her desk, which he had sent her with the comment "I think I look very stupid." Marga was five years older than Paul, of German extraction but brought up in England. She was a musicologist as well as a fine pianist who had played for Clara Schumann and studied with Eugenie Schumann in her youth. She and her sister Helena, a German scholar, had inherited a small fortune from their father, who had been a rich merchant banker, and lived their adult lives together in a Gothic villa called Gunfield, near Lady Margaret Hall in Oxford. There, in the spacious music room, Marga and Helena hosted the concerts of the Oxford Chamber Music Society.

There were many lines of connection between the Denekes and the Wittgensteins, any one of which may have accounted for Paul and Marga's first meeting. There was, of course, the Eugenie Schumann–Marie Fillunger connection. Marga was also a collector of Mendelssohn manuscripts (of which Paul owned several), her mother was a friend of Karl's cousin the violinist Joachim, and she was a friend of the clarinettist Richard Mühlfeld and violinist Marie Soldat-Roeger, regular guests and performers at the Wittgenstein Palais.

For many years Paul joined her and a small group of close companions for holidays of music and nature walks at Overstrand, at St. Margarets-at-Cliffe, near Dover, and at Southwold on the North Sea coast. He was sensitive to nature and very knowledgeable about it. He could name flora and fauna in German, English or French. He adored sunsets and the sea and was observant of the smallest detail. According to Marga, walks calmed his nerves. In this respect he differed from his brother Ludwig, who walked not for exercise or for love of nature, but to discuss his ideas. Ludwig required his companions to participate, not just to listen. "I remember," wrote one of his friends, "how mentally difficult and tiring such walks could be." Paul, on the other hand, did not like to dilute his enjoyment of nature with idle chatter and refused to walk with more than one person on the grounds that "talk for three is tiresome."

> Rain was disregarded [Marga recalled]. He held in contempt any able-bodied person who let it foil plans. Off we set for Dover Castle and completely drenched, on the windswept cliffs far from home, he declared we had talked enough. It was a long way to St. Margarets-at-Cliffe, he walked ahead and I followed like a dripping dog.

Paul insisted on a long walk every day and if anyone was brave enough to accompany him, be it three miles to a restaurant in Manhattan, marching up the White Mountains of New Hampshire, or clambering to the top of the 6,500-foot Schmittenhöhe mountain at Zell am See, his companion was obliged to keep pace and to keep quiet. If the opportunity availed itself, he would also go for a swim in the morning. On Tuesdays he denied himself food and usually went to the cinema, to the theater or to a concert, to distract himself from sensations of hunger. During the film he sat still and absorbed until a few minutes before the end, when he habitually got up and left, regardless of how much he had been enjoying it.

He was what the Germans call *weltfremd*—he lived in a world of his own, quite detached from the details and needs of everyday life and with little idea how everyday living was conducted.

> He was like no one else I have ever known [recalled one of his students]. Shortly after his arrival in New York, I had a lesson in the mid-town hotel where he was temporarily staying. After the lesson we left at the same time. On the way down in the elevator he told me that he was desperate because he needed another pair of shoes and the Vienna Sekretariat [the Wittgenstein staff] had been slow in sending anything. When I asked him "Why don't you buy a pair here on 5th Avenue?" he looked at me in utter astonishment and said "What a wonderful idea. I never thought of that."

There are many stories that attest to Paul's impracticality: his trying to use his front-door key to operate the lift and refusing to understand why it wouldn't work; tangling himself in the string from which a learned book was hung around his neck; walking out into the street in a hat unaware that it was still attached to the hatbox in which it came; being greeted at the airport in Montreal by his American agent, Bernard Laberge, not looking at him properly and wandering off with a member of the public—chatting to him about the evening's concert and trying to get into his car, while Laberge ran frantically round the airport looking for him. At a dinner party in Paul's honor the hostess came into the dining room with a large casserole of goulash. "This," she announced proudly, "has been cooked especially for you." Paul thanked her kindly, put the dish in front of him and proceeded to eat the lot as the rest of the company—too polite to remonstrate—watched in anguished astonishment. He was a serious man but not without a sense of humor. He had a gift for delivering rapid unannounced sentences in a nonsense tongue of his own creation. Leonard Kastle, one of his American students in the late 1940s, remembers him as "the most charming man . . . he was my artistic and spiritual father, and undoubtedly the greatest influence on my life."

Paul was incapable of dissembling. He always spoke his mind and this often led to problems. Marga, who was not afraid of him and took each of his eccentricities in her stride, conceded that he was "difficult . . .

but between him and me acquaintance mellowed into good friendship. He was loyal to his friends and I was older than he and could hold my tongue when he lost his temper." It was never easy to guess when or why Paul would lose it, but storm clouds were never far off and, as his confidante and chief appeaser, Marga found she had "much to do." She smoothed over misunderstandings between Paul and his hotel manager, Paul and a bus conductor, or Paul and any number of her friends. One such saga is recounted with humor:

> One evening at Southwold I asked Paul to play to the Congregational Minister who had kindly lent me a piano so that Paul could use mine. When the minister and his wife came Paul hardly took his eyes off his book and, looking very cross, he hurled himself on the piano stool and gave an almost savage rendering of the Chopin-Godowsky Warsaw Study. Then he left the room abruptly without further ceremony. My sister was horrified: "This was the acme of rudeness!" she said. The next day Paul answered my rebuke by saying he had played as I requested, he never promised to join our futile gossip. In my role as placator I called at the manse with a bunch of carnations from Paul. I was received with great friendliness. They would not accept an apology. The evening had been most enjoyable, the playing marvellous. They took it for granted that such behaviour was just a way of showing off.

Paul was aware of his inability to get on easily with other people and it forced him, despite his charm, erudition and energy for life, to seek a solitary existence. He would never stay in other people's houses but insisted on booking himself and his valet, Franz Kalchschmidt, into a nearby hotel, having a piano brought in, and seeing his friends only when it suited him. When traveling by train, even with his family, he would insist on booking a private carriage for himself. One of his pupils, conductor Steve Portman, remembers Paul having "a shell around him, like a suit of armour that did not permit him to interact with other people—nobody would challenge him for he had an authority that very few people possess." Portman came from a poor and troubled New York background. His lessons with Paul were free. One Christmas he was given an expensive tie. "Oh I've never had anything like this!" Portman exclaimed. "I don't give rubbish!" Paul replied. "My memories of Paul Wittgenstein are absolutely positive," Portman recalls. "He could not have been more forthcoming or helpful."

Paul invited Marga to accompany him on a tour of Holland in April 1929. She asked if she could bring a friend, Michael Lindsay, the Master of Balliol (later Lord Lindsay of Birker), which Paul accepted. On the whole they had a very good time until Marga, thinking that Paul's valet looked lonely and bored, asked him if he would like to come to the cinema.

> Paul was indignant; facing me in real anger he told me it was irksome enough that I had brought Michael but that I should now make friends with his valet was clearly impossible. He shouted "You can choose, I admit, between Franz and me." I interrupted hurriedly, "If it comes to that I shall have you as my companion."

It is easy to understand how many people took against Paul and his brother Ludwig for their outspoken manner, but both had magnetic personalities, and both had their own claque of ardent admirers. In a letter recommending a friend to call on Paul and Ludwig during a visit to Vienna, the distinguished composer and critic Donald Francis Tovey wrote:

> Both of them are, I think, really great people; about as bristling with vitality as Dickens (whose complete works Paul Wittgenstein could probably recite). Ludwig I have only once met. Paul I hope I am not mistaken in thinking to be a close friend; I speak cautiously only because people of my age ought not to presume upon the confiding enthusiasms of the younger generation.

Those who befriended Paul and who could see beyond his neurosis and quick temper found him loyal, generous and warmhearted. He had a habit of sending his friends surprise presents through the post of musical instruments, precious manuscripts, food parcels and money. He never charged any of his pupils for the dedicated lessons that he gave them and in one case gave several thousand dollars to a student in order that he might attend the Spoleto Festival in Italy.

In a 1944 school essay Leonard Kastle, his star student at the time, wrote: "He still makes me shudder when I commit the slightest mistake. But behind that temper is the kindest heart ever to be found," and in her diary four years earlier another student, Philippa Schuyler, commented, "I wept a little at his loud voice. Then he said 'Darling, you must not mind if your teacher shouts a little. He can't help it!' Then when you are ready to leave he kisses you." In her fond recollection of Paul, written shortly after his death, Marga concluded:

> Paul's personality is unforgettable. Those who met him felt it instantly; frequently the impression warded off contact. Highly sensitive to his physical disability, he made self-contained independence his rule of life and met tragedy with fortitude. For those whom he admitted to friendship he was the staunchest of friends.

47 RUSSIA AND RAVEL

Marga went to New York in September 1927 to raise money for Lady Margaret Hall in Oxford, and took with her some records of Paul playing music by Josef Labor with the violinist Marie Soldat-Roeger, which had been made under the auspices of Clara Wittgenstein. Clara (who was three years younger than Karl) was an outstanding maiden aunt who took a special interest in the well-being of her nephews and nieces. Like Gretl she entertained composers and artists and staged private concerts in her spacious flat on the Salesianergasse, at an old Imperial shooting lodge at Laxenburg, and at her summer farmhouse in Thumersbach. Phonograph records, she insisted, were extremely important to an artist's career.

In New York, Marga succeeded in sowing the seeds for a U.S. tour for Paul during which the highlight would be a performance of Strauss's *Panathenäenzug* at Carnegie Hall with the Beethoven Symphony Orchestra under the baton of its founding conductor, George Zaslawsky. On October 31, 1928, Paul performed the Bortkiewicz Concerto in Bucharest, expecting to leave for America two days later, but when news reached him that a sold-out concert of the Beethoven Orchestra at the Carnegie Hall had been suddenly dropped, he decided not to travel. Two reasons were given for the cancellation in New York. On the one hand, Zaslawsky claimed to have suffered a heart attack and on the other his featured violin soloist, Paul Kochanski, was said to have pulled out because his fee had not been paid. The two may have been related. In any case Zaslawsky refused to pay any refund to disgruntled ticket holders and within a few weeks he and his orchestra had filed for bankruptcy.

The successes of Paul's commissions had inspired many young composers to send him unsolicited proposals, suggestions or even complete scores of works they had written for the left hand. They also encouraged figures of higher distinction to join the Wittgenstein carnival. In June 1924, Leopold Godowsky signed a contract for $6,000 (half on signature, half on delivery) for a left-handed piano concerto, but panicked—because he had no experience of orchestration—and in the end offered a masterful caprice on themes from Johann Strauss's *Gypsy Baron* for $3,000. Godowsky wrote to his wife, "It is good music—very likely too good for Wittgenstein." Paul performed it only once.

In his contracts with Korngold, Schmidt, Strauss and Bortkiewicz, Paul had insisted that the contractual details be kept secret. The musical world may have guessed that large sums were involved, but even those young composers who knew nothing of it were excited at the prospect of association with Paul Wittgenstein. Some of their works he performed. In February 1925 he premiered a paraphrase of "Tales from the Vienna Woods" for piano and orchestra by Eduard Schütt in the Musikvereinsaal; a Serenata and Perpetuo Mobile by the blind composer Rudolf Braun led to a commission for a full-scale concerto; a quartet by Hans Gal, which Paul described as "nothing remarkable," was premiered in March 1928 and a concerto by Karl Weigl was rejected. But these were not then or now important composers and Paul always had his eye on higher prospects.

On February 24, 1929, he was booked to perform the *Panathenäenzug* in Paris and instructed his agent, Georg Kügel, to write to Maurice Ravel— a composer at the height of his fame—and ask if he would like to attend the concert, with a view to considering writing his own concerto for Paul.

Ravel, already at work on another piano concerto, expressed regret that he was unable to come but asked if Paul would like to visit him at his small, ornate villa, Le Belvédère, at Montfort-l'Amaury, twenty-five miles west of Paris. The meeting seems to have gone well. Ravel agreed to study some left-hand piano compositions, including the Saint-Saëns and Chopin-Godowsky studies. The prospect excited him. "Je me joue de difficultés," he said and agreed that on his forthcoming trip to Vienna in March he would come to hear Paul in concert playing the *Panathenäenzug*.

In the summer of 1930 Paul toured the Soviet Union. His trip took him to concert halls in Moscow, Leningrad, Baku, Kiev and Kharkov (the birthplace of Sergei Bortkiewicz), where he played the Bortkiewicz Concerto to a clamor of ecstatic applause. In Kiev public enthusiasm was so great that he had to repeat his program two days later. Although he spoke a little Russian, Paul detested the Russian people and their culture and had done so ever since the tough days of his wartime imprisonment. When asked by a polite gentleman in New York in the 1950s if he would like to come and see his splendid collection of Russian antiquities in his newly created Russian Room, Paul answered sharply: "No, I hate everything Russian."

Above all he despised the new communist regime, the ubiquitous propaganda that was used to sustain it and the destitution that it created among its people. "When dark envy dresses up like equality war against privilege becomes the battle cry," he would say, quoting from his favorite Viennese poet, Franz Grillparzer. "I was driven to desperation by the eternal Russian waiting and cursed vehemently," he remembered. In Kharkov he was forced to carry a chair from his hotel bedroom down to the breakfast hall, where there were not enough places to sit. The meal took nearly two hours because nothing ever arrived and ordering was a nightmare:

> "Café au lait." There is no milk. "Then tea with lemon!" There are no lemons. "An egg dish with two eggs!" There are no eggs. "Then bread and butter!" There is no butter, only cheese. A government official who was there told me that he could no longer remember what butter tasted like. And that was in the capital city of an agrarian country like the Ukraine!

In Russia as elsewhere Paul was outspoken in his contempt for the communist regime. In Moscow he rebuked an agent at his concert saying: "If you had kept the Tsar your country would be infinitely better than it is now!" The agent left the room tapping his forehead with his finger. Even as a foreign guest such remarks were risky in the Stalinist Russia of the 1930s, but Paul was having none of it, as he made clear in a written report on his trip to Leningrad:

> The Great Hall, as is generally the case in all public buildings, theatres, concert halls and banks, is draped with red banners. Many of them hang the entire length of the hall, and on them is written: "We shall Conquer and Surpass the Capitalist Countries!" I thought, if instead of these talks, this waste of banner cloth, instead of the countless busts and pictures of Lenin, if instead of these huge and superficial expenditures of money, if instead of all this, only one clean public lavatory were built, then much more would have been achieved for the good and convenience of the people as well as for the "conquering and surpassing" of the capitalist countries.

Just as Paul was leaving for Russia his spritely mustachioed agent, Georg Kügel, had informed him of the good news that Sergei Prokofiev, the famous Russian pianist and composer, now resident in France, was agreeable, in principle, to composing a concerto for him. Kügel, who was paid a retainer by Paul, had approached Prokofiev's agent Michel Astroff at the beginning of June, but had not informed Paul of his intention to help himself to a slice of the fee. While Paul was away, Kügel wrote slyly to Astroff:

> *Mr. Wittgenstein is presently on tour in Russia and will be returning to Vienna at the beginning of July. I shall discuss the whole matter with him then and let you know. In the meantime, I would ask you to say roughly how long Mr. Prokofiev thinks he would need to finish a concerto for the left hand and orchestra.*
>
> *Mr. Wittgenstein would have to have exclusive performance rights for 5 years. The nature of the composition—whether one movement or three,*

whether a set of variations—is, of course, entirely up to Herr Prokofiev. I
hope to be able to get agreement to the requested fee of 5,000 dollars and
would expect my usual 10% agency commission.

I look forward to your favourable reply and sign myself,
Georg Kügel

Returning to Vienna, Paul refused to tell his inquisitive family any-thing about his Russian trip and at a dinner to welcome him back he in-structed his aged Aunt Clara to change the subject immediately if his trip, his concerts or his music were mentioned in the conversation. From Vi-enna he traveled to London and thence to the Overstrand Hotel near Cromer in Norfolk for a seaside holiday with Marga. It was here that news reached him of Prokofiev's final agreement to terms. "Dear Master [he wrote to the composer in Paris], allow me to express my immense joy at the news that I shall one day be playing the concerto that you have agreed to compose for me." On August 29, filled with eagerness and excitement, he flew to Paris to meet Prokofiev for the first time and to hear how Ravel was getting along with his concerto.

At Montfort-l'Amaury Ravel ushered him into his piano room filled with kitsch, neatly arranged ornaments and bibelots—pens made of duck feathers, crystal Gothic candlesticks, seashells and a mechanical bird in a gilded cage that he called Zizi. There the composer struggled to render the orchestral part and the solo line simultaneously with two hands on his piano. Paul was distinctly underwhelmed by the music and told the composer so. One of his complaints concerned the long unaccompanied cadenza with which it begins. "If I had wanted to play without the or-chestra I would not have commissioned a concerto!" he said. "I suppose Ravel was disappointed and I was sorry, but I had never learned to pre-tend." Paul required several changes to be made and when he left Ravel's house was still uncertain whether the composer would be prepared to make them or not. At Rue Valentin Haüy in Paris on September 2, Prokofiev was curious to learn how things were going with Ravel but Paul remained silent. It was not until the end of the month, by which time Ravel had assured him that the changes would be made, that he was able to explain to Prokofiev: "Ravel's Concerto will probably be fin-ished in a few weeks. When I saw you at your house the thing was still uncertain. I am writing to you now, in case you thought I was trying to hide anything."

The deal, which was eventually settled between Paul and Ravel, earned the composer $6,000 and gave the pianist exclusive performing rights in the *Concerto pour la main gauche* for five years from the date of signature. But there were problems. The French premiere was scheduled to take place at the Salle Pleyel in Paris with Ravel himself conducting in April 1932, while the world premiere public performance was to take place in Vienna at the Grosser Musikvereinsaal with the Vienna Symphony Orchestra under Robert Heger in January of that year. As usual the real first performance (on November 27, 1931) took place at a private concert in the Wittgenstein Palais in Vienna with the orchestral part played on a second piano. Within a few months of the announcement that the concerto was ready Paul was booked to play it at concert halls in Berlin, London, Warsaw, Athens, Brno, Lemberg and Poznán.

Ravel was not in the audience at the Vienna premiere on January 5, at which, according to the critic of the *Neue Freie Presse*: "Paul Wittgenstein's virtuoso performance unleashed a storm of applause." Instead he came by train to Vienna from Paris on the 30th accompanied by the pianist Marguerite Long, with whom he was touring his recently completed Piano Concerto in G. They stayed at the French Embassy. In the evening Paul hosted a dinner in Ravel's and Ms. Long's honor. Among those present were Franz Schmidt, the French Ambassador Bertrand Clauzel and various Viennese dignitaries. Paul's intention was to play Ravel's concerto after dinner with his friend the pianist and composer Walter Bricht taking the orchestral part on a second piano. During dinner Paul told Ms. Long that he had made certain alterations to the work, which made her anxious on the composer's behalf, so she advised him to forewarn Ravel before playing it to him. This he did not do. During the performance Ravel's face clouded in fury as he listened to Paul's demolition of his masterpiece. He heard lines taken from the orchestral part and added to the solo, harmonies changed, parts added, bars cut and at the end a newly created series of great swirling arpeggios in the final cadenza. The composer was beside himself with indignation and disbelief. The spirit of his work, he believed, was ruined and his rights had been infringed. Marguerite Long recalled the scene:

As soon as the performance was over, I attempted to create a diversion with Ambassador Clauzel, in order to avoid an incident. Alas Ravel walked slowly over towards Wittgenstein and said to him: "But that is not it at all!" Wittgenstein defended himself: "I am an old hand as a pianist and what you composed does not sound right." That was exactly the wrong thing to say. "I am an old hand at orchestration and it *does* sound right!" was Ravel's reply. Imagine the embarrassment! I remember that Ravel was in such a state of nervous tension that he sent the embassy car away and we returned on foot, hoping a walk in the bitter cold would calm his nerves.

On the walk back Ms. Long tried to put Paul's case as she had sensed that despite everything he adored the music, but Ravel would hear nothing of it and became rigidly opposed to Paul's playing the work in Paris. Rumors circulated in the press that Paul had demanded changes to the concerto because it was too difficult for him to play. The rift between composer and pianist continued to simmer throughout February. Paul wrote to Ravel in Paris protesting that all performers must be accorded a certain lassitude. "Performers must not be slaves!" he said, to which Ravel responded, "Performers *are* slaves." As the composer's mind steadily deteriorated toward the end of his life, this last remark became his mantra-like, knee-jerk response to any mention of the name Paul Wittgenstein.

On March 7, Ravel fired off another angry letter demanding Paul's formal commitment to play the work in future only as written. Paul was in an agitated state, as can always be divined from his handwriting which, at times of stress, came out as a wild, barely legible scrawl. He wrote to the composer Karl Weigl to say that he was thinking of giving up performing in public, and he explained to Marga: "I have cancelled the Paris concert for several reasons too long to be related in one of my sort of letters." His reply to Ravel in a letter of March 17, 1932, gives more detail:

As for a formal commitment to play your work henceforth strictly as written, that is completely out of the question. No self-respecting artist could accept such a condition. All pianists make modifications, large or small, in each concerto they play. Such a formal commitment would be intolerable: I could be held accountable for every imprecise 16th note and every quarter rest which I omitted or added . . . You write indignantly and ironically that I want to be "put in the spotlight." But of course, cher Maître, you have explained it perfectly: that is precisely the reason I asked you to write a concerto! Indeed I wish to be put myself in the spotlight. What other objective could I have had? I therefore have the right to request the necessary modifications for this objective to be attained . . . As I previously wrote, I am only insisting on *some* of the modifications that I proposed, not all of them: I have in no way changed the essence of your work. I have only changed the instrumentation. In the meantime, I have refused to play in Paris, as I cannot accept impossible conditions.

The argument now focused on a two-page section in the middle of the concerto that Paul insisted would be better played by the piano and not, as Ravel had composed it, by the orchestra. "It ruins the concerto," Ravel said. After a long standoff Paul eventually capitulated, admitting in the end that Ravel was right. In the months that he had been studying the work his attitude toward it had changed. He was now "fascinated" by the piece, calling it "a great work . . . It is astonishing. Although averse to any so-called modern music it is just the 6/8 part, the most dissonant of the whole, which I like best!"

A new Paris premiere was agreed for January 17, 1933, at the Salle Pleyel with the Orchestre Symphonique de Paris, which Ravel himself would conduct. Despite lingering frictions between composer and pianist, the concert itself was a monumental success and the official press line was that the two men had mended their bridges. "My quarrel with Ravel has long been settled," Paul told a reporter from the *New York Times* in November 1934. "He and I are on the best of terms." But the whole episode left a bitter taste in both their mouths. Ravel pulled out of a second concert in Monte Carlo in April on grounds of ill health and remained dissatisfied with Paul's alterations to his score. That summer, as the composer was staying with friends at Saint-Jean-de-Luz, he had to be rescued from a swimming pool after finding himself unable to move his arms. These were the first symptoms of a rare dementia known as Pick's disease. His gradual, debilitating decline affected all aspects of his physical and mental coordination. By the end he was unable even to write his name. He died on December 28, 1937, after a failed brain operation at a hospital in Paris.

48 PROKOFIEV

Paul was very excited about his first encounter with Prokofiev. It took place in the lobby of the Hôtel Majestic in Paris and Prokofiev suggested that they lunch at a restaurant with his agent Michel Astroff and afterward repair to his house on the Rue Valentin Haüy, where he had staying the celebrated theater director Vsevolod Meyerhold and his wife, the actress Zinaida Raikh. Paul must have known a bit about Meyerhold already—that he was an official of the theater division of the Soviet Union's Commissariat of Education and Enlightenment and a card-carrying member of the Communist Party—for when Prokofiev invited him home Paul hesitated for a while before exclaiming, "I cannot stand Bolsheviks!" Prokofiev assured him that Meyerhold was an outstanding artist and that he was only a Communist Party member in order that he might continue his work in the Soviet Union undisturbed by the authorities. So Paul agreed to come.

Prokofiev's agent later told the composer that he had been "disappointed by the unattractive look of Wittgenstein," and openly astounded that anyone should pay as much as $5,000 for a concerto. Prokofiev, on the other hand, was impressed by Paul's ability to eat his lunch with only one hand and defended him afterward saying: "So what did you expect— that he would be wearing a frock-coat with medals?" In the evening at Prokofiev's house, he and Paul sat by the piano. Paul demonstrated his technique with pieces by Chopin, Mozart and Puccini after which Prokofiev asked him: "What makes you commission a concerto from me when this is the sort of music you like?" Paul answered that he liked the way Prokofiev wrote for the piano and was hoping for a technically interesting piece, so the composer sat at the keyboard and played him two themes that he was thinking of incorporating into the concerto. He

TOP: Portraits of Karl Wittgenstein's paternal grandparents: Moses Meyer Wittgenstein (Hermann Christian's putative father), and his wife, Breindel (sometimes Bernadine) Wittgenstein (née Simon), c. 1802.

BOTTOM LEFT: Karl in his early twenties, c. 1868.

BOTTOM RIGHT: Karl's father, Hermann Christian Wittgenstein, as a young man, c. 1834.

TOP: Wittgenstein siblings,
c. 1890. From left: Helene,
Rudi, Hermine, Ludwig,
Gretl, Paul, Hans and Kurt.

RIGHT: Karl and Leopoldine
at the time of their silver
wedding in 1899.

The Silver Wedding Party at Neuwaldegg, summer 1899. In sailor suits: Paul (far right) and Ludwig (holding the arm of his aunt Clara). Hermine has a girl on her lap, behind whose straw hat stands Helene. Gretl stands directly behind Ludwig. Among the standing men in white ties can be seen Hans (far right with a cigarette), Kurt (at the top of the picture with a prominent scar on his left cheek) and Rudi (fourth from left, his face between the shoulders of two cousins).

The Musikaal, where Brahms, Strauss and Mahler gathered for the family's musical soirées.

LEFT: Entrance hall at the Wittgenstein Palais, Vienna.

BOTTOM: The Palais, seen here from the Alleegasse (later renamed Argentinierstrasse), was razed to the ground in the 1950s.

TOP: Gretl, Jerome and their son, Thomas Stonborough, with Aimée Guggenheim (Jerome's sister) and Delia Steinberger (Jerome's mother) at St. Moritz, 1906.

LEFT: Karl Wittgenstein, c. 1910.

TOP: Ludwig, Helene and Paul enjoying a joke at Hochreit just before the outbreak of war, July 1914.

ABOVE: On leave from the war at Neuwaldegg, summer 1917. From left: Kurt, Paul and Hermine Wittgenstein, Max Salzer, Leopoldine Wittgenstein, Helene Salzer and Ludwig Wittgenstein.

RIGHT: Kurt Wittgenstein, shortly before his death in 1918.

TOP: The Wittgensteins' mentor, blind composer Josef Labor, at the organ.

ABOVE: Paul, one-armed pianist, c. 1921.

LEFT: Ludwig, schoolteacher, c. 1922.

ABOVE: Villa Toscana, the Stonboroughs' elegant summer house on Lake Traunsee at Gmunden.

LEFT: Leopoldine Wittgenstein is read to by her late-life companion, the retired soprano Marie Fillunger, at Hochreit, c. 1925.

Gretl's new house on the Kundmanngasse in Vienna, partly designed by Ludwig, spring 1929.

Christmas at the Kundmanngasse. From left: Delia Steinberger (now Stonborough), Jerome, Thomas, Gretl and Ji, c. 1929.

LEFT: Paul's friend Marga Deneke with her dog in her garden at Oxford, c. 1928.

BOTTOM LEFT: Gretl Stonborough, c. 1930.

BELOW: Hermine Wittgenstein, c. 1934.

RIGHT: Austrian picnic. From left: John Stonborough, Arvid Sjögren and Marguerite Respinger, c. 1930. Ludwig proposed to Marguerite (originally a Cambridge friend of Thomas Stonborough's) on condition that they would not have to have sex.

BELOW: Christmas at the Palais, 1934. Paul sits with Helene on his right, and Hermine is at the head of the table.

RIGHT: Paul in a photograph taken for his Cuban passport, 1941.

BELOW: Paul performing the premiere of Schmidt's Piano Concerto. The composer (blurred) conducts the Vienna Philharmonic at the Grosser Musikvereinsaal, Vienna, February 9, 1935.

LEFT: Hilde Schania, c. 1936.

BELOW: Hilde with her daughters Elizabeth and Johanna, Vienna, 1938.

LEFT: Paul with Johanna and Elizabeth in Cuba, 1941.

BELOW: Paul with his son Paul Jr., c. 1950.

RIGHT: Ludwig at Cambridge, 1946.

BELOW: A late portrait of Paul, c. 1960.

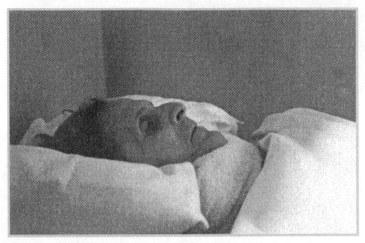

Ludwig on his deathbed at Dr. and Mrs. Bevan's house in Cambridge, April 1951.

The Wittgenstein family grave at the Zentralfriedhof, Vienna—final resting place of Karl, Leopoldine, Hermine and Rudolf Wittgenstein and their servant Rosalie Hermann.

specifically asked Paul to listen to them several times before offering an opinion, but after the first hearing Paul burst out: "You could carry on playing that for two months and I still would not understand it."

From these prickly beginnings Paul put Prokofiev at his ease by telling him that as far as the commission was concerned he could compose whatever he wished at his own discretion. Meyerhold's wife was enraptured with Paul's musicianship, and explained to Prokofiev afterward "how he played with such love. I felt for his spirit that such a man should have lost his arm in the war." But Prokofiev was not impressed and replied to her: "I don't see any special talent in his left hand. It may be that his misfortune has turned out to be a stroke of good luck, for with only his left hand he is unique but maybe with both hands he would not have stood out from a crowd of mediocre pianists."

Paul liked Meyerhold and his wife despite his preconceptions about their Bolshevism, but they were never to meet again. In 1938 the Stalinists closed down Meyerhold's theater in Moscow and murdered Zinaida. Meyerhold was arrested, tortured and shot in prison on charges of "Trotskyite activism."

In January 1931, four months after Paul's first meeting with Prokofiev, he accidentally slipped in the street in Vienna, fracturing his thigh and rupturing a blood vessel, causing a hematoma. On the 20th he performed the Korngold Concerto in Vienna with his leg in a bandage and was still hobbling about in a splint in March when he read in the newspaper that Prokofiev was coming to play in Vienna. Straightaway he sent a letter urging the composer not to stay at the Hotel Imperial but at his Palais instead:

> You will have your own room with your own piano, no one will
> bother you. It is a principle of mine that guests in this house have
> only to say if they wish to be woken in the morning, if they want
> coffee or tea, if they will be in for dinner etc., other than that they
> live here as if they were at a hotel or pension.

Prokofiev spent a happy time with Paul playing Schubert duets on the piano and as soon as he was back in Paris began to concentrate on his left-hand concerto. Paul had asked him for something that was "clearer than Strauss and less childish (from a technical point of view) than Franz

Schmidt." Entitled Piano Concerto No. 4 it was finished in sketch form by the end of July 1931, but the composer was not altogether happy with it. The work is emotionally detached and one senses that Prokofiev's heart was not in it. Right from the start, he harbored plans (initially kept secret from Paul) to turn the piece into a two-handed concerto as soon as the Wittgenstein exclusivity contract had expired. On September 11 he sent the score to Paul with an accompanying note, showing that he was unsure of his reaction:

I hope the concerto will prove satisfactory to you from a pianistic point of view and in terms of the balance between piano and orchestra. I am at a loss to guess what musical impression it will make on you. A difficult problem! You are a musician of the 19th Century—I am one of the 20th. I have tried to make it as straightforward as possible; you, for your part, must not judge too quickly, and if certain passages seem at first indigestible, do not rush to judgement, but wait a while. If you have any suggestions for improving the work, please do not hesitate to tell me them.

If Prokofiev's autobiography can be believed, Paul wrote back bluntly: "Thank you for your concerto, but I do not understand a single note and I shall not play it." The letter has since disappeared, and although Paul may have written those words there was certainly more to his letter than that, as the composer and pianist remained on warm and cordial terms. In an exchange three years later Prokofiev wrote to ask if he would mind his transforming the piece into a concerto for two hands. "Given the excellent relationship that exists between us and not wanting to do something that might be disagreeable to you I thought I should consult you on this matter first." Paul replied that Prokofiev was wrong if he thought the concerto had not pleased him. "That is not fair," he wrote. "Your concerto, or at least a considerable part of it, is comprehensible to me, but there is an enormous difference between a poem that displeases me and one whose meaning I cannot fully grasp."

Paul responded to the delivery of Prokofiev's score with a note to confirm that he would be sending him $3,000 as the second installment of his fee. Prokofiev wrote back to correct him. "You don't owe me $3,000 but

$2,250—that is $2,500 minus the 10% that Kügel [your agent] is taking." Until that moment Paul had no idea that Prokofiev and Astroff had settled for $5,000. He had taken his agent's word for it that the fee was $6,000 payable in two installments. When he discovered the plot to rob him of $1,000 he flew into a rage and sacked his agent on the spot. For a short while he signed himself to the music writer and impresario Paul Bechert, and when Bechert ran off to America in December 1932 leaving all his debts unpaid, Paul was temporarily without representation of any kind.

Many hours were spent poring over Prokofiev's score, but Paul never understood the music and consequently never performed it. The first performance (with Siegfried Rapp as pianist) took place in Berlin in September 1956—three and a half years after the composer's death. As to the proposed two-handed version, Prokofiev never got around to making it, and remained equivocal about the quality of the work: "I have not formed any definite opinion about it myself," he wrote in his autobiography. "Sometimes I like it, sometimes I do not."

49 LOVE STORY

There were reasons why Paul was in such an excitable state at the time of the Ravel debacle that few could have guessed. His girlfriend was in serious trouble. Bassia Moscovici, a beautiful young Rumanian, is said to have been a singer, though no record of any of her public performances survives. Her father was a modest jeweler and watchmaker from Bucharest, and it is possible that Paul first met her as early as November 1928, when he stayed at the Athenée Palace Hotel in Bucharest while rehearsing and performing the left-handed concerto by Bortkiewicz. In the autumn of 1930 Bassia moved to Vienna, where he put her up as a kept woman in a villa on the Vegagasse in Vienna's 19th District. It seems unlikely that he ever intended to marry her as she was born of a humble Jewish family and he, with his nervous temperament, was fundamentally unsuited to married life, but in 1931 her name was registered in the *Austrittsbücher* of the Jewish community in Vienna as a person who, on February 25, had voluntarily left the Jewish faith. It is therefore possible that her subsequent conversion to Roman Catholicism and her adoption of the confirmation name Pauline were intended to clear a way for marriage to Paul. In the event a cruel twist denied her this chance.

In the summer of 1931, Bassia discovered that she was pregnant with his baby. Paul, in desperation, turned to his sisters for help and Gretl, with her big heart and bossy inclinations, took command of the crisis by arranging for the twenty-one-year-old Rumanian to undergo a secret and illegal abortion. Bassia desperately wanted to have the baby but was browbeaten by Gretl into believing that abortion was the only possible and acceptable course of action. The dangerous, late and incompetent backstreet operation went badly wrong.

Bassia became extremely ill and she was still not fully recovered in the late autumn of 1931 when she discovered a swelling on her shoulder caused by rhabdomyosarcoma—a cancer that was spreading through the muscles of her upper arm. At the beginning of November she underwent an operation to have the tumor removed from her shoulder, after which Gretl tried to persuade her to go for a period of recuperation somewhere outside the city. Distrusting her motives, Bassia insisted on remaining close to Paul, but Gretl, determined as always to have her way, booked her into a sanatorium at Mauer bei Amstetten in the Dunkelsteinerwald fifty miles to the west of Vienna, sending an ambulance to her flat in the Vegagasse to pick her up and take her there. The hospital, a well-known clinic for nervous or mentally disordered patients—which was opened in 1902 by the Emperor Franz Joseph with the infamous words "It must be nice being an idiot in Mauer"—was not to Bassia's liking. After a few days she discharged herself and returned to the city, complaining to Paul that Gretl was some kind of evil spirit. By then the cancer had spread to her lungs, the wound from her operation was infected and she was suffering a high fever. Gretl, she claimed, had forced her to have the abortion and deliberately sent her to a dirty hospital where her condition had worsened. None of this, she argued, would have happened if she had only been allowed to have the baby.

At this stage only Gretl and Paul knew that she was dying of cancer. The doctors had not informed Bassia of the severity of her condition. Paul became extremely solicitous, "touchingly good" according to his sister, and Gretl, in a spirit of reconciliation (if not driven by feelings of guilt), offered to take Bassia into her house at the Kundmanngasse for a month. By mid-January 1932 everyone, including the patient herself, knew that she was going to die and there would be no question of her moving out of Gretl's house. Through January, February and March, as Bassia's condition worsened, the relationship between her and Gretl gradually improved, with the occasional smile passing between them. Gretl herself was far from well, suffering from acute fibrillations in her chest, and she spent most of the day lying down. When Marga Deneke came to visit her she recorded: "Putting out her hand to greet me, [Gretl] explained that the doctors were strict in their rules about her heart trouble and remained semi-recumbent lying like a statue on the folds of a red and golden shawl, surrounded by a blaze of coloured flowers."

Gretl rose only for Bassia, hoping to prepare her in some mental or philosophical way for death, but was unsure how to go about it. Bassia's visions or presentiments of her own death struck Gretl as fey and comical and she regretted not being able to take them more seriously. By mid-March Bassia was thin, pale and gaunt. The last vestiges of beauty had forsaken her, but she struggled on with Paul in constant vigil at her side. On April 22 she was visited by Ludwig's friend Marguerite Respinger, who wrote: "Bassia has been in agony since yesterday evening. She will die soon. I am thinking only of Paul . . ." That evening her decline was so severe that Paul stayed with her throughout the night, holding her hand until the moment of death. Miss Respinger returned the following morning to pay her respects. "It made a great impression on me," she wrote. "Not because it was frightening to see a dead person; but to lie there with such a peaceful expression, I wondered: what type of human being would one have to be? Good."

Hermine returned from the Hochreit to find Bassia's mother, Esther Kirchen, holding her dead daughter's hand and speaking to her as though she were still alive, tenderly informing her how pretty she once was, and how sad that she had not been looking so pretty of late—a spectacle that Hermine found both touching and gruesome. She spoke only a little to her brother about it and afterward reported cryptically to Ludwig: "Paul has lost a lot and he admits it. I am not sure though whether he thinks the same as me when he admits it . . ."

Paul undertook all the necessary arrangements and two days later, on Monday, April 25, 1932, Bassia was buried in a prestigious spot close to the main gates at Vienna's Zentralfriedhof. She left no will, but 14,000 Austrian schillings (worth twenty-eight times the average monthly wage) were registered in her possession—presumably a gift from Paul. After the funeral, demonstrably heartbroken, Paul presented Gretl with a glittering tiara and each of the servants in her house with a "most handsome present" for having looked after Bassia; but his distrust of Gretl never healed. Even though she had done so much to help, he continued in his belief that her interference had been detrimental. They discussed their relationship together and both acknowledged that it could never work. Aside from the simple fact that Paul's and Gretl's attitudes to life were entirely opposed, Hermine also thought she detected unpleasant undertones between them. "Paul can only lose here but we cannot change it."

 50   HIS AMERICAN DEBUT

At the time of Bassia's demise Paul's nerves—never his strongest attribute—were strained to their uttermost and, as a direct consequence, his piano playing became inaccurate and aggressive. A Polish tour at the end of the year produced an adverse response from the critics. Pawel Rytel of the *Warsaw Gazette* wrote: "Despite our admiration for the artist we have to stress that there were shortcomings." The *Warsaw Courier* similarly hinted: "Performances by single-handed pianists should not be judged in the same light as two-handed interpretations, but nevertheless I have to say that the pedal was overused." "Obviously one hand cannot replace two," said the critic of *Polska Zbrojna,* while the journal *Robotnik* noted: "As to those compositions composed especially for him, Paul Wittgenstein was expected to play them impeccably but the general impression was not good for reasons of faulty pedalling and lack of technical skill among other things." The critics may have demurred, but audiences did not seem to mind how roughly he played. Even in Poland his concerts were cheered to the rafters as his hypnotic stage presence continued to exert its effect over listeners, in spite of playing that was rough, nervy and inaccurate.

It took him nearly two years from Bassia's death to refind his form and, when it happened, his return was spectacular. An American tour in November 1934 took him to Boston, New York, Detroit, Cleveland, Los Angeles and Montreal. Everywhere he was greeted by a blaze of publicity, packed houses and rave reviews. At a concert in New York he was recalled to the stage for five encores. His performances astonished both critics and audiences. A review in the *New York Herald Tribune* is typical of many:

> Doubtless the greatest tribute that one could pay to Paul Wittgenstein, the famous one-armed pianist, is a simple statement of the fact that after the first few moments of wondering how the devil he accomplished it, one almost forgot that one was listening to a player whose right sleeve hung empty at his side. One found oneself engrossed by the sensitivity of the artist's phrasing and the extent to which his incredible technique was subordinated to the delivery of the musical thought.

Few dared to question what Paul was doing or whether the piano was worth playing with only one hand. One notable exception was the distinguished English critic Ernest Newman. Writing in the *Sunday Times,* after a Proms performance of Ravel's concerto, he wondered whether Paul—as Hermine and Gretl had frequently suggested—was attempting the impossible:

> I have every sympathy with Paul Wittgenstein in a loss of an arm during the war, and the profoundest admiration for the courage that enabled him to work up a one-handed technique afterwards. All the same I wish composers would stop writing one-hand concertos for him, or at any rate inflicting them on us . . . The thing simply cannot be done; the composer is not only hampered in the orchestral portion of his work by consideration of the limitations of the pianist but even in the purely pianistic portions he is driven to a series of makeshifts and fakes that soon become tiresome. This concerto will certainly not help the fast-declining reputation of Ravel. From another point of view, it is true, the regrettable physical dis-

ability of Herr Wittgenstein may have half saved the work as a concerto for only one hand can, in the nature of things, be at worst only half as bad as it might otherwise have been.

After three hectic months in America, Paul returned exhausted to Vienna on February 2, 1935, with just a week to prepare a new concerto by Franz Schmidt that was being premiered with the Vienna Philharmonic as part of the composer's sixtieth-birthday celebrations at the Grosser Musikvereinsaal. Hermine heard him practicing in his room and reported that the piece held little interest for her. "It seems to me that one could continue with the sort of compositions one hears today. It's a shame that he cannot commission anything really good these days." Paul was of a different view. "The first and second movements I think are really *great* music," he wrote to his friend Donald Francis Tovey. The third movement he found a little light so he made some alterations to enrich it that the composer approved and the concert was a storming success—perhaps the greatest single success of his entire career. Schmidt conducted a program consisting entirely of his own works, including the premiere of his great masterpiece, the Fourth Symphony, and fourteen German-speaking newspapers carried reviews extolling the concerto and Paul's inspirational performance of it. With the Ravel concerto, the American tour and now this widely lauded achievement, Paul's career despite its many breaks had reached another high peak. At the same time as all this his personal life was, once again, on the verge of major crisis.

51 FURTHER COMPLICATIONS

What the forty-seven-year-old Paul did not realize, as he boarded the *Majestic* at Cherbourg bound for New York on October 24, 1934, was that one of his piano students, an attractive, dark-haired, eighteen-year-old, half-blind Beethoven enthusiast, was pregnant with his child.

Hilde was the daughter of Franz Schania, an amateur pianist, zither player and a left-wing Roman Catholic, who had worked first for a large brewery at Schwechat, near Vienna, and later as a health inspector for the Wiener Städtische Strassenbahn, the city tram network. He may have been head of a small department, or maybe not. In any case he was considered *nicht standesgemäss* (not of the right class) by Paul's family, who put it about that he was a humble bus conductor: "a *Strassenbahn Kontrolleur*—a man who checked tram tickets—very, very small beer" is how Ji Stonborough later described him. After the First War, in which Herr Schania got his head stuck between a cannon and a rock face at the battle of Isonzo, he became a dedicated socialist and suffered severe depressions. His wife Stefanie, who worked as secretary for a wood-chopping firm, was also depressed. She separated from her husband in 1933 and is said to have taken her own life in January 1936. Hilde was brought up with her elder sister Käthe, first at Rannersdorf and afterward in a council flat in one of "Red Vienna's" new socialist housing experiments on the Geyschlägergasse in the 15th District.

At the age of five, after an attack of measles and diphtheria, Hilde's optic nerve was damaged; her eyesight waned and continued to do so until she was completely blind. When Paul first met her she was partially sighted but so adept at disguising it that he was unaware of any problem. In later life when her sight was considerably worse she still managed to look people in the eye, played the piano with confidence and walked briskly around the house without crashing into things. Visitors were often unaware of her blindness. Some even believed that she was faking it. Her poor vision forced her to stare intently with large dark eyes into people's faces. Men found this attractive in the same way, a generation earlier, as Mahler, Zemlinsky, Klimt, Kokoschka, Werfel and Gropius had fallen for the charms of Alma Schindler, "the loveliest girl in Vienna," whose slight deafness forced her to gaze intently upon men's lips as they spoke.

In the autumn of 1934, Hilde enrolled as a piano student at the New Vienna Conservatoire. Paul had longed to teach advanced pupils since his successes with Ludwig's friend Rudolf Koder in June 1929. His performing schedule was stressful and he never succeeded in controlling his nerves. He was bad at relaxing and needed some sort of supplementary work to fill the hours between practicing and performing. From 1932 he worked as an unpaid assistant music critic on the *Neues Wiener Journal*.

His intemperate reviews had to be reined in by the editor from time to time, but the fact that he would never send an invoice made him an attractive employee.

Though he affected to despise the critics, Paul's admiration for Leschetizky and Labor enabled him to place "great teachers" on an equal plain with "great performers" and his experiences with Rudolf Koder encouraged him to take on several private pupils. In October 1930 he applied, with Franz Schmidt's support, for an unsalaried post at the Hochschule für Musik. Erich Korngold recommended that he send a formal application to the professorial staff:

> I lost my right arm in the war and have had to train myself up exclusively as a left-hand pianist; in this capacity I have given concerts over a number of years both at home and abroad. Although I have had to modify in some respects the standard piano technique taught me by Leschetizky, I believe nonetheless that I am capable of successfully teaching two-handed students . . .

Franz Schmidt had warned Paul that the academy had enough piano teachers already and that his request was likely to be rejected. In the minutes of the professorial staff committee meeting it was recorded: "Both Hofrat Dr. Marx and Professor Mairecker referred to Wittgenstein's remarkable musical talent (upon which the Rector agreed) and to his already proven teaching abilities, whereas others warned of his nervousness that almost amounted to an illness."

As expected Paul was turned down, but a year later he was accepted for the post of unpaid professor of piano at the New Vienna Conservatoire, a private music-teaching establishment that had rented a few tuition rooms from the Gesellschaft der Musikfreunde, the distinguished Viennese music society, at the Musikverein on the Himmelpfortgasse. By all accounts Paul was an unconventional teacher. He would not allow his students to take holidays and when the Conservatoire was closed required them to attend lessons at the Palais or, in the summer, at his house at Neuwaldegg. "I love teaching," he said. "When I have a gifted student to work with I find my greatest happiness." He did not pull his pupils' hair or box their ears as Ludwig had done, but he often lost his temper with them. If they played wrongly he would flick their hands off the keys as they were playing, and throw away or tear up their music. Most of all he deplored them repeating mistakes that they had once learned to correct.

During the lesson and while you played Professor always had to be walking about, up and down the enormous Saal [one student remembered]. In the Neuwaldegger Palais, the dream summer house, he would march right out into the surrounding Wiener Wald and disappear. You might have thought he had gone and would not hear you, but the slightest carelessness on your part would bring him back like lightning and thunder with his shoes covered in mud. He did not worry about his dirty shoes, he was completely unaware of it.

Much of the time was spent working out correct fingering, and the student would have to sit silently while Paul closed his eyes and the stump of his arm twitched with his thinking. He could still feel the fingers of his right hand and was able to work out the best fingering by imagining them moving across the keys. To choose a new piece students would be asked to sight-read the bass line while Paul played the right-hand part with his left hand—and then again the other way round. Maybe it was during just such an exercise that his seduction of Hilde Schania took place. Hilde later remembered Hermine sitting in as a silent chaperone on some of her lessons, but she cannot have been there all of the time.

The trauma of Gretl's interference in Bassia's abortion two years earlier increased Paul's determination that there should be no abortion this time around, that the baby should be born and that his sisters and brother should know nothing whatsoever about it. Hilde was moved into a flat in a small house on the Gersthoferstrasse overlooking the Türkenschanzplatz. It was registered in her father's name, but Paul paid the rent and put a maid at her disposal. On May 24, 1935, a daughter, Elizabeth, was born—named apparently after the late Empress "Sisi," who was stabbed to death by an anarchist as she boarded a steamship on Lake Geneva in September 1898. It may be calculated that the period from Hilde's first formal piano lesson to the less formal consummation of their relationship was a brief one. She had joined as a student of the Conservatoire in the autumn of 1934 and was delivered of her baby at the end of May 1935. Elizabeth's conception must have occurred soon after Hilde's first lesson with Paul.

The secret of Hilde and the new baby was well guarded. Only the Wittgenstein servants knew of it and they were well trained to secrecy. On most evenings Paul's chauffeur drove to and from Hilde's villa in the Gersthoferstrasse. He knew where he was supposed to go without having to be asked. One month after Elizabeth was born Hilde played a Beethoven sonata in a concert of Paul's students at the Conservatoire, but after that she seems to have given up her lessons as well as her ambitions to play in public. Less than two years later, on March 10, 1937, their secret still intact, she gave birth to another daughter, Johanna.

Hilde's father was not impressed. Franz Schania, quiet and withdrawn, seething with irritation and bad temper, was three and a half years younger than Paul, and disliked him intensely. He could never forgive him for seducing and impregnating his daughter, for refusing to marry her, and later for failing to buy him a smart house in Vienna. He referred to him, always with a sneer, as "Herr Graf" (Sir Count). Paul, in his turn, avoided contact with Hilde's family.

52 RISING TENSIONS

Ludwig's effect on both men and women continued to override people's frustrations at not being able to understand his philosophy. When Marga first met him as she and Paul were walking up the staircase that separated the bachelors' quarters from the main part of the Palais, he appeared in a greasy, oil-stained uniform carrying a clarinet in a stocking, but she remembered him still as "extremely handsome with the neck of a Greek god—fresh in colouring—his fair hair sprang up like a wreath of flames, there was a very serious look in his deep blue eyes." This description correlates with another, slightly homosexual, one that the philosophy student and, later, distinguished Buddhist thinker John Niemeyer Findlay has left:

At the age of 40 [Ludwig Wittgenstein] looked like a youth of 20, with a godlike beauty, always an important feature at Cambridge . . . like Apollo who had bounded into life out of his own statue, or perhaps like the Norse God Baldur, blue eyed and fair haired . . . an extraordinary atmosphere surrounded him, something philosophically saintly that was also very distant and impersonal: he was the *philosophe Soleil* . . . the tea one drank with him tasted like nectar.

From 1933 to 1935 Ludwig—tense, stammering, sweating like the Prophet Muhammad as he proclaimed the Koran at Medina—dictated two books of his philosophy to his students at Cambridge. These came to be known as the *Blue* and *Brown* books. As Ludwig himself conceded, "I think it's very difficult to understand them." To a small but ardent group of Cambridge disciples Ludwig was God. That they did not understand him was of small concern, because what mattered to them was to be close to his presence, to be part of his inner circle and to be able to witness the spectacle of his thinking. His lectures were exclusive events to which only the chosen were admitted, and the *Blue* and *Brown* books, which circulated among them, came to be regarded with the same reverence and mystical fascination as the apocalypse gospels that passed surreptitiously under the togas of ancient Christians in the period of Rome's decline.

Paul was probably unaware of Ludwig's Christ-like status among the philosophers of Cambridge or of the fact that he was living some of the time with Francis Skinner, a man twenty-three years his junior, but in neither case would he have minded. He was not censorious. On the rare occasions when they met, the two brothers got on well. Their correspondence during this period is of a mainly frivolous nature. They sent each other newspaper cuttings, pictures and articles that they thought would amuse. Paul posted Viennese delicacies, unprocurable in England, to Ludwig and, on one occasion, a letter from the wife of a rotten composer, Max Oberleithner, inviting him to contribute his favorite recipe to a musicians' cookery book she was compiling. Paul refused to admit to her that scrambled eggs with lots of pepper was what he liked best, but Ludwig drafted a comical response ("Greetings to you from Dr. Ludwig Wittgenstein") in which he asked Frau Oberleithner if he, as a philosopher, might be permitted to make some contribution to her anthology for "Is not philosophy music and music philosophy?" "My favourite food," he added, "is tomatoes in mayonnaise . . . If you should decide to honour me with inclusion in your little book, please quote my full name as I do not wish to be confused with the pianist, Paul Wittgenstein, who may well enter your Pantheon but with whom I have no connection whatsoever."

The brothers' relationship worked because of a tacit agreement between them never to discuss politics or philosophy as on both subjects they profoundly disagreed. Paul, an ardent fan of Schopenhauer, regarded Ludwig's branch of linguistic philosophy as pure nonsense, and like all Austrians at that time who divided themselves between the ultra-right and ultra-left wings, Paul and Ludwig stood at opposite poles of the political spectrum.

Some of Ludwig's students in Cambridge believed him to be a Stalinist. "The important thing," he said of Stalinist Russia, "is that the people have *work* . . . Tyranny doesn't make me feel indignant." In 1933 he started taking Russian lessons and within two years had decided that he wanted to live in the Soviet Union with Francis Skinner. It has been suggested that he served as a recruiting agent for Soviet spies at Cambridge and, though the evidence is inconclusive, his close contact with many known communists and communist agents has long been regarded as suspicious. In 1935 friends arranged for Ludwig to see Ivan Maisky at the Embassy in London, where he succeeded in persuading the Soviet Ambassador of his need for a Russian visa. On a three-week visit to the Soviet Union in September he tried to find himself work as a laborer on a collective farm, but, according to one source, the "Russians told him his own work was a useful contribution and he ought to go back to Cambridge." On his return he reported, "One *could* live there, but only if one was aware the whole time that one could never speak one's mind." But this alone was not enough to put him off. "I am a communist at heart," he told his friend Roland Hutt, and for several years he continued to play with the idea of emigration to the Soviet Union.

Paul's politics were, in contrast, far to the right. He supported the Austro-fascist Heimwehr, the army of the young swashbuckling aristocrat Prince Ernst Rüdiger von Starhemberg, by secretly supplying funds to his campaign for a Heimwehr dictatorship. He paid for huge billboard posters to be erected all around Vienna and for newspaper advertisements urging patriotic Austrians to support the Prince after the *Rote Aufstand* or "Red Uprising" of February 1934. He also financed a sanatorium on behalf of Prince von Starhemberg's paramilitary commander, Major Baron Karg-Bebenburg.

Austria's economy had rallied in the mid-1920s when the krone was replaced by the schilling at a rate of 1:10,000, but there remained high unemployment and an extremely volatile political atmosphere, continually tested by the presence of several private armies. On the left there was the Republikanische Schutzbund (Republican Defense League) run by the Social Democrats and on the right the Frontkämpfer (Battle-Front Veterans) that eventually merged into the Heimwehr (Home Defense). As well as these opposing paramilitary forces was the rapidly growing illegal army of brown-shirt Nazi fascists whose aim was to unite Austria with Germany in a pan-German anti-Semitic Reich under Adolf Hitler, as well as several armed Marxist groups trying to foment communist revolution among the workers.

Violent clashes between these opposing forces were as frequent as they were inevitable. In January 1927 a fight among Schutzbund and Frontkämpfer troops at Schattendorf, Burgenland, resulted in the shooting of a man and child. When the Frontkämpfer paramilitaries responsible were acquitted in court, angry left-wing demonstrators took to the streets, 89 of whom were killed and 600 wounded on the Ringstrasse as the Ministry of Justice building went up in flames. The Stonboroughs were at their villa in the country when all this was going on, feeling nervous that the red towns of Steyrermühl a few miles to the north and Ebensee to the south might stage a "pincer movement" and take Gmunden by force.

In May 1932 a very small but charismatic right-winger called Engelbert Dollfuss, known as the "Millimetternich," became chancellor of Austria at the head of a bickering coalition government. His aim was to make Austria prosperous, drawing it out of the Great Depression, while containing the threat of Hitler's National Socialist movement on the one hand and the agitation of the Marxists on the other. Eight months later Hitler was voted chancellor of Germany by democratic election. Knowing that the Berlin Führer's chief aim was to join Germany with Austria, Chancellor Dollfuss's immediate response was to declare a state of emergency and suspend the Austrian parliament in favor of his own authoritarian Austro-fascist rule by decree. Gretl wrote to her son Thomas to say that the transition from democracy to dictatorship had been painless and to tell him a Dollfuss joke that was doing the rounds in Vienna at the time: "He has had an accident: He fell off the ladder while he was picking strawberries." Soon Dollfuss would establish his *Ständestaat* and outlaw the National Socialists, the communists and all jokes about his size.

In February 1934, Prince von Starhemberg's private Heimwehr army helped the Dollfuss government to crush what was left of the now-banned socialist Schutzbund. On the 12th a forced search of socialist premises in Linz led to violent clashes between left- and right-wing paramilitaries that quickly spread to Vienna, Graz, Judenburg and other towns. In the capital armed members of the Schutzbund barricaded themselves into several of the city's *Gemeindebauten* (council housing-estate buildings), the most famous of which, the half-mile-long Karl Marx Hof, nicknamed the Ringstrasse des Proletariats, came under heavy artillery fire. The socialists were roundly beaten; but the action, which lasted several days and cost many lives, left many of those on the right still feeling nervous of the threat of socialist uprising. Anton Groller, the Wittgensteins' business factotum, recommended that they take Liechtenstein citizenship to save the family fortune in the event of a socialist takeover, but Paul refused on the grounds that he was an "Austrian with his heart and soul" and thought only ill of those who changed their citizenship for purely financial reasons. His brother-in-law, Helene's husband Max Salzer, trustee of the foreign fortune, expressed her fear that by taking Liechtenstein citizenship he might miss some of the hunting season at Hochreit, and thus Herr Groller's idea was roundly rejected.

On the first day of the uprising Paul went shopping in the center of Vienna, unaware of the turmoil that was going on elsewhere in the city, but his twenty-two-year-old nephew, Ji Stonborough, assigned to the charitable Wiener Freiwilligen Rettungsgesellschaft (Viennese Voluntary Rescue Society), spent the day working as an ambulance porter and was very upset by the sight of bleeding agitators on the Floridsdorfer Bridge. He was decorated for his efforts with a medal pinned to his chest by Prince Ernst von Starhemberg in person.

Starhemberg had joined the Heimwehr as a young man and in the

1920s signed up with Hitler's National Socialist movement, taking part in the failed Beer-Hall Putsch of November 1923. Soon afterward he became disaffected with the Nazis and returned to Austria. In 1930 he became head of the Heimwehr, into which he sank most of his fortune (derived from eighteen landed estates), and was soon bankrupted by it, but with donations from Paul, from Fritz Mandl (arms dealer), Benito Mussolini (Italian dictator) and other Austrian millionaires he continued to control the 20,000-man Heimwehr as though it were his own private army. His was the main political voice against Hitler. "Fascism in Austria is represented by the Heimwehr and no one else," he said. "The Nazi Party in Austria is therefore superfluous."

In 1933 he allied his forces to those of Dollfuss's so-called Christian Democrat Party to form the Vaterländische Front (Fatherland Front). His political rallies, his anti-Marxist rhetoric, the *Front heil!* salute and *Kruckenkreuz* symbol in a white circle on a red background have much in common with Hitler's National Socialism. His and Hitler's parties were both fascist and anti-democratic, but the two leaders remained virulently opposed to one another. Hitler called Starhemberg a "traitor," and the prince called Hitler a "liar in charge of a Brown rabble." The anti-Semites who were expelled from Starhemberg's army usually filtered off to join the National Socialists, leaving the Heimwehr with a core support of Austrian patriots (ex-soldiers, war veterans, aristocrats and Catholics) who strove for an independent Austria with dreams of a restored Hapsburg monarchy.

> We have much in common with the German Nazis [Prince von Starhemberg said in a speech]. We are equally enemies of democracy and have many of the same ideas about economic reconstruction, but we in the Heimwehr stand for Austrian independence and support of the Catholic Church. We object to the exaggerated racial theories of the Nazis, as we do to their schemes for a semi-pagan German national religion.

With the crushing of the main core of Marxist socialist resistance in February 1934, Starhemberg and Dollfuss were able to concentrate their efforts on resisting the threat of Hitler, who had been covertly arming and financing Austrian Nazis in order to destabilize the government. In recent months they had dynamited civic buildings, railway lines and power stations and were held responsible for several assassinations and lynchings. Hermine wrote to Ludwig a few days after the uprising: "Who knows what the future will bring? We've only in fact silenced the one hostile party; the other—the national socialists—are more vicious and more hostile than ever. What shall we do with this one? Is it possible that a fight to the finish can end well?"

On July 25, Hitler was attending a performance of Wagner's *Rheingold* at the Bayreuth Festival with his friend Friedelind Wagner, the composer's granddaughter. After the performance one of his aides informed him of the success of the Austrian Nazi plot to assassinate Engelbert Dollfuss. The tiny Austrian chancellor had been shot in the throat at a range of two feet by a rabble of Nazis dressed in Austrian army uniforms who had broken into the Federal Chancellery that evening. There he had been left to bleed slowly to death. According to Friedelind Wagner, Hitler, who was already in an overexcited state because of the opera, "could scarcely wipe the delight from his face" when the news was broken to him.

But to Hitler's intense irritation the coup plot failed to establish a National Socialist government in Vienna. Government troops quickly regained control of the building, several of the conspirators were hanged and a new chancellor, a monochrome lawyer called Kurt von Schuschnigg, was quickly installed. Hitler's ambitions to unite Austria with Germany were far from over. For four years he continued to play a cat-and-mouse game with Schuschnigg that culminated in the latter's ignominious concessions in the spring of 1938. On February 12, Hitler had invited Schuschnigg to private talks at his mountain retreat, the Berghof, situated above Berchtesgaden, high on the German border, with grand, sweeping views across the Austrian countryside. As Schuschnigg arrived at the frontier he was informed that Hitler had invited several of his military generals to attend the meeting. With hindsight, he should have refused to continue, or at least have insisted that Austrian generals be present too, but he did neither. During the fraught exchange that followed, he was insulted, threatened and humiliated by Hitler, who finally presented him with an agreement to sign that stipulated, among other things, that the Austrian Chancellor sack his Chief of Staff and alter the structure of his cabinet to include several named Nazis in key positions. Hitler specifically demanded that the Austrian Nazi Arthur Seyss-Inquart be appointed minister of the interior in charge of home security.

Fearing a full-scale invasion, Schuschnigg capitulated. He was now barely in control of his new German puppet government and his position was weakened to such a degree that he had no choice but to turn to the country. A plebiscite was set for March 13, at which the people would vote for or against an independent Austria. Those under twenty-four years old were excluded from participating on the grounds that they were most likely to want *Anschluss*. Hitler cried foul and dispatched troops to the Austrian border, sending an ultimatum to Schuschnigg that demanded the immediate cancellation of the plebiscite and a complete handover of power to the Austrian National Socialists. Schuschnigg resigned that evening, and in the chaos that followed, a Nazi faction took over the Ministry of the Interior, which controlled the police. The Austrian president Wilhelm Miklas stood out alone against Hitler's demand that Seyss-Inquart be appointed Austrian chancellor. The Germans, impatient for results, published a fake telegram purporting to come from the Austrian government requesting German military assistance, whereupon Hitler—claiming moral responsibility—signed the order for his troops to move in. President Miklas, now convinced that the game was up, begrudgingly signed the order appointing Seyss-Inquart chancellor.

While all this was going on Gretl Stonborough was bobbing about on the Atlantic Ocean with her maid Elizabeth Faustenhammer aboard the SS *Manhattan* bound for New York. Things were not altogether well with her. She had been feeling less than rich and desperately needed to sell her art collection. Before leaving for New York she had arranged for the bulk of it to be packed into sealed crates and sent to a depot in Vienna awaiting shipment. The Heritage Office had granted her an export license and her purpose in going to New York was to arrange for the sale of the pictures as soon as they arrived. By the time her ship reached port on March 18 the country of her birth had ceased to exist—no longer Austria but Ostmark, a province of the German Reich. If rumors of Hitler's *Anschluss* had not already reached her on board ship she would certainly have read all about it in the newspapers on the day of her arrival. "Reich Troops Pour Through Austria" was the *New York Times* front-page headline on that day. This was followed by a long article containing excerpts from a speech of Field Marshal Hermann Göring: "The Greater German Reich has risen. Seventy-five million Germans are united under the banner of the swastika cross. The longings of all Germans for a thousand years have been fulfilled."

What Gretl would not have been able to read in the New York newspapers was the news that her export license had been withdrawn by the new regime and that the sealed crates containing her paintings had been returned to her modern rectangular house on the Kundmanngasse.

PART FOUR

CONNECTION AND MELTDOWN

53 PATRIOT IN TROUBLE

On March 11, 1938—"Austria's longest day"—troops of the German Eighth Army were lined up along the north side of the Austro-German frontier nervously poised for orders to begin Operation Otto. They had no idea what sort of resistance to expect as they crossed the border into Austrian territory but would have been delighted to learn that welcoming swastikas were being unfurled in towns and cities throughout the land in preparation for their arrival. Arthur Seyss-Inquart, not officially chancellor of Austria until the early hours of March 12, was in command of internal affairs and elements of his National Socialist police force, working with Heinrich Himmler's unofficial agents, were given free rein to make sweeping preparations for the German Wehrmacht's imminent mobilization. Any potential threat of resistance had to be neutralized before the German troops advanced. In Vienna the arrest, imprisonment or deportation of all Austrians suspected of the crime of patriotism began in earnest. In the first wave 76,000 men and women were taken in for questioning and 6,000 rumored to have been supporters of Austrian independence or of Schuschnigg's plebiscite, were summarily sacked from their jobs in government, education and other branches of the civil service.

Prince Ernest von Starhemberg's Heimwehr and the Vaterländische Front were primary targets as being the most likely to mount a military resistance to the Wehrmacht. Starhemberg slipped over the border into Switzerland with his Jewish wife, the actress Nora Gregor; Emil Fey, the ex-head of the Vienna Heimwehr, was said to have shot himself—though evidence suggests he was murdered—while Paul's friend Prince Franz Windisch-Grätz, Starhemberg's ADC, fled to France. Kurt von Schuschnigg, ignoring advice to flee the country, was held under house arrest in Vienna. In 1941 he was interned in the concentration camp at Sachsenhausen where it was erroneously reported that he had witnessed his fifteen-year-old son being cudgeled to death by camp guards while employed as a "death-transport commando" burying the bodies of several thousand Russian POWs who had been murdered by Himmler's Schutzstaffel or SS.

Paul's links to the Heimwehr may or may not have been known to Nazi agents. His funding was supposedly secret, but a paper trail from the Heimwehr headquarters in Vienna or from Starhemberg's castle at Waxenberg near Linz may easily have led them to him. In any case Paul's strong patriotic views were never held back, so any number of informants could have tipped off the police. On March 11, the day before the German invasion, Paul was arrested, interrogated by police and sacked from his job as professor of piano at the Conservatoire. No criminal charges were brought against him. He was released under caution and probably kept under surveillance. It is possible that he was forced to swear the Nazi oath, though hard to imagine his having done so with good grace. He was certainly ordered to fly a huge swastika flag from the Wittgenstein Palais. One of his students, Erna Otten, remembers bicycling to her lesson. There was a loud Nazi demonstration going on in the Ringstrasse and she had to take the slip road. When she reached the Palais she saw the swastika flying from the building and remembered Paul's pained and contrite reaction: "As I entered the room, the professor apologised. I can still see him in front of me, how he placed his hand on his heart. He said he had not been able to do otherwise or they would have arrested him immediately."

On March 11, the day of his sacking, Paul secured a letter of recommendation from his boss at the Conservatoire, Josef Reitler, and a week later had it translated into English by the official "sworn interpreter" to the Austrian law courts, Thomas H. Rash:

> Paul Wittgenstein was invited by me to the New Vienna Conservatorium in 1931 and has up to this day conducted a pianoforte finishing class at this institute with exceptional success, which has repeatedly received public acknowledgment and recognition.
>
> The prejudice that the one-armed pianist, to whom the greatest living composers have dedicated works written for the left hand alone, had to contend with were, thanks to his eminent artistic and pedagogic qualities in conjunction with his high seriousness, sense of responsibility and great energy, brilliantly overcome by Paul Wittgenstein. As is unavoidable in a

*conservatorium class he had to test his abilities on pupils of average medi-
ocrity. So much more remarkable are the results of his individualistic
method of instruction. In this connection special mention must be made
of one of Paul Wittgenstein's special characteristics: an idealism, which
has become rare in these days. Both on the concert platform and in the
classroom this beautiful idealism has been his guiding star.*

*In this painful hour of parting I but follow the dictates of my heart
in testifying to the greatness of the artist and the merit of the man.*

(signed): Professor Josef Reitler

Shortly before dawn on the morning after Professor Reitler wrote his
testimonial, German troops started to move across the border. Hitler had
slapped his thigh shouting, *"Jetzt geht's los"* ("Let's be off now!"), giving the
green light to Operation Otto. His soldiers proceeded with caution, fingers poised on their triggers, but were soon relieved to discover that the
Austrian frontier guards had deserted their posts and obligingly dis-
mantled their barriers before they left. Not a shot was fired in the whole
operation and instead of resistance the German army's entry into Austria was fêted with cheers, smiles, salutes, *Heil Hitlers!* and the unfurling
of thousands of swastika banners all the way to Vienna.

At 3:50 that afternoon Hitler crossed the border at the place of his
birth, Braunau-am-Inn. Austria was technically still an independent nation, Seyss-Inquart was chancellor, Wilhelm Miklas president, so the
Führer let it be known that he was entering the country, not as a conquering hero, but simply to "visit his mother's grave." His warm welcome,
however, particularly from the good people of Linz, emboldened his heart
and within two days the description of his actions shifted from the
euphemistic-sounding *Anschluss* (connection) to the more blatant
Machtübernahme (assumption of power). Cardinal Innitzer, head of the
Austrian Catholic Church, who one week earlier had pronounced, "as
Austrian citizens, we stand and we fight for a free and independent Austria," now sent his warmest greetings to Hitler and ordered that all his
churches be draped with swastika flags while the bells tolled to welcome
the Nazi hero. The next day Hitler's demagoguery at Vienna's Helden-
platz was cheered by 200,000 ecstatic Austrian supporters and within a

month an official plebiscite (from which Jews, socialists and Austro-fascists were prohibited from taking part) returned a vote of 99.73 percent in favor of the annexation.

The Führer promised the Austrian people free holidays for their children and cheap "Strength Through Joy" holidays for the workers; he pledged money to buy radio sets so that they could listen to his speeches, and money for fast roads, and money to rid them of unemployment. These were exciting and happy times for most of the Austrian people. Even those who had originally objected to *Anschluss* were beginning to see the light. News that Hitler had canceled Schuschnigg's plebiscite of March 13 failed to reach the remote village of Tarrenz in time. In ignorance the inhabitants went ahead, voting 100 percent in favor of Austrian independence. Less than one month later 100 percent of the Tarrenz electorate recast their votes in favor of the German *Anschluss*.

The joy was not, however, universal. Socialists, Austro-fascists and freemasons all came in for persecution and so did the Jews, who were especially vulnerable to unlicensed mob actions against them. Their shops were smashed, boarded up or daubed with red paint, and their owners pressurized into selling to Aryans. One unruly mob in the Prater forced a group of Jews to eat grass like cows on their hands and knees, others were made to lick the streets or scrub public lavatories with their prayer shawls, while crowds of Austrians gathered round to jeer. On March 17, Reinhard Heydrich, later an important architect of the Holocaust, ordered the arrest of "those National Socialists who in the last few days allowed themselves to launch large-scale assaults in a totally undisciplined way against Jews," but the effect was minimal and official discrimination, which deprived Jews of their rights of citizenship, only served to encourage public acts of violence against them.

In the first days of *Anschluss* some 500 Jews are said to have committed suicide. Many more fled the country; but the majority refused to believe that the anti-Semitic legislation enshrined in the 1935 Nuremberg Laws could be made to work in a city with such a large and integrated Jewish population as Vienna. Sooner or later, they thought, the Nazis would drop their rules and concentrate on something more pressing. No one could have predicted the ruthless efficiency of the city's soon-to-be-formed Central Office for Jewish Emigration under the zealous command of SS-Obersturmführer Adolf Eichmann. The first anti-Semitic decrees were enacted in Vienna on March 12 (the actual day of *Anschluss*) and by May 28 the Nuremberg Laws (retroactive from March 13) were passed into law. Hitler's original scheme—to deprive Jews of voting rights, to stop them holding key jobs in the press, politics, law, the civil service and the arts, to prohibit them from sitting on park benches and so on—was intended to make life in the Reich so disagreeable for the Austrian Jew that he would leave the country of his own volition. But the plan was far more difficult to execute than Hitler or any in his Party had predicted, for not only had *Anschluss* made the Germans responsible once again for all those Jews who since 1933 had fled from Germany and into Austria, but many resident Jews felt either unable or reluctant to emigrate, while thousands more clung to the hope that the restrictions and persecutions against them would be softened or withdrawn over time. Within six months 45,000 Jews are said to have emigrated from the Ostmark. Himmler's urgent task was to find a way of getting rid of the 150,000 that remained.

Three years later the emigration of Jews from the Reich was still incomplete and Hitler was desperate with impatience. "The Jew must clear out of Europe," he reminded Himmler and his staff commander Colonel Zeitzler over lunch.

> When I think about it I realise that I am extraordinarily humane. At the time of the rule of the Popes the Jews were mistreated in Rome. Until 1830, eight Jews mounted on donkeys were led once a year through the streets of Rome. For my part, I restrict myself to telling them they must go away. If they break their pipes on the journey I can't do anything about it. But if they refuse to go voluntarily, I see no other solution but extermination.

One morning in late March, Paul came into the room where Hermine was sitting, his face white with horror, and said to her: "Wir gelten als Juden" (We count as Jews!). Both he and his sister and their siblings suddenly and unexpectedly found themselves subject to all the anti-Semitic restrictions and prohibitions of the new National Socialist regime. Already barred from his post at the Conservatoire for his patriotic fervor, Paul was now banned from teaching in any civic institution and forbidden from performing in public anywhere within the Reich. Soon the Nazi eye would cast its glower on Hermine's Occupational Institute for Boys. A troop of uniformed men waving swastikas would turn up as she was teaching and order her to evacuate the premises by 4 p.m. as the building was needed as a training school for the Hitler Youth. Soon, too, the Nazis would discover Hilde Schania and her two children hidden away in her flat at Gersthoferstrasse 30, and connect them to Paul. The children themselves would be proof enough that a Jew, the father of Elizabeth and Johanna, was guilty of *Rassenschande* (race defilement) as codified in Section 2 of the Nuremberg Law for the Protection of German Blood and German Honor: "Extramarital intercourse between Jews and subjects of the state, of German or related blood, is forbidden."

But before these heavy threats were brought to bear, Hermine and Paul found themselves facing an altogether different charge, for they were in breach of the Führer's decree of March 12 relating to the *Reichsflaggengesetz* or Reich Flag Law, which forbade Jews from displaying the swastika symbol. So by an odd twist of irony the detested flag that the Gestapo had forced Paul to hang from his Palais under threat of arrest was thus ordered down by the same frantic authority, on the basis that the occupants were now Jewish and had no right to fly it.

54 FIRST PLANS

Karl Lueger, the turn-of-the-century anti-Semitic mayor of Vienna, when challenged to define a Jew offered the catchphrase formula "Wer ein Jud' ist, bestimme Ich" (I decide who is a Jew). Hitler reserved this special privilege for himself as well and would occasionally (though rarely) grant an Aryanization certificate to Jews that he liked. He insisted, however, on the right to examine each of their applications personally, poring over photographs and letters of recommendation. Most cases hinged on whether a Jewish ancestor of the male line was the true father or a cuckold to his wife's Aryan lover. In such incidents a signed affidavit was needed, which is precisely what happened in the case of Hitler's trusted ally, Field Marshal Erhard Milch, who responded to the Gestapo's discovery that his father Anton Milch was Jewish by asking his mother to sign a statement swearing that his true father had been the Aryan Karl Bauer—her uncle.

To enjoy full civil rights under the new regime each person required a Reich Citizenship Certificate, which could be obtained only by providing proof of Aryan descent. But this in itself was often problematic. Was a Jew considered Jewish by blood or by religion? What if one of his parents was half Jewish by blood but Christian by upbringing? This muddle was supposedly resolved by the Nuremberg Laws of September 1935, in which it was stipulated that a Jew must be defined as anyone who descends from at least three Jewish grandparents or from two Jewish grandparents if they themselves were, on or after September 15, 1935, either married to a Jewish person or a member of the Jewish community. It was further stated that conversion to Christianity by a Jewish grandparent did not change the racial status of that grandparent, who in law remained a Jew; but even this was not clear enough for all cases and in March 1936 the Reich Association for Non-Aryan Christians issued a question-and-answer booklet for further clarification: "What can be said about the marriage of a half-Aryan with a girl who has one Aryan parent, but whose Aryan mother converted to Judaism so that the girl was raised as a Jew? What can be said further about the children of this marriage?"

In the massive confusion, the system threw up thousands of surprises and anomalies. Many had not the slightest idea about their grandparents' blood or religion. Furthermore investigations showed that there was far more Jewish blood in the system than the Nazis had either hoped or expected to find. When they discovered that Johann Strauss, the "Waltz King," had Jewish blood they simply erased his record from the registry. Similar complications arose with the ancestors of Richard Wagner's wife and of Lorenzo da Ponte, Mozart's librettist, so that special arrangements had to be made in order not to have to ban performances of the *Marriage of Figaro, Don Giovanni* and the "Blue Danube" Waltz, and so that Hitler could continue to enjoy the Wagner Festival at Bayreuth in the company of the composer's granddaughter.

Many active members of the Nazi Party were brought to a rude awakening when they discovered that they themselves qualified as Jews under the Nuremberg rules. Hitler's vapid English friend Unity Mitford wrote to her sister Diana of a woman called Eva Baum: "She was discovered to be a half-Jüdin. Isn't it *amazing* . . . I am really sorry for her, as the Partei & her hate for the Jews were really all she had." In another letter Miss Mitford wrote of her friend Heinz, a member of the SS and a "real Nazi 'aus Überzeugung' " (by conviction) who suddenly found that he too was half Jewish and whose wife sought Miss Mitford's help in bringing his case to Hitler's attention: "Of course poor Heinz was completely erledigt [shattered] when he heard it, & wanted to shoot himself at once, which it seems to me would have been the best way out . . . Isn't it *awful* for them, poor things. I must say it gave me an awful shock when she told me."

The case of the Wittgensteins looked, prima facie, pretty clear-cut. They were all brought up as Catholic Christians. Both their parents (Karl and Leopoldine) had also been brought up as Christians. Their maternal grandmother, Marie Kalmus (née Stallner; 1825–1911), had no Jewish blood and was brought up Catholic, but her husband, their maternal grandfather, Jacob Kalmus (1814–70), was by blood and by upbringing Jewish. In 1832 both he and his mother converted to Catholicism. On the paternal side their grandmother Franziska Figdor (1814–90) was also Jewish—though she too was baptized as a Christian in adulthood, while her husband Hermann Christian Wittgenstein (1802–78) was, according to the wording on his baptismal certificate of 1839, "educated in the Jewish faith." Three out of their four grandparents were therefore Jewish, which made them *Volljuden* (full Jews) under the Nuremberg legislation.

According to Hermine, "Our most intimate family had never considered itself Jewish." This may well be true, but was based on the understanding that they were not Jewish because their ancestors had converted, not on any belief that they had no Jewish blood. Sometime before his father's death Paul had taken a keen interest in family genealogy and produced family trees that demonstrated his descent from several distinguished figures of Viennese Jewry, including direct lines to the court financier and Chief Rabbi Samson Wertheimer (1678–1724), and to the famous banker, imperial court factor and arms dealer Samuel Oppenheimer (1635–1703). Through these connections the charts also reveal his kinship to two of the nineteenth century's greatest Jewish composers, Giacomo Meyerbeer and Felix Mendelssohn. In youth, he and Ludwig had applied to join a sports club in Vienna. When they discovered that membership was limited to Aryans, Ludwig had suggested falsifying the application form, which Paul refused to do. Their uncle Louis when asked about the Wittgensteins' Jewishness answered, "Pur sang!" with an affected grin. He, of course, was an ardent Christian Evangelist. When Nazi anti-Semitism became a talking point in England, Ludwig, filled with remorse, went about rousing his friends at inconvenient hours to make formal confessions to them. He felt that he had somehow allowed them to form the impression that he came from a family of Aryan aristocrats, when he should have told them that he was Jewish all along.

So it seems that the Wittgensteins knew from the start of their Jewish ancestry and that in some respects they were proud of it, but as a family of three generations of practicing Christians they were by 1938 (if not long before) in a state of denial when it came to the crunch question "Are you Jewish?"

Ludwig was surprised when news reached him of the *Anschluss,* as he had never believed it would happen. He was in Ireland at the time and returned immediately to Cambridge, where he wrote to Paul and Hermine telling them that, if needed, he would come to Vienna straightaway. At the same time he took the precaution of soliciting advice from his friend the economist Piero Sraffa. Sraffa told him not to risk a trip to Austria, as the authorities there were unlikely to let him leave again, that he would have to exchange his Austrian passport for a German one and that if they discovered his Jewish ancestry they might refuse even to do this. Caught between the displeasing alternatives of becoming a German citizen (which "even apart from all the nasty consequences is *appalling* to me") and applying for a British passport ("something I have always rejected on the grounds that I do not wish to become a sham-Englishman"), Ludwig chose the latter, receiving a year later (on April 14, 1939) a grant of British citizenship.

By March 18, 1938, he had still heard nothing from his family in Vienna but had worked out for himself that "by the annexation of Austria by Germany I have become a German citizen and, by the German laws, a German Jew (as three of my grandparents were baptized only as adults)." As far as the rest of his family was concerned he took the view that since "they are almost all retiring and very respected people who have always felt and behaved patriotically it is, on the whole, unlikely that they are at present in any danger."

In Vienna, Paul and Hermine were of much the same opinion. Neither had bothered to make a study of the Nuremberg Laws, but they blithely assumed that, even if their Jewish blood were held against them by the new regime, they would probably be protected by virtue of the family's high standing in Austrian public life. All they needed to do was to explain how good, worthy and patriotic the Wittgensteins had always been and that should be enough to ensure them their *Deutschblütigkeitserklärungen,* or German Blood Certificates. Of course it was never going to be that simple. Paul went first on his own to an office in the Minoritenplatz, waited for several hours in a queue in the hallway only to be told when he reached the end of it that rules were rules and his application for special treatment was rejected.

On April 30, Gretl returned from America. She had stopped briefly in Paris for an emergency meeting with Ludwig and to call on Jerome. By the time she reached Vienna she was full of bright ideas about what needed doing. All her adult life she had hosted diplomats, politicians and people in important positions and now, at this moment of national and familial crisis, she sensed the long-awaited opportunity to exhibit her energies and capabilities. First she insisted that Paul had been wasting his time with the authorities in Vienna, they were pettifogging power-maniacs, she knew far more important people in the high echelons of the NSDAP (Nazi Party) in Berlin. These were the people to whom they should apply with a properly drawn-up dossier itemizing all the family's worthy and patriotic achievements.

Hermine was put in charge of collecting the information. She wrote to Ludwig asking if he would lend his weight to their application by sending her a list of his medals, wartime deeds and charitable actions. Fearing, perhaps, that this might jeopardize his own ongoing application for British citizenship, Ludwig wrote back to Paul:

> Although I won't join with you in making this application, *I am however convinced of its justifiability for you.* You may of course cite my war service etc.; it's just that this must not lead to a misunderstand-

ing that as a result I am automatically involved in your application. With much love and good wishes, yours Ludwig.

The stated intention of Hermine's dossier was "to prove the German and Christian nature of the Wittgenstein family and the numerous services performed by the family members for their Fatherland." On a neatly drawn family tree it was also stated that the Wittgensteins wished to carry on making charitable donations in future and to "do everything in our power to prove that we retain a similar attitude towards the common good of the new regime, even though the family assets have been considerably reduced by World War and inflation." A list of Paul's military achievements and some of his less secretive donations was easy to draw up, but Hermine had to write to some of Ludwig's army friends to ask them what they knew, if anything, about his decorations. As to Kurt's army record it was decided that no mention should be made of his men refusing to obey orders, but the dossier should simply state that he had fought with courage and shot himself at the end only in order to avoid capture by the Italians.

As to the list of the family's charitable donations, this too proved to be problematical for upon closer investigation Hermine discovered that a great deal of the money had been misspent—the million kronen that Ludwig had donated for a super-cannon, for instance, had been wasted; the million Kurt had left to charity had disappeared; the 600,000 that Dr. von Eiselsberg had taken in the name of cancer research had never been put to any such use. Hermine found countless lowering examples of this type and each new discovery grieved her. When the authorities discovered her father's 40,000-florin donation toward the cost of building the "Golden Cabbage" (the exhibition hall of the Vienna Secession) in 1898, they demanded the removal of a fixed plaque commemorating this act of Jewish generosity. "Jews who become philanthropists and endow foundations are dirty dogs [said Hitler in conversation]. As a rule, it's the most rascally of them who do that sort of thing. And then you'll hear these poor Aryan boobies telling you: 'You see, there *are* good Jews!' "

At the beginning of June Paul and Gretl, bearing Hermine's "beautiful" dossier, traveled to Berlin, the dynamic and cosmopolitan capital of

Hitler's Reich. Here, in the lion's den, the place where the Nazi Party had its headquarters, Jews felt safer than in Vienna. From the moment they stepped off the train at Berlin's Anhalter Bahnhof, Paul and Gretl noticed how not everybody in Berlin was wearing swastika badges and armbands as they did in Vienna; that there was no red paint daubed on Jewish shops. Here Jews were still permitted to attend theaters and cinemas, to eat in restaurants and cafés, to own and run shops that were still serving Aryan customers. On the Kurfürstendamm, Berlin's main shopping street, only one boutique displayed the sign ubiquitous in Vienna: "No Jewish customers." In sharp contrast to the German capital, Vienna now seemed a thuggish and provincial backwater.

Gretl had succeeded in arranging a meeting with Captain Fritz Wiedemann, Hitler's ADC, at the Chancellery, Berlin W8. The introduction may have been arranged by the Dodds. William Dodd, the American Ambassador to Berlin, knew both Jerome and Gretl, while his daughter, Martha Dodd, was seen at parties in Washington with Ji. But Ambassador Dodd hated all Nazis with the exception of Hermann Göring and had, in any case, left Berlin in December 1937. Martha, his daughter, also disliked Wiedemann, describing him in her book *Through Embassy Eyes* as "exuding eroticism, with heavy face and beetling eyebrows, friendly eyes and extremely low forehead, [and] rather attractive . . . but I got the distinct impression of an uncultivated, primitive mind, with the shrewdness and cunning of an animal, and completely without delicacy or subtlety."

A more likely source of Gretl's introduction to Wiedemann was his mistress, the pushy Princess Stephanie von Hohenlohe-Waldenburg-Schillingfürst, who was in Washington enjoying the same diplomatic-party circuit as Gretl at the beginning of April. The two women had met one another before that in Vienna and also in Paris. In a sense they were rivals—as both were Viennese hostesses, both batting their eyelids at the same small circle of prominent diplomats and both actively seeking to use their connections to their own strategic advantage. The Princess (who had had an illegitimate son by Franz Salvator of Austria-Tuscany, a member of the same family that had leased and subsequently sold the Villa Toscana at Gmunden to the Stonboroughs) had become the lover of Fritz Wiedemann in order to maintain close contact with Hitler, whom she first met when acting as ambassador for the British press baron Lord Rothermere.

Hitler was briefly infatuated by Princess Stephanie, but by the time Paul and Gretl came to see Fritz Wiedemann he had discovered that she was Jewish, that she was the mistress of his adjutant and that, according to his advisers, she might also be a double agent. In his conversations he called her "a scarecrow," adding: "I prefer a friendly little kitchen wench to a politically minded lady!" Because of this, Wiedemann had to explain to Paul and Gretl that he was being cold-shouldered by the Führer and that he could not possibly arrange an audience as he was expecting himself to be sacked at any moment. Instead he arranged for them to see SS-Obersturmbannführer Kurt Mayer, who headed the Reich Agency for Genealogical Research on the Schiffbauerdamm a few streets away. Soon after this meeting Wiedemann was sacked by Hitler and posted abroad as German consul in San Francisco. Gretl later admitted that she had liked him very much despite his being of little help.

At the Agency for Genealogical Research, Paul and Gretl met Kurt Mayer, who had a doctorate in history, running an office staff of eighty-one men and forty-two women, most of whom were in their late twenties or early thirties, struggling to process an avalanche of Aryanization requests from desperate Jewish families. By the end of the war Mayer and his staff had sifted through 52,000 case files, fewer than 10 percent of which resulted in any change to the classification of the applicant.

At his desk Mayer looked courteously over Paul and Gretl's papers and listened to their arguments but concluded that the past glories of the Wittgenstein family had nothing to do with the case: they had three Jewish grandparents and must therefore accept the official classification of *Volljuden*. Their only hope was to discover that one of these grandparents was the illegitimate son or daughter of an Aryan in which case they might be eligible for the status of *Mischling*, or half-breed, which, although unpleasant, would at least exempt them from the more oppressive laws applied to *Volljuden*: "A second Aryan grandparent is essential," he told them.

Rumors had long been circulating among the aunts, uncles and cousins of the family that the progenitor of the Wittgensteins, Paul and

Gretl's grandfather Hermann Christian Wittgenstein, was the bastard son of a German aristocrat, believed to be Prince Georg Heinrich Ludwig, a reprobate scion of the princely house of Sayn-Wittgenstein-Berleburg. A pretty Jewish maid (so the story goes), by the name Breindel Brendel or Bernardine Simon, who worked in the household of Prince Georg at Laasphe, became pregnant by him (or by his brother) and to cover up the scandal was forced to marry the Prince's land agent and factotum, Moses Meyer, and move with him to another Wittgenstein estate to have the baby. It was here then, in Korbach, on September 12, 1802, that Hermann Christian Wittgenstein is supposed to have been born. Except that he wasn't called Hermann Christian Wittgenstein at the time of his birth, but was probably called Hirsch (or Herz) Moses Meyer. Following a Napoleonic decree of 1808 by which all Jews were ordered to adopt fixed surnames, the family took the name Wittgenstein and in 1839 Moses Meyer's son Hirsch converted to Christianity, adopting the name Hermann Christian Wittgenstein.

In the Schiffbauerdamm, Kurt Mayer assured Paul and Gretl in the politest manner that their best bet was to pursue this line of inquiry and that they should hire a professional genealogist to search the records at Korbach and at Laasphe. Both disapproved of the scheme (their father Karl had humorously disclaimed connection to the Sayn-Wittgenstein family by describing his name as "mein Wittgenstein" in distinction from "sein Wittgenstein"), but now it appeared to be their only chance. It was a typical symptom of the craziness of Nazi Party policy that in June 1938 the future security of one man, his daughters, his siblings, his nephews, nieces and cousins all hung in the balance, all dependent upon who had slept with whom way back in January 1802.

COUNTER-ATTACK

Gretl once told her cousin Karl Menger: "I want to be remembered as the daughter of my father, the sister of my brothers, and the mother of my sons." Notable by its absence from this list is any desire to be remembered as the wife of her husband. By June 1938 she was divorced from Jerome and had all but given up on him. She remained loyal however and allowed him to visit her at Gmunden or in Vienna. She also provided him with money. At the time of *Anschluss* he had found himself in the Austrian capital. Immediately he realized that neither funds nor valuables could be removed from the Reich and that his lavish and extravagant Parisian lifestyle would finally have to come to an end. He returned to France in order to sell his furniture and pictures. From Paris he could have proceeded directly to America, but he felt uncomfortable with that idea and went back to Vienna instead. There he fell into a frenzy of depression and agitation, fearing destitution and impending war. It is said that he was suffering from a "severe cancerous illness" that deepened his despair. Not everyone agrees. In any case he was woebegone, and on June 15 for some forgotten reason he lost his temper and shot himself in the head with a hunting rifle while staying at the Villa Toscana in Gmunden.

Gretl moved quickly to prevent the news of his suicide getting into the papers, and the editor of the local *Salzkammergut Beobachter,* working from his offices at Adolf Hitler Platz in Gmunden, duly ignored the sudden and violent death of the lord of the local manor and ran small items on the natural deaths of two old biddies and the attempted suicide of a lovelorn milkmaid instead.

Neither in life nor in death was Jerome much honored. He had used a portion of his wife's money to endow a scientific institute but lost a lot more of it in bad investments. He had failed as a husband to Gretl and was a bad-tempered and absent father to his sons. None of his in-laws liked him much, and after his death, there was little to be said about him. His life had been occupied in restless pursuit of scientific knowledge, in squandering other people's money and causing them grief by his paranoid fits of neurosis. His death, which came at an inconvenient hour for Gretl, must have relieved her and her sons of an irksome burden. He was buried quietly in the town cemetery at Gmunden.

The great love of Gretl's life, in whom she vested her highest aspirations, was her younger son and "golden boy" Ji. Poor stammering Tommy had proved a disappointment. Arrogant and lazy, depressive and not very bright with money, cars or women, he was reckless and feckless and Gretl found herself constantly having to bail him out of trouble. Ji on the other hand was a star in her eyes. To many he seemed to be "just like his mummy." In youth he was effeminate, with a high-pitched voice. He was a late developer who remained a mummy's boy well into his thirties. Once, long before, Gretl had pined for a daughter but now, realizing that she would never have one, she encouraged the softer sides of Ji, while simultaneously pushing him beyond his abilities. "I want my children to become reformers of some kind," she would say. "That is the only career befitting our family." To that end she had Ji thinking about social issues from an early age. As soon as his schooling was finished—he was no intellectual and did not distinguish himself either at his upper-class boarding school in Baden-Württemberg or at Vienna's smart academy, the Theresianum—he was encouraged to attend lectures in political science at the universities of Freiburg and Vienna. After that he became a volunteer for the Vienna Rescue Society, and briefly worked at a Swiss cheese factory and at a Czechoslovakian brewery. In 1933 he covered the World Economic Conference in London for the *Brooklyn Times-Union* and for a while entertained the notion of becoming a political or financial journalist, but his mother had higher ambitions for him. According to their cousin Karl Menger: "For all her social conscience, Mrs. Stonborough seemed to me to belong to that type of very rich Europeans who consider important positions even more than wealth as a birthright of their children." In 1935 she used her diplomatic and political connections to secure him a job, aged twenty-three, at the Department of Labor in Washington, where he worked in the office of Roosevelt's Secretary for Labor, Frances Perkins, the first American woman to hold a cabinet post.

Mother love and early success brought a swagger to young Ji's gait. He was quick tempered, opinionated and conceited. Although no aristocrat, his manner was *de haut en bas* or what the Viennese would call *hopper-tatschig*. Lofty is perhaps the best English word for it. Those whom he did not like were dismissed as "vulgar" and "prole" or berated for their "damned prole insolence" in an accent that was neither American nor German, but even more English than the English. *Odi profanum vulgus* was his oft-stated motto: "I hate the vulgar rabble."

By 1937, Helene's husband, Max Salzer, who had managed the Wittgenstein foreign fortune since 1925, was suffering from senile dementia, so with Gretl's push it was decided that the now twenty-five-year-old Ji should take over his role. This was an odd choice as Ji was young and volatile, knew nothing about business and had no head for maths ("Computing how little there is in my cheque book is well beyond me," he once jokingly admitted), but when Gretl had decided on something, that was that. A company was duly incorporated in Switzerland, in the tax-haven canton of Zug, under the name Wistag AG & Cie. The share or partner capital of one million Swiss francs was to be controlled by Ji, and the interest on that sum was to be used to meet the running costs of a subsidiary trust that held the Wittgensteins' foreign investments. In 1939 these were valued at 9.6 million Swiss francs. Under Swiss law the exact apportionment of the trust shares could be kept secret from everyone except the beneficiaries themselves. The deeds of incorporation stipulated that each of the shareholders could receive a small rate of interest from the trust but that the capital sum must remain with the company (Wistag) for ten years. In other words the trust could not be broken, nor the capital taken out of it until 1947.

Meanwhile Hitler's Four-Year Plan, an expensive program of national reconstruction and rearmament, made him thirsty for revenue and in April 1938 he issued a decree that required all citizens of whatever racial origin to declare their foreign assets. Any currency held abroad was to be brought immediately back into the Reich and exchanged for Reichsmarks at a rate favorable to the government. The form that was sent out to the Jewish population at the beginning of May was an extended version of that which went to the Aryan population and demanded that every Jew provide details of *all* his or her assets, including those held within the Reich—pictures, plates, bank credit, buildings, businesses, photographs and so on. Jews could then be charged the *Judenvermögensabgabe* (Jewish capital levy) of 20 percent of their total asset worth. If they then wished to emigrate they could pay a 25 percent emigration tax and a further 65 percent on whatever was left of their cash reserves. After all these taxes had been submitted it was highly unlikely any Jew would be able to leave the Reich with more than 10 percent of his or her original wealth. At the top of the form entitled "Register of the Assets of the Jews" was printed the warning:

This inventory must be submitted by 30 June 1938. Anyone who is liable to register their assets and have them valued but who either fails to fulfil this obligation or does so either too late or incompetently risks a severe penalty (fine, imprisonment, a jail sentence or confiscation of their assets).

Paul's, Hermine's and Helene's properties were searched and everything of worth that was found in them scrutinized by the art historian, Gestapo agent and valuer Dr. Otto Reich. Gretl, as a Jewess, was also forced to fill in one of these forms, despite her being an American citizen. When Dr. Reich came to her house on the Kundmanngasse she was not at home, but a quick-thinking servant brought out some bauble of interest and, as Dr. Reich was drooling over it, shot into the garden with armfuls of precious manuscripts and hid them in the potting shed. Gretl's form looks a little understated. Her artworks and porcelain collection were together valued at only 11,235 Reichsmarks, her silver and jewelry at 9,000 RM, while her priceless collection of musical manuscripts was not included. Nor is it clear whether the artworks that were packed up for export in March were accounted for in this valuation. As an American Gretl was under no obligation to declare her foreign assets, and while she and her sons were still free to travel in and out of the Reich there was much incentive for her to bury or hide as much as possible and try to smuggle it out bit by bit.

Paul's declaration claims an income of 57,700 Reichsmarks in the year to April 1938, and assets of 4,368,625 RM. The form makes interesting reading as it offers a glimpse into his private financial affairs. It reveals, for instance, that his sister Hermine owed him 107,512 RM (presumably loans against debts she had incurred on her school) and that among his possessions were to be found a sixteenth-century Gobelin tapestry worth 15,000 RM, a Stradivari violin of 1716 valued at 30,000 RM and a viola by Antonius and Hieronymus Amati at 10,000 RM—this last instrument was valued by Machold Rare Violins on April 15, 2002, at $1.8 million. Among his pictures, whose total value was put at 70,080 RM, he owned Monet's oil portrait of Eugenie Graff, *Madame Paul* (now at the Fogg Art Museum at Harvard) and Giovanni Segantini's *Die Quelle des Übels* (The Source of Evil), which Karl had bought at the wildly successful Secession Exhibition of 1898, valued in 1938 at 26,000 RM. At the end of the register, in a space reserved for remarks, Paul had written:

This form has been completed while I and my sisters, Hermine and Helene Salzer (born Wittgenstein), are still in the process of applying to be released from these obligations. My siblings and I are convinced that our grandfather, Hermann Christian Wittgenstein, was not a full Jew by blood. His appearance and his way of life, and the appearance of his direct descendants, demonstrate this and the Department of Genealogical Research [in Vienna] has initiated an inquiry to establish if this confidence of ours is right. If it is the case then we are only two parts Jewish and I would like to point out that all the members of the Wittgenstein family have for 100 years been born and brought up as Christians. The family originates from Germany and came to Austria in 1850.

56 ESCAPE

Paul was convinced that the only sensible course of action was to leave Austria and could think or speak of little else. As a patriot he was heartbroken that 99 percent of the Austrian people had so enthusiastically and perfidiously sold out to the Germans in Hitler's referendum of April 1938. Even if the Reich Agency for Genealogical Research were to grant him *Mischling* status he would still be banned from teaching and performing. Hermine, on the other hand, was able to distance herself from worldly affairs and was content to muddle along, imagining the worst that could happen to her was that a few of her friends might no longer greet her in the street. Paul stood to lose a good deal more.

> Paul [Hermine wrote] suffered indescribably during his long daily walks and wanderings because of the abominable prohibitions that threatened every step in the crassest manner and wounded his self-esteem. He acted like a man whose very foundations of life had been destroyed.

So long as he had money abroad the authorities were not going to let him out. First, they demanded that he bring all of his foreign fortune into the Reich, then he must pay the 25 percent *Reichsfluchtsteuer* (emigration tax) and all the other tariffs that the regime had created to rob the emigrating Jew. Only then would they consider his emigration. But even if he had wished to adhere to government guidelines Paul could not have done so, for his foreign assets were locked into a Swiss trust until 1947. Paul's only hope was to flee the country and to try to gain access to his Swiss funds once he was safely abroad. His passport was stamped with an unexpired Swiss visa but he needed also an exit permit to get out of the Ostmark.

Staying with Marga in England, he used often to play parlor games in the evenings, consisting of quizzes and tests about classical music. It was during one such game that Marga and Paul realized that both of them knew the libretti to various of Mozart's operas by heart, so by using references to them they were now able to communicate without rousing the suspicion of the censors. For instance, Paul's intention of coming to London was suggested by the phrase "Due parole." It is with those words that Count Almaviva, in the short recitative from Act I, scene 6 of Mozart's *Marriage of Figaro,* prefaces his announcement that he is to be sent to London. Marga, who had spent many hours playing cryptic musical games with Paul on their holidays by the sea, knew exactly what they meant. By this means a plan was hatched to create reasonable grounds for the authorities in Vienna to allow Paul to make a brief visit to England. Marga sent letters on bogus "Gunfield Concert Agency" letterhead, offering Paul dates in a series of lecture recitals for which the musicologists Ernest Walker and Donald Francis Tovey were also billed. These nonexistent performances were originally planned for May but Paul was unable to obtain his visa; so she rearranged the dates, sending him another contract for mid-June. Once again, Paul was thwarted by officials and telegraphed to say it was impossible. On June 17, Gretl was coming to London, planning to stay at a hotel in Ebury Street. Paul wired Marga: "SHE WOULD LIKE TO SEE YOU OXFORD OR LONDON—PLEASE LEAVE MESSAGE AT GORING." But two days later he was obliged to send another: "MY BROTHER-IN-LAW STONBOROUGH DIED SUDDENLY THIS EVENING STOP MY SISTER WILL COME LATER STOP HEARTFELT GREETINGS AND REGRETS—PAUL."

Gretl arrived in England a few days after Jerome's funeral and met

Marga briefly in London before traveling to Cambridge, where she handed Ludwig two smuggled parcels. They contained pieces of jewelry and musical manuscripts belonging to various members of the family—Beethoven's Piano Sonata, Opus 109; Haydn's Symphony No. 90 in C; Mozart's A major Violin Concerto; an early Bach cantata ("Meine Seele"), and two piano concertos by Mozart (K 238 and K 467). She asked Ludwig to look after them on behalf of their siblings in Austria who might one day need them. Ludwig placed the two packages in safe-deposit boxes at Barclays Bank on Bennett Street, with entitlement for two people besides himself (John Maynard Keynes and Piero Sraffa) to remove them in his absence.

Marga, meanwhile, was making her own inquiries about how to obtain a British passport for Paul. In one of their coded letters Paul had urged her to visit Ludwig, who, he believed, might be in a position to pull strings. A meeting was arranged between them at a London hotel and was concluded, to Marga's astonishment, in ten minutes flat. A long silence followed, broken eventually by Ludwig: "Everything has been settled now."

"But I have come all the way from Southwold to Charing Cross about your brother's affairs. I think you might at least invite me to lunch."

"Well, if you want that, then all right," said Ludwig wearily, "but what can you want to say to me now?"

"I don't know," Marga replied, "but I expect I shall think of something soon."

So off they went to a Lyons Corner House, where they talked about people they both knew in Vienna while Ludwig agreed or disagreed always with alarming animus. After a while he stood up abruptly and declared, "You have said things that make me want to go on talking. Let us go to the zoo." The caged animals provided ample amusement and afterward they sat and had tea. "I offered him some of my jam, since he had finished his," Marga recalled. "He objected, though it was part of the share the waiter brought me, it was not mine, nor was what he had eaten *his*, it was all 'just jam.'" After that Ludwig escorted her by third-class Underground to Liverpool Street saying, as he did so, that he had talked enough and was only coming to carry her coat, which he had discovered at the zoo was too heavy for her to carry and too hot to wear. As they parted company Marga generously invited him to stay with her at South-wold. "It sounds good," he answered, "but it's no good for me. I know I would hate it."

Back in Vienna Gretl had arranged a meeting with the new Governor of Ostmark, Arthur Seyss-Inquart, to whom she had a line of connection through his brother Richard. Described by Ji Stonborough as a "nice, hon-est and honorable man" Richard Seyss-Inquart had joined the Nazi Party in 1938 shortly before his elder brother became chancellor. According to one report Richard was "a full-hearted Nazi" who was charged with the task of persuading the Catholic Church to support Hitler's *Anschluss*. He had served as a Catholic priest during the First World War and had since worked as a chaplain and teacher in various deaf-and-dumb schools, or-phanages and army hospitals. In 1920 he abandoned the priesthood in order to get married and wrote several books of depressing poems that nobody bought. Richard had met Gretl through his work as head of a young offenders' institution at Langenzerdorf where she had a seat on the board of governors. In 1928, desperate for a divorce, he suffered a ner-vous breakdown and Gretl housed and fed him in the so-called Little Villa at Gmunden during the weeks of his recuperation.

In gratitude for these kindnesses, Richard's brother Arthur Seyss-Inquart, the new head or *Reichsstatthalter* of the Ostmark, agreed to see Gretl. Seyss-Inquart, a *Gruppenführer* of the SS, passionately pro-German and anti-Semitic, has gone down in the annals and almanacs of history as an evil man. As minister of the interior in Schuschnigg's cabinet, he had operated behind the scenes to open the doors to Hitler. Two years after *Anschluss* he was appointed *Reichskommissar* in the Netherlands and in 1946 was hanged at Nuremberg for his culpability for the deaths of 100,000 Jews. Gretl did not take to him much but, for a month at least, she had his ear and used it to plead the case of several distressed friends, includ-ing Paul. She told him that her brother was in a nervous state, that she had looked after Richard when he was similarly distressed, and now she needed his help to save Paul from possible suicide. She accepted that em-igration was out of the question, but argued that since his racial status was not yet resolved it would be reasonable to grant him a short break to give a few concerts in England. Seyss-Inquart told her that he would arrange Paul's visa on condition that she promised he would return to the Reich. This she did, with Paul's authority, and on August 23 her brother obtained a three-week exit permit and left the Reich on the following day.

For a fortnight he stayed in England visiting Marga in Oxford and Ludwig in Cambridge. To both he explained his desperate need to emigrate. Since he could not access his capital share of the Wistag Fund and was forbidden to leave the Reich with money or valuables, he was concerned about his income. Marga invited him to live with her and her sister in Oxford, assuring him that she would provide all the money he needed. Pathologically averse to accepting help from others, Paul wrote to her on his return:

> One thing I can say: that you, dear Marga, are one of the few people from whom, without thinking twice about it and without any bitterness, I would accept help, including material assistance, with the same sincerity with which it was offered. But I do hope, however, that it will not come to that even in the worst case!

Marga tried to persuade him that England was a natural choice. He spoke the language fluently, knew the literature, had visited every year for the past fifteen years, his brother lived there, he was a welcome star of the concert platform and, through her, had made many English friends; but in Cambridge he was deterred from the idea by his younger brother. As Ludwig had earlier been warned by Piero Sraffa: "As to the possibility of war, I do not know: it may happen any moment, or we may have one or two more years of 'peace.' I really have no idea. But I should not gamble on the likelihood of 6 months' peace." It could take a year or two to get British citizenship and if war broke out between England and Germany in the meantime Paul would face deportation or imprisonment as a resident alien.

Five days before his Reich exit visa was due to expire he returned to Vienna but only to find himself, once again, in deep trouble with the authorities. A threatening, formal and bureaucratic letter from the State Commissioner for the Personal Property Sector of the Assets Handling Agency of the Ministry of Economics and Labor lay still unanswered on his desk:

Herr Paul Wittgenstein
   Re: III Jews 29/38 g.

Pursuant to Article 7 of the Ordinance, dated 26 Apr 1938 (Reich Legal Gazetteer I, p 414), relating to the Registration of Assets by Jews, I hereby require you, in exercise of the authority granted me by the Commissioner of the Four-Year Plan, to offer the foreign investment securities registered by you, pursuant to the above-mentioned ordinance, for sale to the Reichsbank branch responsible for your usual place of residence in Vienna and, if so requested, to sell to them. Your offer must be made at the latest within one week of receipt of this demand.

Far worse even than this stifling demand was the realization that the authorities had now discovered Hilde and the children. Paul was served with a court summons on a charge of *Rassenschande* or racial defilement, and the guardianship of Elizabeth and Johanna was taken away from him. According to Section 5, Article 2 of the Nuremberg Law for the Protection of German Blood and German Honor, a Jew who had extramarital intercourse with a subject of the state of German blood would "be punished with imprisonment or hard labor." In 1939 the average sentence for a Jewish man caught with an Aryan woman was between four and five years' imprisonment. Later *Rassenschande* would be treated more seriously and by 1945 it was one of the forty-three crimes punishable by death. By a curious anomaly, among the many codified definitions of what did or did not constitute Jewishness, it was ordained that "the offspring of an extramarital relationship with a full Jew born out of wedlock after July 31, 1936," be classified as a full Jew. This meant that Johanna, Paul's younger daughter (born in March 1937), counted to the Nazis as Jewish while her sister Elizabeth (born May 1935) did not.

Paul's reaction to these pressures was immediate. He packed his bags, taking as many valuables as he could reasonably cram into his pockets or squeeze between the clothes of his suitcase. It was the first time he had ever packed for himself but on this occasion he did not wish for the servants or anyone at the Palais to know what he was doing. He left the building without saying good-bye, hailed a cab to the station and boarded a train bound for the Austro-Swiss border. To his surprise and utter relief, neither German nor Swiss guards attempted to stop him. As soon as he was safely through the border checkpoint he passed a message to Hilde telling her to pack her things and bring the children immediately out of Austria. She would have to go first to Italy and wait on the Italian-Swiss border while he tried to organize their entry visas. Karoline Rolly, her fifty-three-year-old maid from Nymphenberg in Bavaria, was well traveled. She had worked in England and visited the Chicago World's Fair Exposition in July 1933. She had no attachments, disliked the Nazis and adored the children, who called her "Tante." Without a second's thought she agreed to accompany them into exile. It was vital that they left right away and told nobody where they were going for as soon as the police realized that Paul was abroad they would all be in danger of arrest.

Most importantly, Hilde was not to inform her father. Franz Schania was one of the millions of Austrians who had embraced the new regime. He had always been a vacillator, moving quickly to wherever his bread was most thickly buttered. In 1932 he was a member of the red Social Democratic Party, but after the failed uprising of February 1934 had joined the fascist Vaterländische Front. After the *Kristallnacht* pogroms of November 1938 he moved into an apartment on the Kandlgasse (recently expropriated from a family of Jews), joined the Nazi Welfare Movement known as Nazionalsozialistische Volkswohlfahrt, and operated as a *Blockhelfer,* responsible for spreading Nazi propaganda to the residents of his apartment block and relaying information about them and their political loyalties to the *Partei Blockleiter.* In the 1940s ten Jews were deported from Kandlgasse 32. Franz Schania remained resident in Flat 19 at that address until his death in February 1970.

In Vienna Paul had defied his teaching ban by writing to each of his Conservatoire students and inviting them for free private lessons at the Wittgenstein Palais, "because," he said, "I do not want you to suffer any interruption due to any radical political changes." Some refused the offer on the grounds of his Jewishness, but many came. Then suddenly, at the end of August 1938, they turned up for their lessons only to be told by a Palais servant: "He is not here!" Wherever they went to find him they were told the same: "He is not here!" So the rumor soon spread that he had committed suicide—the fourth Wittgenstein brother, so they believed, to have done so.

57 ARREST

In Vienna efforts were continued to ascertain whether Hermann Christian Wittgenstein was a bastard of Prinz Georg of Waldeck and Pyrmont or the legitimate son of Moses Meyer of Korbach, and things were made no less complicated by the discovery in the Vienna City Archive of a family tree, apparently drawn up in 1935 by someone outside the family, which claimed that he was the son of Hirsch Wittgenstein, a Jew from Bielefeld. Genealogists were sent to both places and in neither could they find any record of Hermann Christian's birth. This the family claimed as a small victory, for if he wasn't listed in the Jewish registers, they argued, then he was not a proven Jew.

Officers from the Reich Agency for Genealogical Research in Berlin were not entirely satisfied by this reasoning and at the end of September a cousin, Brigitte Zwiauer (the granddaughter of Karl's sister Millie), sent a bundle of photographs with copies of baptismal certificates and family trees, to add her weight to the case. She argued that neither Hermann Christian nor any of his eleven children looked Jewish—this might seem a frivolous argument but the experts at the Agency took the matter of appearance very seriously—and she insisted that Hermann had been a brazen anti-Semite. The older generation of Wittgensteins were, she claimed, embarrassed by his illegitimacy, which was why they never mentioned it, but now that it all mattered so much even they were prepared to acknowledge it as true. Much of Frau Zwiauer's case smacks of "clutching at straws," but perhaps the most convincing of her arguments was that which she based upon her examination of Hermann Christian's 1839 baptismal certificate—the only document in the family's possession that confirmed his date and place of birth at Korbach, thus scotching the Bielefeld-Hirsch line of inquiry.

It is noteworthy that in Hermann Christian's certificate of baptism (copy attached) his wife is described as born legitimate (conjugal) whereas for Hermann Christian the formula "educated in the Jewish faith" is used, which is clearly not normal, and has been chosen deliberately in order to demonstrate that he is actually not part of the Jewish community but was only raised within it.

Frau Zwiauer's arguments fell on deaf ears. In the orgy of Reich-wide anti-Semitic hooliganism, known as *Kristallnacht,* that took place on the night of November 9–10, the synagogue at Korbach, with all its records of who was born to whom, was burned to the ground. Kurt Mayer at the agency in Berlin ruled that the Wittgensteins were *Volljuden* and that was that—or at any rate Kurt Mayer may have believed that that was that. In fact the situation had taken a new turn and the matter was now being considered by government departments far more powerful than his.

This change of tack was brought about by a realization at the Reichsbank that Paul had fled the Ostmark, that the Wistag Trust, bound by its deeds until 1947, could in fact be broken with the agreement of *all* of its beneficiaries, and that as well as several million Swiss francs in foreign currency the trust also held, in the bank vaults at the Kreditanstalt and Bankverein in Zurich, 215-kilogram bars of fine gold. This may not seem a great deal but Nazi greed for gold (in any amount) is well documented. The Austrian National Gold Reserves worth $99 million were taken to Berlin immediately after the *Anschluss* and the Wittgensteins' hoard, valued in 1938 at $235,000, was worth more than one-tenth of the Czech national gold reserves that were seized by the Germans a year later. Without Paul's signature, however, the Germans would get nothing. Like it or not, they were going to have to negotiate with Paul either in Vienna or in Switzerland. But before the first of these Reichsbank-Wittgenstein confrontations took place at the beginning of November 1938, an appalling new disaster befell the family.

Gretl, as an American citizen, had far more freedom than her siblings. She could flit in and out of the Reich like a brightly colored butterfly without too much interference from the authorities. Shortly after Paul's escape she went to see him in Switzerland, where she gave him one of her famous rockets for having broken his word and caused her to lose face with Arthur Seyss-Inquart. She had also been wearied and disgusted to discover that he had been concealing a young mistress and two illegitimate children from the family all this time, but that was not why she had gone to see him. He had wired her to come to Switzerland as a matter of urgency. Hermine and Helene, he said, had no idea of the acute danger they were in because news censorship in Vienna did not allow them to discover what was really going on, whereas abroad it was well known that war was imminent and that the Jews would soon be locked away in concentration camps, maltreated, malnourished and possibly exterminated. He insisted that Gretl relay this information to them and that they consider doing everything in their power to emigrate.

Gretl returned to Vienna in a state of panic, summoned Hermine and told her to go personally to a certain lawyer in the Kohlmarkt who, she said, could obtain Yugoslavian citizenship for all three of them—Hermine, Paul and Helene. This Hermine did, but with a heavy heart. Personally, she had no wish to leave the Reich and not enough imagination to fear a concentration camp. When Anton Groller, the family's manager and factotum, heard of the plan he was terrified and bitterly hostile to it, but, as he had no alternative scheme of his own, Gretl managed easily to overrule his objection.

At his plush Kohlmarkt office the lawyer assured Hermine that he arranged not false passports but genuine Yugoslavian samples, which the Yugoslav government would sell to any Austrian Jew wishing to emigrate. Hermine swallowed the story and paid a large sum to the lawyer feeling rage inside herself against Paul, whom she blamed for coercing her with scare stories from abroad into taking action that she did not wish to take.

Gretl also put Hermine in charge of telling Helene about the scheme. This was far from the easy task that it seemed, for Helene was nervous and risk averse. Her husband Max, on top of his dementia, was now suffering also from cancer. Any tension could be detrimental to his health. For her part Gretl volunteered to drive to Zagreb to fetch the passports, but when the moment came felt too ill and sent her sister Helene's son-in-law, Arvid Sjögren, instead. As soon as he saw the place Arvid realized that it was no Yugoslavian government office but the grubby demesne of a back-street forger; he took the passports all the same and delivered them, at great personal risk, to Hermine in Vienna. Straightaway she noticed that the dates stamped in them did not correspond to the planned dates for her great escape, so she took them back to the Kohlmarkt lawyer, who assured her that an agent would come in the next couple of days to rectify the error. It was now mid-October 1938.

The deadline passed and the agent never arrived. In panic, the women changed their plans. Hermine would go to Munich instead—a place where she hoped no Wittgenstein would be recognized—and have Swiss visas put into the passports there. On the journey out she discovered that none of the passports had been signed and, in panic, telephoned Gretl, who told her to return at once to Vienna. At Gretl's house the two scheming sisters signed all of the passports except their own with false signatures. These actions made Hermine nearly sick with apprehension. She was terrified that border officials would recognize them and that Max, her senile brother-in-law, might give the game away, but Gretl, the fearless one, urged her to stay calm. This time she would give the passports to her secretary, Hedwig, to take to Munich as she could be trusted to keep her head better than Hermine. That afternoon Gretl, shivering and feverish, retired to bed, only to be roused by her agitated nephew-in-law, Arvid, bearing the news that the soi-disant "passport office" in Zagreb had been busted by the Yugoslavian police, who had passed to the Gestapo a list of all those to whom the fake passports had been issued. A wilier criminal mind would have seen to it that the fake passports were quickly destroyed before the police arrived, but Gretl, in her distress overlooking this obvious expedient, proceeded instead by telling the others how she intended to take all the blame upon herself. It was, after all, she who had forged most of the signatures. She would insist that she had signed them all, even Hermine's, that it was her plan from the start, that she had bought the passports for her siblings without their knowledge, that she had done so as a simple precaution, something for them to put in a drawer in case of emergency. Being a well-connected American citizen she was confident that she would get away with it. No sooner had Hermine and Arvid consented to this improbable scheme than there came a loud banging on the door.

For several hours the police pounded around the house and, after preliminary interviews at which the agreed line was taken by all interrogatees, they departed. Everyone was relieved and Helene, imagining the danger to be over, decided to drive her husband out to the country for a break. But the very next day the police returned in force and arrested Hermine, Gretl and Arvid as well as the lawyer who had taken payment for the passports. Gretl, who by this stage was suffering full-blown pneumonia, was forced out of bed, pushed with her sister into a waiting van and rushed at reckless speed to the central police station on the Rossauerlaende. There each of the accused was individually interrogated and each staunchly glued his or her narrative to the prearranged explanation of events. But the lawyer had not been properly primed and as soon as it was known that Hermine had three times visited his offices on the Kohlmarkt, she, Gretl and Arvid began to crumble. On that same day Helene was also apprehended while out shopping in Gmunden.

Brought before a magistrate, all three agreed that they had lied in their initial statements and, after two nights at the police station, they were carted off to the National Prison. The fate of the Kohlmarkt lawyer is not recorded. Behind the scenes Anton Groller and various nephews and nieces, including Arvid's wife Clara, were working frantically to get them released on bail. A huge sum was demanded and on the sixth day Hermine and Arvid were released.

Without his wife Max Salzer went wild, and his brother, daughter and servants did the best they could to distract him with games and amusements and the lame excuse that Helene was ill and had left the house for a while in order that he should not catch her bug. Most of all they feared that he might read about the scandal in the newspapers and explode with rage and shame. Helene was released as soon as news reached the police station at Gmunden that Hermine and Arvid were out of jail in Vienna. Only Gretl remained behind bars. In her heart Hermine believed this was all her fault for shouting "GRETL!" out of her cell window one night and arousing the guards' suspicions. But it was nothing to do with that.

Why she was held longer than the others and in more deplorable conditions has not been discovered; but by the time Gretl emerged she was in a shocking condition, having been treated very roughly indeed. She had repeatedly demanded to see her friend John Hayes Lord, a diplomat at the American Consulate. Lord and his aristocratic English tennis-playing wife Marjorie had been friends of the Stonboroughs since 1920, when he was posted to the American Consulate in Basel and had lent his weight to Gretl's condensed-milk operation. He and his wife were also friends of Ji's in Washington, which might go some way to explaining the letter that was sent at that time to the *Washington Post* praising the activities of the Vienna Consulate General:

> Sir:
>
> *Having returned from a voyage abroad, may I ask for the hospitality of your pages to put on record my admiration for the work of our diplomatic and consular representatives in Germany.*
>
> *I am particularly referring to the Consulate General in Vienna . . . It is my belief that the officials and their staff, by their earnest endeavor, sympathy and tolerance, are demonstrating democratic ideals through action and are standard bearers of Americanism in a wilderness of lies and scientific sadism.*
>
> J. J. Stonborough

When John Lord arrived at the prison he put on a great show of indignation at the brutish conditions in which Gretl was being held and demanded that her personal doctor be called immediately. Eventually he succeeded in securing her release, but both her American and her fake Yugoslav passports were confiscated and she was ordered to remain in Vienna until her case could be tried. By the time that Hermine (aged sixty-three), Helene (fifty-nine) and Gretl (fifty-six) were finally released on bail they were nervous wrecks. Helene's agitation was unspeakable. She had refused to eat in prison and was now pale and gaunt; Gretl, still suffering from pneumonia, was slumped into a febrile depression, while Hermine could do nothing but fret about her fate from morning to night. Christmas that year was depressing for Gretl. It was her first since 1925 without Paul and Ludwig, Jerome was dead, both of her sons were in America and one of her adopted sons in Berlin. She had only her secretary and the other Zastrow boy to share her chocolate and gingerbread and distract her from the gloomy prospect of an imminent court summons. "These are serious times for the family," Hermine wrote to Ludwig, "a major reckoning and testing of all our relationships, to say nothing of the dangers from without. Sometimes I see everything clearly before me and think: no stone will remain standing."

The good news was that when the summons finally arrived Helene's name was not upon it. She had not been party to the original fraud and it was just as well, for she could now look after her ailing husband in peace. The hearing was set for the beginning of April 1939. With special coaching from their lawyer, Dr. Kornisch, Hermine and Gretl learned their defense statements by heart, but just as proceedings were about to begin and the two ladies and their nephew-in-law were sitting wringing their hands in the dock a sudden announcement was made that due to a new anti-Jewish decree Dr. Kornisch was prohibited from representing them. Arvid, meanwhile, had procured the services of a tall, gray-haired, well-spoken and sinister lawyer of the upper class called Alfred Indra.

The judge offered Gretl and Hermine a chance to postpone the hearing while they found themselves another Aryan lawyer, but they chose to go ahead with their own defense. This Hermine later recalled was a fortuitous turn, for "our appearance and manner of speech were our best defence, far better than all that a decidedly Jewish defence lawyer could have said in our favour." Each in turn took the stand and Gretl, once again, assumed complete responsibility for everything that had happened. Arvid and Hermine admitted their guilt too. Yes, they had bought false passports with intent to deceive government border police; yes, they planned to leave without paying the *Reichsfluchtsteuer,* the emigration tax, and with intent to evade paying all their foreign currency into the Reichsbank; yes, they had forged the signatures of their siblings; and yes, they had told lies to the police when they were first questioned.

Judge Standhartinger, taking all this into account, drew a deep breath and summed the case up to the jury. "A false signature upon a false passport," he said, "is the equivalent of someone attempting to murder an already stiff corpse. In what way, then, can any crime be said to have been committed?" Whereupon judge and jury retired to consider their verdict and after a long wait reappeared to announce the acquittal of all three. The family had always believed that its superior connections could be used to fish it out of any amount of trouble. "We are protected!" they would often say. All were acquitted of all charges on a technicality relating to just one of them. Hermine, Gretl and Arvid were overcome with emotions of relief and joy as it seemed too good to be true.

And sadly for them it *was* too good to be true, for two days later Hermine, Gretl and Arvid received an "evil blow" that would affect them "more deeply than all that had preceded it." The Vienna public prosecutor, unimpressed by Judge Standhartinger's eccentric verdict, appealed against the decision and ordered that the case be reopened.

58 A SECOND EMIGRATION

Paul's sojourn in Switzerland was disagreeable to him. He had no concerts to play, no pupils to teach and no valet to help him in his daily routine. He was anxious for Hilde and his daughters still waiting at the Italian-Swiss border without visas, and worried, for the first time in his life, about money. In the mornings he went for strenuous walks along the banks of the Limmat or swam in the cold waters of the Zürichsee. In the afternoons he practiced at the piano showrooms of the Hug music company on the Füsslistrasse, read French and Latin classics and wrote letters in a fierce, scrawling hand—but none of these activities, either individually or collectively, could calm his agitated state.

Above all he was desperate for news of his sisters in Austria and aware—far more aware than they—of the terrible dangers they were in. Before he left he had beseeched them to emigrate, but Max, Helene's husband, would never agree to leaving his homeland and Hermine was adamant that she would not be parted from her things. Paul had argued forcefully that as Jews in Vienna they were doomed. They should cut their losses, pay the *Reichsfluchtsteuer* and live abroad off the Swiss family fund. If they insisted on staying, he said, the Germans would demand their foreign fortune with threats and intimidation, and once the family had surrendered everything that it owned abroad, it would be effectively ruined. The siblings exchanged bitter, hysterical and often impolite words with one another. "You all behave like cattle who cannot be coaxed out of their stalls when they burn," Paul said. "And you are a crass egoist!" said Hermine.

In his rooms at the luxurious Hotel Savoy Baur en Ville in Zurich

Paul turned these matters over in his mind. He knew that if he returned to the Reich, where he was forbidden from performing or teaching and where the guardianship of his children had been taken away from him, he would be arrested and imprisoned. There was no point in trying to reclaim the fortune and property he had left behind. Instead he must concentrate on that part which was held outside the Reich, in Switzerland. But, as he well knew, his share of the Wistag Fund could not be disbursed without the consent of all the trust's beneficiaries and directors. These included his sisters, his brother in England, various nephews and nieces (most importantly Ji Stonborough in the U.S.), his brother-in-law Max Salzer and the family's financial factotum Anton Groller. A further and graver problem was that officials in Berlin knew about the fund and were demanding that it be paid into the Reichsbank.

It would take time to secure the agreement of all parties and Paul, meanwhile, needed to find some way of paying his mounting hotel bills and providing for Hilde and the children in Italy. With the connivance of Dr. Heinz Fischer, a Swiss concert promoter, a German string quartet was invited to play in Zurich, bringing Paul's precious instruments from Vienna—two violins, one by Stradivari, one by Guadagnini, a viola by Amati and a Rugieri cello. Nobody would notice, as they crossed the border at Haslach, that the instruments in their cases were not theirs. Nor would they spot when the musicians returned to the Reich with cheaper models under their arms than those with which they had left. Dr. Fischer's and the musicians' payment for this risky undertaking is not known, nor is the fate of the two violins (perhaps the instruments were themselves the smugglers' reward), but in October 1938 Paul took the viola and cello to the Swiss violin-maker Stübinger, who valued them at 18,000 Swiss francs each. A quick sale brought him temporary financial relief.

With or without money, he had no intention of staying long in Switzerland and it is unlikely (even if he had wished to remain there) that the Swiss authorities would have continued renewing his visas indefinitely. In Zurich, as elsewhere in the country, the people were edgy and xenophobic. Fear of German invasion and resentment against the growing influx of refugees from the Reich had inspired the authorities to tighten border security and to insist, by October 1938, that all Jews' passports be stamped with a red letter "J." Within a year SS soldiers, acting on orders to rid the *Vaterland* of all lingering Jews, were physically pushing them over the borders. Swiss officials, on the other side, would irritably push them back again.

For Paul, who believed that he looked more Jewish than any of his siblings, the growing anti-Semitism in Switzerland proscribed the country as a safe haven and by early August he had set his sights on America. Getting there, he knew, would not be easy. Like every foreign administration (with the exception of Santo Domingo) the American government refused to increase its quota of immigrants from Germany despite the international crisis. Paul had to pull strings and admitted in a letter to Marga Deneke when his travel plans were finally confirmed: "Although I have obtained the ticket for the ship to New York, I wouldn't have got it without special patronage."

The patronage to which he referred took the form of two professional invitations from America—the first from the Cleveland Orchestra to perform under its Principal Conductor, Artur Rodzinski, and the second to work as an unpaid faculty member at the Westchester Affiliation of the David Mannes Music School at New Rochelle. Both institutions were making strenuous efforts to help stranded Jewish musicians in Europe obtain visas to America, and the David Mannes School sent offers of unpaid employment to many others at that time including Helene's son, the musicologist Felix Salzer. For two years, ever since the storming success of their 1936 concert at the Salzburg Festival, Rodzinski had been promising Paul an invitation to Cleveland. In America the conductor was at the height of his fame and his invitation, which arrived in Zurich in mid-September, was instrumental in securing Paul his transatlantic passage.

By November 1938 Hilde, Fräulein Rolly and the children finally made it into Switzerland on temporary visas. Paul greeted them in Zurich with the news that he would be leaving for America in a week's time. Hilde, twenty-two years old, half blind, a long way from her modest roots on the Stankagasse at Rannersdorf, was entrusted to the care of a Swiss lawyer who had been instructed to provide her with funds and set her up in a rented flat in the French-speaking town of Montreux on the eastern shores of Lake Geneva. It was here on November 28 that Paul said good-bye to her and the children, little realizing that he would not be setting eyes on any of them again for a year and a half.

His ship sailed out of the port of Le Havre on December 1, stopping at Southampton and Cobh in southern Ireland before reaching New York on the ninth. Marga had written to him in Zurich to ask if he could see her in England on his way through. "Unfortunately impossible!" he replied, but:

> *I'll definitely be coming back, earlier perhaps than I might know! My plan is, with the aid of my own reputation and my friends in America, gradually—because it is not conceivable all at once—to get a longer residence and teaching permit. When I have got it and when my circumstances allow, I can come across every year, but that is still pie in the sky! In the meantime let's hope for the best . . . We'll definitely meet again.*
> *Your old friend, P.W.*

They did indeed meet again, just one week later, on December 3. Paul telegraphed to say that he would not be allowed to disembark at Southampton but summoned her to come on board ship and talk to him there before the boat sailed for Ireland. Marga left a scribbled note on a brown-paper bag in the kitchen for her sister:

> *Dearest Lena,*
> *Paul Wittgenstein asked me to see him en route for the USA. He is on the S.S.* Washington *docked at Southampton. Perhaps you would like to come and see him too (He is a good man now). Do it if at all inclined,*
> *Love Marge*

Lena did not come as she still regarded Paul as an ill-mannered and bad-tempered man and would not forgive him his occasional outbursts against her friends, so Marga hurried alone to Southampton, where she found her old friend nervously pacing.

> I took a long walk with him on deck [she later wrote]. He explained to me about his emigration to the US and, with deep emotion, he showed me a photo of a blind pupil to whom he had become at-

tached and for whom he planned to establish a house. I rejoiced at the prospect it opened up for him and told him that without reserves. He continued to give news quoting *Alice* or Goethe's *Faust* and assuring me how glad he was that I had come. From the end of the pier I watched the steamer slide away, till the handkerchief he was waving faded from sight.

59   CHANGING SIDES

Paul was powerless to help his sisters at the time of their prosecution for passport fraud in April 1939 and Hermine was fueled with indignation that he was not around when she most needed him. "Our family lacks the leading man," she complained to Ludwig. "Max is old and unfortunately very sick; Paul's a failure . . . What use is it that Gretl is big-hearted and tries to look after everyone; the problems are insoluble."

On arrival in New York Paul was detained for twenty-four hours by immigration officials, classing him bluntly as "German Hebrew" and voicing suspicions about irregularities in his passport. When they finally agreed to let him go he booked himself a suite at the Hotel Webster on West 45th Street, where he sat for long hours tapping his fingers on his desk and reading Tacitus and Cicero letters to himself in Latin. The David Mannes School was not big enough to offer him his own teaching rooms and for a while he gave lessons on the bar piano at the hotel. Metropolitan life dazed him and he was irritated by a constant bombardment of directives concerning his immigration status. "One comes up against obstacles everywhere and can only hope that they will be successfully overcome," he wrote to Ludwig's old friend Dr. Hänsel in Vienna.

His twenty-six-year-old nephew Ji Stonborough invited him to lunch at his Washington club, the Metropolitan, in order to introduce him to Gerald D. Reilly, the man in charge of visas, and to James Houghteling, Commissioner of Immigration and Naturalization. After lunch these two influential men made some calls and Paul's visitors' visa was temporarily extended. Then and forever afterward Ji was furious that his uncle had not seemed especially grateful.

Back in New York Paul, too impractical to survive on his own, advertised for a bilingual secretary and personal assistant. When Marianne Jarosy Blumen came to be interviewed for the job she found him in his pajamas wrapped in a white sheet looking despondent. He had put his suits and shirts outside the door expecting them to be washed, ironed and returned by the hotel staff next morning. Instead the whole lot had been stolen. Frau Blumen recommended buying some new clothes in the city—an idea that had not occurred to him—and when she returned from her shopping spree with a new wardrobe Paul was delighted and gave her the job. Frau Blumen was a Jewish refugee from Vienna, having arrived in New York in September 1938 with her husband Erwin. She was forty-six years old at the time, and although born in Prague and of Hungarian descent she could speak and type both English and German perfectly. Shortly after her arrival in America her husband ran off to Pittsburgh, leaving her in severe financial difficulties. As soon as he was able, Paul took two adjacent apartments on the nineteenth floor of the Masters Building on Riverside Drive—one for himself and one for her—and both he and she remained there, each dependent upon the other, for the next sixteen years, until her death. Paul was devastated. "How shall I manage without her?" he asked a friend. "Well, you could always get another assistant." "Yes, yes, but what about tomorrow?"

Back in Vienna in April 1939, Gretl and Hermine were worrying over the renewed threat of prosecution for passport fraud. Gretl still had a few friends in high places, but within the Nazi hierarchy her position was growing more equivocal by the day. She had been arrested for passport fraud, and now, on a routine search of her house on the Kundmanngasse, it was discovered that she had failed to declare certain treasures on her list of assets. A hoard of handwritten musical manuscripts by Brahms, Beethoven, Mozart, Schubert, Wagner and Bruckner was confiscated by the authorities. In July she had given her word to Arthur Seyss-Inquart that her brother would return to Vienna after his brief visit to England, but when Paul fled to Switzerland her position with the *Reichsstatthalter* was severely compromised.

Gretl strongly condemned Paul's actions in leaving the country, accusing him of dishonorable conduct. Nothing could be guaranteed to rile her brother more than an assault upon his honor. Anxious lest details of this spat might, at a later time, reach the ears of his children, Paul commissioned an independent report on the breakdown of his relationship with Gretl, instructing a lawyer to ensure that his heirs each received a copy after his death. This report, based on letters and documents in the archives of the solicitors Wachtell, Manheim and Grouf, states at the outset:

> This memorandum will not be seen by Professor Wittgenstein. He has particularly asked that he not be shown a single part of it for he is particularly anxious that this be presented as an objectively prepared historical document and not as an apology. He insists that the writer should feel no obligation except to write the absolute truth.

In the matter of Gretl's dealings with Arthur Seyss-Inquart, the report concludes:

> Mrs Stonborough evidently felt in 1938 and 1939 that there was such a thing as an obligation of honor owed to a Nazi, that the Nazis were people with whom one did business on the basis of honor. If we regard her charitably, the best we can say for her is that she was a very silly woman.

The result of the first passport-fraud trial had been fixed in advance. Quite how is not known, but it now appears that Gretl and Hermine turned down the offer of an adjournment when their Jewish defense lawyer was dismissed because they were confident that they had already "negotiated themselves out of it," and that they knew from the start that Judge Standhartinger was poised and ready to acquit them. The appeal case, however, was likely to be a lot trickier. This time they were terrified that it would be dealt with by a higher authority in Berlin, by people beyond their sphere of influence, who might not "regard us as the eminent ladies Stonborough and Wittgenstein, who had trusted a crook, but rather as two old Jews juggling with false passports." Once again Gretl's contacts came to the rescue, as Hermine revealed: "Gretl and some good friends again found means of preventing the new court proceedings. A suitable man was found who was to change the Public Prosecutor's attitude, and he succeeded. The appeal was withdrawn and we were delivered of this serious anxiety."

This "suitable man" was probably Alfred Indra, the lawyer and Viennese operator who had represented Arvid Sjögren, Helene's son-in-law, at the original fraud trial. Shortly after that he was asked to represent Gretl in various battles with the authorities concerning her property. Ji described him as "a gent and on very good terms with thousands of people. A fixer." Dr. Indra, whose father and uncle were both senior government ministers, was one of only three lawyers during the Nazi period who represented both the Nazi authorities and the well-to-do Jews whose property was threatened with confiscation. In a totalitarian state such as Hitler's Germany, hiring a lawyer to fight the government was not a serious option. A plaintiff wishing to take his case to the courts was offered, by the authorities, a choice of three approved lawyers to represent him. These were Hans Frank, Erich Zeiner and Alfred Indra. Clearly, if any of them fought the case of their clients too brilliantly they would be removed from their posts. Indra's most famous client in 1938 was Sigmund Freud. After the war he represented Freud's heirs in their efforts to retrieve something of the psychoanalyst's confiscated estate, but all his files (so he claimed in 1961) were ransacked first by the SS and later by the Russians.

Dr. Indra had been introduced to Freud by Princess Marie Bonaparte (Gretl's friend from Luzern days) and it was he who organized the Professor's emigration to London and he who drafted the chilling and wholly mendacious declaration for the octogenarian to sign before he left:

> I hereby confirm of my own free will that as of today, June 4th 1938, neither I, nor any of those around me, have been harassed. The authorities and representatives of the NSDAP have always conducted themselves correctly and with restraint towards me and those around me. Prof. Dr. Sigm. Freud

Dr. Indra was forty-four years old in 1938, six foot two inches tall, dark eyed, slick and deceitful. He had been educated at the Theresianum—the same smart Viennese school that Ji attended eighteen years later, and the younger man looked up to him as the impressionable first-year looks up to the square-jawed sporting hero of the upper-sixth. "Indra was a very handsome man," he later recalled. "A wonderful lawyer . . . One who knew how to hunt with the hounds and run with the hare . . . A great help!! . . . He and I were of course on Theresianum terms of 'Du.' " Dr. Indra's trick was to give his clients the impression that he thought the Nazi authorities were stupid and ignorant and that he was entirely on their side against them. This the Stonboroughs swallowed easily, and if Dr. Indra had indeed been instrumental in dissuading the Public Prosecutor from his appeal against Hermine's and Gretl's acquittal, who could blame them?

The aging ladies were, after all, worth more to the Germans outside prison than in it, for they held the keys to the vast fortune in gold and foreign currency that the family kept in Switzerland, a fortune on which the Reichsbank was impatient to get its hands. The house of a German citizen who refused to exchange his foreign savings for Reichsmarks would normally be raided by the Gestapo and its occupants thrown into prison, but the Wittgenstein case was complicated. The assets of the fund, supposedly locked under the terms of incorporation until 1947, belonged to many people, some of whom (Ji and Gretl) were American citizens, and another of whom (Paul) had escaped German jurisdiction. The directors included Ludwig (soon to become a British citizen) and Otto Peyer, a Swiss businessman, neither of them under any compunction to obey German law. If the Nazis were to get their hands on the pot, they needed all parties to be persuaded, but this could hardly be achieved with Gretl and Hermine languishing in prison for passport irregularities, and the authorities soon realized that their best hope was to use them to persuade the others to release the funds.

At the beginning of November 1938 Dr. Indra had asked Ji to go to Zurich to entice Paul back to Vienna as an act of goodwill toward the authorities before leaving for America. The meeting took place over breakfast at the Hotel Savoy Baur en Ville. Ludwig was also present. He had come to help sort out the liquidation of the trust and, since he had given all of his own assets away, was considered a helpful and impartial adviser in the matter of how this might best be done. The Reich-wide anti-Semitic *Kristallnacht* pogroms, during which over 1,000 synagogues and Jewish businesses were destroyed and 100,000 Jews arrested, had taken place only days earlier and the international press was full of it. The risks of returning were too great for Paul. During the discussion Ji told a risqué joke that both his uncles found distasteful.

When the Reichsbank realized that Paul would not return to Vienna it stepped up the pressure concerning the Wistag fortune. Max Salzer and Anton Groller were threatened with imprisonment. An urgent meeting was convened at the Palais, attended by factotum Groller, Max Salzer, Hermine and Gretl. Only Gretl brought her own legal adviser to the meeting (the sinister Dr. Indra), for she it seems had her own agenda.

The purpose of the meeting was to discuss with Dr. Johannes Schoene, the legal representative of the Reichsbank from Berlin, means by which the Wittgenstein fortune could be paid to his bank. Dr. Schoene was an ambitious lawyer in his early thirties, a signed-up member of the NSDAP, very short, very blond with arresting blue eyes—a sort of Hollywood Nazi archetype. "You know," he said to Hermine, "there are those in Berlin who are dismayed to learn that your family still holds such a large fortune abroad. One of them recently said to me: 'And are you saying that these people are still running around free?' " A heavy hint of threat seemed to underscore all of Dr. Schoene's utterances, but he must have had a little charm, for Hermine later described this same meeting as "very friendly."

Gretl had learned from her son Thomas that, in cases where a family's foreign assets were held abroad, concessions could be made if the family was prepared to break up the trust early. This seemingly obvious point filled his mother with optimism and she spoke up at the meeting with an energy that impressed her elder sister as "comparable to that of our father." Her proposition was simple: "if you wish us to liquidate the trust you must pay us to do it, and the price that we demand is full citizenship rights for Hermine and Helene." This Dr. Schoene initially suggested might be possible but, he warned, it would need to be agreed in Berlin with the Reichsbank's Head of Foreign Exchange, Dr. Görlich.

The Berlin meeting, which took place at the bank's offices in the Victoriastrasse on May 2, was attended by many of the same participants as the earlier conference in Vienna. Dr. Görlich put the case to Gretl and Hermine bluntly:

> Either you can emigrate, in which case we shall permit you to keep a small portion of your foreign fortune, or you can stay in the Reich and like everybody else change all your foreign money into Reichs-marks. I assume that you will be choosing the first of these two options as I cannot imagine that you would wish to stay in this country as exception-Jews, against the expressed will of the *Führer*?

Hermine did not answer but hoped, by her silence, that Dr. Görlich would understand that staying in the German Reich was precisely what she intended to do.

As to the sisters receiving Aryan treatment, this, he insisted, was out of the question. They were Jews and that was that, but when Anton Groller mentioned that a branch of the Wittgenstein family was convinced that Hermann Wittgenstein was the illegitimate son of an Aryan prince, Drs. Görlich and Schoene seized upon this information as a possible solution, giving the strong impression that they would do anything to help the family twist it that way. In point of fact they were adroitly playing an old game, pretending, on the one hand, to be sympathetic to the family plight while, on the other, threatening that if matters became too complicated they would have to pass the Wittgenstein file to the Gestapo. Gretl seems to have fallen for the ruse: "Our friendship with the Reichsbank began at that point," she told Hermine. After the meeting her passport was returned to her and three days later she boarded the SS *Washington* at Southampton bound for New York.

60 NAZIS ARRIVE IN AMERICA

Anton Groller had been employed by the Wittgensteins for most of his working life. While shocked by their recent treatment as Jews, he was much in favor of the *Anschluss* and a keen supporter of the NSDAP. Immediately after the meeting in Berlin he contacted Paul. "The Germans," he said, have been very generous. They have made you a definitive offer. From your share of 3.4 million Swiss francs they are going to allow you to keep 2.1 SF, a great sacrifice, I know, but one I expect you to make. Furthermore they will permit you to travel freely in and out of Austria. They will not, however, guarantee any concession concerning the Aryan treatment of your sisters. In return, they require an immediate gesture of goodwill from the family. We suggest you release all the gold to them right away.

Paul's reaction was not enthusiastic. The offer of permission to travel in and out of Austria meant nothing to him, as the criminal charges against him had not been withdrawn and, in any case, he remained always a Jew, stripped of citizenship rights. If he returned to Vienna he would be seized by the Gestapo and forced to surrender even his 2.1 million Swiss francs. Nor was he happy about conceding the gold reserves to the Reichsbank with no guarantees about his sisters' treatment. Ji too was vehemently opposed to such a move and spoke in excitable, high-pitched tones to Paul of his promise to help protect his uncle's fortune from what he called the "prole Nazis," of his resolution to give away as little as possible and to fight the Germans at every turn. Uncle and nephew were in complete agreement that whatever concessions had eventually to be made must be to the greatest possible advantage of Hermine and Helene.

Gretl arrived in New York on May 12, 1939, exactly one week before the German ship SS *Columbus* with Drs. Schoene and Indra on board. Konrad Bloch, a Swiss lawyer representing the Wistag Trust, was also in America but, because his English was poor, he had instructed a bilingual New York solicitor to share his brief. This was Samuel Wachtell, a scrupulous, hard-working and honest attorney whose office had spent thousands of man-hours sorting, free of charge, the immigration papers of Jewish clients fleeing the Reich.

The first meeting of all parties took place on May 19 at the Gladstone Hotel on 52nd Street and Park Avenue. In the days before, Ji's adamantine resolve to prevent the Germans taking all the gold had already crumbled. Gretl had insisted that he sign it over—all 2.5 million SF worth—and she was a formidable woman, "a fighter who brooked no interference."

Anton Groller meanwhile told Paul that the Germans would not allow him to keep any of his fortune if he too did not consent to handing over the gold. This he reluctantly did. "How unexpected," was Dr. Schoene's sarcastic reaction to the news that such a high advance had been conceded. "The Reichsbank would have been satisfied with far less than that."

Gretl swept into the meeting without greeting Dr. Bloch and Dr. Wachtell. She had brought along her own New York attorney, Abraham Bienstock. Dr. Indra, who only a week earlier seemed to be representing her interests against the predations of the Reichsbank in Vienna, was now in New York as Dr. Schoene's understrapper, representing the Reichsbank. Paul had no idea who Indra was and simply remarked, "he never opened his mouth in my presence so that it was not at all clear whom he represented." At the outset Paul stated that he was willing to make sacrifices for his sisters in Vienna, but stressed also the danger that he was in:

> Since I came to America far too late, all available paid positions at conservatories have been taken. I cannot work other than as a piano teacher, for I am no use at anything else— What idiot would employ an impractical one-armed man, when the best-qualified men with two arms in their hundreds are wandering about jobless? Even if a well-paid job were offered me I would not be able to take it for as a "visitor" to the US I am under an obligation to earn no money.

Dr. Schoene's response was icy. Despite the family's goodwill payment of the gold he had now decided that 2.1 million SF was far too much for Paul. The Reichsbank, he said, might consent to 500,000, or maybe less. Paul, predictably, lost his temper and the meeting was adjourned.

Gretl and Ji departed immediately for Washington. Dr. Bloch took Paul to one side and told him that he mistrusted his sister as, on more than one occasion, she appeared to be siding with the Nazis against him. This Paul dismissed. "It is only apparent," he replied. "My sister has not the slightest reason to favour the Reichsbank over me. We are not on good terms, but she is not capable of dishonourable conduct." At the next meeting, however, he changed his mind.

It was crucial that all parties on the Wittgenstein side should agree a common strategy against the Reichsbank, but during their absence in

Washington Gretl and Ji neither could nor would allow themselves to be contacted. Dr. Bloch telephoned their lawyer only to be told that he had been instructed to speak to no one. On the day of the meeting Gretl rang to say that neither she nor her son would be able to come early but would instead be arriving at the same time as Indra and Schoene. Dr. Bloch sprang a surprise, so that when she entered the room she brusquely demanded: "Where are the Germans?" "We have canceled them," he said, "so that we may first decide what we are going to tell them." Gretl was visibly shaken but took her seat while Dr. Wachtell opened proceedings with a recapitulation of the case in a few short words. When he had finished Ji, adopting a ministerial tone, said: "I listened with considerable interest to your somewhat lengthened explanations, but I wish to say that there are people present who do not understand anything and I do not wish them to be here."

"If you are referring to me," Dr. Wachtell answered, "you are mistaken. I have fought similar disputes with the Germans and I know how to treat the matter."

"I am not referring to you."

"Then to whom do you refer?" Paul asked, bridling at what he later termed the "loutish impudence of my stinking louse of a nephew."

"I allude to my uncle Paul and Dr. Bloch," Ji said. "I have no time to hear them and in any case everything must be settled in thirty minutes as I have a train to catch."

"I don't give a damn about your train!" shouted Paul, infuriated by the suggestion that a million-dollar fortune should be negotiated according to a railway timetable.

"And I don't give a damn about your money!" screamed Ji, slamming the table with his fist.

Gretl immediately summoned her brother into an adjacent room where she told him: "You have no right to defend your money. You would not be here at all if it were not for me."

When they returned the quarrel flared up again and just as Paul was on the point of conceding his whole fortune in a temper to the Nazis, a high-decibel shriek brought the assembly to sudden silence. "STOP!!" Samuel Wachtell, the Wistag attorney, seeing the danger that Paul was in was calling for an immediate adjournment. Ji and Gretl rushed off angrily to the station. The next day Paul received a letter from his nephew enclosing a bill for his and his mother's travel expenses to Washington. "It would have been better," he wrote, "if we could have come to some understanding." Paul sent a telegram by return: "PERSONALLY SHALL TAKE NO MORE PART IN PROCEEDINGS. ADVISE YOU TO GET IN TOUCH WITH MY LAWYER DR WACHTELL."

"Back then," Paul later recorded, "Wachtell literally saved me from starvation. If he had not yelled 'STOP' I would have left this meeting a beggar—a beggar who does not even know in which country he is allowed to beg!" From that day Paul never spoke to Gretl again, nor did he have any further dealings with his "louse" of a nephew.

61 THE STONBOROUGHS' MOTIVATION

Why were Gretl and Ji apparently so anxious that Paul should hand the whole of his fortune to the Reichsbank? Konrad Bloch believed that the reason was connected to Ji's prospects of inheritance as he was an heir to Hermine and she would receive Paul's fortune, which even at the Reichsbank's rate of exchange would be worth something in years to come. Paul had other suspicions. He sensed that the Stonboroughs were trying to bring about the liberation of their art treasures in Gmunden and in the Kundmanngasse. "That is only a suspicion—I explicitly emphasise that," he wrote. "Nevertheless I consider it to be very likely that Schoene, for whom, as a representative of the Reichsbank, no means would be too base, held out this prospect to them."

There is another possibility. The evidence shows that the Germans used the threat of Hermine's imprisonment and confiscation of all her Austrian property to exert pressure on the family—and in particular on Paul—to relinquish its entire interest in the Wistag Trust to the Reichsbank for conversion into Reichsmarks. While Gretl was in America she was safe from criminal prosecution, but her extensive Austrian properties were vulnerable. Gretl and Hermine may have been threatened that if Paul did not agree to the Reichsbank's demand for the total sum of the Wistag Trust, the Germans would pursue them for the shortfall, seizing both their properties and imprisoning Hermine for failure to comply with foreign currency laws. This may explain a throwaway remark in Hermine's memoirs. Referring to the Reichsbank meeting in Berlin at the beginning of May 1939 she wrote, "Finally it was decided to allow Paul a sum of foreign currency that seemed to me rather high." Why, when his share in the fund was worth 3.5 million SF, did she consider 2.1 million "rather high"? What difference did it make to her how much of his own fortune her brother was allowed to retain? Unless, of course, she believed that she and Gretl would have to make good the difference.

One wonders at the role played by Dr. Indra, "the fixer," in New York. When he came to America, apparently as a legal representative of the Reichsbank, he was, unbeknown to Paul, simultaneously acting as Gretl's solicitor in dealings with the Reichsbank in Austria. So whose interests was he really there to serve? The Reichsbank's? Gretl's? Or both? When Paul's solicitor discovered that Dr. Indra had found out secret information about the Wistag Trust, it was assumed that Dr. Groller was guilty of the leak.

Back in New York Indra remained intent on luring Paul back to Germany and proposed that since it was not German policy to negotiate on foreign soil, a top official from Berlin should be sent to conduct meetings with him on board a German ship. Paul's lawyers warned that this would be "extremely dangerous." At the same meeting Gretl burst out: "That Paul does not give his money to the Reichsbank is shabby and unaccountable. Every damned thing my brother owns he owes to his family . . . He has no right to defend his fortune since it is only through me that he is here!" Dr. Schoene, when he heard this, was unable to suppress a satisfied grin, but Dr. Wachtell wryly asked: "Do you want to be paid for that, Madam?" It was comments such as this that inspired Ji to describe Wachtell as "a real shit."

An intercepted report from Dr. Schoene to his bosses in Berlin explained that he had been frustrated in his efforts to seize the Wistag fortune for Germany "by the Jewish lawyers, Wachtell and Bloch, who are ill disposed towards the Reich." Wachtell, Schoene complained, "is obstinately resting his case upon an unassailable legal standpoint," but, he reported, John Stonborough is demonstrating "an altogether fair attitude towards Germany's interests." Part of this "fair attitude" consisted in Ji's doing exactly what the Germans told him to do. "Alfred Indra dictated a letter to me in the middle of Wall Street," he later admitted, and "Dr. Schoene also told me what to say, write, maintain . . . in the end I consented to sign this or that complicated document." His explanation (unlikely in the extreme) was that Schoene and Indra were both "double-agents" working secretly for the Stonboroughs against the Reichsbank in order to secure a *Mischling* solution for Hermine and Helene.

By July 1939 the matter was still unresolved and the Reichsbank was resorting to heavier tactics in order to force Paul to capitulate. In Vienna Hermine, Herr Groller and all the Salzers were advised that they would be severely punished if the money was not forthcoming and that delays over the negotiations for *Mischling* status in New York were the cause. Together they sent a telegram: "DO NOT INSIST ON HALF-BREED STATUS. OTHERWISE ACUTE IMPENDING DANGER TO UNDERSIGNED PERSONS." By striking terror into the relatives in Austria, Dr. Schoene was hoping to force Paul's hand, but Gretl, knowing full well it was bluff and that no one in Austria would be harmed so long as negotiations were ongoing in New York, continued with her unflinching demands for *Mischling* status, while insisting that Paul surrender his whole fortune.

On July 12, Ludwig, Anton Groller and Freda Marie Schoene (Dr. Schoene's wife) sailed together on the *Queen Mary* for New York. Ji cabled his uncle Ludwig, "DON'T GIVE IN OR AUNT IMPRISONED." Dr. Wachtell, aware of the escalating burden on his client, had already taken countermeasures to save Paul from the new wave of pressure. "I would like you to take some time off," he said to him. "Go on vacation without leaving your address. I value your presence at all times, but in this negotiation I could do very well without it." To Ludwig on the *Queen Mary*, he sent the following:

Dear Professor Wittgenstein:

. . . The announcement of your trip to America was the latest of a se-
ries of efforts, which had been made in order to exert pressure on your
brother to yield to the demands of the Reichsbank. No doubt as a result
of threats and intimidation, your sisters in Vienna have not merely sup-
ported these demands passively, but sent, through Dr. Schoene, letters and
cablegrams urging compliance and intimating serious and impending
dangers otherwise. I have no means of measuring the degree of pressure

*applied against the sisters in Vienna and through them transmitted to you
and Mrs. Stonborough. But I am in a position to measure the pressure
applied from all directions on Paul Wittgenstein.*

*That pressure has been unrelenting, in spite of the fact that Paul has
made offers of compromise which are more than fair and which I am certain would have been acceptable to the Reichsbank had the latter not
found it so easy to induce the sisters in Vienna to permit themselves to
be used as the instruments in the application of a pressure which has
defeated itself by its own lack of moderation and sensible restraint.*

The letter went on to explain that Paul would be happy to meet his
brother in New York but only if Ludwig would agree to seeing Dr.
Wachtell first so that "when you and Paul meet both of you may be saved
any possible annoyances and disagreeable differences due to lack of
knowledge on your part of the facts involved."

Ludwig went, as advised, to see Samuel Wachtell and although he had
marked the 22nd in his pocket diary as the day he intended to meet Paul,
he did not in the event either see or speak to his brother during his week-
long visit to America. He did however send a letter to him (now lost) from
which Paul later quoted: "the Stonboroughs' behaviour was certainly rash
and stupid."

The American visit had exhausted Ludwig and he achieved very little
before returning, in flattened spirit, to Cambridge. He seems to have par-
ticipated joylessly in the application of pressure on Paul to give up his
fortune and many years later admitted with sadness and seriousness in his
voice: "Had I realised then how insane Paul was, I would never have
treated him so harshly." Paul and Ludwig's meeting in Zurich eight
months earlier in November 1938 turned out to be their last. The two
brothers never met, spoke or corresponded with one another again.

62 THE THREAT OF WAR

Hitler's avaricious foreign policies continued to rouse indignation abroad,
but the last thing he wanted was an all-out war with Russia, France, En-

gland or Italy. His stated plan was to unite, as peacefully as possible, all of German-speaking Europe into one German Reich under his leadership, but, on the principle of the end justifying the means, he lied, reneged, pushed beyond his stated intentions and exhibited too often a contemptuous disregard for the conventions of international diplomacy. Even he had been surprised at how smoothly the *Anschluss* with Austria in March 1938 had passed off. Foreign countries had voiced their disapproval but in the end they had all found a way to acknowledge the new expanded Reich without loss of face. The annexation of the Czech Sudetenland in October had been far riskier for Hitler, and war was only narrowly avoided by his repeated assurances that he had no further territorial claims in Europe and by his soliciting the prior agreement of Neville Chamberlain, Édouard Daladier and Benito Mussolini. When, on March 15, 1939, he ordered the Wehrmacht into Czech-speaking Prague the international community unanimously condemned his action. Prime Minister Chamberlain responded with over 100 measures indicating Britain's preparation for war, and four months later, as the Germans were poised to snatch the free port of Danzig, he vowed that Britain would come to Poland's military aid in the event of a conflict with Germany.

Hitler's efforts to discourage all countries from warring against him were carried on in earnest, even as his troops were rudely annexing Germany's neighbors. In order not to ruffle the feathers of the American administration it was decided (among many other things) that Ji Stonborough should be handled with care. Nazi diplomats in America had reported to Berlin that he was a man of importance. His job title—Commissioner of Conciliation in the Department of Labor—was nervously interpreted in Berlin as something far more powerful than it actually was. In point of fact Ji's daily routine consisted in little more than writing gray reports on American industrial disputes. In Berlin it was known that he was well connected in political circles in Washington. His name was frequently appearing in the gossip columns of the Washington press as an invitee at high-society cocktail parties. His friend James Houghteling was married to a cousin of President Roosevelt and the Germans believed (wrongly) that Ji might have the ear of the President. It was further assumed in Berlin that his frequent trips between Vienna and Washington were exploited by the U.S. administration to gain intelligence about Nazi Germany, and it was for this reason, primarily, that the Germans wished to fill Ji's youthful head with favorable impressions of their dynamic new Reich. This unofficial protection was known to the Stonboroughs and used by Gretl in her negotiations with the Reichsbank over the distribution of the Wistag funds.

By August 1939 the Wistag-Reichsbank dispute was still not settled. Paul had withdrawn entirely from the proceedings, leaving his attorney to fight his corner. The next round, it was decided, should take place in Switzerland. Paul stayed in America, sending Dr. Wachtell written instructions:

> You have my entire confidence to act and conclude in Zurich in my name . . . My honour (which would be the target of all calumny should anything happen in Vienna) is at stake, as is my own conscience and peace of mind . . . Do what you think is right, but remember, a moral claim can never be waived.

The Zurich negotiations proved no easier than those that had taken place in New York the previous month. Ludwig came and left early without achieving anything. Gretl and Ji refused to talk to Samuel Wachtell for he, as far as they were concerned, was still the enemy. Dr. Indra tried, but failed, to make Wachtell sign a false memorandum, while Anton Groller tried to appeal to his conscience. He told him that he knew Paul far better than Dr. Wachtell did, that although Paul had said he had no intention of returning to Vienna, his heart truly belonged there and that if he did not pay up, the Palais to which he was so deeply attached would be confiscated and never returned.

All the while the assembled company was waiting anxiously for official news from Berlin about *Mischling* status. Kurt Mayer, whom Paul and Gretl had met at the Reich Agency for Genealogical Research, had refused to accept the flimsy evidence that Hermann Christian Wittgenstein was the son of an Aryan prince, but the head of the Reichsbank had succeeded in sidelining Mayer and placing the Wittgenstein file in the hands of higher authority. Now the family was hoping, not for genealogical proof of Aryan descent, but for some sort of "pardon." This would need the

Führer's consent. The first that Dr. Wachtell knew of Hitler's possible involvement was from Dr. Indra. At a meeting at the Hotel Dolder in Zurich, Wachtell had voiced his concerns that the Germans, having awarded *Mischling* status, might later revoke it in order to force Paul to pay more. Dr. Wachtell's memorandum of the meeting continues:

> Dr Indra said that no one would dare do that in view of the high standing of the official who would sign the *Mischling* decree. I remained unconvinced. But Dr Indra insisted that that was so since the one who would sign such a decree, if it were granted, would be the Führer himself. I thought this was a fantastic expectation and told Indra so, but Indra assured me that that was entirely likely.

Hitler was on the brink of invading Poland and thus, if Chamberlain's assurances were to be trusted, on the brink also of war. And yet it seems that he found the time to sign the order allowing the Wittgensteins to be accorded half-breed status. His ruling that Hermann Christian be considered of Aryan descent was passed to Wilhelm Frick, Minister of the Interior, who on August 29 sent instructions to Kurt Mayer at the Agency for Genealogical Research in Berlin. The next day Mayer was forced to issue *Mischling* certificates to all relevant descendants. This volte-face aroused the suspicion of the district office for Genealogical Research in Vienna, whose director wrote to Berlin demanding an explanation. Kurt Mayer's reply survives in the Vienna archives:

> *In the matter of the origins of the Wittgenstein family and its descendants, I came to my decision in accordance with the directive issued on 29 August 39 by the Interior Minister, a directive which rests in turn upon an order issued by the Führer. Given these facts, the family origins and circumstances were not independently scrutinised in any closer detail by this office. The decision of the Führer applies immediately and without restriction to Hermann Wittgenstein (born Korbach 12/9/1802) who should be regarded as the German blood ancestor of all the descendants . . . In the meantime family origin certificates have been issued to the numerous descendants of Hermann Wittgenstein so that their racial classification*

within the meaning of the Reich Citizenship Act should present no more
difficulties. If necessary in cases of doubt, relevant family origin certifi-
cates can be requested from the Reich Agency for Genealogical Research.
   Signed Dr Kurt Mayer

Of course none of this would have come to pass if Paul had not finally
been persuaded to waive his rights to a substantial portion of his fortune.
Dr. Wachtell's persistence on his behalf had resulted in the Reichsbank's
agreeing to his keeping 1.8 million Swiss francs. A further 300,000 SF
from Paul's share was paid to the lawyers Bloch, Wachtell and Bienstock
of which Paul recouped 200,000 from Ji as well as a further 300,000, being
slightly less than his share in the capital of the Wistag holding company.
All in all then Paul succeeded in retaining 2.3 million SF of his foreign assets at a cost of just over 1.2 million SF. All of his cash and real estate in
Germany including his half-share in the great palace and his third share
of the Neuwaldegg estate were transferred for no consideration to his sisters Hermine and Helene. On an Internal Revenue Service tax form for
August 1945 Paul estimated the value of his assets in the U.S., as of December 31, 1944, at $924,821. Using calculations based on the Consumer
Price Index this amount in 1944 can be said to have had a value in the
year 2000 equivalent to $9,066,875—a substantial sum of money by most
people's standards but nothing compared to Paul's real worth if the Nazis
had not intervened.

No sooner had Paul's money been taken into German hands than all
departments fell upon it like a pack of hungry hyenas and a great bureaucratic confusion ensued between the Reichsbank, the Central Office
for the Protection of Historical Monuments, the Assets Control Office,
the Reich Emigration Tax Office and the Gestapo. The Reichsbank had
signed an agreement with Paul that he could remove all his non-fixed assets, at least those that were not subject to export control. Everything was
packed and ready to go when the Central Office for the Protection of Historical Monuments stepped in and overruled the Reichsbank. On his 1944
IRS return Paul had declared: "I have no knowledge as to whether personal belongings in Austria are still intact and what they are worth. These
included at one time at least valuable works of art, manuscripts and furniture."

Part of the agreement with his sisters had stated that his emigration tax should be paid out of the cash he had transferred to them, and when the Assets Control Office revalued Paul's domestic fortune at 6.4 million Reichsmarks the Reich Emigration Tax Office immediately demanded 25 percent or 1.6 million RM of it. Hermine and Helene hired the services of Dr. Indra, who had so recently succeeded in wrestling the money from Paul, to protect their newfound fortune from the tax man.

63 VALUABLE MANUSCRIPTS

Two days after the Wittgenstein family had received its certification of *Mischling* status, at 5:35 a.m. on the morning of September 1, 1939, some 1.25 million officers and men massed along the German border with Poland in East Prussia were given orders to advance. *"Achtung! Panzer, marsch!"* The roar of airplanes, motorcycles, armored cars, tanks and supply trucks smashed the silence of the clean morning air and within minutes the sound of explosives and gunfire was added to the din. The huge cavalcade advanced at extraordinary speed toward Warsaw and within eight days the German Blitzkrieg was over. Poland was transformed into yet another province of Hitler's expanding Reich. On September 3, before the fighting was concluded, the British and French Prime Ministers declared war on Germany.

Ji was still in Vienna when the news came through. As an American citizen he was in no immediate danger, but he and his mother were desperate to smuggle as much valuable property out of the country as they could before things got any worse. On September 10 he packed his suitcase in preparation for his return to Washington, stuffing furtively, under a pile of pants and socks, a significant number of original musical manuscripts: the Scherzo of Beethoven's Quartet Opus 130; the song "Lied aus der Ferne"; nineteen Beethoven holograph letters; Brahms's Handel Variations and two versions of the D minor Piano Concerto; Mozart's Serenade (K 361) and the String Quintet in C (K 515); six songs by Schubert, including the famous "Die Forelle" (The Trout); a piano duet sonata; and a collection of sketches by Wagner for *Die Walküre*.

Karl and Leopoldine had been avid collectors of musical manuscripts. Gretl inherited some of them and expanded her collection with new acquisitions after her father's death. In the 1920s, before Jerome had disgraced himself in the Wall Street Crash, she had charged him with the task of buying musical manuscripts, as well as French paintings and Oriental and Egyptian art. These were to be seen as long-term investments bought with her money using his apparently expert eye. In this way Jerome amassed several significant collections. Many of the manuscripts that were in Vienna in June 1938 were hidden from the Nazi inspectors and not listed on Gretl's declaration of assets. At the time of the passport trial some were discovered and placed by the authorities in the vaults of the Austrian National Library, but there were others still hidden away. It was these that Ji pushed into his suitcase, in the hope of slipping them out of Austria.

His plan was to pass by train over the Buchs border into Liechtenstein and Switzerland. From Zurich he would send the manuscripts by diplomatic courier to Washington before proceeding via Paris to the port of Le Verdon in western France, where he hoped to board the SS *Manhattan* bound for New York. But, on the Austrian side of the border in Vorarlberg, his train was brought to a halt. Enthusiastic Gestapo and Grepo (border police) ran up and down the carriages searching through all the passengers' bags. When they found the manuscripts at the bottom of Ji's suitcase he was hauled off the train and was still being interrogated as it pulled out of the station without him. In an account of this exploit penned many years later Ji recalled:

> I was bright enough to assert loud and clear that only idiots would try and remove such valuable manuscripts from the Reich and that each one was a neat and beautiful modern copy. The Gods of Olympus kept their hands over me and the dolts believed me and allowed me, ungraciously, as an American of importance, to take the next train in 6 hrs to Zurich.

If this is to be believed then the customs officers and border police really were the thickest of dolts, for they were trained in the very task of stopping valuables from being smuggled out of the Reich. They must have heard the "these-are-only-copies" excuse a thousand times and presumably had recourse to experts in case of doubt. That three or more of these men could have examined Ji's manuscripts and agreed among themselves that they were no more than "beautiful modern copies" is unlikely; more probably is that the border police made some quick inquiries and discovered that, as far as Berlin was concerned, Ji Stonborough was "an American of importance."

He was held at the border for six hours, during which time he was invited to take a walk with a man who had been pulled off the same train and who claimed to be a baker from St. Gallen, but whom Ji suspected of being a Swiss intelligence officer. On their long stroll together, Ji apparently told him nothing, but only talked about the weather. This, at least, was his version of events. If true, it was not typical of him, for in general he could not easily refrain from boasting. No sooner had he arrived safely back in America than the gossip columnist Dudley Harmon reported in her column for the *Washington Post* that: "The liner *Manhattan*, which docked at New York Saturday positively bulging with passengers, brought back several Washingtonians, among them John Stonborough who is fascinating his friends at cocktail time with tales of the difficulties of getting out of Europe."

Whether Ji revealed anything to the Swiss baker is not known. The Grepo, however, turned out to be a little less doltish than he claimed, for no sooner had he passed with his precious cargo over the border than his mother, still in Vienna, was visited by the Gestapo. This time they went through her inventories with a fine-tooth comb and, learning about the six manuscripts that she had smuggled into England for Ludwig's safekeeping in June 1938, promptly threatened her with criminal prosecution for the illegal export of national treasures. Once again, with the aid of Dr. Indra, she was able to negotiate her way round the trouble. Indra recommended that she offer for sale to the state both her own and Ji's manuscripts for a "reasonable price" in return for immunity from prosecution. These were the manuscripts that had been confiscated from her home at the time of her arrest and placed in the National Library. They included Gretl's holographs of symphonies by Bruckner and Wagner, Ji's manuscripts of Brahms's Piano Quintet and a quintet by Weber, other pieces by Brahms and Schubert and an autograph letter by Beethoven. Dr. Indra requested that, in return for selling these treasures to the library at a knockdown price, she be allowed to export just one of them—the manuscript of the Brahms Third Symphony (which had once belonged to the conductor Hans von Bülow and was now owned by her reprobate son Thomas)—free of tax.

It was this last suggestion that prompted the Austrian officer in charge of the case, Friedrich Plattner (head of the Department of Education, Culture and National Instruction at the Viennese Ministry for Internal and Cultural Affairs), to seek advice from higher authority in Berlin. On January 9, 1940, he wrote to the notorious head of the Reich Chancellery, Hans Heinrich Lammers, explaining how the "threat of prosecution" had inspired the widow Stonborough to offer her own and her sons' manuscripts to the National Library for just 50,000 RM. The letter continues:

> In order to lend particular weight to this offer, the Stonborough family draws attention to the fact that, during the negotiations which are shortly to take place about how the remaining assets of roughly 1 million Swiss francs in Zurich are to be divided up, the family will be in a position either to bring about or to prevent the transfer of this sum in favour of the German Reich; further emphasis has recently been given to this fact by a representative of the Reichsbank through intervention in favour of the Stonborough family on the part of the Central Heritage Protection Agency in Vienna.
>
> Also worth mentioning is the possibility that the Stonborough family—Dr. John Stonborough has an allegedly influential position in the Labor Department in Washington—might, possibly through diplomatic channels, be able to bring some pressure to bear for the Brahms symphony to be exported without anything being given in return.

Lammers, not unnaturally, refused permission for the last symphony autograph score by Brahms remaining in the Reich to be exported, and commanded Plattner to enforce the sale of the manuscripts to the library and demand the million Swiss francs in return for Gretl's immunity from prosecution. This million was the same million that Ji had sworn to Paul would be held aside as an emergency fund for Hermine and Helene in the event of their needing to emigrate. That money would now have to be found elsewhere.

64 COLD WAR

In Switzerland Paul had occupied himself extensively with the case of Daniel Goldberg, a Viennese doctor who had looked after Hilde and the children in Vienna. He and his Aryan wife had fled to Paris in August where they were living in a squalid hotel on the outskirts of the city. When Paul discovered this he sent large sums of money and campaigned with friends in England and America to find the doctor a position. Gretl too made vigorous efforts to save old family friends from Nazi anti-Semitism and succeeded in bringing two of them first to Cuba and later into America; but by 1940 she had played out all her cards and was decidedly persona non grata with the German authorities. As soon as her deal with the National Library was concluded she was required to leave the country. Of her two properties at Gmunden the National Socialists commandeered the larger and would soon occupy her Viennese mansion as well. Dr. Indra helped, in the hours before her emigration, to bury various of her treasures in the garden at Kundmanngasse. To him she entrusted full power of attorney during her absence and left, full of sorrow, for the port of Genoa. On February 8, 1940, she arrived in New York on board the SS *Washington*. This was her second, forced emigration from Austria and it left her, once again, feeling listless and depressed. To Ludwig she wrote: "There is no place I can find rest and I cannot be of any use to anyone. So God willing I will find a meaningful occupation."

In the end she occupied these barren months by selling off her possessions. In October two massive sales of furniture, paintings and Oriental artifacts, described as "The Property of the Estate of the Late Jerome Stonborough," were held at the Parke-Bernet Galleries on 57th Street. Picassos, Corots, Gauguins, Matisses, a twenty-foot coromandel lacquer Pekingese screen, ancient Roman statuary, Athenian vases, horses, jugs and bibelots from the days of Tang, Ming, Yuan and Sung. These treasures cannot have come from New York since Gretl had no fixed abode there. Extant passenger lists give Jerome's U.S. address in February 1937 as the Waldorf Astoria Hotel. A year later, Gretl gave hers as 44 Wall Street— the office of her son's stockbroker. The sale catalogue states that the items were all collected by Jerome in Paris. It is not known whether she succeeded in negotiating an export license for any of her artworks in Vienna. The manager at Parke-Bernet Galleries gave the Stonboroughs an estimate for the paintings of between $59,015 and $91,615. But the sale was a disappointment. The highest price for a single item was paid for Lot 71, *Nature morte* by Henri Matisse, which went for $10,400. No more than $5,200 was paid for Toulouse-Lautrec's severe portrait of *La Femme au noeud rose;* $4,100 for Gauguin's *Le Violoncelliste* and $3,800 for Picasso's 1921 *Le Chien.* Almost everything else went for under $2,000, including a splendid Modigliani portrait, *La Femme au collier,* for $400, whose sister picture *La Femme au collier vert* was valued by Christie's, New York, in May 2007 at between $12 million and $16 million. The picture sale raised a total hammer price of $56,705. It was a bad time to sell.

Several months later Ji sold cheaply all the manuscripts that he had smuggled through the border at Buchs to the Clarke-Whittall Collection at the Library of Congress in Washington. Some of the money was put into offshore accounts in Bermuda and some into an investment trust in the joint names of John Stonborough and Abraham Bienstock.

Since Hermine and Helene's so-called emigration fund had been paid to the Nazis Gretl and Ji resolved to make it up in other ways, both writing to Ludwig to ask him to release the manuscripts deposited at Barclay's Bank in Cambridge, so that they too could be offered for sale in Washington. At least one of them (Mozart's Piano Concerto K 467) actually belonged to Paul. Ludwig wrote to Ji to dissuade him from selling at a time when the market was low, to which Ji responded with a "damned aggressive" letter in which he accused his uncle of "going off half-cock." "I have done fairly well in the administration of 2 and a half fortunes since approx '39," he wrote, "and I am entitled to more regard for my opinions and decisions in financial matters than you have shown me."

65 A FAMILY REUNION

In Switzerland young Hilde's life was far from easy, for with time-limited visas she, the children and Fräulein Rolly were under imminent threat of extradition. At the beginning of March 1939 she received instructions from Paul's lawyer to pack everything and proceed to Genoa by overnight train. Tickets were booked on the Italian liner *Rex* bound for New York. When they got there they found a riot of desperate people hoping to clamber aboard. Their luggage was loaded, only to be unloaded again when it was discovered that their immigration papers were not in order.

For two and a half weeks they waited at Genoa before securing places on board a smaller boat bound for Panama and Valparaiso. The *Virgilio,* built for no more than 640 passengers, was packed with a needy, dispossessed rabble of over 1,100 people fleeing Hitler's Europe. Hilde, who had never been on board a ship before, was feeling sick with longing for Austria by the time she had reached the Straits of Gibraltar. The journey took them via the Canaries, Venezuela, the Isthmus of Panama and the twin cities of Cristóbal and Colón (where they were caught in a dramatic fire that burned down half the city) and eventually to Havana, where they bought Cuban visas, took a house by the sea and waited, for a year and a half, for Paul to come and rescue them.

He could do nothing immediately, for by leaving America Paul risked not being allowed back in. Only when his visitors' visa had finally expired in August 1940 was he able to fly to Havana. For seven months he stayed in the Hotel Nacional de Cuba on the San Lázaro Cove visiting his mistress and his children at weekends. At every turn his attempts to secure both his and their permanent visas for the U.S. were thwarted and for a while he considered moving with his family to Argentina.

Hilde, by nature, was religious. She had been brought up in the Catholic faith and longed for her relationship with the father of her children to be dignified by marriage. In the past few years she had suffered and sacrificed much, confronting each new difficulty with courage and fortitude. She had persuaded Paul, despite his antipathy to the Catholic Church, to allow their daughters to be baptized in Vienna and now, on

August 20, 1940, in Havana, Cuba, he and she became man and wife in a private, formal, Catholic ceremony.

In New York, Gretl and Paul had made no attempts to meet one another, but Gretl learned about her brother through information supplied by a shared acquaintance. "I would go to see him with joy if it would be of any use," she wrote to Ludwig, "but I know that I am the last person he could stand. I understand it so well." During the war she was forced to write to her youngest brother in English to avoid the suspicion of the censors. This she found uncomfortable, but it was the only way that Ludwig could obtain news of his brother: "Paul's friend (with her children) is now in Cuba & he will bring her here & marry her as soon as he can get the permission. In the old days I used to think of such a possibility as being about the greatest misfortune that could befall him, but now!—I look at you & we say: 'naturally.' May his soul rest in peace."

66 BENJAMIN BRITTEN

In April 1934 Paul had performed Ravel's Concerto with Hermann Scherchen conducting at the ISCM Festival in Florence. In the audience sat the twenty-year-old English composer Benjamin Britten, who had come to hear his own Phantasy Quartet performed on the following evening. *The Times* critic regarded Paul's performance as the best of the whole festival, but Britten was so taken by Scherchen's thirteen-year-old son Wulff (later the inspiration behind his music for "Young Apollo") that he may not have been concentrating especially hard. As a schoolboy in Norfolk he had heard Strauss's *Parergon* on the radio and had written in his diary: "In the afternoon after a lie down I listen to the wireless, a concert, orchestra and Paul Wittenstein (I think that's his name, the left handed pianist). Quite good, tho' I didn't like the programme very much."

In 1940 Britten was living in America where he had arrived shortly before the outbreak of war, having left England to escape his intricate entanglements with Wulff. Paul, unsure if he liked Britten's music, approached the matter of a commission gingerly. Britten's boyfriend Peter

Pears recorded: "We went and had a long talk with him [Wittgenstein]. He was rather stupid, couldn't understand Ben's music(!), & Ben *nearly* got terribly cross, but just managed to contain himself." A few days later Paul invited the young composer and his publisher, Hans Heinsheimer, to his apartment on Riverside Drive to discuss the possibility further. When they left the matter was still undecided. Eager for a firm commitment (the fee was $700) Heinsheimer rang him the next day and reported back to Britten:

> I called Mr. Wittgenstein once more this morning and asked him if he could please make up his mind quite clearly and sincerely. He said that this is exactly what he did yesterday and if it sometimes looked a little bit strange, the reason was that he wanted to be as sincere as possible. He didn't see this meeting as the proper occasion or the proper opportunity to pay nice compliments, but as a sort of meeting of a doctor and a patient, where the utmost sincerity should be applied. He apologises if he made the impression of being a little too persistent and he really thinks that your music would be the right thing for him. He highly appreciates your offer to show him parts of the work before the deal is completed . . . I think I should encourage you to try it.

Within a matter of days Britten had completed his first sketches and took them to Paul for approval. After a good "Austrian" supper, he was able to report: "I pulled off the deal with Wittgenstein. I had dinner with him, which was much more pleasant than I'd feared. He's much easier to manage alone! I've even started the piece which I think may be quite nice." And to his sister Britten wrote, "I've been commissioned by a man called Wittgenstein . . . he pays gold so I'll do it."

For a while relations between composer and patron ran smoothly. Britten finished the work in sketch form by August 12, just over a week after Paul had arrived in Havana. By October Paul was playing the piano part by heart and seemed pleased with it, but the two men were separated—Paul unable to enter the U.S. and Britten afraid of visiting Cuba lest he too be denied reentry to the States. This situation frustrated the pianist more than the composer. Britten arranged a private performance on two pianos for the distinguished conductor of the Cincinnati Symphony Orchestra, Eugène Goossens, who was so impressed that he wrote immediately to Heinsheimer: "This is a truly amazing work and confirms again one's knowledge of the fact that Britten is the outstanding young man in the world of creative music today."

Paul (aged fifty-three) flew from Havana to Florida on February 10, 1941, leaving Hilde (twenty-five), his daughters Elizabeth (five) and Johanna (three) and Fräulein Rolly (fifty-five) to follow on by boat three days later. On the landing papers next to Hilde's name is scribbled in the rough hand of an immigration official: "Husband shows from statement that he has $200,000 but she a marked deficiency of vision almost to complete blindness." On arrival she and the girls moved to a comfortable house at Huntington, Long Island. "A nice place," Paul called it, "with a view to the bay and a charming garden where I shall plant some strawberries and redcurrants. Most important thing about it is that it is only ten minutes from the beach." For the rest of her married life Hilde lived with the children on Long Island while Paul stayed at his apartment on Manhattan's Riverside Drive, visiting them at weekends and for part of the school holidays.

At Huntington Hilde proudly announced that she was pregnant once again and Paul, who longed for a son, was delighted by the news. With Britten, however, his relationship was starting to become strained. As with Strauss, Korngold, Ravel and Schmidt, Paul once again accused the composer of making his orchestra far too loud. Britten, he said, was a typically modern composer who "feels unwell" if he is not allowed to over-score; "playing against the noise of your orchestra is a hopeless strife," he wrote, "a roaring like a lion . . . a deafening noise . . . No human strength on the piano can be a match for 4 horns, 3 trumpets, 3 trombones and double woodwind, all making noise at the same time." The young composer stood his ground at first, refusing to make any changes. The premiere of the piece, which would eventually be called *Diversions,* was set for January with the Philadelphia Orchestra under the Hungarian conductor Eugene Ormandy. Britten wrote to his English publisher: "I'm having a slight altercation with Herr von Wittgenstein over my scoring—if there is anything I know about, it is scoring so I am fighting back. The man really is an old sour puss." Peter Pears unsurprisingly agreed: "Wittgenstein is being stupid and recalcitrant about the scoring of the *Diversions* and has been trying to get Ormandy on his side. It means a series of tactful but firm letters from Ben."

"Our battle," as Paul openly referred to it, continued by letter for several weeks without either side offering the smallest concession. Resenting the impasse, Paul wrote again to Britten:

> In the museum in Vienna I have seen a terrible weapon used in the Middle Ages—it looks like an easy chair but when you sit down the two sides snap over your body and you can't get out again. The German word for it is *Fangstuhl*. My idea was to have privately constructed a sort of *Fangstuhl*, then to invite you, let you sit down in it and only let you out of your prison when you have conceded the different alterations to your concerto that I am going to propose.

Eventually the composer agreed to a few small changes but, ever after, felt extremely bitter about them. The premiere took place in Philadelphia on January 16, 1942. Britten agreed to attend, if only "to hear Wittgenstein wreck my *Diversions*" and was distinctly put out by the changes that the pianist had forced upon his score. All but one review was highly favorable—the most influential being the critic Linton Martin of the *Philadelphia Inquirer*:

> A one-armed pianist, whose right sleeve hung empty at his side while his left hand swept the keyboard with fairly magical mastery, thrilled the Philadelphia Orchestra audience in the Academy of Music yesterday with a performance of virtuoso brilliance that would have spelled triumph for a greatly gifted artist exercising all ten digits.

Two months later, on March 13, 1942, *Diversions* received its New York premiere at a broadcast concert from the Town Hall with Charles Lichter conducting the Columbia Concert Orchestra. Britten did not attend and Peter Pears wrote to a friend: "Wittgenstein is playing his piece on Friday 3:30–4:30 on CBS. Do listen if you can, tho' I expect it will be bad." Gretl, however, did turn up, to see her brother for the first time since May 1939.

Paul did not notice her and a friend slip into their seats at the back of the auditorium. To Ludwig she wrote:

> I felt I wanted to see him (unseen by him) & also to hear him. He looks well & astonishingly young & as sympathetic as always on the podium. But his playing has become much worse. I suppose that is to be expected, because he insists on trying to do, what really cannot be done. It is *eine Vergewaltigung* [a violation]—Yes, he is sick . . .

67   THE WITTGENSTEINS' WAR

At the beginning of 1938, embarrassed by his continued sensual interest in Francis Skinner, Ludwig scribbled in his diary: "Thought: it would be good and right if he had died, and thereby rid me of my folly . . . Although, there again, I only half mean that." For years Ludwig and Francis had been inseparable until on October 11, 1941, the twenty-nine-year-old gardener and mechanic died from a severe and sudden attack of polio—the same disease that had taken the life of Ludwig's nephew Fritz Salzer after the First World War. Ludwig was devastated. Fed up with teaching philosophy at a time of international crisis, he sought and was offered a 28-shilling-a-week job as ward-porter at Guy's Hospital in London. When a doctor there recognized him as the distinguished Cambridge philosopher and went up to greet him, Ludwig "turned white as a sheet and said 'Good God, don't tell anybody who I am.' "

"My soul is *very* tired. It isn't at all in a good state." His job was to carry pills from the dispensary to the wards where he apparently advised patients not to take them. At Guy's the emotional void left by Francis Skinner's death was filled to some degree by a twenty-one-year-old man of humble East End origins and modest mind who worked in the dispensary. His name was Roy Fouracre, and his affectionate name for Ludwig was Old So-and-so. He and Ludwig remained close friends until Ludwig's death in 1951 when he left Roy a little money in his will. From the position of lowly porter Ludwig was soon promoted to that of "ointment maker" and surprised his boss by devising improved methods of ointment preparation that had never been previously considered. His stint at Guy's came to an end when Roy joined the army and Ludwig moved to Newcastle to work as a laboratory assistant to two doctors who were studying an irregular breathing disorder known as *pulsus paradoxus*. Once again Ludwig demonstrated his originality by devising an altogether novel method by which a patient's pulse might be recorded—"an ingenious departure from standard practice which worked well," as one of the doctors recalled.

That was Ludwig's English war. In Vienna, the people's enthusiasm for National Socialism, for fighting and even for Hitler himself had started to wane with news of defeat at the battle of Stalingrad. Of the 50,000 Austrian troops of the German Sixth Army that had been surrounded by Russian forces, only 1,200 had survived. Wiener Neustadt was bombed by the Americans in August 1943 and when the heavier bombing of central Vienna started in September 1944 a bleak mood of defeatism spread for the first time among the hearts and minds of the Viennese people.

Towards Hermine and Helene the Nazis had held true to their word, and the two old ladies lived without interference from the authorities for the duration of the war. Helene's husband Max Salzer died in April 1941. His debilitated mental state had played heavily on her nerves, as had the emigration of her only surviving son, Felix, to America. With three of her grandsons fighting in the Wehrmacht, two of whom went missing at the end of the war, these were taxing years for Helene. Hermine too, always shy, now reclusive, had long given up drawing and teaching. Encouraged by members of her family she set about writing her memoirs—a collection of selective, sentimental and sometimes bitchy reminiscences of the family. At first she stayed at Hochreit (the mountain retreat she had inherited from her father). In October 1944, fearing Russian invasion from the east, she fled to Vienna, and as soon as the capital looked set to become a bloody battlefield she moved to a house on Gretl's estate at Gmunden. The Wittgenstein Palais, now entirely hers, was converted for use as a hospital for wounded officers.

Of Gretl's two adopted sons the eldest, Wedigo, fought on the German side and was killed. "It goes very near me," Gretl wrote to Ludwig. "I was very fond of him in spite of all of his weaknesses and nothing he could ever have done could have changed that. In fact he was damned innocent.—He was made of a material alien to ours and was built for a different environment than ours and I was always amazed and troubled by his evident affections . . ." Jochen, the younger, fought for the Allies, was captured by the Germans and tortured as a traitor. He did however survive the ordeal. When Hitler declared war on the United States in December 1941, Gretl's house on the Kundmanngasse was expropriated and put to Nazi use. Many of the things in it were stolen.

In Washington, Ji fell in love with an unusual woman, a mechanically minded enthusiast for Heinz baked beans and fast cars called Veronica Morrison-Bell. She was the third daughter of an obscure Northumberland baronet and was twenty-nine years old when she arrived in America for the first time. As a woman of independent spirit, she had taken a holiday in Tokyo before the war broke out only to find that her route back to Europe was blocked by warships and mines. So she headed east across the Pacific, arriving in California on October 2, 1940. A friend of her parents, the rich patroness Dorothea Merriman, had found her a secretarial post in the Washington office of the Allied Combined Chiefs of Staffs, where they were making hush-hush plans for a Churchill government in exile. Veronica, whose brother was a captain in the 7th Lancers, was fiercely patriotic and it was rumored that her consent to marrying Ji depended upon his giving up his desk job and joining the army to fight the Nazis. In the spring of 1941 Ji duly enlisted as a volunteer officer cadet with the Duke of York's Royal Canadian Hussars, and on July 17, 1942, the couple were married at an officer-training camp at Brockville, Ontario, with a taxi driver as witness. Gretl mourned the loss of her "golden boy" but accepted the situation as best she could. "I like Veronica," she wrote to Ludwig, "I like her very much although I realize that she has a hard & bitter kernel under the soft cover."

Ji, or Stoney as he was known to his fellow officers, trained hard and was considered a proficient soldier, even though he swore too much, and denigrated the Canadian army as "a damned inefficient bunch of dolts." Once his detachment had arrived in France in 1944, he saw action in battles against the Hitler Youth's specially formed Panzer Division. His fluent German made him a useful interrogator, translator and intelligence officer, but he never rose beyond the rank of major as "some bastard of a

Canadian General" blocked his advancement. The problem came at the end of the war when he was involved in the trial of SS Brigadeführer Kurt "Panzer" Meyer, a highly decorated German soldier, wrongly accused of ordering the assassination of Canadian POWs in Normandy in 1944. Ji was working for the prosecution and even before the trial had begun had let it be known that a guilty verdict was a foregone conclusion and that Meyer would be sentenced to death. During the proceedings, at which he was serving as interpreter, it was revealed that he had tried to influence a witness statement by shouting and intimidation, at which point "some bastard of a General," that is the Judge Advocate, dismissed him from the court, summoning a new interpreter to take his place. Meyer was sentenced to death but, after vigorous campaigning by both Germans and Canadians, was released from prison in September 1954.

The battles of Paul's war assumed a very different form. In New York he joined an exile group calling itself Austrian Action, run by Count Ferdinand Czernin, the son of the Austrian Foreign Minister during the First World War. The group's membership was made up of all types and all political persuasions, and was formed to campaign for an overthrow of the Nazi regime in Austria. Paul gave his money and time to supporting the group, playing in several high-profile Austrian Action fund-raising concerts in New York; as a result he was treated with suspicion by the jittery American administration, which believed that all members of Austrian Action were communists. During the war years Paul also gave concerts to rally American troops, performing, for soldiers at Oakland, Camp Shanks and Gulfport Field, an arrangement of Ravel's Concerto with military brass band accompaniment. In New York in April 1944 he gave a concert in support of the Hebrew Immigrant Aid Society. Every week he sent weekly parcels of food and money to old friends and old retainers in Austria, France and England.

With no control over what was happening musically in Europe, he became suspicious that the great repertoire of left-handed piano pieces he had spent his fortune commissioning and which had brought him his career's successes was being stolen from him. There were two sorts of theft. One consisted in rearranging his original left-handed pieces for two hands, and the other in *his* works being performed by other two-armed or single-armed pianists. Already, before the war, Ravel, incensed by the liberties Paul had taken with his concerto, had championed the French pianist Jacques Février to play his work as soon as the Wittgenstein contract had expired. To Paul's irritation, Février recorded Ravel's Concerto in 1943. At the same time Richard Strauss, in a move guaranteed to enrage Paul, rededicated his *Panathenäenzug* to the young German pianist Kurt Leimer, who went on to make the first recording.

In Austria, due to the exodus of Jewish composers, Franz Schmidt became the new embodiment of pure-blood German musical genius. Schmidt was a sick man at the time of the *Anschluss* and the excitement of long-awaited official recognition went straight to his head. At the premiere of his oratorio *Das Buch mit sieben Siegeln* (The Book of Seven Seals), he gave a Nazi salute from his balcony seat at the Musikverein and undertook to compose another work in praise of the Nazi Party called *Die deutsche Auferstehung* (The German Resurrection). He died before completing it, but these acts severely limited Schmidt's posthumous international reputation.

Paul, who revered Schmidt almost as a father, was heartbroken to discover, shortly after the composer's death in 1939, that a young fascist pianist called Friedrich Wührer was making and performing two-handed arrangements of all the six works originally composed for Paul's left hand. Wührer was an ex-student of Schmidt's who Paul later claimed "went about for ten years shouting 'Heil Hitler!' and now only plays music to erase the past." He detested Paul as vehemently as Paul detested him. "In Austria," he wrote to a fellow pianist, "we do not take Herr Wittgenstein seriously. A choleric neurasthenic—rich, presumptuous and, as a pianist, lousy."

Wührer claimed to have visited Schmidt on his hospital deathbed, where he had pointed out to the composer that he had not yet written anything "right" for the piano. Schmidt is said to have replied: "But I have already written a piano concerto. You only need to arrange it for two hands!" This, Wührer claimed, gave him sanction to rearrange all the works for two hands. Paul wrote furious letters of protest to the composer's widow from America but her replies were muddled and equivocal. She had become unbalanced and was later "put to death" under the Nazi euthanasia scheme. "I know that Wührer is lying but how can I prove it?" Paul wrote to Koder in frustration.

During these years Wührer performed all of Schmidt's left-hand works in his own two-hand arrangements, ignoring the fact that they were still exclusively contracted to Paul. He had agreed to print a short notice in each concert program—"This work was composed for Paul Wittgenstein and is an arrangement of an original composition for the left hand"—but since Paul was an exiled Jew, listed in the official Nazi handbook *Lexikon der Juden in der Musik* as a banned concert artist, nobody in Vienna had to agree to any of his transatlantic demands. Wührer's programs consequently appeared without the notice.

By late 1944 support in Vienna for Adolf Hitler had all but evaporated. The American planes that came to bomb the Viennese were called Liberators. In sortie after sortie their pilots pounded the city from the air believing that they were freeing the people below from the heavy yoke of German oppression. And this is how many of the Viennese saw it too—not as a punishment for having welcomed a hellish, compatriot ideologue, surrendered their country to him, implemented his savage schemes with more vim and enthusiasm than the crazed dictator himself could have dreamed possible, or for having defended his brutal regime for five years with their guns, their bombs and their lives—no, the Americans were to be seen as "liberators" and with the bloodthirsty Russian army now approaching at speed from the east it became crucial to the Viennese that the more lenient Americans should get to their city first.

In December 1944 on a wet, wintry day, a U.S. Liberator bomber on a routine mission released a cluster over Vienna's once prosperous Wieden district. A bomb landed on the roof of the Wittgenstein Palais. The explosion tore through the back of the building, smashing the garden elevation and bringing down half of the rear exterior wall—the lavish bedroom where Karl had lain dying in 1913 was reduced to rubble; the ceiling of the *Musiksaal* where Brahms, Mahler and Hanslick had once sat in rapt attention came crashing down to the floor; and the great glass dome that for seventy years had allowed the sunlight through to the marble staircase below was shattered into thousands of fragments of twisted metal and broken glass. After a deafening report, the air was filled with dust. Distant sirens disturbed the monotonous patter of rain.

68 ROADS' END

In the years after the war Vienna was divided into French, British, Soviet and American sectors of occupation. Movement between these zones was restricted. The Palais found itself in the Russian sector. For a month the great building stood open to the elements and, for nearly a year after that, was boarded up and abandoned. The task of repairing the damage fell to Hermine, but it was not until the spring of 1947 that she was able to move back in. Pictures, furniture, manuscripts and a porcelain collection held in storage that had belonged to Paul were shipped out to him in America, but there was no reconciliation, nor any contact with him except through lawyers. If Hermine was elated to be back in the old home, even without her brother as companion, the sensation did not last long, for within six months of her return she was diagnosed with a fatal gynecological cancer.

Ludwig returned to Vienna for the first time in nine years to visit her. He had not been feeling too well himself and had given up his professorship at Cambridge in order to write, moving to Ireland, where he had been hopping from address to address in a state of near nervous collapse. In Vienna he found his eldest sister in a bad way and throughout 1948 her condition worsened. After a big operation at the beginning of 1949 she was told she had but a short time to live—two or three years at most. She then had a slight stroke, followed by another, heavier one, and it was soon apparent to everyone that her death was imminent. Gretl and Helene were at her side as she slipped in and out of consciousness.

Ludwig wanted to return to Vienna again in March, but Gretl tried to block his visit on the grounds that it would only upset Hermine, who was incapable now of recognizing anybody. Rudolf Koder wrote a slightly different account to Ludwig, who replied furiously:

> It seems that my sister Gretl gave me false news by implying that Hermine is not able to recognise anyone at all. It's very unpleasant to receive contradicting pieces of information. Please don't get influenced by anyone and continue to write the truth as you see it. Don't trust Gretl's judgement, it's too temperamental.

In March 1949, Paul, who had stayed clear of Vienna for over eleven years, was invited to play in two concerts to mark the tenth anniversary of Franz Schmidt's death. Ludwig wrote to Marga Deneke to tell her to inform his brother that Hermine was dying. Presumably she did this, but Paul, who played Schmidt's Beethoven Variations with the Vienna Philharmonic on March 13 and two quintets in the Brahmssaal on the nineteenth, did not go to see his ailing sister.

Vienna was no longer the safe and grandiose city that he remembered from his eager youth, nor did it any longer resemble the quick, cosmopolitan, cultural hub of the inter-war years. The cityscape of 1949 still bore the scars of the war; and the flame of the people, bereft of its Jewish energy, dimmed by the shame of complicity in the Nazi terror, was now reduced to a tragic ember. Paul had long ago thrown in his lot with the Americans and, though he remained at heart a patriotic Austrian, he came to Vienna in 1949, not as an exile yearning for his home, but as a visitor, a hotel guest and an international concert artist. He did not visit the Palais nor even look at it from the street. His heart was full of bitterness.

Ludwig, rashly (for his health was also failing), accepted an invitation from a former philosophy student, Norman Malcolm, to stay at Ithaca in New York State. In April, before leaving for America, he went to see Hermine in Vienna. Paul had already left the city, and Ludwig found his sister's life hanging by its final thread. He wrote to Professor Malcolm: "I haven't done any work since the beginning of March & I haven't had the strength of even trying to do any. God knows how things will go on now." The doctor in Dublin told him that he was suffering from a pernicious, atypical anemia that could be corrected with iron and liver pills. An X-ray of his stomach where a growth was suspected revealed no abnormalities. On July 21 he sailed on the *Queen Mary*.

Ludwig found America hot and bewildering. The Malcolms were kind to him but he felt like "an old cripple" and "too stupid" to write letters. He paid a surprise visit to Paul's house on Long Island but found it empty except for a maid and left without leaving a note. Once again he felt ill, bad enough to submit himself to the rigors of a medical inspection, and once again nothing seriously wrong was found. The day before he had murmured to Malcolm in a breathless frenzy: "I don't want to die in

America. I am a European. I want to die in Europe. What a fool I was to come!"

Returning to London he had himself checked again and was finally told the proper cause of his malaise. He had an inoperable and advanced cancer of the prostate, which had spread to his bone marrow, causing anemia. The treatment, a regular oral administration of the female hormone estrogen, was prescribed to arrest his production of testosterone. The side effects of this therapy include sickness, diarrhea, hot flashes, impotence and breast swelling. Unable to work and still feeling restless he decided to return to Austria for Christmas, where he imagined he would die in his old room at the Palais. "I am thinking of going to Vienna for some time as soon as possible. There I'll just do nothing & let the hormones do their work." He gave instructions to his friends not to mention his illness to anyone as it was "of the greatest importance" that his family should not get to hear about it while he was staying there.

On Christmas Eve Ludwig arrived at the Palais and retired to bed. It was on such a Christmas thirty-seven years earlier that Karl had lain dying of cancer and now—another grim Yuletide in the same palatial surroundings—it was the turn of Karl's eldest and youngest children. For two months Ludwig remained in Vienna, spending most of his time prostrate. Each day he went to see Hermine but she could hardly talk to him and when she did it was impossible to understand what she was trying to say. On February 11, 1950, she died. Ludwig wrote to a friend in England: "My eldest sister died very peacefully yesterday evening. We had expected her end hourly for the last 3 days. It wasn't a shock."

Most of Hermine's seventy-five years had been occupied in maidish time-filling activities, spoiled by feelings of inferiority and social inadequacy. She had produced one or two pictures of average merit, the best being of Josef Labor on his deathbed. Her friendships were few but loyal. Above all she had been keeper of the family flame. She had worked hard since her father's death to maintain his estates, standards and values and to honor his memory. She had maintained the Viennese Palais and made significant improvements to Hochreit and the Palais at Neuwaldegg. Her unpublished memoir, written for her great-nephews and -nieces, portrays the Wittgensteins in a fairytale aspect and reveals her to have been fonder and prouder of her uncles and aunts than of most of her siblings or even her mother. Only Ludwig and Gretl are honored in this work. Hans, Rudi, Kurt, Helene and Paul are dismissed with few words. For all Hermine's obvious faults the effect of her death on Ludwig was profound. "Great loss for me and all of us," he wrote in his diary. "Greater than I would have thought."

Ludwig was himself expecting to die, but for a year after Hermine's demise he continued writing and moving from place to place. In April 1950, he went to Cambridge, then, after a brief sojourn in London, moved to Oxford, took a holiday in Norway in August, settling on his return into the house of his doctor Edward Bevan and his wife in Cambridge. By February his decline was such that it was decided any further treatment would be pointless. Bucked by this, Ludwig told Mrs. Bevan, "I am going to work now as I have never worked before." Immediately he set about writing a large portion of the book now known as *On Certainty*. He made it (just) to his sixty-second birthday. "Many happy returns!" said Mrs. Bevan. "There will be no returns," he answered. On the following morning he composed his last philosophical thought:

> Someone who dreaming says "I am dreaming," even if he speaks audibly in doing so, is no more right than if he said in his dream "it is raining," while it was in fact raining. Even if his dream were actually connected with the noise of the rain.

That night Ludwig's condition deteriorated considerably and when Dr. Bevan told him that he was not likely to survive more than a couple of days he said, "Good!" Before passing out for the last time he murmured to Mrs. Bevan: "Tell them I've had a wonderful life!" His final moments—unconscious and oblivious—were attended at his bedside by four of his former students and, at their behest, a Dominican monk. He was buried the next day (April 30, 1951) by Catholic rite in the cemetery of St. Giles, Cambridge. None of his family or friends from Vienna was present.

If ever there were a case to show that cancer is a genetic disease, the Wittgenstein family should be submitted as the first exhibit of concluding proof. Eighteen months before Hermine's death Maria Salzer (Helene's daughter) was killed by cancer. In time both of Helene's daughters and several of her granddaughters as well as her great-granddaughters would be stricken by the same disease. Helene herself died of it in 1956. She had not seen her brother Paul since 1938.

As for Gretl, she outlived Helene by a couple of years, but they were not especially happy ones. She returned to Vienna but with none of the old gaiety or sense of purpose. Her social life was not the same as it had been in the 1920s and 1930s and she was lonely. The burden she felt at the antics of her rakish elder son (who married five times and was a constant financial drain) was compounded by her disappointment over the post-war idleness and lack of ambition of her younger son. After 1945, Ji had turned his back on his high-flying Washington career; he opted instead for the indolent life of an English country squire, settling in Dorset, where he and Veronica raised a family.

Of Paul, Gretl never spoke again, but she mentioned him in letters to Ludwig before he died. "For a time I really believed that Paul would get over his attitude," she told him, "but now I see that we have really lost him. He is not a forgetter & I don't see that age is going to make him mellower. I understand him so much better now than in the old days, when his outward overbearingness fooled me."

In 1958 the heart which had given her trouble since the days of her maidenhood finally gave in. She had three strokes in quick succession, rallied enough to pretend to her grandson that she had plenty of energy and would be all right, but spent the remainder of her days struggling for consciousness at an expensive private clinic on the Billrothstrasse. It was in a small bedroom here, in the Rudolfinerhaus, that she died on September 27. Of the Wittgenstein siblings, Gretl was the warmest, the most humorous and the kindest, but she was also the bossiest, the most ambitious and the most worldly. She hated these traits in herself but lacked the strength to resist them. Despite her knack for irritating and interfering she was remembered with deep affection by her many friends and descendants. She was buried on October 1, 1958, in the town cemetery at Gmunden, next to her husband.

69 THE END OF THE LINE

Paul Wittgenstein died on March 3, 1961. He was seventy-three years old. Like his younger brother, he too had fallen prey to cancer of the prostate and its attendant anemia, but in the end it was an acute attack of pneumonia that killed him.

In outward appearance his last years in America had been successful. His family, which by the end of November 1941 included a son, Paul Jr., moved from Huntington to a comfortable mock-Tudor residence with land and views across Long Island Sound at Great Neck. He continued to spend most of his time, except for the weekends and the longer holidays, in Manhattan, but despite this unconventional arrangement and the disparity of age between him and his wife, the marriage was, by some accounts at least, a happy one. In 1946 he and his family were granted full American citizenship and Paul never repined. During semiretirement from the concert platform in 1958 he published three books of piano music for the left hand, including some of his own arrangements, of which he was exceedingly proud. In the same year he was awarded an honorary doctorate, in recognition of his services to music, by the Philadelphia Musical Academy.

He had many piano pupils, all of whom he taught for free, and the work brought him fulfillment. One of his students, the talented composer and later award-winning film director Leonard Kastle, became his closest friend. His playing during this period, however, deteriorated sharply. At its peak, in the period between 1928 and 1934, he was a world-class pianist of outstanding technical ability and sensitivity who was able to galvanize an audience by his arresting stage manner. His posthumous reputation as a pianist is however low. This is partly caused by his altering the music of famous composers who subsequently railed against him. Ravel continued to complain about him until his death, Prokofiev insulted him in his autobiography and Britten revised the score of his *Diversions* after 1950 in order to create an "official version" that would stop Paul playing it by rendering his version obsolete. It is also the case that Paul made very few recordings, most of which are bad. A 1928 piano-roll performance of his own arrangement of the Bach-Brahms D minor Chaconne is faultless, but the two recordings he made of the Ravel Concerto and one of Strauss's *Parergon* are not so good. Clumsy errors, thoughtless phrasing and unnecessary tampering with the music spoil all three performances.

It would appear that the nervous strain of concert-giving was too great for him. While in the early years he could turn in performances of high quality, his playing was occasionally harsh and ham-fisted. As the years progressed the physical and mental effort overwhelmed him and he produced more of the latter and fewer of the former. Orchestras and conductors that had invited him once, seldom sought to rebook him. In England Marga continued to search for work for her old friend but found it increasingly difficult. The conductor Trevor Harvey, who had performed *Diversions* with Paul in Bournemouth in October 1950, wrote to her eight years later:

> I think I am going to have a great deal of difficulty in getting much for Paul. I'm sure I know you well enough to say exactly what I think and that you won't be offended because of your old friendship with P.W. The question is—how does he now play? Because last time he was here he didn't create a good impression—frankly, the Britten performance with me in Bournemouth had lots of moments of brilliance but there was a good deal of hard playing and as a performance it sometimes misunderstood Britten's intentions . . . Paul may, of course, be playing infinitely better than he was last time but it's going to be difficult to persuade people without any evidence.

Two weeks after that Bournemouth performance Paul played *Diversions* again under Sir Malcolm Sargent at the Royal Albert Hall in London. *The Times* critic recorded "a warm reception" but continued: "familiarity with these works has bred in him a certain contempt for refinement of detail, which he could well remedy by studying each afresh from the printed score."

The pianist Siegfried Rapp, who had lost his right arm during a battle in the Second World War, was especially bitter. He wrote to Paul asking permission to perform some of the works that he had commissioned and was bluntly refused:

You don't build a house [Paul told him] just so that someone else can live in it. I commissioned and paid for the works, the whole idea was mine . . . Constructing this house has cost me a great deal of money and effort—I was in any case far too generous with contracts as in the Ravel case, and I am now being punished for it. But those works to which I still have the exclusive performance rights, they are to remain mine as long as I still perform in public; that's only right and fair. Once I am dead or no longer give concerts, then the works will be available to everyone because I have no wish for them to gather dust in libraries to the detriment of the composers.

Rapp was determined to wrestle something from Paul's catalogue of commissions and after Prokofiev's death succeeded in getting a copy of the left-hand concerto from the composer's widow, and in 1956, to Paul's acute irritation, he gave the world premiere performance in Berlin. His attitude to Paul was aggressively negative. Writing to the Czech pianist Otakar Hollmann, Rapp remarked: "I had imagined that there might be nothing special about Wittgenstein's playing but what I heard on the records was indescribably bad . . . I am mightily horrified and disappointed. He's no pianist at all! To me Wittgenstein is now nothing but a rich dilettante."

Paul should have retired earlier from the concert platform, but he was a fighter and continued to view each performance as a test of his endurance and his nerve. To give up would have been, for him at least, an unacceptable admission of failure. He continued giving tours and public performances of ever-decreasing merit through his final illness, and right up until the year before his death. It was not vanity that compelled him, for at heart he was a modest man. "You are overrating me by far," he wrote to his student Leonard Kastle shortly before his death. "I have only a few redeeming points, the rest isn't worth much, and that's not fishing but the truth."

It was of course the same cocktail of pride, honor and obstinacy that stood in the way of any reconciliation with his siblings, but here each of the Wittgensteins was similar and each equally to blame. When Gretl and Paul were summoned to a court hearing in New York to swear on behalf of a friend applying for U.S. citizenship, they both sent representatives as they could not face meeting one another. Or as Gretl put it: "I was sure that he would have hated meeting me, so I sent my lawyer." Hermine said that she thought often of Paul on her deathbed but would not go the length of asking to see him, and as she lay dying Ludwig speculated: "I believe that she wants to make peace, so to speak, from her side and to extinguish all the bitterness." But nothing was done about it.

A similar situation had arisen with a memorandum that Paul drew up concerning the great Wistag quarrel. He commissioned it "since it is possible that at a later date it might be needed in order to save my honour" but sent instructions to his lawyer: "I would ask you initially not to send a copy to my brother, but to do so only if he expressly requests it." Of course Ludwig did nothing of the sort and therefore never read it, despite the fact that, in its final form, the memorandum was headed with a note: "The following was not originally intended as an appendix to my testament or for my children, but was much more intended for my brother who lives in England to read."

If Paul had been at home when Ludwig breezed by in 1949, the bitter feud—at least as it existed between the brothers—might well have ended there. Both felt miserable about the rift but with the exception of that one ad hoc visit neither was prepared to make the first move. Marga tried, on several occasions, to bring them together but her efforts were clumsy and caused great offense:

> Paul is in Oxford with the Denekes [Ludwig wrote to Rudolf Koder in March 1949] and recently I received a strange invitation, which filled me with disgust, from Miss Deneke, asking to visit her during Paul's stay. I wrote back stating my reasons about my unwillingness to accept the invitation . . . I am certain it was not written on Paul's instructions. I believe rather that she wanted to bring about the get-together and my brother gave her the permission to invite me, which she, because of her stupidity, did in a most stupid way.

A year later, when Paul was in England playing *Diversions,* Marga, undaunted by Ludwig's previous response, tried him again. This time she went to see him in person at his attic lodgings in St. John Street, Oxford:

He was sitting in a dressing gown over a fire [she recalled]. His voice still had its old musical huskiness but it sounded weak and suffering was written on his pale face. After a minute he asked me to leave him. He said it made him shudder to recall old memories and seeing me brought back thoughts of Vienna and his home that were too much for him.

Paul rarely spoke to his children about Ludwig or about his sisters. In 1953 he wrote to Rudolf Koder: "I kept out of contact with my brother from 1939; he wrote me one or two letters when I was visiting England, in response to Miss Deneke's invitation. I did not answer them. I do not know whether I would have done anything if I had been aware that he was terminally ill." By then Paul had managed to put his past behind him. Ludwig and Gretl believed that he had to estrange himself from his family in order to lead a free, fulfilled and happy existence.

After Hermine's death the once glorious Palais Wittgenstein was sold for development. Razed to the ground by cranes, bulldozers and wrecking balls, the final demolition marked the symbolic end to the Wittgenstein story. Paul and his son were the last surviving descendants in the male line from Karl and without the slightest hope of a return to the Palais in Vienna they looked to find a new identity and a new hope in the brash, optimistic life of America.

That our house in the Alleegasse is not only to be sold but razed to the ground is very sad but, I suppose, unavoidable [Paul wrote to Rudolf Koder]. But who can nowadays live in and upkeep a palais of such extravagance of space and grandiosity? Just think of the staircase and the salons on the first floor. Even at the time when I and my late sister were living there, the maintenance costs were far more than we could afford.

On Monday, March 6, 1961, friends were invited to pay their last respects in the American way. Paul's body had been moved from the North Shore Hospital where he had died to the Fliedner Funeral Home on Middle Neck Road where, on the following day at 10 a.m., a service was given.

No words were said. A small congregation assembled. A man at the front stood up and placed a phonograph needle on a 33 rpm recording of Brahms's German Requiem. Each time a side was finished the man went forward and turned the record over until, at length, the music reached its winding conclusion:

> *Selig sind die Toten, die in dem Herrn sterben, von nun an. Ja der Geist*
> *spricht, daß sie ruhen von ihrer Arbeit; denn ihre Werke folgen ihnen nach.*

(Blessed are the dead who die in the Lord from henceforth: Yea, saith the Spirit, that they may rest from their labors; and their works do follow them.)

Nobody came to the front to speak, no epicedium was read, no prayers. The needle arm was lifted and returned to its position of rest and, when the turntable had ceased its spinning, everyone filed out.

The *New York Times* ran a long obituary highlighting the important incidents of Paul's career. In London Trevor Harvey praised his exceptional generosity, concluding his obituary in the *Gramophone* magazine: "As a personal friend Paul Wittgenstein will never be forgotten while those who knew him are alive; but long after his friends are no more, music lovers will have reason to remember him with gratitude for the music he caused to be written." Marga's tribute to her eccentric old friend appeared in the London *Times,* eleven days after his death: "Loyalty to his friends was part of his strong personality. Paul Wittgenstein has indeed added a distinguished page to the history of music."

POSTSCRIPT

Hilde Wittgenstein lived until March 2001, by which time she was completely blind and insensible from Alzheimer's disease. Thirty years earlier she had moved from Long Island, New York, to Newfoundland, Pennsylvania, where she lived in a house that she had designed using plastic Lego bricks. Paul's body was exhumed from its grave on Long Island and reinterred at the Pine Grove cemetery nearby. As the years passed she became increasingly suspicious of everyone around her and estranged herself from her staunchest allies: Karoline Rolly, Dorothy Lutz (the lady who looked after her), her son Paul Jr., and one of her daughters. Despite her suspicious nature she gave a large portion of her fortune to a cultish Pennsylvanian Christian group. For years she kept Paul's library of valuable manuscripts jealously locked in a room of her house, to which no one was permitted entry. After her death it was discovered to contain many treasures, including the long-lost manuscript of Hindemith's *Piano Music with Orchestra*. After Hilde's death Paul's library, consisting of three and a half tons of books and manuscripts, was auctioned off at Sotheby's in London. It was bought by a Chinese entrepreneur called Ng, who had made his fortune by introducing the Big Mac burger to the people of Hong Kong.

Elizabeth, Johanna and Paul (Jr.) Wittgenstein were brought up strictly by both their parents on Long Island. They remembered their father as "a stern, incomprehensible and a somewhat distant and imposing figure" who was exceptionally enthusiastic about Christmas. All three spoke English at home in Long Island and could not understand when their parents talked to one another in German. They were taught to play the piano by Paul's former pupil Erna Otten, but none of them was, or is, particularly musical. Elizabeth had no children. After school she gravitated toward the caring professions, but suffered from her father's nervous temperament and died in an accident, which has never been fully explained, at Flushing, Queens, in February 1974. Johanna, whose name was changed to Joan in childhood, married a Dane and has five children, the eldest of whom was born during Paul's lifetime. She is presently retired from the book trade and lives on her own in a remote house in the woods of Virginia. Paul Jr. suffered ill-health from his teens. He was a gifted mathematician and for a while worked as a computer programmer. In the early 1960s he learned how to paint at a psychiatric clinic, and soon after his discharge from the hospital moved permanently to Austria, where he has mounted several successful exhibitions of his paintings using the name Louis Wittgenstein.

The Stonborough brothers, Thomas and Ji, were never on especially good terms. Thomas died in 1986, having sold off most of his inheritance, including Gretl's modernist dwelling on the Kundmanngasse, Klimt's famous painting of his mother and several Ludwig Wittgenstein manuscripts to which he had no proper title. Threatened for years with demolition, the Kundmanngasse Palais was eventually rescued by architectural enthusiasts and is presently the Viennese home of the Bulgarian Cultural Institute. Thomas's only surviving child, Pierre, works in private banking and has two daughters.

Ji Stonborough died in 2002 at Glendon in Dorset. For some time he had been troubled by his obligations to the Lloyd's Insurance Company and was fitted in his last years with a pacemaker. His wife Veronica died shortly before him. They had three children but only one grandchild, who is a poetess. The Glendon estate was sold in 2007.

The Salzer line has flourished numerically even though many of its members have been stricken by cancer. Most of Helene's descendants continue to live in Austria, where they share (in ever-decreasing apportionment) the ownership of the Wittgenstein summer retreat at Hochreit. Helene and Max's second son, Felix Salzer, the famous musicologist, died in 1986. Four years later his widow sold his manuscript collection for $1.85 million—it included the original manuscript of Beethoven's A major Cello Sonata, a letter by Schubert and a rondo by Mozart. In 1958 Felix had inherited the Palais at Neuwaldegg. He never lived there. For a while it became a convalescent home for 200 ethnic-German displaced persons. He later sold it for 23 million Austrian schillings. The land was divided up. Some of it was made into private housing estates, while a large slice of land passed into government ownership. In 2006 Paul's heirs succeeded in winning back a small portion of the Neuwaldegg estate through the Constitutional Court for Victims of National Socialism.

ACKNOWLEDGEMENTS

❖ ❖ ❖

This book could not have been written without the extraordinary kindness, willingness and enthusiasm of hundreds of people from all around the world. I am extremely grateful to everyone who helped and relieved that I got only two rebuffs. Most of all I wish to thank Joan Ripley, Paul Wittgenstein's daughter, who put all her papers at my disposal, allowed me to interview her for hours on end and never tried to censor anything. The British Academy gave me a generous grant without which I would not have been able to find such detail in so many countries.

To the following and to countless numbers whose names do not appear below I give heartfelt thanks: Gillon Aitken (literary agent), Dr. Otto Biba (Gesellschaft der Musikfreunde, Vienna), Richard Bidnick (for information on Paul Wittgenstein), Antonia von Boch (for translation and research), Tricia Boyd (Edinburgh University Library), Hans Brofeldt (expertise on left-handed piano music), Peter von Brücke (Wittgenstein cousin), Paula Byrne (advice on research grants), Julie Courtenay (Lady Margaret Hall Archive), Martin Cullingford (*Gramophone* magazine), Damian Dlaboha (translation and research), Michael Fishwick (publisher and editor), Charles Fitzroy (introductions in Vienna), Dr. Edwin Frederick Flindell (expert on Paul Wittgenstein), Alexander Fraser (Russian translation), Georg Gaugusch (for research in the Vienna archives), Colin Harris (Bodleian Library), Berkant Haydin (Joseph Marx Society), Monica Herren (Passionist Historical Archives, New Jersey), Dr. Thomas Höhne, of Höhne, In der Maur und Partner Rechtsanwälte (legal adviser in Vienna), Gerald Howard (American publisher), Peter James (copy editor), Peter Janus (Library of Congress, Washington), Glyn Jones (expert translator), Leonard Kastle (student and friend of Paul Wittgenstein), Johannes Koder (son of Rudolf Koder), Anne Marie Kollgaard (Danish translation), Sandy McGinnis (Paul Wittgenstein's granddaughter), Professor Brian McGuinness (expert on Ludwig Wittgenstein), David McKitterick (Trinity College Library) and the Master and Fellows of Trinity College, Cambridge, Fiona McKnight and Noëlle Mann and the Prokofiev Archive at Goldsmiths' College, London, Dr. Deborah Mawer (Ravel expert at Lancaster University), James Miller (Sotheby's), Dr. Hans Mohnl (Central Institute of Meteorology and Geodynamics, Vienna), Rosemary Moravec (Austrian National Library, Vienna), Michael Nedo (Wittgenstein Archive, Cambridge), Professor Arbie Orenstein (Juilliard School of Music), Erna Otten (student of Paul Wittgenstein), Jesse Parker (Paul Wittgenstein student), Catherine Payne (*Strad* magazine), Wendy Perez (New York Public Library), Peter Phillips (*Musical Times*), Stephen Portman (Paul Wittgenstein student), Ursula Prokop (biographer of Margaret Wittgenstein), Sally Riley (translation rights), Anna Sander (Balliol College Archives), Albert Sassmann (expert on Paul Wittgenstein and left-hand piano repertoire), Ed Scarcelle (Scherman Music Library, New York), Professor Carl Schachter (music professor, friend of Felix Salzer), Erhard Schania (half-brother of Hilde Wittgenstein), Tony Simpson and the Bertrand Russell Peace Foundation Ltd., Peter Stadlbauer (General Settlement for Victims of National Socialism, Vienna), Roberta Staples (Lady Margaret Hall Library), Glenn Stefanovics (expert on the eastern front, 1914–18), Maria Stracke (descendant of Helene Wittgenstein), Alan Tadiello (Balliol College Library), Dr. Bob Thompson (Universal Edition, New York), Mark Thomsen (Paul Wittgenstein's grandson), Frits van der Waa (correction to the first draft), Stephen Walsh (music professor at Cardiff University), Peter Ward-Jones (Bodleian Music Library), Eliza Waugh (proofreading and Italian translation), Christopher Wentworth-Stanley (archival research in Vienna) and Geoffrey Williams (University of Albany).

NOTES

✳ ✳ ✳

ABBREVIATIONS

BL   Bodleian Library, Oxford
BR   Bertrand Russell
GBW   Gesamtbriefwechsel, digital database
HW   Hermine Wittgenstein
HW1   Hermine Wittgenstein, "Familienerinnerungen"
HW2   Hermine Wittgenstein, Aufzeichnungen "Ludwig sagt . . ."
JSt   John Stonborough ("Ji")
KW   Karl Wittgenstein
LpW   Leopoldine Wittgenstein (née Kalmus)
LW   Ludwig Wittgenstein
MD   Marga Deneke
MSt   Margaret Stonborough ("Gretl")
NYT   New York Times
ÖNB   Austrian National Library, Vienna
PA   Prokofiev Archive
pc   private collection
PW   Paul Wittgenstein
WMGA   Wachtell, Manheim and Grouf Archive
WP   Washington Post

I. VIENNESE DEBUT

3   "The interiors of the houses are unspeakably squalid." Lansdale, p. 19.
3   "A man who had been but a short time." Unsigned article, Harper's Magazine, 3/1898, quoted in ibid., p. 11.
4   "Whereas in politics, in administration." Zweig, p. 19.
5   "Quite apart from the price." PW to MD, 12/30/1936, BL.
7   "he perpetually finds himself feeling contempt." David Pinsent, Diary, 9/24/1913, reprinted in Flowers, vol. 1, p. 225.
7   "The feeling that I shall have to die." LW to BR, 9/20/1913, GBW.

7   "He can't stand either of them." LW's aversion to his sister and brother-in-law is recorded by both Russell and Pinsent; see Flowers, vol. I, p. 226.

7   "UNFORTUNATELY I have to go to Vienna." LW to BR, undated [12/1913], GBW.

3. KARL'S GREAT REBELLION

10 "1864 Advised to leave school." Quoted in HWI, p. 37.

12 "Main activity was to distinguish between." Ibid.

12 "I cannot write to my parents." KW to his sister Bertha, 9/29/1865, quoted in ibid., p. 39.

12 "Mother's letter made me terribly happy." KW to his brother Louis, 10/30/1865, quoted in ibid., p. 38.

13 "You may think that I am a rotten son." KW to his mother, 2/7/1866, quoted in full in ibid., p. 39.

4. ENTREPRENEUR

13 "If it is Father's urgent wish." KW to his brother Louis, 1/27/1866, quoted in HWI, p. 41.

15 "Karl has a good heart but he left." Fanny Wittgenstein to LpW, undated (Sept. 1873), quoted in full in ibid., p. 52.

16 "Well, they are all like that." Quoted in ibid., p. 53.

16 "Dear Miss, My son Karl, unlike his brothers." Hermann Wittgenstein to LpW, 9/16/1873, quoted in full in ibid., p. 54.

17 "To hell with you!" Quoted in ibid., p. 55.

18 "An industrialist must take chances." KW, "Die Ursachen der Entwicklung der Industrie in Amerika," 1898; reprinted in KW, Politico-Economic Writings, p. 59. KW's gambling enthusiasms may be traced in Daily North Western, "The American Way—C. M. Schwab Gives Austrians Some Lessons," 1/28/1902, and American Heritage Magazine, "When the Headlines Said: Charlie Schwab Breaks the Bank," 4/1958, vol. 8, issue 3, in which he is confusingly referred to as "Dr. Griez Wittgenstein."

18 "had been estimated at 200 million kronen." Karl Menger, Reminiscences of the Wittgenstein Family, reprinted in Flowers, vol. I, p. III.

5. MARRIAGE TO AN HEIRESS

19 Jerome Steinberger was the son of a bankrupt kid-glove importer. The stories of Herman and Jacob Steinberger, M. J. Steinberger & Sons, Maurice Wertheimer & Co. and the death of Mrs. Wertheimer may be followed in: New York passenger lists; US census returns 1860, 1880, 1900; New York City Directories, and articles and notices in the New York Times including: "Important Business Failures," 6/13/1877; "Disappearance of Lady," 6/27/1878; "The Wertheimer Mystery," 6/28/1878; "Body Not Yet Discovered," 6/30/1878; "Mrs. Wertheimer Found Drowned," 7/2/1878; "Hebrew Fair," 12/13/1895; "Home for Aged Hebrews," 6/4/1897; "Failure of Glove Firm," 1/18/1898, p. 12; "Affairs of Wertheimer & Co.," 1/19/1898; "New Corporations," 1/22/1898; "Legal Notices," 2/17/1898; "Legal Notices," 4/7/1898; "In the Real Estate Field,"

3/31/1900; "Bankruptcy Notices," 7/11/1900; "Deaths Reported; Manhattan and Bronx," 12/27/1900.

19 His sister, Aimée, married William. "Weddings of the Day—Guggenheim—Steinberger," *NYT,* 10/18/1904. After Aimée Steinberger's marriage to William Guggenheim a previous wife took him to court for bigamy. See: "Says Her Divorce Isn't a Valid One," *NYT,* 1/19/1909, p. 5; judge's summing up quoted in Davis, *The Guggenheims,* p. 281.

20 "She possessed a 'rare' beauty." MD, "Memoirs," vol. 2, p. 78.

6. THE DEATH OF RUDOLF WITTGENSTEIN

21 "my perverted disposition." Magnus Hirschfeld in *Jahrbuch für sexuelle Zwischenstufen,* vol. VI (1904), p. 724, quoted in Bartley, 3rd ed., p. 35, n. 16.

22 "Forsaken, forsaken, forsaken am I!" *Verlassen bin ich.* Trans. Glyn Jones from a German version in Häseler, p. 6.

7. THE TRAGEDY OF HANS

23 "When my seven-year-old brother, Rudi." HW1, p. 96.

25 "It was tragic that our parents." Ibid., p. 102.

25 "Industrialist Karl Wittgenstein has suffered." *Neues Wiener Tagblatt,* 5/6/1902, quoted in Gaugusch, p. 14, n. 65.

26 "My father's frequent joking." *Die oft glühende Lustigkeit meines Vaters schien mir nicht lustig, sondern nur gefährlich.* MSt, Notebook, quoted in Prokop, p. 14.

26 "known to be homosexual." See Bartley, *Wittgenstein,* 3rd ed., p. 36.

26 "in 1903 the family was informed." Monk, p. 12.

27 "Of course a man can take a pistol." JSt to Brian McGuinness, 6/18/1989, pc.

27 "I believe that my gifts are such." Otto Weininger, *Taschenbuch,* quoted in Abrahamsen, p. 97.

8. AT HOME WITH THE WITTGENSTEINS

30 "a uniform reminiscent of an Austrian hunting outfit." Erna Otten to E. Fred Flindell, 6/20/67, pc.

30 "always festive occasions." HW1, p. 79.

31 "Nothing more should be played now." Anecdote told by PW to his pupil Steve Portman in the late 1940s, who relayed it to the author, 5/2007.

31 "Dear and esteemed and gracious lady." Eduard Hanslick to LpW, 4/11/1904, ÖNB.

32 "Who is Dr. Stonborough?" Marquise de Fontenoy, "Buys Archduke's Palace," *WP,* 1/8/1914, p. 6.

9. THE BOYS

32 *"Schmarren!"* Told to the author by PW's daughter Joan Ripley, 9/2006.

33 "To my dear brother Paul for Christmas 1922." *Meinem lieben Bruder Paul zu Weihnachten 1922. Möge dieses Buch, wenn es wertlos ist, bald spurlos verschwinden.* Inscription, pc.

33 "mentally deranged, and quite a few." Hitler's disparaging remarks about his teachers may be found in Trevor-Roper, 3/3/1942, p. 288; 4/12/1942, pp. 347–9; 8/29/1942, pp. 547–8; and 9/7/1942, pp. 566–8.

35 "Suicide is not a sign of courage but of cowardice." Otto Weininger to Moriz Rappaport, undated (8/1903), in Weininger, p. 157.

35 "I know that to kill oneself is always a dirty thing." *Ich weiss dass der Selbstmord immer eine Schweinerei ist.* LW to Paul Engelmann, 6/21/1920, GBW.

36 "It seemed that I had sung so wonderfully." Somavilla, p. 73.

36 "Does he have to pound the piano like that?" *Man muss das Piano ja nicht so bearbeiten.* Quoted in Kross, p. 7.

10. THEIR MOTHER

37 "We simply could not understand her." *Wir standen ihr eigentlich verständnislos gegenüber, aber auch sie hatte kein wirkliches Verständnis für die acht sonderbaren Kinder, die sie geboren hatte, ja bei aller ihrer Menschenliebe hatte sie merkwürdigerweise kein wirkliches Verständnis für Menschen überhaupt.* HWI, p. 95.

37 "My mother's devotion to duty made me." *Die Pflichttreue meiner Mutter war mir zu unbequem und ihr erregtes Wesen war mir unerträglich. Meine Mutter litt an einer unaufhörlichen Überlastung der Nerven.* MSt, Notebook, quoted in Prokop, p. 19.

37 "From a very early stage we children had." *Was wir Kinder von Jugend auf stark empfanden, war eine merkwürdige Erregtheit in unserem Elternhaus, ein Mangel an Entspannheit, der nicht allein von der Aufgeregtheit meines Vaters herrührte. Auch meine Mutter war sehr erregbar, wenn sie auch ihrem Mann und ihrer Mutter gegenüber die freundliche Ruhe nie verlor.* HWI, p. 94.

38 "I believe that our mother, as we knew her." *Ich glaube, dass meine Mutter, wie wir sie kannten, nicht völlig mehr sie selbst war . . . Wir begriffen unter anderem nicht, dass sie so wenig eigenen Willen und Bewusstsein hatte, und bedachten nicht, wie unmöglich es war, neben meinem Vater eigene Meinung und Willen zu bewahren.* Ibid.

38 "It would have been impossible." Ibid., p. 91.

39 "They rocked with the rhythm of the dance." MD, "Memoirs," vol. 2, p. 76.

11. THE OTHER BROTHER

40 "stands for quality, flexibility, reliability." See Stahl Judenburg's website at http://www.stahl-judenburg.com/englisch/index.html.

40 "there is no depth to his character." *Tiefe darf man bei ihm nicht suchen, aber wenn sie nicht gebraucht wird, vermisst man sie ja auch nicht.* HW to LW, May/June 1917, GBW.

13. PAUL'S EARLY TRAINING

41 "had secured a 'social position.' " Zweig, p. 81.

41 "All those qualities of youth, freshness." Ibid.

43 "he was both an artist and a teacher." PW, "The Legacy of Leschetizky."

44 "What binds you and me together." LW to PW, undated (1928?), pc.

44 "Labor. He's lost for ever." Beaumont, 10/15/1901.

45 "You know, ever since I can remember." Ibid., 2/28/1899.

45 "commanded to applaud super-vigorously." JSt to Brian McGuinness, 10/7/1993, pc.

45   "I could never hear enough of Labor's music." *Ich nie genug hören konnte und bei dessen Spiel ich oft meinen Tränen freien Lauf liess, da er sie ja nicht sah.* HW1, p. 78.

14. LUDWIG'S PREDICAMENT

46   "All the women I know are such idiots." David Pinsent, Diary, 2/7/1913, reprinted in Flowers, vol. 1, p. 201.

46   By June 1911 Ludwig had patented. See *Wittgenstein Studies,* 2/25/1995, and online at http://sammelpunkt.philo.at:8080/archive/00000487/01/25-2-95.TXT.

46   "neither taste nor talent." David Pinsent, Diary, 2/7/1913, reprinted in Flowers, vol. 1, p. 201.

46   "His greatness lies in that with which we disagree." LW to George Edward Moore, 8/23/1931, GBW.

47   "Improve yourself, that is the only thing." LW in conversation with Heinrich Postl, quoted in Monk, p. 213.

47   "Perhaps the most perfect example." BR, *Autobiography,* p. 329.

47   "very tall with a long thin face." Ibid., p. 213.

47   "an unknown German, speaking." BR to Ottoline Morrell, in Griffin, 10/18/1911.

47   "My German friend threatens to be an infliction." BR to Ottoline Morrell, in ibid., 10/19/1911.

48   "My ferocious German came and argued at me." BR to Ottoline Morrell, in ibid., 11/16/1911.

48   "I am getting to like him." BR to Ottoline Morrell, in ibid., 11/29/1911.

48   "At the end of his first term he came." BR, "Philosophers and Idiots," in Flowers, vol. 1, p. 147.

48   "He has pure intellectual passion." BR to Ottoline Morrell, in Griffin, 3/16/1912.

49   "The poor man is in a sad state." Lytton Strachey to Saxon Sydney-Turner, 11/20/1912, pc.

15. THE NEWLYWEDS

50   "I do not think that my marriage." MSt to HW, 2/26/1905, quoted in Prokop, p. 53.

50   "The parting was terribly hard." *Der Abschied war doch furchtbar schwer.* MSt to HW, 1/8/1905, quoted in ibid., p. 52.

50   "The Egyptian ruins do not impress me." MSt to LpW, 2/1/1905, quoted in ibid., p. 53.

51   "Six of these women." MSt to HW, 5/12/1905, quoted in ibid., p. 58.

51   "I cannot tell you how much." MSt to HW, 10/27/1910, quoted in ibid., p. 70.

16. KARL'S LOSS OF CONSCIOUSNESS

52   "On arriving here I found my father very ill." LW to BR, 12/26/1912, GBW.

52   "as the illness of my poor father." LW to BR, 1/6/1913, GBW.

52   "Although it is certain that he will not recover." LW to Walter Morley Fletcher, 1/10/1913, GBW.

52   "He is not yet in any great pain." LW to BR, 1/10–20/1913, GBW.

52   "Dear Russell, My dear father died yesterday." LW to BR, 1/21/1913, GBW.

17. IN MEMORIAM K.W.

53   "Karl Wittgenstein was a man." Kupelwieser, "Karl Wittgenstein als Kunstfreund." p. 10.
53   "The Austrian Iron Industry." Ibid.
53   "Karl Wittgenstein had a wild temperament." Ibid.

18. PAUL REVIEWED

54   "Please accept the enclosed joke." Albert Figdor to PW, 12/1913, Paul Wittgenstein Collection, New York Public Library.
55   "My opinion of your playing." LW to PW, undated (1928?), pc.
55   "You do not, I believe, seek to hide." Ibid.
55   "From an artistic point of view." PW to MD, his English agent, 1/30/1928, BL.
55   "Any young man, a member." Max Kalbeck review in *Neues Wiener Tagblatt*, 12/6/1913.
56   "Under the fading light of our feelings." Ibid.
56   "further practice would add greater perfection." Unsigned review, *Fremdenblatt*, 12/22/1913, reproduced in Suchy, Janik and Predota, p. 161, n. 15.
57   "The Austrian Heir Apparent has announced." *Srbobran*, 12/3/1913, quoted in Corti and Sokol, p. 408.

19. MONEY MATTERS

61   "extremely distasteful . . . ignoble." *Die anderen Briefe hätte ich als Belege nicht gebraucht; als Dank waren sie mir—offen gestanden—größtenteils höchst unsympathisch. Ein gewisser unedler fast schwindelhafter Ton.* LW to Ludwig von Ficker, 2/13/1915, GBW.
61   "ethical"/"bourgeois." HW's ideas on *ethisches Geld* vs. *bürgerliches Geld* appear in HW2, p. 97.
61   "It would be healthy . . . if destiny." MSt. *Tagebucheintragung,* 10/11/1917, quoted in Prokop, p. 96.
62   "Nothing is more dangerous." Beaumont, 2/28/1899.
62   "very beautifully and had received praise." *Labor und Mendelssohn und ganz besonders den Letzten soll er sehr schön gespielt haben.* HW to LW, 1/20/1914, GBW.

20. PRELUDE TO WAR

63   "He was never seen to smile." Zweig, p. 216.
64   "This world of peace, which has." Thomas Mann in *Gedanken im Kriege,* 1915, quoted in Clare, p. 56.

21. SIGNING UP

67   "My life has been one nasty mess." *Mein Leben war bisher eine grosse Schweinerei— aber soll es immer so weitergehen?* LW to BR, 3/3/1914, GBW.
67   "I keep on hoping that things will come." LW to BR, 12/1913, quoted in McGuinness, *Wittgenstein: A Life,* p. 192.
67   "I knew very well that Ludwig." *Es war ihm, wie ich genau weiss, nicht nur darum zu*

tun, sein Vaterland zu verteidigen, sondern er hatte den intensiven Wunsch, etwas Schweres auf sich zu nehmen und irgendetwas Anderes zu leisten als rein geistige Arbeit. HWI, p. 103.

67   "It seems to me as good as certain." LW, Notebook, 10/20/1914, typescript, pc.
67   "I think it is magnificent of him." David Pinsent, Diary, 8/1914, reprinted in Flowers, vol. 1, p. 232.

22. DISASTERS

68   "if the Monarchy must perish it should." Emperor Franz Joseph remark to Franz Conrad von Hötzendorf, quoted in Beller, *Austria*, p. 185.
68   "Aid has come to us from an unexpected quarter." MSt to HW, 8/22/1914, quoted in Prokop, p. 78.
68   "lack of attention in the riding school." Quoted in Janik and Veigl, p. 218.
71   "As regards my allegedly heroic deeds." PW to LpW, 2/2/1915, GBW.

23. PRISONER OF THE RUSSIANS

73   "Everybody had to face either to the left." Bruno Prochaska, "Tjeploschka," in Weiland, vol. 1, p. 101.
73   "how they still recurred as my sporadic nightmare." MD, "Memoirs," vol. 2, p. 24.
74   "It took three hours, but I did it." Zichy, p. 15.
74   "A young man lay in the corner." Brändström, p. 87.
75   "Letters have been received lately." Quoted in Rachaminov, p. 73.
75   "My dear beloved Ludwig, I have written." LpW to LW, 10/7/1914, GBW.
76   "I've not heard any more from Paul." LpW to LW, 10/13/1914, GBW.
76   "Received a lot of mail today." LW, Coded Notebook, 10/28/1914, typescript, pc.
76   "Headache and tiredness in the morning." Ibid., 10/29/1914.

24. KURT WITTGENSTEIN IN AMERICA

77   "My Dear Mrs. Wittgenstein, I have obtained." Alfred von Rettich to LpW, quoted in Flindell, "Dokumente," with corrections by the author.
78   "I am most anxious at the moment for Kurt." *Fast am leidesten tut mir jetzt Kurt, er wird eine böse Zeit haben, wenn jeder geleistet und gelitten hat nur er nicht! Er wird sich fortwährend zurückgesetzt vorkommen!* HW to LW, 4/26/1915, GBW.
78   "I'm always having to think of poor Kurt." *Immer muss ich an den armen Kurt denken und wie schrecklich es ist dass er diese Zeit nicht miterlebt, man kann das jetzt gar nicht leben nennen was er in Amerika tut.* HW to LW, 6/5/1915, GBW.
78   "It is not difficult to find a reason." "Has Faith in German Allies," unsigned article, *WP*, 1/18/1915, p. 6.
78   an elderly lady of German extraction. Delia Steinberger's 1920 U.S. Census entry, which can be found online, contains several fictions. She wrongly states her age and declares that her parents were English born and bred. Her father was born in Germany, her mother in Paris.
79   "The reports I have from home." Quoted in unsigned article, "Has Faith in German Allies," *WP*, 1/18/1915, p. 6.
79   "The Imperial and Royal Austro-Hungarian Embassy." Quoted in unsigned article, "Austrian Propaganda Costs Forty Millions," *NYT*, 9/15/1915.

80   "ARRIVED ROTTERDAM TODAY." *Soeben Rotterdam gesund angekommen mittwoch Wien Kurt.* Kurt Wittgenstein to LpW, quoted in LpW to LW, 5/21/1917, GBW.

80   "I've just learned that Kurt has arrived." HW to LW, 5/21/1917, GBW.

26. THREE SOURCES OF INSPIRATION

83   "the greatest marvel of modern times." Quoted in Abell, p. 10. Liszt, in a letter to Baroness Meyendorff, described Zichy's left hand as "remarkably dextrous to the point that the greatest pianists would be hard pushed to match him." Waters, p. 421.

83   "You must learn how to put your pants on." Zichy, p. 21.

83   "This book will comfort the amputee." Baron von Eiselsberg, *Vorwort,* quoted in Zichy, p. 7.

84   "I can assure you I am the topic of Vienna." Leopold Godowsky to Maurice Aronson, 2/6/1904, quoted in Nicholas, p. 63.

27. A GLIMMER OF HOPE

85   "Paul transferred to small hotel Omsk." *Paul seit zweiter Hälfte Jänner kleines Hôtel Omsk übersiedelt. Bewegungsfreiheit innerhalb der Stadt, dreimal wöchentl. sich melden.* Otto Franz to LpW, 2/20/1915, ÖNB.

85   "My dear, well-beloved and darling mother." PW to LpW, 2/2/1915, ÖNB.

86   "Paul seems to be practising industriously." LpW to LW, 4/15/1915, GBW.

86   "You were quite correct to suppose." HW to LW, 4/26/1915, GBW.

87   "dear Labor fully immersed in his composition." LpW to LW, 5/24/1915, GBW.

28. BURIED ALIVE IN THE KREPOST

89   "as the weeks and months go by." Brändström, p. 109.

89   "dung-shack, an ice-hole." Meier-Graefe, p. 48.

91   "GOOD NEWS. NAME APPEARS." *Bien portant, inscrit sur listes préliminaires des prisonniers à être échangés, commission finale bientôt, bonne chance.* Wire from Danish Consulate to LpW, copied in letter to LW, 3/16/1915, GBW.

91   "You can imagine how happy I am!" LpW to LW, 3/16/1915, GBW.

91   "I have had good news from Paul." LpW to LW, 5/20/1915, GBW.

91   "Mama is, of course, really upset." HW to LW, 7/8/1915, GBW.

92   "The men lie side by side." Hans Weiland, "Stilles Heldentum," in Weiland, vol. I, p. 192.

29. A CHANCE OF ESCAPE

93   "This amazing individual." *Der bewunderungswürdige Mensch ist sehr heiter, trotzdem er sich hier jetzt zum Zwecke der Prothesen allen möglichen Operationen unterziehen muss.* LpW to LW, 9/20/1915, GBW.

93   "I was extremely pleased that both." *Ausserordentlich gefreut hat es mich dass beide ausgetauschten Offiziere mit grosser Achtung und Liebe von Paul sprechen und seine Güte Anständigkeit u. Idealismus rühmen.* HW to LW, 10/5/1915, GBW.

93   "If this is really an obstacle to Paul's release." *Denn wenn das wirklich ein*

Hindernis für Pauls Freigabe wäre, würde man doch irgendeine Anordnung herbeiführen müssen. HW to LW, 10/6/1915, GBW.

94 "Perhaps we may have to be grateful." *Vielleicht wird man noch dafür dankbar sein müssen, momentan aber da wir uns doch schon etwas Hoffnung machten daß er bald zum Austausch kommen könnte, bedeutet das eine furchtbare Enttäuschung!* Ibid.

94 "That represents at least a glimmer." *Das bedeutet doch einen Hoffnungsschimmer!* LpW to LW, 10/29/1915, GBW.

94 "As to whether Paul will be exchanged." *Ob Paul ausgetauscht wird? Ich habe eigentlich wenig Hoffnung und der Gedanke an eine mögliche Enttäuschung von ihm und Mama ist mir schrecklich.* HW to LpW, 11/3/1915, GBW.

94 "They sold their patients' food." Brändström, p. 184.

95 "My dear, good Ludwig, Just imagine." LpW to LW, 11/12/1915, GBW.

30. FAMILY REUNION

96 "Paul's appearance and nature." *Es war ganz anders als ich dachte, denn Paul ist so unverändert in seinem Aussehen u. Wesen (abgesehen natürlich von seinem Arm) dass auch das Wiedersehen nicht viel anders als das nach einer sehr langen Reise war wo man sich alle Neuigkeiten erzählt und gar nicht aufhören kann damit.* HW to LW, 11/16/1915, GBW.

96 "I took much delight in Paul's calm." *Die Ersten erhielt ich am 21, am Tag von Paul's Ankunft und konnte mich in Folge dessen ruhigeren Gemüts der Freude hingeben.* LpW to LW, 11/25/1915, GBW.

96 "he speaks of his misfortune in such." *Er spricht so natürlich von seinem Unglück dass man nie das Gefühl hat vorsichtig reden zu müssen weil ihm dies oder jenes weh tun könnte und das macht es riesig leicht.* HW to LW, 11/16/1915, GBW.

31. A TRANSFORMATION

98 "I am not afraid of being shot." *Ich fürchte mich nicht davor erschossen zu werden aber davor meine Pflicht nicht ordentlich zu erfüllen. Gott gebe mir Kraft. Amen. Amen. Amen.* LW, Coded Notebooks, 9/12/1914, typescript, pc.

98 "a bunch of pigs . . . unbelievably crude." *Die Bemannung ist eine Saubande. Keine Begeisterung, unglaubliche Roheit, Dummheit und Bosheit.* Ibid., 8/15/1914.

98 "Have been through terrible scenes." *Habe furchtbare Szenen erlebt . . . fühle mich sehr schwach und sehe keine äussere Hoffnung. Wenn es mir jetzt zu Ende geht, so möge ich einen guten Tod sterben eingedenk meiner selbst. Möge ich mich nie selbst verlieren.* LW, Diary, 9/13/1914, quoted in Rush Rhees, "Postscript," in Flowers, vol. 3, p. 269.

98 "There is nothing between us and the enemy." *Wir sind in unmittelbarer Nähe des Feindes . . . Jetzt war mir die Gelegenheit gegeben, ein anständiger Mensch zu sein, denn ich stehe vor dem Tod, Auge in Auge. Möge der Geist mir erleuchten.* Ibid., 9/15/1914.

98 "In Siberia, all men search for God." Meier-Graefe, p. 56.

98 "Religion is the masterpiece of the art." *Die Religion ist ein Meisterstück in der Kunst der Tierdresseur, denn es bringt den Menschen bei, wie sie denken sollen.* Arthur Schopenhauer (attrib.).

99 "This book virtually kept me alive." *Dieses Buch hat mich seinerzeit geradezu am Leben erhalten.* LW to Ludwig Ficker, 7/24/1915, GBW.

99 "neither pure revelation nor a phase." Tolstoy, p. 8.

99 "From time to time I become an *animal.*" *Ich werde von Zeit zu Zeit zum Tier. Dann kann ich an nichts denken als an essen, trinken, schlafen. Furchtbar! Und dann leide ich auch wie ein Tier, ohne die Möglichkeit innerer Rettung. Ich bin dann meinen Gelüsten und Abneigungen preisgegeben. Dann ist an ein wahres Leben nicht zu denken.* LW, Diary, 7/29/1916, quoted in Monk, p. 602.

99 "It is a matter of indifference to me." *Ja, was ich hier geschrieben habe, macht im Einzelnen überhaupt nicht den Anspruch auf Neuheit; und darum gebe ich auch keine Quellen an, weil es mir gleichgültig ist, ob das was ich gedacht habe, vor mir schon ein anderer gedacht hat.* LW, *Tractatus Logico-Philosophicus,* preface.

99 "That which we cannot speak about." *Worüber man nicht sprechen kann, darüber muß man schweigen.* Ibid., point 7.

100 "The foundation and beginning of all things." Tolstoy, p. 158.

100 "The world is all that is the case." *Die Welt ist die Gesamtheit der Tatsachen, nicht der Dinge. Die Welt ist durch die Tatsachen bestimmt und dadurch, dass es alle Tatsachen sind. Denn, die Gesamtheit der Tatsachen bestimmt, was der Fall ist und auch, was alles nicht der Fall ist. Die Tatsachen im logischen Raum ist die Welt.* LW, *Tractatus Logico-Philosophicus,* points 1–1.13.

100 "This present life in time is the food." Tolstoy, p. 3.

100 "If we take eternity to mean." *Wenn man unter Ewigkeit nicht unendliche Zeitdauer, sondern Unzeitlichkeit versteht, dann lebt der ewig, der in der Gegenwart lebt. Unser Leben ist ebenso endlos, wie unser Gesichtsfeld grenzenlos ist.* LW, *Tractatus Logico-Philosophicus,* point 6.4311.

101 "Even if Paul should by chance." MSt to HW, quoted in HW2, p. 72, n.41.

101 "There are two godheads: the world." *Es gibt zwei Gottheiten: die Welt und mein unabhängiges Ich.* LW, *Notebooks 1914–1916,* 7/8/1916, p. 74.

101 "Ludwig had all the characteristics." Max Bieler to Sister Mary McHale, quoted in Monk, p. 132.

101 "The solution of the problem of life." *Die Lösung des Problems des Lebens merkt man am Verschwinden dieses Problems. (Ist nicht dies der Grund, warum Menschen, denen der Sinn des Lebens nach langem Zweifeln klar wurde, warum diese dann nicht sagen konnten, worin dieser Sinn bestand?)* LW, *Tractatus Logico-Philosophicus,* point 6.521.

32. GRETL'S ISSUES

102 "with all my strength. To do my utmost." *mit allen meinen Kräften beteiligen. Körperlich & geistig mein äusserstes tun.* MSt to HW, 8/22/1914, quoted in Prokop, p. 78.

102 "This war affects me just as it does you." *Genauso wie Dir geht es mir mit diesem Krieg; nichts aber auch gar nichts kann ich realisieren. Aber ich gäbe etwas darum, wenn ich etwas leisten könnte in diesem Feldzug. Es kommt mir so schrecklich vor, dass man so etwas miterlebt hat & doch eigentlich nicht miterlebt.* MSt to HW, 8/22/1914, quoted in ibid., p. 79.

102 "I can hardly say how much I love." *Wie ich sie liebe u. bewundere kann ich gar nicht sagen! Warum hat sie doch solche Eigentümlichkeiten die Anlass zu schärferem Tadel geben als manchem zu Teil wird der nicht in grossen Dingen so gut u. gross handelt wie sie! Das tut mir immer bodenlos leid!* HW to LW, 8/31/1916, GBW.

103 "inner life." *Man kann von seinem äußeren und seinem inneren Leben schreiben . . . Das innerer Leben war früher klar und ist jetzt verworren und das äußere Leben spielt*

sich jetzt nicht mehr wie in den vergangenen Jahren nur unter Dingen ab, sondern unter Menschen. MSt to HW, quoted in Prokop, p. 82.

33. PAUL'S ONE-HANDED DEBUT

104 "very beautifully, with great warmth." *Paul spielte es auch sehr schön, mit grosser Wärme u. Feuer.* HW to LW, 10/29/1916, GBW.

105 "Paul's case has naturally made me." *Denn natürlich geht der Fall "Paul" mir doch sehr nahe u. so wie ich wegen mancher Rohheiten ihm das Recht absprechen möchte Musik zu betreiben, so freudig spreche ich ihm das Recht zu, um eines empfundenen Stückes willen.* Ibid.

105 "It was like trying to climb a mountain." Wechsberg, p. 25.

106 "Although it was only elderly and weak women." *Gestern waren es allerdings nur alte und schieche, aber er könnte auch junge hübsche haben, so nett u. liebenswürdig ist er gegen Damen (fast so conciliant als er gegen Männer schroff und arrogant sein kann).* HW to LW, 10/29/1916, GBW.

107 "all fired up and dead keen as regards Paul." *Er ist wieder Feuer und Flamme für Paul.* LpW to LW, 1/10/1917, GBW.

107 "Paul Wittgenstein does not play the piano." Julius Korngold review, *Neue Freie Presse,* 12/19/1916.

34. WAR IN EUROPE RAGES

108 "Within myself I am full of hatred." *Und ich bin innerlich hasserfüllt und kann den Geist nicht in mich einlassen. Gott ist die Liebe.* LW, Notebook, 3.1916, quoted in Rush Rhees, "Postscript," in Flowers, vol. 3, p. 272.

108 "So I am nearly always surrounded." *So bin ich jetzt fast immer umgeben von Leuten, die mich hassen. Und dies ist das einzige, womit ich mich noch nicht abfinden kann. Hier sind böse, herzlose Menschen. Es ist mir fast unmöglich eine Spur von Menschlichkeit in ihnen zu finden.* Ibid.

109 "Perhaps you are not such an odd person." HW to LW, 4/16/1916, GBW.

109 "It would have meant certain death." Ibid.

109 "Perhaps nearness to death will bring light." *Vielleicht bringt mir die Nähe des Todes das Licht des Lebens.* LW, Notebook, 5/4/1916, quoted in Monk, p. 600.

35. AMERICA JOINS THE WAR

110 " 'Oh my God! It's starting.' " *Oh Gott, das ist der Anfang & sterbe so die tausend unnötigen Tode, die der Feige stirbt.* MSt, *Tagebucheintragung,* 8/22/1918, quoted in Prokop, p. 106.

110 "I am always thinking of death." *Immer denke ich an meinen Tod & muss ihn mir immer ausmalen. Ich traue mich gar nicht mehr an eine Heimkehr zu glauben: so sicher scheint mir, dass ich früher sterben werde.* Ibid.

111 "I am well, apart from my health." *Ich bin guter Dinge, ganz unabhängig von meiner Gesundheit, weil ich ein gutes Gewissen habe. Wie es beim Tolstoj heißt: gebunden durch das Fleisch, aber frei durch den Geist.* MSt to HW, 4.1917, in Prokop, p. 86.

111 "What can I do then?" MSt to HW, 6/15/1917, in Prokop, p. 89.

111 "Kurt is back home just the same big child." *Kurt ist als der Kindskopf heimgekehrt als der er vor 3 Jahren auszog aber das macht momentan nichts; er ist bei der Abrichtung*

in Stockerau, kommt Sonntags nach Hause, hetzt mit den Kindern wie ein Kind und das steht ihm immer sehr gut. HW to LW, 6.1917.

112   "Thank God that such things exist." *Gottseidank dass es so etwas gibt, das ist in jeder Lebenslage ein Segen!* HW to LW, 7/10/1917, GBW.

36. PAUL'S ALTERED CHARACTER

113   "If necessary Gretl's rocket will be repeated." *Im Bedarfsfall wird man dann eben das Kopfwaschen wiederholen und, wie er selbst schon vorher gebeten hat, in eventuell verstärktem Mass.* HW to LW, 4/7/1917, GBW.

113   "I cannot begin to imagine it." *Pauls Kopfwaschung durch Gretl kann ich mir gar nicht recht vorstellen. Aber es gibt eben Sachen die man sich nicht vorstellen kann.* LW to HW, 4/12/1917, GBW.

113   "Between Mama and me there is no contact." *Auch sonst kommt durch Paul ab und zu jemand ins Haus während es doch, wenn nur ich zu Hause wäre, recht tot wäre. Kontakt ohne Reibung gibt es bei uns und Mama nicht.* HW to LW, 1/12/1917, GBW.

113   "The hours passed in stimulating company." *Die Stunden der Gemütlichkeit und Anregung durch eine kleine Szene (und selbst durch mehrere) nicht um ihren Wert gebracht werden.* HW to LW, 1/20/1917, GBW.

114   "Unfortunately, to my really great distress." *Leider, wirklich zu meinem grossen Leidwesen, kommt sie in seinem Klavierspiel zum Vorschein, ach nicht ein Takt ist nach meinem Sinn und Gefühl wenn ich ihn oben spielen höre und das ist eine momentane Qual und ein nachhaltiger Kummer.* HW to LW, 7/11/1918, GBW.

115   "abominable places full of cheap knickknacks." PW, "Notes on Two Russian Tours," 1935?, pc.

115   "And that is really something!" *Er spricht gar nicht darüber, freuen tut es ihn aber doch sehr, denn das ist wirklich etwas.* HW to LW, 3/20/1917, GBW.

37. ENDGAME

117   "One hardly knows what is the best thing." *Da weiss man auch nicht was man ihm wünschen soll, denn was eine Verwundung jetzt, da er doch nur mehr ein halber Mensch ist, bedeuten würde, kann man gar nicht aussprechen wenn man bedenkt wie leidenschaftlich er das Klavierspielen liebt.* HW to LW, 2/18/1918, GBW.

118   "It was a good thing that your more finely tuned apparatus." *Da ist es gut dass Dein feiner Apparat nicht zugegen war, der sicherlich eine leise Spannung herausgefühlt hätte (die Brüder sind ja auch zu verschieden) und sie dadurch verstärkt hätte.* Ibid.

118   "a very efficient, lively, and energetic general." *Sehr tüchtiger, energischer General, sehr lebhaft, ein Meister treuer Pflichterfüllung. Entspricht als Abschnittskmdt. In jeder Hinsicht vorzüglich. Ein sehr willensstarker General, der zweifellos die volle Eignung zum Kommandanten einer Infanteriedivision besitzt.* www.weltkriege.at/Generalitaet/04%20Feldmarschalleutnant/Schiesser/schiess er.htm.

119   "When this happened I saw my future." Bob Dorman, "Germany for Germans, says New Leader who Drills his Troops to Enforce his Idea: Picturesque New Figure," interview with Adolf Hitler, NEA News Service, reproduced in *Modesto Evening News,* 4/15/1923, p. 26.

120   "My dearest son, After the dreadful anxiety." LpW to LW, 12/27/1918, GBW.

120   "I'm indescribably happy to know." HW to LW, 12/30/1918, GBW.

121   "Kurt fell on 27th September, it's very sad." *Kurt fiel am 27.IX, es ist sehr traurig!* HW to LW, 1/10/1919, GBW.

121   "My brother Kurt shot himself." HW1, p. 102.

121   "A special poignancy marks Kurt Wittgenstein's death." MD, "Memoirs," vol. 2, p. 45.

123   "the most interesting and worthwhile of my brothers." *[Ludwig scheint mir] der interessanteste und wertvollste Brüder.* HW1, p. 106.

123   "finally die from a lack of the 'hard must.' " Ibid., p. 103.

123   "Many die too late, and some die too early." *Viele sterben zu spät, und Einige sterben zu früh. Noch klingt fremd die Lehre: "stirb zur rechten Zeit!"* Friedrich Nietzsche, *Also sprach Zarathustra,* first lines of Part I, XXI, "Vom freien Tode" (Voluntary Death).

39. FAMILY TENSIONS

130   "Have you had any tragedies in your life?" Theodore Redpath, "A Student's Memoir," reprinted in Flowers, vol. 3, p. 32.

131   "Good old Paul has managed one piece." *Der gute Paul führt ein hirnverrücktes Stückerl nach dem anderen auf, mit Papas Allüren aber ohne jeden Kopf, bringt er mich in die scheusslichsten Lagen.* MSt to HW, 3/25/1919, quoted in Prokop, p. 117.

131   "It is no way to do business!" Ibid.

131   "And he is right!" Ibid.

131   "Everything in the Alleegasse." *In der Alleegasse alles wie sonst . . . Abends grosser Streit mit Paul über Politik.* MSt, *Tagebucheintragung,* 6/29/1919, quoted in Prokop, p. 118.

131   "The Austrians are desperate, they preferred." *Die Österreicher sind verzweifelt. Die alte Schlamperei war ihnen lieber als die neue Unordnung & doch enthält die Letztere zum Unterschied von der Ersteren Keime zu neuem Leben.* Ibid., 1/5/1919, quoted in Prokop, p. 108.

131   "I have always had red tendencies." *Ich, die immer schon rote Tendenzen hatte, nun noch viel röter geworden bin.* MSt to HW, 4/29/1919, quoted in Prokop, p. 117.

132   "It is not in the nature of us 5 siblings." LW to HW, 11.1929, GBW.

132   "Hearing the music in the next-door room." MD, "Memoirs," vol. 2, p. 16.

133   "as far as my state of mind is concerned." *Es geht mir nicht sehr gut (nämlich geistig).* LW to Paul Engelmann, 8/25/1919, GBW.

133   "A man with your philosophically trained mind." *Wenn ich mir ihn mit seinem philosophisch geschulten Verstand als Volksschullehrer vorstellte, so schien es mir, als wollte jemand ein Präzisionsinstrument dazu benützen, um Kisten zu öffnen. Darauf antwortete mir Ludwig: "Du errinerst mich an einen Menschen, der aus dem geschlossenen Fenster schaut und sich die sonderbaren Bewegungen eines Passanten nicht erklären kann; er weiss nicht welcher Sturm draussen wütet und dass dieser Mensch sich vielleicht nur mit Mühe auf den Beinen hält."* HW1, p. 110.

134   "Do not lay up store on earth." Tolstoy, p. 57.

134   "If you wish to be perfect, go and sell." St. Matthew 19:21.

134   "everything to fulfil Ludwig's wishes." *Ich habe alles getan, um bis ins Kleinste Ludwigs Wünsche zu erfüllen.* HW1, p. 110.

135 "began with the Jews." PW, Russian Notes, p. 5, pc.
135 "Is there any shady undertaking . . . ?" Hitler, p. 42.
136 "In the face of that revelation." Ibid., p. 43.
136 "Should the Jew, with the aid." Ibid., p. 46.
136 "in matters of honour one does not consult." Quoted in McGuinness, *Wittgenstein: A Life*, p. 2.
137 "the woman is particularly likeable." *Die Frau ist besonders sympatisch, obwohl natürlich jüdisch.* HW to LW, 1939, GBW.
137 "Aryan and Jewish races are diametrically opposed." *Ich glaube dass die arische und die jüdische Rasse in Vorzügen und Mängeln diametral entgegengesetzt sind und sich offen oder verstreckt bekämpfen müssen.* HW2, p. 97.
137 "dishonesty lies at the heart of every Jew." *Paul verficht mit grösster Heftigkeit dass auf dem Grund jedes Juden die Unehrlichkeit liegt.* Ibid.
137 "If he ever named Jews." MD, "Memoirs," vol. 2, p. 32.
137 "nothing to do with the communist Jews." *Ludwig sieht nur Wirtschauspfründner mit denen er ebenso wenig zu haben will als mit den kommunistischen Juden.* HW2, p. 113.
137 "unnatural creatures." *Ludwig machte mich darauf aufmerksam dass die Juden durch das Leben in fremden Staaten unter fremden Gesetzen und Lebensbedingungen und Zwängen unnatürliche Wesen geworden sind.* Ibid., p. 97.
137 "Must there be a Jew behind every indecency?" *Ich denke: muss denn hinter jeder Unanständigkeit ein Jude stecken?* LW dream, 12/1/29, quoted in Monk, p. 612.
137 a *Beule* in Austrian society. LW compares the Jewish race to a *Beule* in *Culture and Value*, p. 18. A long discussion about what he meant by *Beule* may be found in David Stern, "Was Wittgenstein a Jew?," reprinted in Klagge, pp. 259-60.

138 "In truth he led two or three lives." JSt to Brian McGuinness, 8/19/1993, pc.
138 "Concerning the biography of my brother." *Was die Biographie meines Bruders betrifft: ich glaube wohl, dass mein Bruder Ludwig sich gegen jede Biographie gewehrt hätte. Denn Biographie heisst: Indiskretion. Eine Biographie die keine Indiskretion enthält, ist so gut wie keine. Da nun aber einmal alle bedeutenden Männer sich gefallen lassen müssen, dass man ihre Biographie schreibt, wird das wohl mein Bruder nach seinem Tode auch über sich ergehen lassen müssen; und da ist es jedenfalls besser, es stehen richtige Daten in dieser Biographie als falsche, von unsinnigen Gerüchten ganz abgesehen.* PW to Friedrich Hayek, quoted in PW to Rudolf Koder, 10/7/1953, pc.
138 "Observe attentively the passers-by." Lansdale, p. 11.
139 "had endless mistresses and all from the scum." JSt to Brian McGuinness, 8/19/1993, pc.
139 "I disliked Paul intensely and, I admit." JSt to Brian McGuinness, 2/2/1989, pc.
139 "female wares were offered for sale." Zweig, p. 83.
139 "Try as I might I cannot recall." Ibid., pp. 88-9.
140 "Do not seek delight in sexual gratification." Tolstoy, p. 55.
140 "If by pressing a button it could." G. E. M. Anscombe, quoted in Engelmann, p. xiv.

140 "rough young men were ready to cater." Bartley, p. 40.

140 "a book of obscene denigration." JSt, untitled essay incorporated at end of Rhees, "Wittgenstein," p. 80.

140 "Lay with him two or three times." *Zwei oder dreimal mit ihm gelegen. Immer zuerst mit dem Gefühl, es sei nichts Schlechtes, dann mit Scham.* LW, Notebook, 9/22/1937, quoted in Monk, p. 620.

42. A LITTLE TEACHING

141 "very unhappy about his condition." MSt to HW, 2/12/1920, quoted in Prokop, p. 128.

143 "It is out of the question." PW to LW, 11/17/1920, pc.

143 "That it was unavoidable that your origins." PW to LW, 11/20/1920, pc.

144 "Why should you care about clothing?" Tolstoy, p. 57.

144 "But I tell you that everyone is worthy." Ibid., p. 51.

144 "Every day I think of Pinsent." *Täglich denke ich an Pinsent. Er hat mein halbes Leben mit sich genommen. Die andere Hälfte wird der Teufel holen.* LW to BR, 8/6/1920, GBW.

144 "I have continually thought of taking my own life." *Ich habe fortwährend daran gedacht, mir das Leben zu nehmen und auch jetzt spukt dieser Gedanke noch in mir herum. Ich bin ganz & gar gesunken.* LW to Paul Engelmann, 5/30/1920, GBW.

144 "I am in a state of mind that is terrible to me." *Ich bin nämlich in einem Zustand, der mir sehr furchtbar ist.* LW to Paul Engelmann, 6/21/1920, GBW.

144 "or else all the devils in hell will break loose." *Die Arbeit in der Schule macht mir Freude und ich brauche sie notwendig; sonst sind bei mir gleich alle Teufel los.* LW to Paul Engelmann, 10/11/1920, GBW.

144 "obnoxious, good-for-nothing and irresponsible." LW to BR, 10/23/21, GBW: *hier sind sie viel mehr als anderswo nichtsnutzig und unverantwortlich.* In letters to Engelmann LW described the Otterthalers as "Unmenschen" and the Hassbachers as "ekelhafte Larven."

145 "went far beyond my own mental grasp." Engelmann, p. 82.

145 "You see, from the very beginning." *Sie sehen: ich verfange mich gleich anfangs in Zweifel über das, was Sie sagen wollen, und komme so nicht recht vorwärts . . .* Gottlob Frege to LW, 6/28/1919, GBW.

145 "he doesn't understand a word." LW to BR, 8/19/1919, GBW.

145 "superficiality and misunderstanding." *Oberflächlichkeit und Mißverständnis.* LW to BR, 5/6/1920, GBW.

146 "My propositions serve as elucidations." LW, *Tractatus Logico-Philosophicus*, 6.54, p. 74.

146 "My work consists of two parts." *Mein Werk bestehe aus zwei Teilen: aus dem, der hier vorliegt, und aus alledem, was ich nicht geschrieben habe. Und gerade dieser zweite Teil ist der Wichtige.* LW to Ludwig von Ficker, Sept.-Oct. 1919, reproduced in Engelmann, p. 144.

146 "It's terrible when he says." Frank Ramsey to his mother, Agnes Ramsey, 9/20/1923, reproduced in McGuinness, *Wittgenstein in Cambridge*, p. 139.

146 "We really live in a great time." Frank Ramsey to his mother, Agnes Ramsey, 7/22/1924, pc.

147 "Shaking their heads, they found it amusing." Bernhard, p. 75.

147 "It is not easy having a saint for a brother." HW to Ludwig Hänsel, 12/13/1920, in Somavilla, Unterkircher and Berger, p. 40. The "English" proverb HW quotes is, in fact, from Ecclesiastes 9:4: "Better be a live dog than a dead lion."

148 "Dear Mr Koder, I have a request." PW to Rudolf Koder, 11/13/1923, pc.

148 "that totally insane fellow who wanted." Unascribed quotation from Luise Hausmann and Eugene C. Hargrove, *Wittgenstein in Austria as an Elementary School Teacher,* reprinted in Flowers, vol. 2, p. 102.

149 "I'm curious to know what the psychiatrist." *Ich bin übrigens neugierig, was der Psychiater zu mir sagen wird. Ich bin von Ekel vor der Untersuchung, wie vor der ganzen schweinischen Angelegenheit erfüllt.* LW to Rudolf Koder, Autumn 1926, GBW.

43. PAUL'S RISE TO FAME

150 "it is perhaps only due to an accident." HW says of both PW's and LW's propensity to suicide: *Paul und Ludwig waren so nahe daran, dasselbe zu tun, dass es vielleicht nur einem Zufall zu danken ist, wenn sie in dieser Welt geblieben und später mit dem Leben fertig geworden sind.* HW2, p. 102.

152 "subtler than anything else." *ist besonders schwer zu verstehen. Es ist in gewissem Sinne subtiler als alles andere . . .* LW, *Culture and Value* (MS 107 184), c. 11/7/1929, p. 5.

152 "Labor's feeling well again!" *Labor geht es wieder gut!* HW to LW, 5/15/1922, GBW.

152 "One cannot praise enough the miracle." *Das Wunder dass in diesem Falle dem Homöopathen gelungen ist kann man nicht genug preisen. Die vollständig veränderte Ernährung hat sofort das physische und moralische Befinden gehoben und Labor ist wieder der Alte, der jugendliche Musiker geworden.* LpW to LW, 5/23/1922, GBW.

152 "My dear Labor, The joy it gives me." PW to Josef Labor, 6/1/1922, Wiener Stadt und Landesbibliothek.

153 "Every conductor in Germany will automatically." *Alle Dirigenten in Deutschland ein neues Stück von mir automatisch aufführen.* Erich Korngold to PW, 6/19/1923, reprinted in Flindell, "Dokumente," p. 425.

154 "I think I should have everything ready." *Ich glaube, dass ich bis zum Ende der nächsten Woche alles fertig habe. Es würde mir Leid tun, wenn Ihnen das Stück keine Freude machen würde—vielleicht ist es Ihnen anfänglich ein wenig ungewohnt zu hören—ich habe es mit grosser Liebe geschrieben und habe es sehr gern.* Paul Hindemith to PW, 5/4/1923, reprinted in ibid., p. 425.

154 "I hope that your terror will have abated." *Ich hoffe, dass sich nach Durchsicht der Partitur Ihr Schrecken wieder legen wird. Es ist ein einfaches, vollkommen unproblematisches Stück und ich glaube sicher, dass es Ihnen nach einiger Zeit Freude machen wird. (Vielleicht sind Sie am Anfang ein wenig entsetzt, aber das macht nichts.) Verstehen werden Sie das Stück auf jeden Fall.* Paul Hindemith to PW, 6/1923, reprinted in ibid., p. 426.

155 "the contrast between the sound of the piano." PW to Leonard Kastle, 6/13/1960, Special Collection, University at Albany Library.

155 "Dear Herr Korngold, Please find enclosed." PW to Erich Korngold, 5/18/1926, ÖNB.

156 "Paul Wittgenstein, who achieved with one hand." Review signed "e.d.," *Neues Wiener Tagblatt,* 2/4/1924.

156 "astonishing, concisely crafted and truly inspired work." Review signed "r.," *Neue Freie Presse,* 9/27/1924.

156 "Paul Wittgenstein, having been robbed of his right arm." Unsigned review, *Neues Wiener Tagblatt*, 9/30/1924.

157 "Strauss is very avaricious." PW to MD, 1/30/1928, BL.

157 "had to be changed *de fond en comble*." PW to MD, 3/25/1927, BL.

157 "How can I with my one poor hand." Quoted in MD, "Memoirs," vol. 2, p. 45.

157 "It is easy to understand that this pianist." Adolf Weissmann, quoted in unsigned article, "A Radio Opera Premiere," *NYT*, 2/19/1928, p. 116.

158 "uninteresting opinions of uninteresting persons." PW to MD, 3/21/1928, BL.

158 "I am so sorry that the Berlin press tore you." *Es tut mir sehr leid, dass die Presse von Posuwitz Berlin Ihnen mein Stück so zerrissen hat. Ich weiss, dass der Panathenäenzug nicht schlecht ist, aber für so gut, dass er die Ehre einer einstimmigen Ablehnung erfährt, habe ich ihn nicht gehalten.* Richard Strauss to PW, 2/8/1928, printed in Flindell, "Dokumente," p. 426.

158 "Paul Wittgenstein finds here a wealth of activity." Julius Korngold review, *Neue Freie Presse*, 3/15/1928.

159 "Paul Wittgenstein has been much sought here." Unsigned article, "One Armed Pianist to Play," *NYT*, 8/2/1928, p. 25.

159 "Having to work and moreover to earn money." PW to MD, 9/21/1927, BL.

44. THE DEATH OF MRS. WITTGENSTEIN

160 "My mother tried to smooth the surface." HW1, p. 104.

161 "Gentlemen, I am old and sick and easily tired." HW1, p. 94.

161 "It was weird. Mama slept." MSt to Thomas Stonborough, 6/8/1926, quoted in Prokop, p. 161.

161 "It was a gentle death." *Lieber Freund! Heute früh ist meine Mutter gestorben. Es war ein sanfter Tod.* LW to Rudolf Koder, 6/3/1926, GBW.

161 "It was a very beautiful night!" *Es war eine sehr schöne Nacht.* MSt to Thomas Stonborough, 6/8/1926, quoted in Prokop, p. 161.

161 "Yes, it can be said that my mother." *Ja, meine Mutter hatte in vielen Stücken fast etwas von einer Heiligen an sich und sie wurde auch so geliebt, verehrt und betrauert von unzähligen Menschen! Und doch wäre dieses Bild nicht vollständig und nicht einmal ganz ähnlich, wenn nicht noch einige sonderbare Eigentümlichkeiten erwähnt würden, die meiner Mutter das Leben schwer machten, und die es auch für uns Kinder oft schwer machten, ihr gerecht zu werden.* HW1, p. 94.

45. FROM BOOM TO BUST

162 "Paul played so splendidly today." Marie Baumayer to HW, 9/21/1926, ÖNB.

163 "I come home very depressed with a headache." Jacques Groag to his brother, Emo Groag, *c.* 2/1927, quoted in Paul Wijdeveld, *Ludwig Wittgenstein: Architect*, reprinted in Flowers, vol. 2, p. 146.

163 "two great people had come together." *Zwei grosse Menschen waren da als Architekt und Bauherr zusammengekommen und so konnte bei diesem etwas in seiner Art Vollendetes geschaffen werden.* HW1, p. 114.

164 "all the anger that he felt against himself." MSt to Thomas Stonborough, 12/29/1928, quoted in Prokop, p. 184.

164 "He is my husband and I cannot destroy." *Er ist mein Mann und ich kann nicht*

um Geld das Menschliche zerstören. MSt to Thomas Stonborough, 11/12/1929, quoted in ibid., p. 195.

46. MORE ON PAUL'S CHARACTER

166 "I remember how mentally difficult." Dr R. T. Grant, undated letter, to Georg von Wright, pc.

166 "Rain was disregarded." MD, "Memoirs," vol. 2, p. 27.

167 "He was like no one else." Erna Otten-Attermann to Fred Flindell, 6/20/1967, pc.

167 "the most charming man." Leonard Kastle to the author, 2/23/2007.

168 "between him and me acquaintance mellowed." MD, "Memoirs," vol. 2, p. 29.

168 "One evening at Southwold I asked Paul." Ibid., p. 37.

168 "a shell around him, like a suit of armour." Steve Portman to the author, 10/2006.

169 "Paul was indignant; facing me in real anger." MD, "Memoirs," vol. 2, p. 38.

169 "Both of them are, I think, really great people." Donald Francis Tovey to Stuart Deas, 1/1930, Edinburgh University Library.

170 "He still makes me shudder." Leonard Kastle, "Paul Wittgenstein; Teacher and Friend," reprinted in Suchy, Janik and Predota, p. 68.

170 "I wept a little." Philippa Shuyler, Scrapbook, 7/10/1941, quoted in Talalay, p. 91.

170 "Paul's personality is unforgettable." MD, "Memoirs," vol. 2, p. 58.

47. RUSSIA AND RAVEL

171 "It is good music—very likely." Leopold Godowsky to Frieda Godowsky, 5/6/1928, quoted in Nicholas, p. 135.

172 "Je me joue de difficultés." PW to Joachim Wechsberg, 2/5/1958, pc.

172 "When dark envy dresses." *Als Gleichheit brüstet sich der dunkle Neid. Gilt jeder nur als Mensch, Mensch sind sie alle Krieg jedem Vorzug heisst das Loesungswort.* Franz Grillparzer, *Libussa,* Act V.

172 "I was driven to desperation." PW, Russian Notes, *c.* 1935, p. 7, pc.

172 " 'Café au lait.' There is no milk." Ibid.

173 "If you had kept the Tsar." JSt to Brian McGuinness, 1/18/1996, pc.

173 "The Great Hall, as is generally the case." PW, Russian Notes, *c.* 1935, p. 11, pc.

173 "Mr. Wittgenstein is presently on tour." Georg Kügel to Michel Astroff, 6/25/1930, PA.

174 "Dear Master, allow me to express." PW to Sergei Prokofiev, 8/27/1930, PA.

174 "If I had wanted to play without." Quoted in Prokofiev, *Autobiography,* p. 293.

174 "I suppose Ravel was disappointed." Wechsberg, p. 28.

174 "Ravel's Concerto will probably be finished." PW to Sergei Prokofiev, 9/29/1930, PA.

175 "Paul Wittgenstein's virtuoso performance." *Paul Wittgensteins virtuose Leistung entfesselte stürmischen Beifall.* Review signed "r," *Neue Freie Presse,* 1/18/1932.

176 "As soon as the performance was over." Long, p. 40.

176 He wrote to the composer Karl Weigl. *Ich habe gedacht mein öffentliches Spielen langsam aufzugeben.* PW to Karl Weigl, 2/22/1932, Yale University Library.

176 "I have cancelled the Paris concert." PW to MD, 4/2/1932, BL.

176 "As for a formal commitment to play." PW to Maurice Ravel, 3/17/1932, quoted in Orenstein, p. 594.

177 "It ruins the concerto." Seroff, p. 262.

177 "a great work." PW to Donald Francis Tovey, 6/22/1932, Edinburgh University Library.

177 "My quarrel with Ravel." Unsigned interview with PW, "One-Armed Pianist Undaunted by Lot," *NYT*, 11/4/1934, p. N7.

48. PROKOFIEV

178 "I cannot stand Bolsheviks!" Prokofiev, *Diaries,* 9/2/1930.

178 "disappointed by the unattractive look." Ibid.

178 "So what did you expect." Ibid.

178 "What makes you commission." Ibid.

179 "You could carry on playing." Ibid.

179 "how he played with such love." Ibid.

179 "You will have your own room." PW to Sergei Prokofiev, 3/20/1931, PA.

179 "clearer than Strauss." PW to Sergei Prokofiev, 10/22/1930, PA.

180 "I hope the concerto will prove satisfactory." Sergei Prokofiev to PW, 9/11/1931, PA.

180 "Thank you for your concerto." Prokofiev, *Autobiography,* p. 293.

180 "Given the excellent relationship." Sergei Prokofiev to PW, 10/8/1934, PA.

180 "That is not fair. Your concerto." PW to Sergei Prokofiev, 10/11/1931, PA.

180 "You don't owe me $3,000 but $2,250." Sergei Prokofiev to PW, 9/16/1931, printed in Flindell, "Dokumente," p. 429.

181 "I have not formed any definite opinion." Prokofiev, *Autobiography,* p. 293.

49. LOVE STORY

181 Bassia Moscovici. Details concerning Bassia Moscovici are hard to find. Her *Verlassenschaftsakt* in the Vienna City Archives, BG Landstrasse 6A 414/1932, gives her parents' names and occupations, and her property at time of death. The Jewish Community *Austrittsbücher* simply record: IKG *Austrittsbuch No.108/1931; 25. II. 1931: Bassia MOSCOVICI, geb. 23 [sic]. XII. 1910 Bukarest, ledig, XIX., Vegagasse 14. Im Verzeichnis der Verstorbenen in Wien* (Hrsg.vom Magistrat der StadtWien), Vienna 1936, it is recorded: *MOSKOWICI, Bassia (Pauline), Juwelierstochter, 22 J. (geb. 22. XII. 1910), gest. Sa., 23. April 1932 in Wien, 3. Bezirk, Kundmanngasse 19, Sarkom des Oberarms, röm.-kath; begr. Mo., 25. April 1932 Zentralfriedhof Wien, Gruppe 30b, Reihe 7, Grab Nr. 14.*

183 "Putting out her hand to greet me." MD, "Memoirs," vol. 2, p. 55.

183 "Bassia has been in agony." *Die Bassia liegt seit gestern Abend in Agonie. Sie wird bald sterben müssen. Ich denke oft an den Paul.* Marguerite Respinger to LW, 4.22.1932, GBW.

183 "It made a great impression on me." *Es hat mir einen grossen Eindruck gemacht. Nicht weil der Anblick eines Toten etwas erschreckendes für mich hat—aber um einmal friedlich so daliegen zu können, wie muss man da gewesen sein! Gut.* Marguerite Respinger to LW, 4.23.1931, GBW.

183 "Paul has lost a lot and he admits it." *Er hat viel verloren und gibt es auch zu,*

obwohl ich nicht ganz sicher bin, dass er dasselbe denkt wie ich, wenn er es zugibt! HW
to LW, 4/26/1932, GBW.

184 "Paul can only lose here." *Verlieren kann dabei natürlich nur der Paul aber zu*
ändern ist nichts! HW to LW, 5/7/1932, GBW.

50. HIS AMERICAN DEBUT

184 "Despite our admiration for the artist." P. Rytel, "Z Filharmonii: XII Koncert
Symfoniczny," *Gazeta Warszawska,* 1932, no. 378, trans. Krystyna Klejn.

184 "Performances by single-handed pianists." F. Szopski, "Georg Heoberg, Pawel
Wittgenstein," *Kurier Warszawski,* 1932, no. 341.

184 "Obviously one hand cannot replace two." Review signed "W.F.," *Polska Zbrojna,*
1932, no. 343.

184 "As to those compositions composed." Review signed "H.D.," "Z Filharmonii,"
Robotnik, 1932, no. 421.

185 "Doubtless the greatest tribute." Review in *New York Herald Tribune,* 11/18/1934,
p. 16.

185 "I have every sympathy with Paul Wittgenstein." Ernest Newman review in
Sunday Times, 8/21/1932.

186 "It seems to me that one could continue." *Es scheint mir immer, als könne man ad*
infinitum so fortreden wie diese Art der Kompositionen jetzt sind. Schade für Paul dass er
in dieser Zeit nichts wirklich Gutes mehr bekommen kann! HW to LW, 2/7/1935, GBW.

186 "The first and second movements I think." PW to Donald Francis Tovey,
1/14/1935, Edinburgh University Library.

51. FURTHER COMPLICATIONS

187 "a *Strassenbahn Kontrolleur*—a man who checked tram tickets." JSt to Brian
McGuinness, 8/19/1993, pc. In various Viennese forms and directories Franz
Schania gives his job as: *Strassenbahnbeamter* (Lehmann directory, 1935-7),
Strassenbahn-Vizeinspektor (Lehmann, 1940), *Obersekretär der Städtische*
Strassenbahn (Wiener Stadt und Landesarchiv: Politische Beurteilung, PB
265247, 1942), *Wiener Verkehrsbetriebe Beamter* (Lehmann, 1950) and
Kanzleioberkommissar (in his will).

188 "I lost my right arm in the war." PW, Application for a teaching post at the
Hochschule für Musik, 10/11/1930, reproduced in Suchy, Janik and Predota, p. 122.

188 "Both Hofrat Dr Marx and Professor Mairecker." Minutes from the
Hochschule staff committee meeting, 1930, in Archiv der Universität für Musik
und darstellende Kunst, Vienna, reproduced in ibid., p. 121.

188 "I love teaching." Article signed "G.N.," "Teaching Field in the United States
Gains Adherent in Viennese Pianist," *Musical Courier,* 1/1939.

189 "During the lesson and while you played." Erna Otten-Attermann interview
with Albert Sassmann in Suchy, Janik and Predota, p. 37.

52. RISING TENSIONS

190 "extremely handsome with the neck." MD, "Memoirs," vol. 2, p. 66.

191 "At the age of 40." J. N. Findlay, "My Encounters with Wittgenstein,"
Philosophical Forum, vol. 4, 1972-3, p. 171.

191 "I think it's very difficult to understand them." LW to BR, autumn 1935, GBW.

191 "Greetings to you from Dr Ludwig Wittgenstein." LW to Frau Oberleitner, copied to PW, pre-April 1932, pc.

192 "The important thing is that the people have *work*." Rhees, *Ludwig Wittgenstein,* p. 226.

192 "Russians told him his own work." Told by George Sacks in the play *A Thinking Man as Hero,* broadcast BBC2, 4/1973, quoted in Monk, p. 351.

192 "One *could* live there." Fania Pascal, "Wittgenstein: A Personal Memoir," reprinted in Flowers, vol. 2, p. 222.

192 "I am a communist at heart." Quoted in Monk, p. 343.

194 "He has had an accident." *Der neuste Witz über ihn ist, dass er einen Unfall gehabt hat. Er ist beim Ribisel Pflücken von der Leiter gefallen.* MSt to Thomas Stonborough, undated, quoted in Prokop, p. 213.

194 "Austrian with his heart and soul." HWi, p. 155.

195 "Fascism in Austria is represented by the Heimwehr." Unsigned article, "Heimwehr Leader in Offer to Hitler," *NYT,* 1/29/1934.

195 "We have much in common with the German Nazis." Unsigned profile of Ernst Rüdiger von Starhemberg, "New Chancellor Foe of Anschluss," *NYT,* 7/27/1934.

196 "Who knows what the future will bring?" *Aber eigentlich weiss doch niemand wie es weitergehen wird. Wir haben ja doch die eine feindliche Partei nur zum Schweigen gebracht, die andere—die Nationalsozialisten—ist bissiger und feindlicher denn je. Was wird man mit dieser machen? Kann man einen Kampf aufs Messer ausfechten mit gutem Ausgang?* HW to LW, 2/1934, GBW.

196 "could scarcely wipe the delight from his face." PW, Testament Appendix, 1/31/1945 [sic], p. 10, WMGA, pc.

197 "Reich Troops Pour Through Austria." Front page, *NYT,* 3/18/1938.

198 "The Greater German Reich has risen." Ibid.

53. PATRIOT IN TROUBLE

202 "As I entered the room, the professor." Erna Otten-Attermann, interview with Albert Sassmann, in Suchy, Janik and Predota, p. 43.

202 "Paul Wittgenstein was invited by me." Josef Reitler, endorsement of Paul Wittgenstein as piano teacher, 3/11/1938, copy of official English translation, 3/19/1938, pc.

204 "those National Socialists." In Michael Wildt, *Die Juden Politik des SD,* quoted in Friedländer, p. 242.

205 "The Jew must clear out of Europe." *Der Jude muß aus Europa heraus. Wir kriegen sonst keine europäische Verständigung. Er hetzt am meisten überall. Letzten Endes: Ich weiß nicht, ich bin kolossal human. Zur Zeit der päpstlichen Herrschaft in Rom sind die Juden mißhandelt worden. Bis 1830 wurden acht Juden jedes Jahr durch die Stadt getrieben, mit Eseln. Ich sage nur, er muß weg. Wenn er dabei kaputtgeht, da kann ich nicht helfen. Ich sehe nur eines: die absolute Ausrottung, wenn sie nicht freiwillig gehen.* Trevor-Roper, 1/23/1942, p. 193.

205 "Wir gelten als Juden." HWi, p. 156.

54. FIRST PLANS

207 "What can be said about the marriage." From *Mitteilungsblatt des Reichsverbandes der Nichtarischen Christen,* 3/1936, quoted in Friedländer, p. 158.

207 "She was discovered to be a half-Jüdin." Unity Mitford to her sister Diana Guinness, 12/23/1935, in Mosley, p. 68.

208 "Of course poor Heinz was completely erledigt." Unity Mitford to her sister Diana Guinness, 7/18/1938, in ibid., p. 125.

208 "Our most intimate family." HWi, p. 155.

209 "Pur sang!" Quoted in McGuinness, *Wittgenstein: A Life,* p. 1.

209 "even apart from all the nasty consequences." LW to John Maynard Keynes, 3/18/1938, GBW.

209 "something I have always rejected." Ibid.

209 "by the annexation of Austria by Germany." Ibid.

209 "they are almost all retiring." Ibid.

210 "Although I won't join with you." LW to PW, 5/30/1938, pc.

211 "to prove the German and Christian nature." *Durch die beigefügten Daten und Legenden die deutsch-christliche Einstellung der Familie W. und ihre zahlreichen Verdienste um ihr Vaterland beweisen . . . diese Einstellung zum Gemeinwohl auch unter dem neuen Regime nach Kräften zu beweisen, obwohl das Familienvermögen durch die Einwirkungen des Weltkrieges und insbesondere der Inflation sehr bedeutend geschmälert wurde.* Quoted in *Schiedsinstanz für Naturalrestitution,* 206/2006, 7/12/2006, article 53.

211 "Jews who become philanthropists." Trevor-Roper, 1/23/1942, p. 193.

212 "exuding eroticism, with heavy face." From Martha Dodd, *Through Embassy Eyes,* quoted in Schad, p. 44.

213 "a scarecrow." Trevor-Roper, 9/2/1942, p. 556.

213 "A second Aryan grandparent is essential." *Ein zweiter arischer Grosselternteil sei nötig.* HWi, p. 157.

55. COUNTER-ATTACK

214 "I want to be remembered as the daughter." Karl Menger, *Reminiscences of the Wittgenstein Family,* reprinted in Flowers, vol. 1, p. 115.

216 "I want my children to become reformers." Ibid.

216 "For all her social conscience." Ibid.

217 "Computing how little there is." JSt to Joan Ripley, 1/2/2000, pc.

217 "This inventory must be submitted." PW's completed form: "Verzeichnis über das Vermögen von Jüden," no. 19710, signed 7/15/1938, copy, pc.

219 "This form has been completed." Ibid.

56. ESCAPE

219 "Paul suffered indescribably." HWi, p. 157.

220 "SHE WOULD LIKE TO SEE YOU OXFORD." PW to MD, 6/13/1938, BL.

220 "MY BROTHER-IN-LAW STONBOROUGH." *Mein Schwager Stonborough ist heute Nacht plötzlich verschieden. Meine Schwester wird später kommen. Herzliche Grüsse und Bedauern.* Telegram PW to MD, 6/15/1938, BL.

221 "Everything has been settled now." MD, "Memoirs," vol. 2, p. 60.

221 "I offered him some of my jam." Ibid.

222 "nice, honest and honorable man." JSt to Brian McGuinness, 1/22/1989, pc.

222 "a full-hearted Nazi." *Ein offenherziger Nazi.* Viktor Matejka, *Anregung ist alles,* quoted by Herbert Exenberger in *Gefängnis statt Erziehung Jugendgefängnis Kaiser-Ebersdorf 1940–1945* on the website of the Dokumentationsarchiv des österreichischen Widerstandes, www.doew.at/thema/kaiserebersdorf/jugendgef.html.

223 "One thing I can say: that you, dear Marga." PW to MD, 10/15/1938, BL.

223 "As to the possibility of war, I do not know." Piero Sraffa to LW, 3/14/1938, GBW.

224 "Herr Paul Wittgenstein; Re: III Jews 29/38 g." Staatskommissar in der Privatwirtschaft Franz Roitner to PW, 8/5/1938, copy, pc.

225 Franz Schania was one of the millions of Austrians. Details of Franz Schania's affiliations with the Nazi Party may be found in his *Gauakt* (District NSDAP file) in the Wiener Stadt-und-Landesarchiv. The *Gauakt* is described as a "Politische Beurteilung" (political assessment), file no. PB 265247, compiled at the end of 1942 following a request by the Wiener Städtische Strassenbahnen to the NSDAP Gauleitung, Vienna. Information from the Meldeamtsarchiv shows that Flat 19, Kandlgasse 32, into which Schania moved after the *Kristallnacht* pogroms of November 1938, was previously occupied by the Jewish family of Wulwek, whose son, the musician Leo Wulwek, fled to safety in Palestine via Czechoslovakia. Leo's parents, Benjamin and Scheindel Wulwek, were first removed to an inferior flat nearby and on October 28, 1941, deported to the Lotz (Litzmannstadt) Ghetto, or *Sammelhaus,* at Schottenfeldgasse 53/7. Their names appear on a list of murdered Holocaust victims at http://www.avotaynu.com/holocaustlist/w.mt.htm. The names of Jews deported from Kandlgasse 32 where Schania acted as *Blockhelfer,* or Nazi informant, may be found on the Holocaust website http://www.lettertothestars.at/liste_opfer.php?searchterm= kandlgasse+32&action=search&x=31&y=8. In Franz Schania's will (3/1/1964), located in his *Verlassenschaftsakt* (probate file), EStLA, Verl. Abh. BG Innere Stadt I, Franz Schania, A4/9A238/70, he leaves nothing to Hilde or Käthe (daughters by his first marriage), because they "have only paid me the very slightest attention" (*um mich ja nur allerwenigsten kümmerten*). On official forms during the war he denied the existence of Hilde. The villa at Gersthoferstrasse 30, where Hilde and her children were secreted in a flat from 1934 to 1938, belonged to the famous singer and friend of PW, Ruzena Herlinger. The flat was registered in Franz Schania's name to preserve the anonymity of PW, Hilde and the two illegitimate children. Ms. Herlinger, who was Jewish, fled to England in 1938. Franz Schania attempted to enlist PW's help to buy the villa but was refused. It was bought instead by an Aryan dentist called Anton Haller and demolished in 2005.

225 "because I do not want you to suffer." *Denn ich wünsche nicht, dass der Unterricht meiner Schüler durch die politische Umwälzung eine Unterbrechung erleidet.* PW to Ernst Schlesinger "Henry Selbing," 8/16/1938, quoted in Suchy, Janik and Predota, p. 22.

57. ARREST

227 "It is noteworthy that in Hermann Christian's certificate." *An diesem Taufschein, dessen beglaubigte Abschrift ich beifüge, ist bemerkenswert, dass wohl seine Frau, nicht*

aber er als ehelich geboren bezeichnet wird. Ebenso ist die Formel "im jüdischen Glauben erzogen" nicht gewöhnlich; sie ist wohl bewusst gewählt worden um auszudrücken, dass er eigentlich der jüdischen Kultegemeinde nicht angehörte, sondern nur in ihr erzogen wurde. Brigitte Zwiauer to Reichsstelle für Sippenforschung, Vienna, 9/29/1938, copy, Wittgenstein Archive, Cambridge.

231 "Sir: Having returned from a voyage." JSt to WP, 9/6/1938, printed 9/8/1938.

231 "These are serious times for the family." *Jetzt sind ernste Zeiten für die Familie, ein grosses Abrechnen und Prüfen aller Verhältnisse, abgesehen von den äusseren Gefahren. Manchmal sehe ich alles deutlich vor mir und ich denke mir: Kein Stein wird auf dem anderen bleiben.* HW to LW, 10/15/1938, GBW.

232 "our appearance and manner of speech." HWi, p. 173.

233 "evil blow." Ibid., p. 174.

58. A SECOND EMIGRATION

233 "You all behave like cattle." PW, Testament Appendix, 1/31/1945 [*sic*], p. 12, n. 10, WMGA, pc.

235 "Although I have obtained the ticket." PW to MD, 11/1938, BL.

236 "I'll definitely be coming back." Ibid.

236 "Dearest Lena, Paul Wittgenstein asked me." MD to her sister Helene Deneke, in Deneke Papers, BL.

236 "I took a long walk with him on deck." MD, "Memoirs," vol. 2, p. 64.

59. CHANGING SIDES

237 "Our family lacks the leading man." *Es fehlt unserer Familie der leitende Mann. Max ist alt und leider sehr krank, Paul versagt, Fritz fehlt es an Tiefe und Gewicht. Was hilft es da, dass Gretl ein grosses Herz hat und sich um alle bekümmert; die Probleme sind zu unlösbar.* HW to LW, 10/15/1938, GBW.

237 "One comes up against obstacles everywhere." *Man stösst überall auf Schwierigkeiten, kann nur hoffen, dass es gelingen wird sie zu überwinden.* PW to Ludwig Hänsel, 1/9/1939, in Somavilla, Unterkircher and Berger, p. 154.

238 "How shall I manage without her?" Anecdote told to the author by Leonard Kastle, 5/2007.

239 "This memorandum will not be seen." Harold Manheim, "Memorandum with Regard to Paul Wittgenstein's Relations with his Sister in Vienna," 2/17/1944, p. 2, WMGA, pc.

239 "Mrs Stonborough evidently felt in 1938 and 1939." Ibid., p. 6.

239 "negotiated themselves out of it." *Der Krieg ist abgewendet und mit ihm auch die imminenteste andere Gefahr, aus der heraus wir gehandelt haben.* HW to LW, 10/22/1938, GBW.

239 "Gretl and some good friends again found means." HWi, p. 175.

240 "a gent and on very good terms." JSt to Brian McGuinness, 1/13/1989, pc.

240 "I hereby confirm of my own free will." *Erklärung. Ich bestätige gerne, dass bis heute den 4. Juni 1938, keinerlei Behelligung meiner Person oder meiner Hausgenossen vorgekommen ist. Behörden und Funktionäre der Partei sind mir und meinem Hausgenossen ständig korrekt und rücksichtsvoll entgegengetreten. Wien, den 4. Juni 1938. Prof. Dr. Sigm. Freud.* Statement by Sigmund Freud 6/4/1938, in "A Sale in

Vienna," printed in *Journal de l'Association Internationale d'Histoire de la Psychanalyse,* vol. 8, 1989.

241 "Indra was a very handsome man." JSt to Brian McGuinness, 2/8/1989, pc.

242 "You know, there are those in Berlin." HW1, p. 176.

243 "Either you can emigrate." Ibid.

243 "Our friendship with the Reichsbank began." HW1, p. 178. In a letter to Brian McGuinness (1/13/1989) JSt says, "The Reichsbank in Berlin were honest and honorable," and describes Hans Schoene as "young and nice."

60. NAZIS ARRIVE IN AMERICA

243 "The Germans have been very generous." PW, Testament Appendix, 1/31/1945 [*sic*], p. 7, WMGA, pc.

244 "a fighter who brooked no interference." JSt to Brian McGuinness, 1/22/1989, pc.

245 "he never opened his mouth in my presence." PW, Testament Appendix, 1/31/1945 [sic], p. 2, WMGA, pc.

245 "Since I came to America far too late." Ibid., p. 7.

245 "My sister has not the slightest reason." Ibid., p. 6.

246 "Where are the Germans?." Ibid., p. 5.

246 "I listened with considerable interest." Ibid.

247 "It would have been better if we could." Ibid., p. 9.

247 "PERSONALLY SHALL TAKE NO MORE." PW to JSt, quoted in ibid., p. 14.

247 "Back then, Wachtell literally saved me." Ibid., p. 9.

61. THE STONBOROUGHS' MOTIVATION

247 "That is only a suspicion." PW, Testament Appendix, 1/31/1945 [*sic*], p. 15, n. 12, WMGA, pc.

248 "Finally it was decided to allow Paul." HW1, p. 178.

248 "extremely dangerous." Konrad Bloch to Samuel Wachtell, 6/20/1939, WMGA, pc.

248 "That Paul does not give his money to the Reichsbank." PW, Testament Appendix, 1/31/1945 [*sic*], p. 15, WMGA, pc.

248 "a real shit!" JSt to Brian McGuinness, 2/2/1989, pc.

248 "by the Jewish lawyers, Wachtell and Bloch." Hans Schoene to Reichsbank, quoted in PW, Testament Appendix, 1/31/1945 [*sic*], p. 17, WMGA, pc.

249 "Alfred Indra dictated a letter to me." JSt to Brian McGuinness, 1/13/1989, pc.

249 "DO NOT INSIST ON HALF-BREED STATUS." Quoted in PW, Testament Appendix, 1/31/1945 [*sic*], p. 11, WMGA, pc.

249 "DON'T GIVE IN OR AUNT IMPRISONED." *Ji—nicht nachgeben oder Tante eingesperrt.* Recorded in LW's diary, 7/24/1939, Trinity College Library, Cambridge. The singular *Tante* refers to Hermine.

249 "Dear Professor Wittgenstein, The announcement." Samuel Wachtell to LW, 7/14/1939, WMGA, pc.

250 "the Stonboroughs' behaviour was certainly rash." PW, Testament Appendix, 1/31/1945 [*sic*], p. 10, WMGA, pc.

250 "Had I realised then how insane Paul was." JSt to Brian McGuinness, 8/19/1993, pc.

252 "You have my entire confidence." LW to Samuel Wachtell, 7/24/1939, WMGA, pc.

253 "Dr Indra said that no one would dare." Samuel Wachtell, Internal Memorandum, 8/17/1939, WMGA, pc.

253 "In the matter of the origins of the Wittgenstein family." Kurt Mayer to Gauamt für Sippenforschung der NSDAP, Vienna, 2/10/1940, copy, pc.

254 "I have no knowledge as to whether personal belongings." PW completed form: Aliens' Questionnaire, p. 3, Statements of Assets and Liabilities as of 12/31/1944, signed 8/17/1945, pc.

63. VALUABLE MANUSCRIPTS

255 *"Achtung! Panzer, marsch!"* Kurt Meyer, p. 1.

256 "I was bright enough to assert loud." JSt to Brian McGuinness, John and Jerome Stonborough, 3/12/1999, pc.

257 "The liner *Manhattan,* which docked at New York." Dudley Harmon, "About the Town," *WP,* 10/3/1939, p. 12.

258 "In order to lend particular weight." Friedrich Plattner, *Schnellbrief* to Hans Heinrich Lammers, 1/9/1940, copy, pc.

64. COLD WAR

259 "There is no place I can find rest." *Es gibt auch hier keine Oase in der man sich ausruhen könnte & ich kann auch niemandem in meiner Umgebung wirklich nützlich sein. So Gott will finde ich, wenn ich hier bleiben muss, irgendeine nützliche Beschäftigung.* MSt to LW, 1940, GBW.

260 "I have done fairly well in the administration." JSt to LW, 12/2/1944, GBW.

65. A FAMILY REUNION

262 "I would go to see him with joy." MSt to LW, 9/1940, GBW.

262 "Paul's friend (with her children)." Ibid.

66. BENJAMIN BRITTEN

262 "In the afternoon." Benjamin Britten, Diary, 2/14/1929, quoted in Mitchell and Reed, vol. 2, p. 828, n. 1.

262 "We went and had a long talk." Peter Pears to Elizabeth Mayer, 7/4/1940, quoted in ibid., p. 826.

263 "I called Mr. Wittgenstein." Hans Heinsheimer to Benjamin Britten, 7/2/1940, quoted in ibid., p. 826.

263 "I pulled off the deal with Wittgenstein." Benjamin Britten to Elizabeth Mayer, 7/29/1940, quoted in ibid., p. 834.

263 "I've been commissioned by a man." Benjamin Britten to Beth Welford, 6/26/1940, quoted in ibid., p. 831.

264 "This is a truly amazing work." Eugene Goossens to Hans Heinsheimer, 9/27/1940, quoted in ibid., p. 874, n. 5.

264 "A nice place with a view to the bay." *Das Haus ist schön gelegen mit der Aussicht auf*

eine Meeresbucht, hat einen hübschen Garten, in dem ich im nächsten Jahr Erdbeeren
und Ribisel zu ziehen gedenke, und, was das Wichtigste ist, bis zum Badestrand sind es
nur 10 Minuten zu gehen! PW to Rudolf Koder, 7/31/1941, pc.

264 "playing against the noise of your orchestra." PW to Benjamin Britten,
7/31/1941, Britten-Pears Archive.

264 "I'm having a slight altercation." Benjamin Britten to Ralph Hawkes, 7/23/1941,
quoted in Mitchell and Reed, vol. 2, p. 956.

264 "Wittgenstein is being stupid." Peter Pears to Elizabeth Mayer, 8/23/1940,
quoted in ibid., p. 957, n. 6.

265 "In the museum in Vienna I have seen." PW to Benjamin Britten, 7/31/1941,
Britten-Pears Archive.

265 "to hear Wittgenstein wreck my *Diversions.*" Benjamin Britten to Albert
Goldberg, 1/20/1942, quoted in Mitchell and Reed, vol. 2, p. 1014.

265 "A one-armed pianist, whose right sleeve." Linton Martin review, *Philadelphia
Inquirer,* 1/17/1942.

265 "Wittgenstein is playing his piece on Friday." Peter Pears and Benjamin Britten to
Antonio and Peggy Brosa, 3/10/1942, quoted in Mitchell and Reed, vol. 2, p. 1024.

266 "I felt I wanted to see him." MSt to LW, March–April 1942, GBW.

67. THE WITTGENSTEINS' WAR

266 "Thought: it would be good and right." LW, MS 120, 1/4/1938, quoted in Monk,
p. 387.

266 "turned white as a sheet." Dr. R. Grant to Georg von Wright, undated, pc.

266 "My soul is *very* tired." LW to Rowland Hutt, 11/27/1941, GBW.

267 "an ingenious departure from standard practice." Dr. R. Grant to Georg von
Wright, undated, pc.

267 "It goes very near me." MSt to LW, c. end of September 1944, GBW.

268 "I like her very much although." MSt to LW, 3/14/1944, GBW.

268 "a damned inefficient bunch of dolts." JSt to Joan Ripley, 9/13/1999, pc.

268 "some bastard of a Canadian General." Brian McGuinness, John Stonborough
obituary, *Independent,* 6/4/2002.

270 "went about for ten years shouting 'Heil Hitler!' " *Zehn Jahre lang hat er Heil
Hitler gerufen.* PW to Rudolf Koder, 1/6/1957, pc.

270 "In Austria we do not take Herr Wittgenstein seriously." *Wir in Oesterreich nehmen
Herrn W. nicht ernst. Ein cholerischer Neurastheniker, reich, anmassend und als Pianist
miserabel.* Friedrich Wührer to Siegfried Rapp, 12/26/1949, quoted in Siegfried
Rapp to Ottakar Hollmann, 12/1/1956, quoted in Suchy, Janik and Predota, p. 119.

68. ROADS' END

272 "It seems that my sister Gretl gave me." *Aus ihr geht hervor, daß mir meine
Schwester Gretl wieder eine falsche Nachricht gegeben hat, als sie sagte, Mining erkenne
niemand mehr. Es ist schrecklich für mich, widersprechende Nachrichten zu erhalten.
Bitte laß Dich durch neimand beeinflußen & schreib mir nach wie vor die Wahrheit, so
wie Du sie weißt. Bitte verlaß Dich nicht auf das Urteil meiner Schwester Gretl, es ist viel
zu temperamentvoll.* LW to Rudolf Koder, 3/2/1949, GBW.

273 "I haven't done any work since." LW to Norman Malcolm, 5/17/1949, GBW.

273 "I don't want to die in America." Malcolm, p. 77.

274 "I am thinking of going to Vienna." LW to Jean Rhees, 11/28/1949, GBW.

274 "My eldest sister died very peacefully." LW to Georg Henrik von Wright, 2/12/1950, GBW.

275 "Great loss for me and all of us." *Grosser Verlust für mich und alle. Grösser als ich geglaubt hätte.* LW, MS 138, 2/10/1949, quoted in HW2, p. 38.

275 "I am going to work now as I have." Ray Monk interview with Joan Bevan, quoted in Monk, p. 577.

275 "Many happy returns!" Ibid.

275 "Someone who dreaming says." LW, *On Certainty,* point 676, p. 90.

276 "For a time I really believed that Paul would get over his attitude." MSt to LW, May 1942, GBW.

69. THE END OF THE LINE

278 "I think I am going to have a great deal." Trevor Harvey to MD, 8/19/1959, BL.

278 "familiarity with these works has bred." Review, *The Times,* 10/31/1950.

279 "You don't build a house." PW to Siegfried Rapp, 6/5/1950, quoted in Suchy, Janik and Predota, p. 172.

279 "I had imagined that there might be." Siegfried Rapp to Ottakar Hollmann, 12/1/1959, quoted in ibid., p. 118.

279 "You are overrating me by far." PW to Leonard Kastle, 6/13/1960, University at Albany, Special Collections.

280 "I was sure that he would have hated." MSt to LW, 6/1942, GBW.

280 "I believe that she wants to make peace." *Ich glaube, sie will gleichsam von ihrer Seite Friede machen & in sich alle Bitterkeit, die doch existiert haben muß, auslöschen.* LW to Rudolf Koder, 8/23/1949, GBW.

280 "since it is possible that at a later date." PW to Konrad Bloch, 6/26/1939, WMGA, pc.

280 "The following was not originally intended." PW, Testament Appendix, 1/31/1945 [*sic*], p. 1, WMGA, pc.

280 "Paul is in Oxford with the Denekes." *Paul ist jetzt mit den Denekes in Oxford, & ich erhielt neulich eine sehr seltsame mir ekelerregende Einladung von Miss Deneke, sie dort während Pauls Anwesenheit zu besuchen. Daß, & warum, ich diese Einladung weder annehmen kann, noch will, habe ich ihr geschrieben. Ich bin sicher, daß die Einladung der Miss Deneke nicht in Pauls Auftrag geschrieben war. Ich glaube vielmehr, daß sie eine Zusammenkunft herbeiführen wollte, & mein Bruder ihr die Erlaubnis gab, mich einzuladen, was sie, ihrer Dummheit entsprechend, in der dümmsten Form getan hat.* LW to Rudolf Koder, 2/22/1949, GBW.

281 "He was sitting in a dressing gown." MD, "Memoirs," vol. 2, p. 80.

281 "I kept out of contact with my brother." PW to Rudolf Koder, 10/7/1953, pc.

281 "That our house in the Alleegasse is not." PW to Rudolf Koder, 5/21/1955, pc.

282 "Selig sind die Toten." Words of the final chorus of Brahms's *Ein Deutsches Requiem,* taken from Revelation 14:13.

282 "As a personal friend Paul Wittgenstein." Harvey, "Paul Wittgenstein: A Personal Reminiscence," in *The Gramophone,* June 1961, p. 2.

282 "Loyalty to his friends was part." MD, "Mr. Paul Wittgenstein. Devotion to Music."

POSTSCRIPT

283 "a stern, incomprehensible." Ripley, "A Memory of My Father," pc.

BIBLIOGRAPHY

* * *

I. BOOKS

Abrahamsen, David: *Otto Weininger: The Mind of a Genius.* New York 1946
Alber, Martin: *Wittgenstein und die Musik.* Innsbruck 2000
Barchilon, John: *The Crown Prince.* New York 1984
Barta, Erwin: *Die großen Konzertdirektionen im Wiener Konzerthaus 1913–1945,* Frankfurt am Main 2001
Bartley, William Warren III: *Wittgenstein.* Philadelphia 1973
Beaumont, Anthony (ed.): *Alma Mahler-Werfel: Diaries 1898–1902.* Ithaca 1999
Beller, Steven: *Vienna and the Jews 1867–1938.* Cambridge 1989
Beller, Steven: *A Concise History of Austria.* Cambridge 2006
Bernhard, Thomas: *Wittgenstein's Nephew,* trans. Ewald Osers. London 1986
Black, Max: *A Companion to Wittgenstein's Tractatus.* Cambridge 1964
Botstein, Leon and Hanak, Werner (eds): *Vienna, Jews and the City of Music.* Annandale 2004
Brändström, Elsa: *Among Prisoners of War in Russia and Siberia.* London 1929
Bree, Malwine: *The Leschetizky Method.* New York 1913
Brook, Donald: *Masters of the Keyboard.* London 1946
Brook-Shepherd, Gordon: *Anschluss: The Rape of Austria.* London 1963
Burghard, Frederic F.: *Amputations.* Oxford 1920
Carroll, Brendan G.: *The Last Prodigy: A Biography of E. W. Korngold.* Portland 1997
Clare, George: *Last Waltz in Vienna.* London 1981
Cornish, Kimberley: *The Jew of Linz.* London 1998
Corti, Egon and Sokol, Hans: *Kaiser Franz Joseph.* Cologne 1960
Crankshaw, Edward: *The Fall of the House of Habsburg.* London 1963
Davis, John H.: *The Guggenheims: An American Epic.* New York 1978
Del Mar, Norman: *Richard Strauss: A Critical Commentary on His Life and Works* (3 vols). London 1978
Deneke, Margaret: *Ernest Walker.* Oxford 1951
Duchen, Jessica: *Erich Wolfgang Korngold.* London 1996
Edel, Theodore: *Piano Music for the Left Hand.* Bloomington 1994
Edmonds, David and Eidinow, John: *Wittgenstein's Poker.* London 2001

Engelmann, Paul: *Letters from Ludwig Wittgenstein, with a Memoir,* ed. B. F. McGuinness, trans. L. Furtmuller. Oxford 1967

Flowers, F. A. III (ed.): *Portraits of Wittgenstein* (4 vols). Bristol 1999

Fox, Winifred: *Douglas Fox: A Chronicle.* Bristol 1976

Friedländer, Saul: *Nazi Germany and the Jews,* vol. 1: *The Years of Persecution 1933–39.* New York 1997

Griffin, Nicholas (ed.): *The Selected Letters of Bertrand Russell: The Private Years, 1884–1914.* London 1992

Haider, Edgard: *Verlorenes Wien: Adelspaläste vergangener Tage.* Vienna 1984

Häseler, Adolf (ed.): *Lieder zur Gitarre oder Laute: Wandervogel—Album III.* Hamburg 1912

Hitler, Adolf: *Mein Kampf,* trans. James Murphy. London 1939

Janik, Allan: *Wittgenstein's Vienna Revisited.* London 2001

Janik, Allan and Toulmin, Stephen: *Wittgenstein's Vienna.* New York 1973

Janik, Allan and Veigl, Hans: *Wittgenstein in Vienna.* New York 1998

Kaldori, Julia: *Jüdisches Wien.* Vienna 2004

Kinflberg, U.: *Einarmfibel.* Karlsruhe 1917

Klagge, James: *Wittgenstein: Biography and Philosophy.* Cambridge 2001

Knight, W. Stanley Macbean: *History of the Great European War,* vol. 4. London 1924

Koppensteiner, Susanne (ed.): *Secession: Gustav Klimt Beethovenfries.* Vienna 2002

Koppensteiner, Susanne (ed.): *Secession: Die Architektur.* Vienna 2003

Kross, Matthias: *Deutsche Brüder: Zwölf Doppelporträts.* Berlin 1994

Kupelwieser, Paul: *Aus den Erinnerungen eines alten Österreichers.* Vienna 1918

Lansdale, Maria Hornor: *Vienna and the Viennese.* Philadelphia 1902

Levetus, A. S.: *Imperial Vienna.* New York 1905

Levy, Paul and Marcus, Penelope (eds): *The Letters of Lytton Strachey.* London 1989

Liess, Andreas: *Franz Schmidt: Leben und Schaffen.* Graz 1951

Lillie, Sophie: *Was einmal war. Handbuch der enteigneten Kunstsammlungen Wiens.* Vienna 2003

Long, Marguerite: *At the Piano with Ravel,* trans. Olive Senior-Ellis. London 1973

MacCartney, C. A.: *The Social Revolution in Austria.* Cambridge 1926

MacDonald, Mary: *The Republic of Austria 1918–1934.* London 1946

McGuinness, Brian (ed.): *Wittgenstein and His Times.* Bristol 1982

McGuinness, Brian: *Wittgenstein: A Life: Young Wittgenstein (1889–1921).* London 1988

McGuinness, Brian: *Approaches to Wittgenstein.* Oxford 2002

McGuinness, Brian (ed.): *Wittgenstein in Cambridge: Letters and Documents 1911–1951.* Oxford 2008

McGuinness, Brian, Pfersmann, Otto and Ascher, Maria Concetta (eds): *Wittgenstein Familienbriefe.* Vienna 1996

Malcolm, Norman: *Ludwig Wittgenstein: A Memoir.* Oxford 2001

Mayer, Arno J.: *Why Did the Heavens Not Darken? The Final Solution in History.* New York 1988

Meier-Graefe, Julius: *Der Tscheinik.* Berlin 1918

Meyer, Kurt: *Grenadiers.* Mechanicsburg 2005

Mitchell, Donald and Reed, Philip (eds): *Letters from a Life: Selected Letters and Diaries of Benjamin Britten* (2 vols). London 1991

Monk, Ray: *Ludwig Wittgenstein: The Duty of Genius.* London 1990

Mosley, Charlotte (ed.): *The Mitfords: Letters Between Six Sisters.* London 2007

Natter, Tobias G. and Frodl, Gerbert: *Klimt's Women.* Vienna 2000

Nedo, Michael and Ranchetti, Michele: *Ludwig Wittgenstein: Sein Leben in Texten und Bildern*. Frankfurt am Main 1983

Nemeth, Carl: *Franz Schmidt: Ein Meister nach Brahms und Bruckner*. Vienna 1957

Neuman, H. J.: *Arthur Seyss-Inquart*. Vienna 1970

Nice, David: *Prokofiev: A Biography 1891–1935*. New Haven and London 2003

Nicholas, Jeremy: *Godowsky, the Pianists' Pianist*. Hexham 1989

Nietzsche, Friedrich: *Also Sprach Zarathustra*. Leipzig 1886

Orenstein, Arbie: *A Ravel Reader. Correspondence, Articles, Interviews*. New York 1990

Prater, Donald: *Stefan Zweig: European of Yesterday*. Oxford 1975

Prokofiev, Sergei: *Autobiography, Articles, Reminiscences*. New York 2000

Prokofiev, Sergei: *Diaries (1907–1933)* (privately printed edition in Russian). Paris 2002

Prokop, Ursula: *Margaret Stonborough-Wittgenstein: Bauherrin, Intellecktuelle, Mäzenin* Vienna 2003

Rachaminov, Alon: *POWs and the Great War: Captivity on the Eastern Front*. Oxford 2002

Redpath, Theodore: *Ludwig Wittgenstein: A Student's Memoir*. London 1990

Rhees, Rush (ed.): *Ludwig Wittgenstein: Personal Recollections*. Oxford 1981

Robinson, Harlow: *Sergei Prokofiev: A Biography*. New York 2002

Russell, Bertrand: *Autobiography* (one-volume ed.). London 2000

Ryding, Erik and Pachefsky, Rebecca: *Bruno Walter: A World Elsewhere*. New Haven and London 2001

Schad, Martha: *Hitler's Spy Princess*, trans. Angus McGeoch. Stroud 2002

Schonberg, Harold C.: *The Great Pianists*. New York 1964

Schorske, Carl E.: *Fin-de-Siècle Vienna*. New York 1980

Schreiner, George Abel: *The Iron Ration: Three Years in Warring Central Europe*. London 1918

Schuschnigg, Kurt von: *The Brutal Takeover*, trans. Richard Barry. London 1971

Seroff, Victor: *Maurice Ravel*. New York 1953

Shirer, William: *The Rise and Fall of the Third Reich*. New York 1959

Smith, Nigel J.: *Lemberg: The Great Battle for Galicia*. London 2002

Somavilla, Ilse (ed.): *Denkbewegungen: Tagebücher und Briefe, 1930–1932, 1936–1937*. Electronic edition, Innsbruck 1997

Somavilla, Ilse, Unterkircher, Anton and Berger, Paul (eds): *Ludwig Hänsel-Ludwig Wittgenstein: Eine Freundschaft*. Innsbruck 1994

Spitzy, Hans: *Unsere Kriegsinvaliden*. Vienna 1917

Stone, Norman: *The Eastern Front 1914–1917*. London 1975

Suchy, Irene, Janik, Alan and Predota, Georg (eds.): *Empty Sleeve: Der Musiker und Mäzen Paul Wittgenstein*. Innsbruck 2006

Talalay, Kathryn: *Philippa Shuyler: Composition in Black and White*. Oxford 1995

Tolstoy, Count Leo: *The Gospel in Brief*. London 1896

Tovey, Donald Francis: *Essays in Musical Analysis*, vol. 3: *Concertos*. Oxford 1936

Trevor-Roper, H. R. (ed.): *Hitler's Secret Conversations*. New York 1953

Unger, Irwin and Debi: *The Guggenheims: A Family History*. New York 2005

Walter, Bruno: *Theme and Variations*. London 1947

Waters, Edward N.: *The Letters of Franz Liszt to Olga von Meyendorff, 1871–1886*, trans. William R. Tyler. Cambridge, Mass. 1979

Weiland, Hans (ed.): *In Feindes Hand* (2 vols). Vienna 1931

Weininger, Otto: *Über die letzten Dinge*, trans. Steven Burns. Lewiston 2001

Weissweiler, Eva: *Ausgemerzt! Das Lexikon der Juden in der Musik und seine mörderischen Folgen.* Cologne 1999

Williams, Gatenby [a.k.a. Guggenheim, William]: *William Guggenheim.* New York 1934

Witt-Dörring, Christian: *Josef Hoffmann: Interiors 1902–1913.* New York 2006

Wittgenstein, Hermine: *Die Aufzeichnungen "Ludwig Sagt."* Berlin 2006

Wittgenstein, Karl: *Politico-Economic Writings,* ed. N. C. Nyiri. Amsterdam 1984

Wittgenstein, Ludwig: *Philosophical Investigations.* Oxford 1953

Wittgenstein, Ludwig: *The Blue and Brown Books.* Oxford 1958

Wittgenstein, Ludwig: *Notebooks 1914–1916.* Oxford 1961

Wittgenstein, Ludwig: *Zettel.* Oxford 1967

Wittgenstein, Ludwig: *On Certainty.* Oxford 1969

Wittgenstein, Ludwig: *Geheime Tagebücher 1914–1916.* Vienna 1992

Wittgenstein, Ludwig: *Culture and Value.* Oxford 1998

Wittgenstein, Ludwig: *Tractatus Logico-Philosophicus,* with introduction by Bertrand Russell and parallel text translation by David Pears and Brian McGuinness. London 2000

Wright, G. H. von (ed.): *Ludwig Wittgenstein: Letters to Russell, Keynes and Moore.* Oxford 1974

Zichy, Géza, Count: *Das Buch des Einarmigen.* Stuttgart 1916

Zweig, Stefan: *The World of Yesterday.* London 1943

2. ESSAYS, ARTICLES AND OTHER WORKS

Abell, Arthur M.: "Count Géza Zichy." *Musical Courier,* 7/17/1915, p. 20

Albrecht, Otto E.: "The Adventures and Discoveries of a Manuscript Hunter." *Musical Quarterly,* vol. 31, no. 4, Oct. 1945, pp. 492–503

Anon: "Freiherr Prof. von Eiselsberg's Clinic at Vienna." *British Journal of Surgery,* issue 6, 1914

Anon: "L'Opera del S. P. Benedetto XV in favore dei prigionieri di Guerra." *La Civiltà Cattolica,* Mar. 1918, vol. 2, pp. 293–302

Anon: "One-Armed Pianist Undaunted by Lot," interview with Paul Wittgenstein. *New York Times,* Nov. 4, 1934, p. 7

Attinello, Paul: "Single-Handed Success: Leon Fleisher's Keyboard Comeback." *Piano & Keyboard,* no. 163, Jul./Aug. 1993

Bauman, Richard: "Paul Wittgenstein: His Music Touched Our Hearts." *Abilities Magazine,* no. 50, Spring 2002

Bellamy, Oliver: "Concerto pour la main gauche: La Force du destin." *Le Monde de la Musique,* Dec. 2004.

Boltzmann, Ludwig: "On Aeronautics," trans. Marco Mertens and Inga Pollmann, in Susan Sterrett, *Wittgenstein Flies a Kite,* London 2005, p. 255

Bonham's sale catalogue: *European Paintings from the Estate of Hilde Wittgenstein,* June 6, 2006. New York

Bramann, Jorn K. and Moran, John: "Karl Wittgenstein: Business Tycoon and Art Patron." *Austrian History Yearbook,* vol. 15-16, 1979–80

Chinkevich, E. G.: *Rapport sur la visite des camps des prisonniers austro-hongrois dans l'arrondissement militaire d'Omsk (Sibérie).* Petrograd 1915

Czernin, Hubertus: "Der wundersame Weg der Eugenie Graff." *Der Standard,* Feb. 27, 1988, p. 34

Davis, Gerald H.: "National Red Cross Societies and Prisoners of War in Russia, 1914–18." *Journal of Contemporary History*, vol. 28, no. 1, Jan. 1993, pp. 31–52

De Cola, Felix: "The Elegant Art: Playing the Piano with the Left Hand Alone." *Clavier*, vol. 6, no. 3, Mar. 1967

Deneke, Margaret: "Memoirs" (unpublished typescript, 1962–4, 2 vols.), Lady Margaret Hall, Oxford

Deneke, Margaret: "Mr. Paul Wittgenstein. Devotion to Music." Obituary, *The Times*, Mar. 14, 1961

Fitzmaurice-Kelly, Capt. M: "The Flapless Amputation." *British Journal of Surgery*, vol. 3, issue 12, 1915

Flindell, E. Fred: "Ursprung und Geschichte der Sammlung Wittgenstein im 19. Jahrhundert." *Musikforschung*, vol. 22, 1969

Flindell, E. Fred: "Dokumente aus der Sammlung Paul Wittgenstein." *Musikforschung*, vol. 24, 1971

Flindell, E. Fred: "Paul Wittgenstein (1887–1961): Patron and Pianist." *Music Review*, vol. 32, 1971

Gaugusch, Georg: "Die Familien Wittgenstein und Salzer und ihr genealogisches Umfeld." *Adler: Zeitschrift für Genealogie und Heraldik*, 2 (XXXV), 2001, pp. 120–45

Godowsky, Leopold: "Piano Music for the Left Hand." *Musical Quarterly*, vol. XXI, July 1935

Harvey, Trevor: "Paul Wittgenstein: A Personal Reminiscence." *Gramophone*, June 1961

Kennard, Daphne: "Music for One-Handed Pianists." *Fontes Artis Musicae*, vol. 30, no. 3, July/Sept. 1983

Kim-Park, So Young: "Paul Wittgenstein und die für ihn komponierten Klavierkonzerte für die linke Hand" (unpublished dissertation). Aachen 1999

Klein, Rudolf: "Paul Wittgenstein zum 70. Geburtstag." *Österreichische Musikzeitschrift*, Dec. 12, 1957

Kong, Won-Young: "Paul Wittgenstein's Transcriptions for Left Hand: Pianistic Techniques and Performance Problems" (unpublished dissertation) Denton, Texas 1999.

Kundi, L. P.: "Josef Labor: Sein Leben und Wirken, sein Klavier- und Orgelwerk nebst thematischem Katalog sämtlicher Kompositionen" (unpublished dissertation). Vienna 1963

Kupelwieser, Paul: "Karl Wittgenstein als Kunstfreund," *Neue Freie Presse*, no. 17390, 1/21/1913

Lau, Sandra Wing-Lee: "The Art of the Left Hand: A Study of Ravel's 'Piano Concerto for the Left Hand' and a Bibliography of the Repertoire" (unpublished dissertation). Stanford 1994

McKeever, James: "Godowsky Studies on the Chopin Etudes." *Clavier*, vol. 19/3, Mar. 1980

Malone, Norman: "The Technical and Aesthetical Advantages of Paul Wittgenstein's Three Volumes of Music 'School for the Left Hand' " (unpublished dissertation). Chicago 1973

Parke-Bernet Galleries Sale Catalogue: *French & Other Period Furniture (Property of the Estate of the Late Jerome Stonborough)*, Oct. 18, 1940

Parke-Bernet Galleries Sale Catalogue: *Important Works by Celebrated Modern French Painters Collected in Paris by the Late Jerome Stonborough*, Oct. 17, 1940

Patterson, Donald L.: *One-Handed: A Guide to Piano Music for One Hand*. Westport 1999

Pegelow, Thomas: "Determining 'People of German Blood,' 'Jews' and 'Mischlinge': The Reich Kinship Office and the Competing Discourses and Powers of Nazism." *Contemporary European History*, issue I, vol. 15, pp. 43-65

Pelton, Robert W.: "The Indomitable Paul Wittgenstein." *Contemporary Keyboard*, vol. 3, Aug. 1977

Penrose, J. F.: "The Other Wittgenstein." *American Scholar*, vol. 64, no. 3, Summer 1995

Pickard Bonni-Belle: "Repertoire for Left Handers." *Clavier*, vol. 25, no. 9, Nov. 1986

Reich, Howard: "Rediscovered Score: Pianist's Last Legacy." *Chicago Tribune*, Aug. 11, 2002

Rhees, Rush: "Wittgenstein," *Human World*, February 1974

Ripley, Joan: "Empty Sleeve—The Biography of a Musician." Mary Baldwin College, Staunton, Virginia 1987

Ripley, Joan: "A Memory of My Father," 3pp, typescript, pc

Salehhi, David: "Ludwig Wittgenstein als Schüler in Linz." *Wittgenstein Studies*, Jan. 15, 1997

Sassmann, Albert: "Aspekte der Klaviermusik für die linke Hand am Beispiel des Leschetizky-Schülers Paul Wittgenstein" (unpublished dissertation). Vienna 1999

Sassmann, Albert: "Ein Klavierschüler Paul Wittgensteins: Henry Selbing war Dirigent und Komponist." *Allgemeine Zeitung für Rumänien*, July 16, 2004

Seekircher, Monika, McGuinness, Brian and Unterkircher, Anton (eds.): *Ludwig Wittgenstein: Briefwechsel*, Innsbrucker elektronische Ausgabe, Charlottesville 2004

Sotheby's Sale Catalogue: *Music, Including the Paul Wittgenstein Archive*, May 22, 2003. London 2003

Stack, S.: "Media Impacts on Suicide: A Quantitative Review of 293 Findings." *Social Science Quarterly*, vol. 81, Mar. 2000, pp. 957-81

Stonborough, John J.: "Germans Back Hitler—Now!" *Sign*, Dec. 1939

Stonborough, John J.: "The Totalitarian Threat." *Sign*, Nov. 1940

Thormeyer, F. and Ferrière, F.: *Rapport sur leurs visites aux camps de prisonniers en Russie. 14. Omsk*. Geneva, Mar. 1915

Turner, J. Rigbie: "Infinite Riches in a Little Room: Music Collections in the Pierpont Morgan Library." *Notes*, 2nd Ser., vol. 55, no. 2, Dec. 1988

Unger, Aryeh L.: "Propaganda and welfare in Nazi Germany. *Journal of Social History*, vol. 4, no. 2, Winter 1970, pp. 125-40

Wechsberg, Joachim: "His Hand Touched Our Hearts." *Coronet*, vol. 25, no. 8, June 1959

Wittgenstein, Paul: "The Legacy of Leschetizky." *Musical Courier*, vol. 132, no. 2, Aug. 1945

Wittgenstein, Paul: "Preface," in his *School for the Left Hand*. Vienna, Zurich and London 1957

Wittgenstein, Paul: *Über einarmiges Klavierspiel*. Austrian Institute, New York 1958

3. MANUSCRIPT LETTER COLLECTIONS

Hermine Wittgenstein and Margaret Stonborough to Ludwig Wittgenstein: MSS Austrian National Library, Vienna (Stonborough Collection)

Margaret Stonborough to Hermine Wittgenstein and Margaret Stonborough
 diaries, etc.: Pierre Stonborough, private collection
Ludwig Wittgenstein to Paul Wittgenstein: MSS private collection
Ludwig Wittgenstein to his sisters and mother: MSS Austrian National Library,
 Vienna (Stonborough Collection)
Paul Wittgenstein to Benjamin Britten: MSS Britten-Pears Library, Aldeburgh
Paul Wittgenstein to Marga Deneke: MSS Bodleian Library, Oxford (Deneke
 Collection)
Paul Wittgenstein to Rudolf Koder: MSS private collection, Vienna
Paul Wittgenstein to Erich Korngold: MSS Austrian National Library, Vienna; MSS
 Erich Wolfgang Korngold Archive, Hamburg
Paul Wittgenstein to Josef Labor: MSS Wiener Stadt und Landesbibliothek, Vienna
Paul Wittgenstein to Donald Francis Tovey: MSS Reid Music Library, Edinburgh
Paul Wittgenstein to Ernest Walker: MSS Balliol college Library, Oxford
Paul Wittgenstein to Karl Weigl: MSS Yale University Library, New Haven

INDEX

❖ ❖ ❖

American Relief Administration (ARA), 129–30

Anti-Semitism
  Bolshevism fears and, 135–36
  of Hitler, 135–36, 205, 211
  Kristallnacht pogroms, 227, 242
  Nazis' anti-Semitic policies in Austria, 204–5
  "racial defilement" issue, 224
  in Switzerland, 234–35
  taxes on Jews, 217–18
  of Wittgenstein family, 15–16, 136–37
  Wittgensteins' Jewish ancestry issue, 205–6, 208–14, 219, 226–27, 243, 249, 252–54

Astroff, Michel, 173, 178, 181

Austrian Action group, 269

Bartley, William Warren, III, 140, 141, 147

Bauer, Karl, 207

Baum, Eva, 207–8

Baumayer, Marie, 36, 132, 162

Bechert, Paul, 181

Benedict XV, Pope, 90

Berchtold, Leopold, 64

Bevan, Edward, 275

Bieler, Max, 101

Bienstock, Abraham, 245, 254, 260

Bloch, Konrad, 244, 245, 246, 247, 248, 254

Blue and *Brown* books (L. Wittgenstein), 191

Blumen, Marianne and Erwin, 238

Boltzmann, Ludwig, 45–46

Bonaparte, Princess Marie, 240

Bortkiewicz, Sergei, 153, 154, 172

Boult, Adrian, 159

Brahms, Johannes, 9, 30, 160

Brändstrom, Elsa, 74–75, 89, 94

Braun, Rudolf, 171

Bree, Malwine, 43, 105

Brendel, Breindel, 214

Briand, Aristide, 129

Bricht, Walter, 175

Brillin, Isaac, 15

Britten, Benjamin, 262–65, 277

Brusilov, Alexei, 108

Bülow, Hans von, 258

Busch, Fritz, 158

Carnegie, Andrew, 32

Chamberlain, Neville, 251, 255

Charles I, Emperor, 116, 127

Christianity, 99

Clauzel, Bertrand, 175, 176

Concerto pour la main gauche (Ravel), 174–77

Conrad von Hötzendorf, Franz, 64, 69–70

Croy-Dülmen, Princess Cunigunde von, 87–88

Cunliffe-Owen, Marguerite, 32
Czernin, Count Ferdinand, 269
Czerny, Karl, 42

Daladier, Édouard, 251, 255
Danner, Sebastian, 40, 128
David Mannes Music School, 235, 237
Deneke, Helena, 165, 236
Deneke, Marga, 121, 137, 169, 170, 174,
    176, 183, 190, 220–21, 223, 235,
    236–37, 273, 278, 280–81
  Paul W.'s relationship with, 165–66,
    167–68
Diaz, Gen. Armando, 119
Diversions (Britten), 264–65, 277
Dodd, William and Martha, 212
Dollfuss, Engelbert, 193–94, 195, 196
Dostoevsky, Fyodor, 89
Dumba, Konstantin, 80

Eichmann, Adolf, 205
Eiselsberg, Baron Anton von, 8, 83, 96,
    211
Engelmann, Paul, 144, 145, 162
Epstein, Julius, 25

Faustenhammer, Elizabeth, 197
Février, Jacques, 270
Fey, Emil, 201
Ficker, Ludwig von, 146
Field, John, 6
Figdor, Albert, 54
Figdor family, 14
Fillunger, Marie, 160
Findlay, John Niemeyer, 190–91
First World War
  Austro-Hungarian mistakes, 69–70, 79
  Austro-Hungarian victory against
    Russia and Russia's withdrawal,
    116–17
  ending of, 127
  Gretl W.'s involvement, 102
  impact on Austria-Hungary, 127
  Italian front, 119–20
  onset of, 63–65
  U.S. entry into, 110

See also under Wittgenstein, Konrad
    "Kurt"; Wittgenstein, Ludwig;
    Wittgenstein, Paul
Fischer, Heinz, 234
Fouracre, Roy, 266, 267
Frank, Hans, 240
Franz, Otto, 85, 86, 91, 94
Franz Ferdinand, Archduke, 63–64
Franz Joseph, Emperor, 63, 68, 115, 116,
    182
Frege, Gottlob, 145
Freud, Sigmund, 129, 137, 240
Frick, Wilhelm, 253
Friedman, Ignacy, 42
Furtwängler, Wilhelm, 158

Gal, Hans, 171
Georg V of Hanover, King, 44
Georg of Waldeck and Pyrmont, Prince,
    214
Geschlecht und Charakter (Weininger), 28
Godowsky, Leopold, 83–84, 171
Goldberg, Daniel, 259
Goldmark, Karl, 38
Goossens, Eugène, 264
Göring, Field Marshal Hermann, 198,
    212
Görlich, Dr., 242–43
Gospel in Brief, The (Tolstoy), 98–101,
    134, 140, 144
Gregor, Nora, 201
Grillparzer, Franz, 172
Groag, Jacques, 162, 163
Groller, Anton, 194, 228, 230, 242,
    243–44, 245, 248, 249, 252
Guggenheim, William, 32
Gürtler, Lt., 93

Haidbauer, Josef, 162
Hall, Lady Margaret, 170
Hänsel, Dr., 147, 162, 237
Hanslick, Eduard, 31, 83
Harmon, Dudley, 257
Harvey, Trevor, 278, 282
Heger, Robert, 175
Heimwehr army, 192, 193, 194–95, 201,
    202

Heinsheimer, Hans, 263, 264
Hermann, Rosalie, 95, 112–13
Heydrich, Reinhard, 204
Himmler, Heinrich, 201, 205
Hindemith, Paul, 153–55
Hirschfeld, Magnus, 21
Hitler, Adolf, 127, 193, 213, 217
    anti-Semitism of, 135–36, 205, 211
    "Aryanization of Jews" policy,
        206–7
    early years, 33
    First World War service, 119
    Nazi takeover of Austria, 195–97,
        203–4
    territorial successes of 1938–39,
        250–51
    Wittgensteins' Jewish ancestry issue,
        253
Hoffmann, Joseph, 50
Hohenlohe-Waldenburg-Schillingfürst,
    Princess Stephanie von, 212–13
Hollmann, Otakar, 279
Hoover, Herbert, 130
Houghteling, James, 237, 251
Hutt, Roland, 192

Indra, Alfred, 232, 240–41, 242, 244,
        245, 248, 249, 252, 253, 257–58,
        259
Innitzer, Cardinal, 203

Jews. See Anti-Semitism
Joachim, Joseph, 30, 43

Kalbeck, Max, 5, 55–56
Kalchschmidt, Franz, 168, 169
Kalmus, Jacob, 208
Kalmus, Marie, 208
Karg-Bebenburg, Maj. Baron, 193
Kastle, Leonard, 167, 170, 277, 279
Kerensky, Alexander, 116
Keynes, John Maynard, 49, 221
Kirchbach auf Lauterbach, Karl Graf
        von, 118
Kirchen, Esther, 183
Kleiber, Erich, 158

Klimt, Gustav, 20–21
Knepler, Hugo, 105
Kochanski, Paul, 171
Koder, Rudolf, 148, 149, 187, 188, 270,
        272, 280, 281
Kokoschka, Oskar, 61
Korngold, Erich Wolfgang, 188
    compositions for Paul W., 153, 154,
        155–56
Korngold, Julius, 5, 6, 56–57, 107, 158
Kornisch, Dr., 232
Krepost prison, 89–92
Kristallnacht pogroms, 227, 242
Kügel, Georg, 171, 173–74, 181
Kun, Béla, 135
Kusmanek, Hermann, 79

Laberge, Bernard, 167
Labor, Josef, 62, 83, 107, 162
    compositions for Paul W., 87, 104,
        114, 151, 152–53, 154, 155
    death of, 159
    eightieth birthday, 151–52
    personal qualities, 43–44
    Wittgenstein family and, 44–45
Lammers, Hans Heinrich, 258
Lansdale, Maria Hornor, 3, 138–39
Lehnert, Julius, 151
Leimer, Kurt, 270
Leschetizky, Theodore, 36, 42–43, 84,
        104
Lichter, Charles, 265
Liel, Capt. Karl von, 93
Life of Jesus (Renan), 101
Lindsay, Michael, 169
Liszt, Franz, 83
Long, Marguerite, 175–76
Loos, Adolf, 61
Lord, John Hayes, 230–31
Lueger, Karl, 136
Lutz, Dorothy, 283

Mahler, Gustav, 31, 153
Maisky, Ivan, 192
Malcolm, Norman, 273
Mandl, Fritz, 195
Mann, Thomas, 64

Maresch, Rudolf, 29
Marie of Greece, Princess, 129
Martin, Linton, 265
Mayer, Kurt, 213, 214, 227, 252, 253–54
Mecklenburg, Grand Duke of, 109
Meier-Graefe, Julius, 89, 96, 98
Mein Kampf (Hitler), 135–36
Mendelssohn, Felix, 208
Menger, Karl, 18, 214, 216
Menzel, Rosine, 87, 104
Merriman, Dorothea, 268
Meyer, Kurt "Panzer," 269
Meyer, Moses, 214
Meyerbeer, Giacomo, 208
Meyerhold, Vsevolod, 178, 179
Miklas, Wilhelm, 197, 203
Milch, Field Marshal Erhard, 206–7
Mitford, Unity, 207–8
Monk, Ray, 140, 141
Monteux, Pierre, 158
Moore, George, 48, 67, 98, 145
Morrell, Lady Ottoline, 47
Morrison-Bell, Veronica, 268, 276, 284
Mortiz, Gen., 85, 88
Moscovici, Bassia, 181–84
Moser, Koloman, 50
Mühlfeld, Richard, 166
Mussolini, Benito, 195, 251

Nazi rule in Austria
    Anschluss, 196–98, 201, 203–4
    anti-Semitic policies, 204–5
    appropriation of Wittgensteins'
        foreign assets, 218, 223–24, 227,
        241–50, 252, 254–55, 256–57, 280
    "Aryanization of Jews" policy, 206–8
    Austrians' turn against Nazis, 267,
        271
    Kristallnacht pogroms, 227, 242
    "liberation" of Austria by Allies, 271
    passport fraud prosecution of
        Wittgenstein sisters, 228–33, 237,
        238, 239–41
    patriotic Austrians, persecution of,
        201–2
    Paul W.'s escape, 219–23, 224–26,
        227–28, 238–39
    pre-takeover chaos, 193–96

"racial defilement" issue, 224
revenue-generating measures, 217–18
Schania's role, 225
Wittgensteins' Jewish ancestry issue,
    205–6, 208–14, 219, 226–27, 243,
    249, 252–54
Wittgensteins' smuggling of
    valuables out of Austria, 220–21,
    234, 255–59
Nedbal, Oskar, 5, 105
Newman, Ernest, 185–86
Nilius, Rudolf, 154
Nuber, Alexander von, 66, 80

Oberleithner, Mrs. Max, 191
On Certainty (L. Wittgenstein), 275
Oppenheimer, Samuel, 208
Ormandy, Eugene, 264, 265
Otten, Erna, 202, 283

Paderewski, Ignaz, 42
Panathenäenzug (Strauss), 157–58
Parak, Franz, 133
Paramilitary forces of Austria, 193
Parergon zur Sinfonia Domestica (Strauss),
    157
Pears, Peter, 262–63, 264–65
Perkins, Frances, 216
Petty, Sir William, 163
Peyer, Otto, 241
Philosophical Investigations (L.
    Wittgenstein), 147
Piano Music with Orchestra (Hindemith),
    154–55
Pinsent, David, 49, 67, 144
Plattner, Friedrich, 258
Plavsky, Gen. Alexei, 87–88
Poliakov, Samuil, 17
Ponte, Lorenzo da, 207
Portman, Steve, 168–69
Prokofiev, Sergei, 173–75, 178–81, 277
Prostitution, 139

Raikh, Zinaida, 178, 179
Ramsey, Frank, 146
Rapp, Siegfried, 181, 278–79

Rash, Thomas H., 202
Ravel, Maurice, 171–72, 174–78, 269–70, 277
Redpath, Theodore, 130
Reich, Otto, 218
Reilly, Gerald D., 237
Reitler, Josef, 202–3
Renan, Ernest, 101
Respinger, Marguerite, 140, 183
Réti, Rudolph, 62
Rettich, Col. Alfred von, 77
Rhené-Baton, 159
Rilke, Rainer Maria, 61
Rodzinski, Artur, 235
Rolly, Karoline, 225, 235, 261, 264, 283
Rosé String Quartet, 54
Russell, Bertrand, 46, 47–49, 52, 67, 98, 101, 145
Rytel, Pawel, 184

Salvator, Franz, 212
Salzer, Felix, 41, 159, 235, 267, 284
Salzer, Fritz, 266
Salzer, Hans, 40–41
Salzer, Helene Wittgenstein. See Wittgenstein, Helene "Lenka"
Salzer, Maria, 275
Salzer, Max, 40, 137, 194, 216, 228, 229, 230, 233, 242, 249, 267
Sargent, Sir Malcolm, 278
Schaafgotsche, Capt. Erwin, 70, 71
Schania, Franz, 186–87, 190, 225
Schania, Hilde. See Wittgenstein, Hilde Schania
Schania, Käthe, 187
Schania, Stefanie, 187
Scherchen, Hermann, 262
Scherchen, Wulff, 262
Schiele, Egon and Edith, 119
Schiesser, Gen. Anton von, 118, 120
Schindler, Alma, 44, 45, 62, 187
Schmidt, Franz, 162, 175, 188, 270
    compositions for Paul W., 153, 154, 155, 156, 186
Schnabel, Artur, 42
Schoenberg, Arnold, 31, 44, 153
Schoene, Freda Marie, 249

Schoene, Johannes, 242, 243, 244, 245, 247, 248, 249
Schopenhauer, Arthur, 98
Schrödinger, Erwin, 46
Schumann, Eugenie, 160, 165
Schuschnigg, Kurt von, 196–97, 201–2
Schütt, Eduard, 171
Schuyler, Philippa, 170
Schwab, Charles, 32
Schwer von Schwertenegg, Maj. Gen. Otto, 70
Second World War, 255, 266–69, 271
Seyss-Inquart, Arthur, 197, 201, 203, 222–23, 228, 238
Seyss-Inquart, Richard, 222
Siebert, Gen. Josef von, 117, 159
Simon, Bernardine, 214
Sjögren, Arvid, 228, 229, 230, 232, 233, 240
Skinner, Francis, 140–41, 191, 192, 266
Soldat-Roeger, Marie, 62, 166
Spanish flu pandemic, 119
Sraffa, Piero, 209, 221, 223
Standhartinger, Judge, 232, 239
Starhemberg, Prince Ernst Rüdiger von, 192–93, 194–96, 201
Steinberger, Delia, 78–79
Steinberger family, 19
Stonborough, Jerome (born Steinberger), 7, 61, 96, 104, 129, 131, 256
    death by suicide, 215
    divorce, 214–15
    early years, 19
    legacy of, 215
    marriage to Grerl W., 19–20
    married life, 50, 51, 102, 103, 111, 141, 163–64
    as mysterious figure for Wittgenstein family, 31–32
    psychological problems, 31, 51, 103, 141, 164–65
    Switzerland move in 1917, 110–11
Stonborough, John Jerome "Ji," 45, 138, 139, 140, 142, 164, 187, 194, 222, 240, 241, 283
    birth of, 51
    death of, 284
    education and work experiences, 216

English country squire life, 276
Gretl W.'s relationship with, 215–16
Kurt W.'s death, 121
management of Wittgensteins'
    foreign investments, 216–17
marriage of, 268
Nazis' appropriation of
    Wittgensteins' foreign assets, 241–
    42, 244, 246–47, 248–49, 252, 254
Nazis' interest in, 251–52, 257
passport fraud prosecution of
    Wittgenstein sisters by Nazis, 231
Paul W.'s relationship with, 237, 247
personal qualities, 216
sale of family valuables, 260
Second World War service, 268–69
smuggling of valuables out of Nazi-
    ruled Austria, 255, 256–57
Stonborough, Margaret Wittgenstein.
    See Wittgenstein, Margaret "Gretl"
Stonborough, Pierre, 103, 284
Stonborough, Thomas, 51, 111, 142,
    163, 164, 194, 215, 242, 258, 276,
    283–84
Stovall, Pleasant, 129
Strachey, Lytton, 49
Strauss, Johann, 207
Strauss, Richard, 30–31, 43, 153, 159, 270
    compositions for Paul W., 156–58
Sudeten crisis, 251
Suicide epidemics, 28–29

Tarnowski, Count Adam, 80
Through Embassy Eyes (Dodd), 212
Tolstoy, Leo, 98–101, 111, 133–34, 140,
    144
Tovey, Donald Francis, 169, 186
Tractatus Logico-Philosophicus (L.
    Wittgenstein), 33, 99–100, 101,
    145–47
Trakl, Georg, 61
Trotsky, Leon, 117
Turner, Saxon Sydney, 49
Typhus epidemic, 91–92

Vienna
    character in 1900, 3–4

Jewish population, 135
post–First World War conditions,
    127–29
post-Second World War conditions,
    272, 273
prostitution in, 139

Wachtell, Samuel, 244, 245, 246, 247,
    248, 252, 253, 254
Wadsted, Otto, 85, 86, 87, 91
Wagner, Friedelind, 196
Wagner, Richard, 137
Wagner-Jauregg, Julius, 103
Walter, Bruno, 158
Washburn, Albert Henry, 141
Weigl, Karl, 171, 176
Weiland, Hans, 92
Weingartner, Felix, 159
Weininger, Otto, 27–29, 35, 46, 136, 137
Weissmann, Adolf, 158
Wertheimer, Samson, 208
Wiedemann, Capt. Fritz, 212–13
Willstätter, Richard, 51
Wilson, Woodrow, 110
Windisch-Grätz, Prince Franz, 201
Wistag AG & Cie company, 217. See also
    appropriation of Wittgensteins'
    foreign assets under Nazi rule in
    Austria
Wittgenstein, Clara, 170, 174
Wittgenstein, Clothilde, 14
Wittgenstein, Dora, 40
Wittgenstein, Elizabeth, 189–90, 206,
    224, 235, 261, 264, 283
Wittgenstein, Franziska "Fanny" Figdor,
    12, 13, 15, 34, 208
Wittgenstein, Helene "Lenka" (married
    Max Salzer), 104, 150, 164
    death of, 276
    funds for living in Nazi-ruled Austria,
        259, 260
    Hermine W.'s death, 272, 274, 275
    Ludwig W.'s divestiture of his
        fortune, 134
    Nazis' appropriation of
        Wittgensteins' foreign assets, 218,
        242, 249, 254, 255
    passport fraud prosecution, 228–32

personal qualities, 40–41
Second World War years, 267
sex life of, 137
sibling relations, 132
Wittgenstein, Hermann Christian, 9, 10,
    11, 14
  anti-Semitism of, 15–16, 136
  Jewish ancestry issue, 208, 213–14,
    226–27, 252, 253
Wittgenstein, Hermine "Mining," 11, 17,
    23, 24, 25, 30, 40, 45, 51, 62, 67, 68,
    77, 78, 80, 86, 91, 94, 104, 106, 108,
    109, 111, 112, 115, 118, 131, 133,
    141, 150, 152, 159, 160, 162, 163,
    164, 183, 184, 186, 189, 196, 233
  anti-Semitism of, 137
  artistic pursuits, 9–10, 142
  Christmas of 1929, 165
  day-care school run by, 142, 206
  death of, 272–73, 274–75
  funds for living in Nazi-ruled Austria,
    259, 260
  Gretl W.'s relationship with, 50,
    102–3
  Jewish ancestry issue, 205, 206, 208,
    210, 211, 243
  Karl W.'s relationship with, 9–10
  Kurt W.'s death, 120–21, 122, 123
  legacy of, 274–75
  on Leopoldine W., 37–38
  Leopoldine W.'s death, 161
  Ludwig W.'s divestiture of his
    fortune, 134
  Ludwig W.'s estrangement from
    Wittgenstein family, 147
  Ludwig W.'s religious beliefs, 100–101
  maidish life, 142
  memoirs of, 123, 267, 274–75
  Nazis' appropriation of
    Wittgensteins' foreign assets, 218,
    241, 242–43, 247–48, 249, 254, 255
  palace redecorating, 116
  passport fraud prosecution, 228–33,
    237, 238, 239–41
  Paul W.'s First World War service, 117
  Paul W.'s one-handed playing, 104–5
  Paul W.'s psychological problems,
    113, 114
  Paul W.'s relationship with, 280

Paul W.'s reunion with family
    following release from POW camps,
    96
  personal qualities, 9
  Second World War years, 267
  sex life of, 137
  sibling relations, 132
  wealth of, 61
Wittgenstein, Hilde Schania, 186, 187,
    206, 224, 225, 233, 235, 264
  children born to, 189–90, 277
  final years, 282–83
  marriage to Paul W., 261–62
Wittgenstein, Hirsch, 226
Wittgenstein, Johanna, 122, 190, 206,
    224, 235, 261, 264, 283
Wittgenstein, Johannes "Hans," 34, 35,
    37
  disappearance and possible suicide,
    24, 25–29
  early years, 24–25
Wittgenstein, Karl, 22, 30, 31, 45, 48, 50,
    211, 256
  anti-Semitism of, 136
  business career, 14–15, 17–18
  death of, 7–8, 51–54
  early years, 10–11
  education of his children, 34
  as father, 23, 26, 36–37
  Hermine W.'s relationship with, 9–10
  Jewish ancestry issue, 208, 214
  marriage of, 15–17
  politics of, 116
  U.S. stay in 1860s, 11–13
  wealth of, 18, 150
Wittgenstein, Konrad "Kurt," 37, 68,
    118, 211
  death by suicide, 120–23
  First World War service, 111–12,
    121–22
  diplomatic/propaganda efforts in
    United States, 77–80
  personal qualities and business
    pursuits, 39–40
  U.S. stay, 65–66, 77–80, 95
Wittgenstein, Leopoldine "Poldy"
    Kalmus, 8, 22, 45, 54, 80, 111, 115,
    152, 256
  death of, 159–61, 162

health problems, 104
Jewish ancestry issue, 208
Kurt W.'s death, 120–21, 122
marriage of, 15–17
as mother, 23, 37–38
musical talent, 38
Paul W.'s prisoner-of-war experience,
    75–76, 77, 85–86, 90–91, 93–94, 95
Paul W.'s psychological problems, 113
Paul W.'s reunion with family
    following release from POW camps,
    95–96
personal qualities, 38
Wittgenstein, Ludwig, 43, 44, 45, 62, 75,
    78, 80, 86, 87, 91, 93, 94, 95, 102,
    104, 105, 106, 118, 152, 160, 169,
    183, 196, 223, 231, 237, 259, 260,
    262, 266, 267, 268, 276
anti-Semitism of, 137
architectural work, 162–63
Blue and Brown books, 191
British citizenship, 209
Cambridge return in 1929, 164
as Cambridge student, 46–49
Cambridge teaching career, 191
Christmas of 1929, 165
communist sympathies, 192
death of, 275
divestiture of his fortune, 133–34
early years, 32–35, 36
education of, 33, 34
engineering enthusiasms, 45–46
estrangement from Wittgenstein
    family, 143, 147–48
First World War service, 66–67, 70, 95,
    97–98, 108–9, 117, 120
    prisoner-of-war experience, 120,
    132–33
Gretl W.'s relationship with, 130, 134
health problems, 148, 273–74, 275
Hermine W.'s death, 272, 273
as icon of twentieth century, 32
Jewish ancestry issue, 208–11
Karl W.'s death, 52–53
Kurt W.'s death, 122, 123
Leopoldine W.'s death, 161
medical work during Second World
    War, 266–67
musical gifts, 36

Nazis' appropriation of
    Wittgensteins' foreign assets,
    241–42, 249–50, 252
Norway exile, 6–7
On Certainty, 275
Paul W.'s escape from Nazi-ruled
    Austria, 221–22
Paul W.'s prisoner-of-war experience,
    76
Paul W.'s psychological problems, 113
Paul W.'s relationship with, 32–33,
    34, 54–55, 191–92, 250, 280–81
philosophical career, 33, 46–49,
    99–100, 101, 145–47, 191, 275
Philosophical Investigations, 147
physical appearance, 190–91
politics of, 192
psychological problems, 7, 108, 144
religious beliefs, 98–101, 109, 132–33
schoolteaching career, 133, 143, 144,
    148–49, 162
sex life of, 140–41
sibling relations, 132
smuggling of valuables out of Nazi-
    ruled Austria, 221
social shortcomings, 34, 108
Soviet Union visit, 192
suicidal thoughts, 35, 37, 49
Tractatus Logico-Philosophicus, 33,
    99–100, 101, 145–47
U.S. stay in 1949, 273–74
walking regimen, 166
wealth of, 61
Wittgenstein, Ludwig "Louis," 12, 13,
    150, 159, 209
Wittgenstein, Margaret "Gretl" (married
    Jerome Stonborough), 7, 22, 26, 31,
    68, 104, 194, 217
adopted children of, 142, 267–68
children born to, 51
Christmas of 1929, 165
death of, 276
divorce, 214–15
emigration from Austria in 1940, 259
extortion incident, 141–42
final years, 276
First World War service, 102
health problems, 183
Hermine W.'s death, 272

Hermine W.'s relationship with, 50,
102–3
Jewish ancestry issue, 210, 211–14,
243, 249
Kurt W.'s death, 122
on Leopoldine W., 37
Leopoldine W.'s death, 161
Ludwig W.'s architectural work for,
162–63
Ludwig W.'s divestiture of his
fortune, 134
Ludwig W.'s relationship with, 130,
134
Ludwig W.'s religious beliefs, 100–101
marriage of, 19–20
married life, 50, 51, 102, 103, 111, 141,
163–64
Nazis' appropriation of
Wittgensteins' foreign assets, 218,
241, 242–43, 244–48, 249, 252,
256–57
passport fraud prosecution, 228–33,
238, 239–41
Paul W.'s escape from Nazi-ruled
Austria, 222–23, 227–28, 238–39
Paul W.'s psychological problems, 113
Paul W.'s relationship with, 130–32,
184, 238–39, 247, 262, 265–66, 276,
279–80
Paul W.'s relationship with
Moscovici, 182–83, 184
personal qualities, 102–3
physical appearance, 20–21
politics of, 131–32
psychological problems, 110
relief efforts following First World
War, 129–30, 141
scientific pursuits, 50–51
selling of her possessions, 197, 198,
259–60
sex life of, 137
sibling relations, 132
smuggling of valuables out of Nazi-
ruled Austria, 220–21, 255–56,
257–58
social connections, 129
Ji Stonborough's marriage, 268
Ji Stonborough's relationship with,
215–16

Switzerland move in 1917, 110–11
wealth of, 61–62, 131, 164, 218
Wittgenstein, Paul, 127, 129, 135, 163,
164, 194, 195, 272
anti-Semitism of, 137
arm wound and amputation, 71–72,
74, 77, 96–97
Blumen's relationship with, 238
charitable activities, 128–29
children born to, 189–90, 277
Christmas of 1929, 165
communism, hostility toward, 172,
173
courage, testing of, 83
death of, 277, 281–82
Deneke's relationship with, 165–66,
167–68
early years, 32–35, 36–37
eccentricities of, 166–69
education of, 33, 34
escape from Nazi-ruled Austria,
219–23, 224–26, 227–28, 238–39
exhumation and reburial, 282–83
finger injury, 104
First World War service, 97
combat participation, 68–69, 70–72,
117–19
prisoner-of-war experience, 72–76,
77, 80–95
"welfare" work, 107–8
friendship, capacity for, 169–70
Goldberg and, 259
Gretl W.'s relationship with, 130–32,
184, 238–39, 247, 262, 265–66, 276,
279–80
health problems, 118–19
R. Hermann and, 112–13
Hermine W.'s death, 273
Hermine W.'s relationship with,
280
Hilde W.'s marriage to, 261–62
Hilde W.'s premarital relationship
with, 186, 189–90
Jewish ancestry issue, 205–6, 208–9,
210, 211–14, 219, 253, 254
Kurt W.'s death, 121, 122, 123
Leopoldine W.'s death, 161
Ludwig W.'s divestiture of his
fortune, 134

Ludwig W.'s estrangement from
Wittgenstein family, 143, 147–48
Ludwig W.'s First World War service,
109
Ludwig W.'s relationship with, 32–33,
34, 54–55, 191–92, 250, 280–81
Ludwig W.'s religious beliefs, 100–101
military decorations, 109
military service (pre–First World
War), 68
Moscovici's relationship with, 181–84
Nazis' appropriation of
Wittgensteins' foreign assets, 218,
223–24, 227, 241–42, 243–44,
245–50, 252, 254–55
memorandum on, 280
Nazis' targeting of Paul for patriotic
activities, 202
New York living arrangements, 264,
277
palace redecorating, 116
passport fraud prosecution of
Wittgenstein sisters by Nazis, 228,
237
pianist career, 34, 162, 164, 170–71
Berlin debut, 114–15
choice of career, 36
commissioning of compositions,
86–87, 104, 114, 151, 152–58,
171–72, 173–77, 178–81, 186,
262–65
concert debut, 4–6, 42, 54, 55–57
continuation of career despite loss
of arm, decision on, 82–84
criticism, attitude toward, 54–55
decline in ability in later years,
277–79
early training, 36, 42–44
experience-gaining concerts, 62–63
"major artist" status, 158–59
one-handed debut, 104–7
one-handed playing, training in, 84,
86
one-handed techniques, 105–6
Polish tour of 1932, 184
recordings, 277–78
repertoire of one-handed pieces,
151
Soviet Union tour of 1930, 172–73

teaching, 187–89, 202–3, 235, 237,
277
"thefts" of commissioned works,
269–71, 278–79
U.S. tour of 1928, 159
U.S. tour of 1934, 185–86
wartime playing for troops, 114, 269
wealth's complications, 62
writings on piano music for left
hand, 277
politics of, 62, 192–93
privacy, obsession with, 138, 168
psychological problems, 112–14
"racial defilement" charge brought by
Nazis, 224
religious beliefs, 98
reunion with family following release
from POW camps, 95–96
Second World War activities, 269
sex life of, 138–40
sibling relations, 132
smuggling of valuables out of Nazi-
ruled Austria, 234
social shortcomings, 34
Ji Stonborough's relationship with,
237, 247
suicidal thoughts, 35–36, 37
suicide rumor about, 225–26
Swiss stay during Nazi rule in
Austria, 233–36
temper of, 168
U.S. move in 1938, 235–37
Vienna visit in 1949, 273
walking regimen, 166
wealth of, 61, 62, 131, 149–50, 218,
254
withdrawn period, 150
women's attraction to, 106
Wittgenstein, Paul, Jr., 277, 283
Wittgenstein, Paul (uncle Paul), 11, 134
Wittgenstein, Rudolf "Rudi," 35, 37,
54
death by suicide, 21–22, 23–24,
25–26, 29
Wittgenstein family crypt, 54
Wittgensteins' musical soirées, 30–31,
39
Wittgenstein Winter Palais, 29–30, 267,
271, 272, 281

Wood, Sir Henry, 159
World of Yesterday, The (Zweig), 139
Wührer, Friedrich, 270-71

Zaslawsky, George, 170, 171
Zastrow, Jochen and Wedigo, 142, 163, 165, 231, 267-68

Zeiner, Erich, 240
Zeitzler, Col., 205
Zemlinsky, Alexander, 31, 44
Zichy, Count Géza, 74, 83, 105
Zitkovsky, Willi, 68
Zweig, Stefan, 4, 41, 63-64, 66, 115, 139
Zwiauer, Brigitte, 226-27

ALSO BY

ALEXANDER WAUGH

FATHERS AND SONS
The Autobiography of a Family

If there is a literary gene, then the Waugh family most certainly has it—and it clearly seems to be passed down from father to son. Alexander Waugh tells this extraordinary tale of four generations of scribbling male Waughs in *Fathers and Sons*, one of the most unusual works of biographical memoir ever written. In this remarkable history of father-son relationships in his family, Waugh exposes the fraught dynamics of love and strife that have produced a succession of successful authors. Based on the recollections of his father and on a mine of hitherto unseen documents relating to his grandfather, Evelyn, the book skillfully traces the threads that have linked father to son across a century of war, conflict, turmoil, and change. It is at once very funny, fearlessly candid, and exceptionally moving—a supremely entertaining book that will speak to all fathers and sons, as well as the women who love them.

Biography & Autobiography

ANCHOR BOOKS
Available wherever books are sold.
www.anchorbooks.com

Meet with Interesting People
Enjoy Stimulating Conversation
Discover Wonderful Books

Printed in the United States
by Baker & Taylor Publisher Services